TRANSFORMING
P·A·R·I·S

Adolphe Yvon, *Napoléon III Presenting Haussmann with a Decree Annexing the Communes Surrounding Paris* (1859)

TRANSFORMING

P·A·R·I·S

The Life and Labors of

BARON HAUSSMANN

by

DAVID P. JORDAN

THE UNIVERSITY OF CHICAGO PRESS

Published by arrangement with The Free Press, a division of Simon & Schuster, Inc.

Frontispiece: Copyright © 1995 Artists Rights Society (ARS), New York / SPADEM, Paris

Credits for the photographic inserts are listed on pages 453–55.

The University of Chicago Press, Chicago 60637

ISBN 0-226-41038-2 (pbk.)

Library of Congress Cataloging-in-Publication Data

Jordan, David P., 1939–
    Transforming Paris : the life and labors of Baron Haussmann / by
David P. Jordan.
        p.   cm.
    Includes bibliographical references and index.
    1. Urban renewal—France—Paris—History.   2. City planning—
France—Paris—History.   3. Haussmann, Georges Eugène, baron,
1809–1891.   I. Title.
HT178.F72P345   1996
307.1′216′092—dc20
[B]   96-1208
                                                   CIP

⊛ The paper used in this publication meets the minimum requirements
of the American National Standard for Information Sciences—
Permanence of Paper for Printed Library Materials, ANSI Z39.48—1984.

FOR JUDITH

For many reasons

BOOKS BY DAVID P. JORDAN

Gibbon and His Roman Empire
The King's Trial: Louis XVI vs. the French Revolution
The Revolutionary Career of Maximilien Robespierre

· CONTENTS ·

List of Maps   viii
About the Maps   xi
Preface   xv
Acknowledgments   xxi

Prologue: "The Muscular Generation to Which I Belong"   1

I   Paris Before Haussmann   13

II   Haussmann Before Paris   41

III   Climbing the Greasy Pole   55

IV   Paris in Crisis   91

V   "My Combative Prefectship"   115

VI   "This Province I Have So Loved"   135

VII   "A State Within the State"   165

VIII   "The Implacable Axes of a Straight Line. . ."   185

IX   "The Vice-Emperor Is the Prefect of the Seine"   211

X   Money   227

XI   "Lackey of a Good House"   247

XII   "Organs of the Large City"   267

XIII   "The Vandalism of Triumph"   297

XIV   Haussmann After Paris   315

XV   Paris After Haussmann   341

Epilogue: "One of the Most Important Men of Our Time"   369

Notes   373
Works Cited   423
Index   441

· MAPS ·

Tourist's map, c. 1900   xii–xiii

Successive Walls of Paris   21

Stages in the Construction of the Louvre   25

Grande Croisée   187

Boulevards Richard Lenoir & Voltaire   189

Rues Gay-Lussac, Claude Bernard, & Monge   190

Boulevards St. Germain & Henri IV   195

Boulevards Malesherbes, Friedland, & Haussmann   196

Haussmann's Boulevards   360–61

· ABOUT THE MAPS ·

I WROTE THIS BOOK WITH A MAP, "PARIS EN 1871," ABOVE MY DESK, A constant reminder of the physical reality of the city and Haussmann's transformations. The maps reproduced here are meant to give the reader the same visual reinforcement for the descriptions that I had in writing them.

A map, however beautiful or geometrically accurate, is only a two-dimensional representation of the complexities of Paris. It is a rational distortion. I have chosen three distinct modes of cartographic distortion of the city to provide an image of what I am writing about, and I reproduce a few of the famous historical maps of the city among the illustrations. These latter require no explanation here.

The map on pages xii and xiii is a reproduction of a tourist's map of the city, dating from about 1900. Dozens have survived. The one reproduced here is in the collections of the University of Chicago. I have overlaid the grid so the reader can easily find the map coordinates given in the text in parentheses and thus more easily locate what I am describing. The Hôtel de Ville, for example, is in the upper left-hand corner of F 4. This is not an eminently precise reference system for two reasons. First, the map emphasizes important buildings rather than the street systems. Numerous streets built by Haussmann and mentioned in the text are not indicated. Now and then the reader will come across map coordinates in the text, as B 5 for Porte de St. Cloud, which does not appear on the map. In such cases the coordinates indicate not the precise location but the general area of the street, landmark, or building in question. Some streets and buildings vanished in the *grands travaux:* the rue Transnonain is gone and the map reference is only to the area of its original existence.

Second, there are spatial distortions. The monuments of Paris are not drawn to scale, nor is the amount of cityscape they occupy. Notre Dame (E-F 4) does not fill more than half the Ile de la Cité. The distances between monuments, consequently, are inaccurate; virtually everything appears closer than it is. And the entire area occupied by Paris has been "compressed" from north to south. Only from east to west does the city show something of its actual shape.

Using this map also entails some anachronisms. It is neither Haussmann's Paris nor present-day Paris. The Eiffel Tower (C 4) was built after his fall, while the gare Montparnasse (D 5) was demolished to make way for the Montparnasse Tower. Some streets have undergone a name change. The Avenue du Bois de Boulogne (B 3) is now the Avenue Foch; it was the Avenue de l'Impératrice when Haussmann cut it. Yet for all these distortions, I find this an attractive and legible map that gives a sense of place not easily found in some more accurate renditions. It presents Paris as a whole, and is easily taken in at a glance. The monuments are recognizable and well drawn; the city's remarkable endowment of public buildings is obvious, as is their diversity of style.

The map on pages 360–61, Haussmann's Boulevards, was adapted and drawn by my colleague, Raymond Brod, the University of Illinois at Chicago cartographer, as were all the other line maps reproduced in the text. Its very density, a spider's web of Paris streets, conveys the complexity of the urban fabric Haussmann created. By no means are all the streets of Paris indicated on the map, but the contrast of thick lines (the streets the prefect cut) and thinner lines (existing streets) gives some idea of the axial groups he built and their implantation in an old city. It also conveys how much of the old city he left intact.

The five small maps are based on a completely different order of distortion. Everything has been removed from Paris except Louis-Philippe's defensive wall—the crimped line enclosing the city—the Seine and the two islands, and a few indications of *places* and landmarks. Several of Haussmann's most important axial groups have been drawn into this template of Paris, not absolutely to scale but accurately enough to give a picture of their place (and role) in the city. These maps have been placed as close as possible to the discussion of their construction.

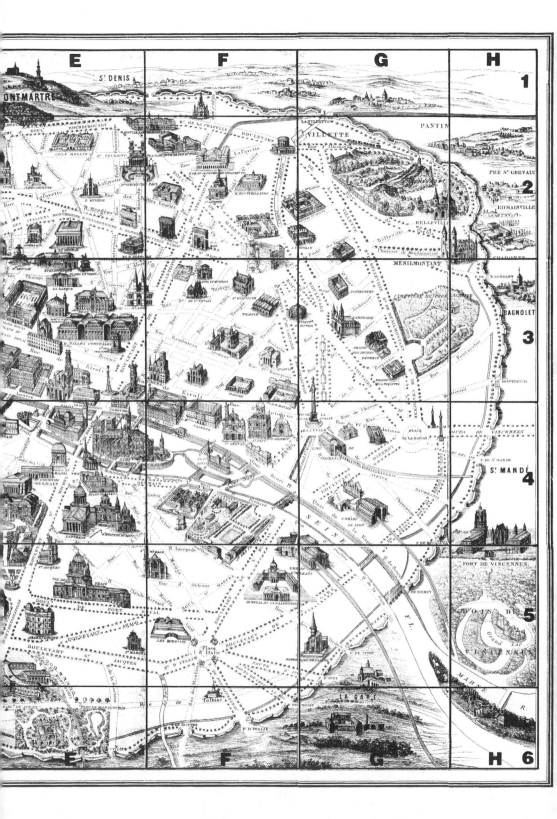

· PREFACE ·

OF THE TWO TASKS I RITUALISTICALLY PERFORM WHEN I COMPLETE A book—clearing my desk of the accumulation of notes, books, and scribbled reminders whose order and relevance is apparent only to me, and writing a preface—the latter is far and away the more satisfying. Even when it merges on the mawkish, publicly thanking friends for easing long solitary labors, for comfort and encouragement, and for quality control is a pleasure.

I intended a much different book from the one you are reading. Indeed, writing about Baron Haussmann had never entered my mind. In 1987, with the bicentennial of the French Revolution rapidly approaching, I was negotiating with my editor and friend, Joyce Seltzer, to write something on the revolution, the subject I professed and wrote about, the only subject whose literature, sources, and controversies I knew adequately. Joyce, however, had a bright idea: why not write a biography of Haussmann? He was an important figure who had yet to find his biographer.

Everything seemed wrong about her proposal—century, subject, timing—and I had no empathy for the man. Hadn't he destroyed Paris so the army could deploy rapidly and shoot down demonstrators? My sympathies were on the other side of the barricades that Haussmann—so the cliché ran—had made obsolete. Why would I want to study him? But as I thought about the project it became more interesting, for I deliberately misconstrued Joyce's proposal. I didn't have to write about Haussmann, who did not much intrigue me. I could write about Paris, which did.

I had been visiting or living there almost every year since 1968 (an auspicious introduction), and had resided, for varying lengths of time, in many *arrondissements*—the fourth, fifth, sixth, ninth, and thirteenth. Once I began this book I even spent some weeks in an extraordinary apartment built in the Haussmann era, not far from the parc Monceau, in the very heart of New Paris. Living in such a posh neighborhood, I assured friends, was research.

I had an old and deep affection for the city. If I thought about it, I knew my way around Paris as well as I did around Chicago, where I had lived for more than twenty-five years, and knew considerably more about Parisian history and lore (and restaurants). Over the years I had read, not very systematically it is true, many of the writers—Mercier, Balzac, Baudelaire, Zola, among others—who passionately loved and described Paris. I was emotionally engaged with the city, and Haussmann would provide the pretext to write about it. But I had to be persuaded to abandon the familiar terrain of the eighteenth century for the alien topography of the nineteenth.

What are friends for? Jonathan Marwil argued that taking on Haussmann and Paris would stretch my mind and shake my complacency. Richard Levy, himself a historian of the nineteenth century as well as an old Paris hand, reinforced these views. Stanley Mellon, who first taught me French history and continues to do so, insisted approaching Haussmann and Paris from the perspective of the eighteenth century was precisely the strength I brought to the project. All three convinced me they were right. And having prodded me to write this book, they assumed the corvée of reading what I had written. Each bears some responsibility for whatever virtues of clarity, fluency, empathy, and intellectual rigor it has. I keep, as a bulky souvenir of my own labors and theirs, a box containing copies of the manuscript at various stages, amply annotated with the comments, suggestions, queries, and rebukes of my friends, as I groped my way toward a final version. Joyce Seltzer, too, did much more than inspire the work, which became the last manuscript she edited for the

Free Press before moving on. Her sure sense of a book's architecture, as well as a highly refined abhorrence of excess verbiage, are everywhere apparent to me. You, dear reader, benefit almost as much as I did from the collective sensibility, intelligence, and wisdom of my friends, but you have not experienced the immeasurable gift of their friendship.

John Merriman, of Yale University, had shown some interest in tackling Haussmann but, fortunately for me, became diverted by other projects. He would have written a different book on Paris and her great prefect. Instead, he shared all that he knew of Haussmann, encouraged me to take up the task, and then read my manuscript in a nearly penultimate incarnation, bestowing upon it his incomparable knowledge of French cities in the nineteenth century. Virtually every chapter was improved by John, whose erudition and good sense saved me from potential embarrassment as I picked my way through the sources and historiography of a field where I was finding my footing.

Another friend, François Furet—who also took the time to read my manuscript and make a number of luminous suggestions, all of which I incorporated—thought Haussmann should not be a pretext for writing about Paris. He suggested I write a traditional biography, a genre so highly developed in Anglo-American historiography, so neglected in France. There were promising inducements to writing Haussmann's life, including a three-volume autobiography by an important public figure who died only a hundred years ago. His children would have lived into our century; their children might still be alive; their grandchildren would be my age. In addition, Haussmann was an administrator who dealt daily in paperwork, who communicated in writing rather than by telephone. Surely there would be abundant personal papers, as well as a vast yet manageable public record. Unlike the French revolutionaries I had been studying for years, here was a man whose life was fully recorded.

I was quickly disillusioned. Haussmann's *Mémoires* presented only the bureaucrat, deliberately excluding or masking the private man. His personal papers were in none of the obvious national or regional public repositories. I turned to his descendants. His oldest daughter, Henriette-Marie, had predeceased him. His youngest daughter,

Valentine, died in her fifty-eighth year; her son, Haussmann's only
male grandchild, had been killed in a boating accident in 1909, not
long after his mother's death. By French law, which requires a century to elapse from the date of death before the financial settlement
of an estate is made public, I could not see either Valentine Haussmann's will nor that of her son, Didier Pernety-Haussmann. Presumably Haussmann's papers passed to his surviving daughter—
although the distribution made at his death is vague about the precise contents of boxes and boxes of papers that had nothing to do
with family finances and what became of them—and thence to his
grandson. Here the trail abruptly goes cold. An early biographer reported that Haussmann's personal papers had been burned by a distant relative because they contained numerous extramarital love
letters. The story is uncorroborated. According to M. Roland
Hecht, a descendant of Henriette-Marie's second daughter, who
kindly made inquiries of his family at my request, whatever papers
there were survived until World War I, when the Germans destroyed the family property in Alsace, where Haussmann's papers
were stored.

Even the public record was seriously compromised: the Hôtel de
Ville, where Haussmann lived and worked for seventeen years, had
been burned by the Paris Commune in 1871. Documents, maps,
dossiers, correspondence, photographs—all had been incinerated.
A traditional "life" was not possible. The man would have to be approached from the outside, glimpsed through the eyes of contemporaries, reflected in his creations.

The plan I adopted was to weave Haussmann and Paris together,
making, I hope, an interesting and authentic pattern. Haussmann is
not a very intriguing character, the kind of man whose company I
would have sought, although his creation of what was reputed the
finest wine cellar in Paris is a notable exception to this judgment.
He is significant and interesting for what he did and represented.
His autobiographical presentation of self as a bureaucrat whose private life was of little interest to contemporaries or posterity, however unhelpful to the biographer, is a faithful reflection of this reality.
Haussmann's contemporaries took little interest in his character;
and his motives seemed obvious: he was considered a careerist, an

opportunist, a man bereft of culture or taste, a great administrator who loved wielding power ostentatiously for its own sake. For us his life turns on a central paradox: he was not a great man so much as a representative figure—the professional, bourgeois bureaucrat, an early and impressive example of the expert, the technocrat, the urban planner—yet his life's work, the transformation of Paris, is a great and enduring accomplishment. Beautiful, bejeweled, endlessly fascinating, it is not the kind of work we associate with bureaucrats and bureaucracies. The undeniable splendor of the city is his monument, before which the bureaucrat and the philistine pale. And rightly so.

The best part of this undertaking, for me, was tracking Haussmann's papers, although I came up empty-handed. I visited the towns where he served, searched the archives there (as well as those in Paris), contacted surviving distant relatives, and even visited his only surviving residence, Cestas, near Bordeaux. I spent an exceptionally pleasant day there at the invitation of the present owner, Mme Bellemer, drinking champagne on the front stairs, climbing the rusted waterworks with Françoise, her daughter, trying to imagine the house when he, his furniture and his books were still there, while listening to Mme Bellemer tell stories of growing up in the house that had been Haussmann's.

Tracing my hero's footsteps did not reveal his inner self to me, but it is the way I enjoy working. I found archivists, both in Paris and in the provinces, uniformly cordial and helpful, and got to know a part of France—the departments of the Gironde, the Lot-et-Garonne, and the Ariège (including the charming town of St. Girons, which he so hated)—that were unfamiliar. I found a few items unknown to earlier historians or biographers—his subprefect's log from St. Girons, nearly fourscore letters sent to a friend when serving in the Yonne, and a number of individual documents surprisingly scattered in unlikely files—and I was the first to see, in 1991, the financial settlement of his estate and the inventory of his worldly goods. But, alas, I did not stumble upon the treasure I sought.

My wife, Judith, accompanied me on all these pilgrimages and paper chases, and whenever we were in Paris, both above and below ground, listened to my interminable explanations of what Hauss-mann had done, what had once stood on the ground where we walked, and precisely how and where his Paris was being destroyed, the skyscrapers and high-rise apartments that were ruining the uni-form scale he had imposed. I had become a talking *Guide Bleu*. She helped me choose the illustrations and find the right tone for the opening chapter. These are only the least significant reasons for dedicating this, my most ambitious book, to her.

Studying Haussmann and Paris has been generously supported by the National Endowment for the Humanities, who awarded me a fellowship in 1992–93 during whose tenure I wrote most of the first draft. The Campus Research Board of the University of Illinois at Chicago made smaller but crucial grants that allowed me to spend a summer in the departmental and municipal archives of Bordeaux and, on another occasion, in those of the Ariège, the Lot-et-Garonne, and the Archives Nationales, in Paris. The Humanities Institute of the University of Illinois at Chicago also responded fa-vorably to two requests to plug holes in the emerging manuscript: one to scan Bordeaux and Paris newspapers, the other to defray the expenses of acquiring many of the photographs, especially the splendid work of Charles Marville, that enhance this book.

Paris-Chicago, July 1994

· ACKNOWLEDGMENTS ·

FIRST MY THANKS TO BRUCE K. NICHOLS AND LORETTA DENNER OF the Free Press who saw this book through the press. They were uniformly kind, calm, efficient, and helpful, as was Edward B. Cone, who scrupulously copyedited my manuscript. David Van Zanten's erudite *Building Paris: Architectural Institutions and the Transformation of the French Capital, 1830–1870* (Cambridge: Cambridge University Press, 1994) arrived too late for me to plunder. Fortunately I had been picking his brain over lunch for a couple of years. Colin Lucas provided a forum, at the University of Chicago, for me to present a very early formulation of some of my ideas, and my colleague Gerald Danzer did the same when he invited me to speak to "The City in History Conference" in 1992. He also, successfully, nagged me about including maps, for which I am grateful. John Spielman, who taught me history when I was a freshman at the University of Michigan—and along with Stanley Mellon inspired me to emulation—invited me to talk about Haussmann at Haverford College.

Daniel Ollivier, the former cultural attaché at the French Consulate in Chicago, introduced me to his wife's cousin, Marianne (and her husband, Dr. Bruno) Richard-Molard, who became not only my agents in Bordeaux but friends as well. M. Jean Valette, the *conservateur en chef* and director of the departmental archives of the Gironde, went well beyond extending professional courtesy: he offered to let me work through the August closing. And Thomas Pappadis . . . he listened to my bright ideas, my enthusiasms, my anxieties.

TRANSFORMING
P·A·R·I·S

· PROLOGUE ·

"The Muscular Generation to Which I Belong"

"TWO HUNDRED TWENTY LITERS OF WINE IN THE BARREL VALUED AT 140 francs, 900 bottles of Bordeaux red valued at 540 francs, 120 bottles of Bordeaux red valued at 100 francs," the *notaire* droned on, "280 bottles of Bordeaux white valued at 168 francs . . . twenty-eight bottles of wine from Cestas . . . fourteen bottles of champagne, seventeen bottles of Pontet-Canet, fourteen bottles of Léoville-Poy-ferré, fifteen bottles of Mouton-d'Armagnac, fifteen bottles of Chateau Issan, fourteen bottles of Haut-Brion, twenty bottles of Chateau Margaux, twelve bottles of Gruaud-Larose. . ." He was reading the Inventory of the worldly goods of Georges-Eugène Haussmann and his wife, Louise-Octavie de la Harpe, who had died within seventeen days of each other: fifty-two married years of material accumulations.[1] At their marriage the Haussmanns had chosen the regulation of community property for all goods acquired since the marriage, with the provision that should one predecease the other, the remaining spouse would have the use of the deceased spouse's property until his or her death, when the entire estate would be distributed. Present for the reading, which would continue, with some interruptions, from February 7, 1891, to May 1, 1891, were the chief inheritors: Valentine Haussmann (their surviving daughter) and their son-in-law and his two children.[2]

1

The apartment, where Haussmann and his wife died (12 rue Boissy d'Anglas, not far from the Place de la Concorde and the Tuileries Garden), was in a good bourgeois neighborhood. It has been demolished, as has been his place of birth. Haussmann rented it, along with stabling for two horses and a parking area for two carriages, from the widow Languillet. The rent was equal to his annual pension as a retired prefect.

Spacious, as Paris apartments go, yet not ostentatious, the apartment was densely and eclectically furnished, comfortably cluttered. The salon was in the style of Louis XVI, with white lacquered furniture—a *canapé*, or kind of couch, with six armchairs—and Beauvais tapestry. The dining room could seat fourteen, and the Haussmanns owned porcelain service for eighteen guests, along with sixteen crystal carafes for his collection of excellent Bordeaux wine, and silver worth 7,600 francs.

The apartment "looked as though it had been furnished, certainly regardless of expense, from a bric-à-brac shop. In the drawing-room . . . the furniture was rococo, but there was a magnificent suite of Louis XV chairs amidst this harlequinade. A large and beautiful water-color of Empress Eugénie hung over the gilt consoles." Only the study had "a strong individual character. All the man, one might say, was in this room," where the furniture was in the *style administratif*. There were "numerous photographs of members of the Bonaparte family, signed by the givers" and "a large portrait of Napoléon III met one's eye as one entered." The study "was the office of a Cabinet Minister not too certain of his majority."[3] This room contained a large desk, a map cabinet, two tables, a lacquered cabinet, a green leather easy chair, two side chairs upholstered in ribbed silk, one armchair upholstered in velour, another in heavy cotton, two chairs upholstered in green ribbed silk, a wooden chair, a small safe, a clock, two bronze gas fixtures (Empire style), a desk clock with barometer, a pendulum clock (Byzantine design from the time of Louis XVI), two maps of Paris mounted on the wall, a couple of insipid paintings of country scenes, a pastel of his wife, marble busts of himself and his wife, a portrait of the Prince Imperial and another of Prince Victor Bonaparte, as well as a bronze of himself. One bookcase held 180 bound volumes of the *Mémoires de l'Académie des Sciences*, another contained 150 volumes of jurisprudence.

His many decorations, presented by his own and foreign sovereigns, forty-two in all (including a diamond-encrusted cross of the Legion of Honor), fill two pages of the Inventory. His clothing consisted of thirteen shirts, twelve night shirts, fifteen pair of socks, eighteen handkerchiefs, a prefect's dress uniform, and an academician's uniform. The family papers, an enormous accumulation of stuffed boxes and cartons, the very essence of a bureaucrat's life, were not described, dismissed by the *notaire* as "of no value," no financial significance for the estate.[4]

In addition Haussmann left debts. The estate at Cestas, near Bordeaux, part of his wife's inheritance, was encumbered with debts and mortgages, mostly incurred by borrowing to pay for his extensive transformations of the property.[5] He owed sizable sums to architects and banks, one of which held a judgment against the estate, and his savings account was overdrawn. Two other bank accounts showed current balances of a few hundred francs. Death dues and debts necessitated the sale (at auction) of his chateau. When these transactions were completed there were 428,450 francs left to be distributed. Haussmann and his wife were to be buried in Père Lachaise cemetery, in the Haussmann family plot, six meters owned and paid for in perpetuity. A Parisian by birth, Haussmann had returned to his natal city to die and be buried.

With the exception of a few dozen decorations, two maps of Paris, two uniforms for state or institutional functions, and two autographed photographs of Bonapartes, this melancholy material enumeration of a life of public service gave little sense of Haussmann's unique and stunning achievement, little evidence that he was among the most powerful and influential men of his generation. He had lived too long, into a regime that despised and calumniated him. "I have, for the Republic," he wrote with atypical irony, "a degree of gratitude proportional to this demonstration of munificence toward me."[6]

The Empire, this regime called despotic, impartially protected all believers, all cults. The republican government, this imagined regime of liberty for all, showed its impartiality in an inverse sense, by proscribing, generally, the outward expression of intimate convictions with which it had no sympathy.[7]

His funeral, modest, private, and ordinary, underlined the paltriness of his mementos, his vanished greatness. The Third Republic denied him a state burial. The world had forgotten Haussmann. In his last, sorrowful years he sought to remind the world:

> May death strike me standing up [he wrote in his *Mémoires*], as it has so many men of the muscular generation to which I belong: this is now my only ambition. However it comes I will depart this world if not with my head held high as I formerly did in my public life, at least with a strong heart; as for the things of Heaven, [I am] hopeful of the merciful justice of God."[8]

Haussmann's motives for writing an autobiography were an intricate web of pride, egotism, vanity, vengeance, and self-justification. Despite his bold anticipation of death, he felt the need to issue a final prefect's report to the present and the future on his achievements, his *res gestae*. He was, although the world seemed to have forgotten, the man who transformed Paris. His work had been embraced and celebrated, an essential part of the nation's life and culture, the subject of literature, painting, photography, the object of tourism. The city had taken on new vitality just as he himself approached his end. The workman had been forgotten. His only distinct memorial was the boulevard Haussmann, and several attempts had been made to remove his name.

Autobiography was the only historical act available to him, and literature was foreign to his nature and his gifts. He was a man of deeds, not descriptions. He began his *Mémoires* at the urging of a friend, Jules Lair, who convinced Haussmann that he owed himself, his family, and his friends "a summary of my public life," especially "a presentation of my administration of Paris, so diligent, so vigorous," and "a decisive refutation of the errors, often unintentional, of the attacks that were as violent as they were unjust, of the systematic and passionate hostilities, which time has still not completely effaced."[9] The emotional spring of Haussmann's memories was anger. "These are recollections written at a distance, after a long retirement, favorable to reflection and impartiality,"[10] but such literary clichés did not preclude rage and bitterness. Almost liturgically he reiterated that his was a life "of legitimate satisfactions, but was filled, above all, with sharp suffering, cruel disillusionments, and petty miseries."[11]

Haussmann's autobiographical purpose was not to lay bare his innermost self, but to remind the French and the world of what he did, and to have them marvel at his achievement:

> In my long life, the only period that appears to me to excite the interest, the curiosity, of the public, is that when I filled, as prefect of the Seine, the functions of mayor of all Paris, and during which was acquired, without having been sought in the least, the almost universal notoriety that now attaches to my name.[12]

All else is banished from his *Mémoires*. The man he presents and wants remembered is "quite simply a parvenu Parisian, determined to make a name for himself, even a controversial name, in his beloved natal city."[13] A proudly ambitious man: "I followed a direct route, without letting myself be diverted. This was not always easy, but it was a very simple rule of conduct and it was mine." Tenacity and lack of duplicity gave him an advantage over his adversaries, who were much more devious than he: "clever men, little accustomed to the straight and narrow, did not lie in wait for me along this road."[14] And let those who got in his way beware. As he explained to an unidentified "Grande Dame," he gave better than he got: "I strike back with usury."[15]

His fundamental views and assumptions, his personal credo, he assures the reader at the outset, will not be dissembled. Politically he believes in democracy and is "very liberal" but authoritarian: "The only practical form of Democracy is the Empire," and "I was an Imperialist by birth and conviction."[16] But above all he was a dedicated administrator, unattached to any coterie: "absorbed . . . by the substantial mission that I had been given . . . I did not seek to see or know more than what directly concerned me."[17] He is a man, Haussmann assures his readers, they can trust. "After a sincere search of my conscience, I have the profound conviction of never having, in these *Mémoires* or in my life, knowingly caused pain to anyone or given in to feelings that I might [later] regret." The faults he confesses, but does not explore, are "too much faith in the solidity of the Imperial regime" and consequently "too little concern for our future interests."[18] His character is faithfully reflected, he insists, by the very simplicity and precision of his writing. "I hardly concern myself with style." "Mine is not mannered, it is the style of a familiar account, of a conversation among friends." He prefers "the language of the Law," in which he was trained, where "there are no synonyms. Every word has its own value and one must know it." Such writing may lack elegance but it has precision, which can be seen to best advantage in "my prefectorial orders."[19] But the true language of haussmannization is statistics:

> As arid as might be the terrain of numbers, they are a support that one rarely disregards without perishing, and which never lie. They hold the secret of many forces. Moreover, if the language of numbers is without charm, it is without illusion. Numbers are the prose of business: they are also its eloquence. Clear and precise, they do more than persuade, they provide certainty.[20]

His *Mémoires* are constructed like a prefect's report: dense, detailed, carefully argued, technically well informed, full of statistics and administrative and historical erudition, of which he wrote dozens, all equally masterful and unscintillating. In the very monotony, the accumulation of examples, the lists of figures, a powerful eloquence inculcates his heroic accomplishments.[21]

The *Mémoires* present his own view of the transformation of Paris, "this great and difficult work . . . for which I was the devoted instrument, from 1853 to 1870, and for which I remain the responsible editor, in a country where everything is personified."[22] He is the self-confident hero of his own book. The few regrets he confesses are overwhelmed by the vanity of accomplishment. His editor has provided an apt and accurate appraisal:

> What would we not today give [he asked rhetorically] to possess the account of the transformation [of Rome] by Augustus, and how many minor poems would we not sacrifice in exchange for a work that would reveal to us the practical administration of the Romans?[23]

For all his shortcomings and shortsightedness, Haussmann was essentially correct about himself and his achievement. The *Mémoirs* are not braggadocio. What he missed, what no one of his generation could have seen, was that he was almost an ideal type, a modern bureaucrat *avant la lettre*. So many of the important characteristics of France at midcentury converged in Haussmann, often in exaggerated form because oversized, that his story takes on representative dimensions. The self-conscious administrator devoted to state service (whoever its master), the bureaucrat devoted to the emerging age of statistics and quantification, the urban planner convinced that reason rather than self-interest or sentiment drove his decisions, the hard-working bourgeois disdainful of the more idle and privileged, the citizen who scorned democracy as disorderly and inefficient— all these aspects of his remarkable career he presents and celebrates. It was Haussmann's good fortune to preside over the greatest urban renewal project in history, and he left an indelible imprint on Paris. He shaped none of the primal energies of his century, nor did he articulate their meaning. He was not a master spirit of the age, a great man in our usual understanding of an increasingly ambiguous classification. But he shaped a city that reflected the imperatives of capitalism and centralized imperial power, he integrated the important public works of his age–railroads, sewers, water supply–into the city, he implanted a new commercial city into a decaying urban fabric and gave it new life, he imposed patterns on Paris that had not previously existed, and he permanently altered the city's appearance. To have grasped the route so many careening juggernauts were taking, and to have cleared their irresistible paths, was a kind of greatness.

No name is so attached to a city as is Haussmann's to Paris. The great founders of cities in antiquity, both mythological and actual, even Alexander the Great or the Emperor Constantine, who gave their names to their creations, have not left so indelible an urban imprint. But some parallels with antiquity are apt. The Greco-Roman world was an essentially urban culture and civilization, apparent first in the Greek city-states and then the Roman Republic and Empire, when the provinces looked to the capital, where was concentrated all that represented the Roman world–emperor, aristocracy, administration, culture, wealth, education, law courts, altars. The provincial cities, which emerged from Roman military camps, including Paris, sought to emulate or copy Rome.

Haussmann enjoyed comparing Paris with Augustan Rome. Not merely because it was flattering to himself and his master, Napoléon III, or a familiar contemporary conceit among the educated. Ancient Rome had been transformed by an emperor and his aediles, imperial officers charged with city administration. The parallels were irresistible; Augustan Rome haunts Haussmann's *Mémoires* as metaphor, model, and benchmark. But this linkage of antiquity to the present was more rhetorical than real. Haussmann preferred a more recent parallel: the Marquis de Tourny, the intendant of Louis XV who transformed Bordeaux in the eighteenth century.

The choice was both excellent and revealing. Cities had ceased being the creation of conquerors or heroes and become the task of bureaucrats and administrators. Tourny did his work in the infancy of the new phenomenon, Haussmann during the adolescence and young adulthood of city planning. The evolution of European cities is more apposite and carries no burden of myth. Besides, for Haussmann, who was insular and chauvinistic, only a French comparison would do. He was emotionally and aesthetically attached to eighteenth-century urbanism, whose dominant elements–rectilinear, planted boulevards leading to monuments or *places*, public parks and promenades, markets in the center of the city, rational street patterns, the city divided into functional "zones," with government separated from commerce and "dirty" industry banished from the city, a hierarchical architectural regularity–were designed to glorify the ruler. In addition Tourny's Bordeaux, where Haussmann spent more than a dozen years before his summons to Paris, had several striking similarities to Haussmann's Paris: a dominant river with embellished quays, grand public buildings inherited from the past, an opera house at the center of the city, a stable commercial bourgeoisie, and an old medieval core that had been successfully integrated into the new city. Haussmann's invocation of the obscure Tourny was also flattering. There were similarities between the eighteenth-century servant of Louis XV and Haussmann's own position, but the comparison was patently to Haussmann's advantage: Bordeaux was not Paris, the Second Empire was not the old monarchy. The eighteenth century, before the culmination of the centralized state under Napoléon, was not the nineteenth. In Tourny's day provincial capitals might successfully vie with Paris in beauty and modernity. Bordeaux, Nancy, even Arras (where Robespierre was born) could boast stunning new centers that replaced medieval cores with uniform buildings in the best classical style, built of the finest cut stone, which declared local pride and prosperity. The last century of the ancien régime was a great age of urban building and beauty, but none of these renewed French cities was conceptualized on the scale Haussmann brought to Paris, none was rebuilt to represent an empire anxious to assert, in stone, its power and permanence.

There was no city like Paris. The concentration of money, energy, people, and institutions, the dominance of Paris over France, was unparalleled. This characteristic was pushed so far by Haussmann and Napoléon III that Paris burst its old urban integument. Glasgow and Edinburgh, Berlin and Munich, Milan and Turin and Rome, Madrid and Barcelona define the competitive tensions between cities for national dominance. No city in France, or Europe, could compare with Haussmann's Paris. Madrid and Berlin had been built to represent and reflect the requirements of power, imperial power in the former. London had grown more organically, although it provided, with Regent's Street, an early example of a planned quarter and a new street cut through a dense urban fabric. Rome, long shaped by the preponderance of the Papacy, seemed stuck in the Renaissance, and Vienna was about to undergo a transformation nearly as extensive as Haussmann's Paris, although on a smaller scale. Contemporaries recognized the significance of Haussmann's work and sought comparisons. The most apt was likening Haussmann's work to the rebuilding of Lisbon after the earthquake and fire of 1755, stressing the relationship of the Portuguese king and his first minister, Pombal.

The railroads, symbolic of the extraordinary energies of capitalism unleashed, the nation-state solidified, an expanding population, a global economy, the available marvels of industrialism—all united to make the transformation of Paris necessary, possible, and gigantic. Haussmannization—a contemporary coinage meaning drastic, centralized, violent urban renewal—was made possible by the sharp convergence of the forces of authoritarian urbanism, the new structures of capitalism, and the urban crisis that overwhelmed Paris. The alliance between public and private investment, all accomplished under the intimidating intervention and symbols of imperialism, made Haussmann's work possible.[24] The city itself, with its long history as a royal capital, the center of the kingdom in every possible way, meant that the task of transformation would be on the grandest scale. Once underway Paris became the model of a national city. Not only was it imitated throughout France–Lyon and Marseilles had similar and simultaneous transformations–but throughout the West. Paris became what ancient Rome had been: an urban ideal to which all aspired through emulation or imitation. For the nineteenth century, it was St. Augustine's City of Man, the modern city par excellence. Its boulevards and buildings were exported to the rest of the world as easily as the luxury goods that formed the foundation of the city's economy, while hundreds of thousands went on pilgrimage to the secular Mecca.

The mythic proportions of the place, the pull of Paris, sometimes despite the Parisians, is seemingly universal. The Paris that magnetically attracts still remains Haussmann's Paris.[25] The boulevards, the Place de l'Etoile, indeed all the major *places*, most of the bridges over the Seine, all the squares and small parks, the Bois de Boulogne and Bois de Vincennes, to mention only a few of the aspects that define Paris, were all Haussmann's work. How we walk or drive about the city was determined by him, as was our focus on the various monuments closing the perspectives he created. And the architecture. The overwhelming impression of Paris as a uniform, harmonious urban tapestry accented with charming scenes from an earlier age that survived Haussmann's wreckers, endures. What he left intact is as important in the overall design of Paris as what he demolished. The bits of the old city, alive in the midst of the new, old gems in a new setting, have an appeal all their own. Even in its architectural regularity Paris provides the kind of aesthetic satisfaction unavailable in a city built in many styles over many centuries.

There is an irony to Haussmann's intimate identification with Paris. His is almost a household name, both of admiration and scorn. Yet few know precisely what he did or what he was. He is assumed to have been an architect–he despised them–or, alternately, an engineer–he valued them but thought they lacked vision. In fact he was a bureaucrat, perhaps the most famous or successful administrator in urban history. It is difficult to name another. Only Robert Moses, the individual chiefly responsible for the highways, bridges, public beaches, and power stations of New York City, comes close; and Moses was a great admirer of Haussmann. Not unexpectedly, he valued in Haussmann what he valued in himself: boldness of conception, the ability to grasp the enormous complexity of a great city and treat it as a whole, integrating all the parts, great and small, into a single organism, the predominance of transportation, the importance of parks, administrative genius, contempt for democratic procedures, and a penchant for bullying.

Our distrust for administrators—reflected in presidential promises to trim the bureaucracy, streamline government, make things work—would have been incomprehensible to Haussmann and his contemporaries. He believed administration could and should confront and solve the great questions of the day. Good government was good administration for Haussmann, one of the earliest French proponents of a professional civil service, foreshadowing our own age of the expert, our reliance on technocrats. Haussmann now seems a familiar figure: in his own day he was a new breed of bureaucrat.

He had no patience with abstractions or ideology. He was an administrator who did things, made things, built Paris. He knew and boasted that his achievement and his fame would outlast the personal calumnies he endured. By the time he wrote his *Mémoires*, transformed Paris had not only outlived the Second Empire but had been reaffirmed by the completion of many of his projects, several of which were not fully realized until our century. A few jewel-encrusted decorations, signed photographs of Bonapartes, uniforms no longer worn, boxes of prefectorial reports are all that Haussmann would have left behind had he not been summoned to Paris in 1853 by Louis Napoléon, emperor not by the grace of God but by his own coup d'état, and given the task of translating the emperor's vague vision of a new capital into reality. Haussmann imprinted himself on history not because of his *Mémoires* or the greatness of his character and life but because he was responsible for one of the modern wonders of the world, the new Paris, whose transformation he oversaw, from the most grandiose conceptions to the most minute detail.

· I ·

Paris Before Haussmann

LONG BEFORE HAUSSMANN, VISITORS WERE AMAZED AT THE CITY IN the bend of the Seine. Paris first seen etched a sharp and sometimes monstrous image in the memory. The city was larger than life, beyond the limits of perception. Its size, density, complexity, both wonderful and terrific when viewed from a distance, were confirmed in the days of more intimate examination that followed the first glimpse. Once experienced at street level, its particular charms and beauties singled out from the overwhelming whole, the city could become Paris remembered, the most familiar form of celebration in memoirs, letters, novels, poetry, and song. In recollection sentiment, sentimentality, and nostalgia softened first impressions, replacing them with a sense of specific loss or regret.

Those who loved or loathed Paris wrote similarly of their first view, struck by the stark contrasts of two cities in one. "I had imagined a city as beautiful as it was big, of the most imposing aspect, where one saw only superb streets, and palaces of marble and gold," wrote Rousseau:

> Entering through the faubourg Saint Marceau, I saw only small, dirty and stinking streets, ugly black houses, an air of filth, poverty, beggars, carters, sewing women, women hawking tisanes and old hats.[1]

"So this is Paris," said the Russian traveler Nikolai Karamzine to himself as he trudged through the mud of the narrow streets of the faubourg Saint Antoine, "the city that seemed so magnificent to me from afar."

> But the decor changed completely when we arrived at the banks of the Seine. There arose before us magnificent edifices, six-story houses, rich shops; what a multitude of people! What variety! What noise![2]

"Leaving Villejuif," wrote Réstif de la Bretonne, who would devote his literary life to prowling Paris streets to record the vitality of the city in all its abundance and perversity,

> we alighted upon a great mass of houses overhung by a cloud of smoke. I asked my father what it was? "It's Paris. It's a big city, you can't see it all from here." "Oh, how big Paris is father, it's as big as Vermanton to Sacy, and Sacy to Joux." "Yes, at least as big. Oh, what a lot of people! So many that nobody knows anyone else, not even in the same neighborhood, not even in the same house. . ."[3]

Here, in three contrasting eighteenth-century perceptions of Paris are the themes of the city's history. Created by a long and turbulent past, Paris presented the stark contrast of two cities on the same site, one beautiful, one squalid, the physical strains of urban hurly-burly, anomie, and a sense of menace. Long after Haussmann imposed new patterns of movement, space, and residence, transforming the city in the name of salubrity and order, commerce and progress, the same historical forces, forced into new channels, would continue to flow. Long before he laid violent hands on Paris, thoughtful men knew something had to be done.

No one knew where the city began or ended. For years the kings had tried to check the growth of Paris, first with walls, then with decrees, milestones, and markers. The city absorbed, overran, or ignored them all. "I marvelled at the way Paris devours its surroundings, changing nourishing gardens into sterile streets," wrote Réstif de la Bretonne. No one knew how many people lived in Paris, including the government, and there was no accurate map of the city. There were proposals aplenty for Paris, and criticism was socially and intellectually diverse. Virtually all the would-be city planners deplored the existence of two cities and wanted to liberate monumental, public, wealthy Paris from the squalid accumulation of centuries of haphazard growth. In the century before the French Revolution the city itself had recoiled from its own spreading decay and decrepitude. Those who could had been moving westward, leaving behind the old medieval core of Paris.

Among those who observed the city at street level, Sébastien Mercier and Réstif de la Bretonne had a deep affection for Paris despite its horrors. But Voltaire, the most famous of these urban critics, loved with less compassion and sentimentality. Lacking a taste for the underbelly of urban life, he deplored the overcrowding, the danger, the filth that everywhere assaulted his gaze. Paris was ugly, low, vulgar, disorderly. Voltaire lamented the lack of public markets, fountains, regular intersections, theaters; he called for widening the "narrow and infected streets," for uncovering the beauties languishing beneath Gothic sprawl and squalor. "One passes the [east side of the] Louvre and grieves to see this facade, a monument to the grandeur of Louis XIV, to the zeal of Colbert, and to the genius of Perrault, hidden by the buildings of the Goths and Vandals." He excoriated the clutter that hid or deformed classical monuments. The center of Paris, with the exception of a few buildings and streets "that equal or surpass the beauties of ancient Rome," (the Louvre, the Tuileries, the Champs-Elysées) is "dark, hideous, closed in as in the age of the most frightful barbarism." He celebrated Christopher Wren's London and regretted the neighborhoods that had escaped the London fire in 1665.[4]

What was needed was light and air, not more monumental buildings or *places* implanted in the medieval tangle but liberation from urban strangulation. In a passage that became a favorite of Haussmann's, Voltaire pronounced the problem soluble in ten years with the aid of a graduated tax levied on Parisians for beautifying their city, for making it "the wonder of the world."[5] Voltaire concluded a 1749 pamphlet with a prayer:

> May God find some man zealous enough to undertake such projects, possessed of a soul firm enough to complete his undertakings, a mind enlightened enough to plan them, and may he have sufficient social stature to make them succeed.[6]

He had imagined Haussmann a century before he appeared.

Montesquieu, as had all the intellectuals of the day, also proposed improvements. He wondered why fountains were not as prevalent in Paris as they were in Rome. He suggested two set in the middle of a square—Paris fountains were habitually fixed to a wall rather than freestanding—built where the Pont-Neuf joined the Right and Left Banks.[7] He might have pointed to the use of fountains in his native Bordeaux, later an important influence for Haussmann, but Rome carried more prestige. Most critics, however, proposed far more drastic solutions in which few buildings would escape demolition. The Collège de Quatre-Nations (D 4, the present Institut), the Place des Victoires (E 3), Perrault's Louvre colonnade, and the churches of St. Gervais (F 4, Voltaire's favorite) and St. Sulpice (D 4) would be spared but the eighteenth-century critics unhesitatingly sacrificed virtually the entire medieval heritage of Paris. The more severe extended their dreams of urban renewal to the monuments of the Renaissance and Age of Louis XIV. They wanted streets cut through the lovely *places* Royale and Louis-le-Grand. New streets were offered as the solution to all urban problems; they would give Paris movement while fumigating and aerating the city. For the first time streets took priority over buildings, an emphasis that would dominate all subsequent thinking about Paris.

The desire for urban movement meant not only access to the city's monuments and buildings but to the setting of those buildings. Public space had to be made rational. The theater became the most significant public building in the eighteenth century, replacing church and palace. Not only was it an institution now open to a general public and consequently a freestanding structure outside the châteaux of the nobility, but its very function necessitated a transformation of the immediate neighborhood. The demand for theaters and their importance in eighteenth-century cities was another indication of the growing importance of public opinion: cities had to build spaces in which many could legally gather for functions other than admiring the grandeur of court and king, who in France had deserted Paris for Versailles. In the seventeenth century, tennis courts and reception rooms had served as theaters. In such ill-adapted spaces had all Molière's plays been staged in the Palais-

Royal. The Odéon theater (E 4) was built on land alienated by the Prince de Condé, who also put up some of the money. Deliberately intended to give Paris a theater worthy of its playwrights, it was designed as something entirely new by Charles de Wailly and Marie-Joseph Peyre. The theater extended into the city, endowing the immediate neighborhood with theatrical qualities and inviting a general audience, so long as they could afford a ticket. Around the same time Wailly also built the structure on the Right Bank today still used by the French National Theater. The urban landscape was being secularized and democratized, the street scene incorporated into architecture.

Before the eighteenth century the theatricality, and the theaters, of Paris were confined to the aristocracy and their haunts. From the habit of a public life, an extension of being at court, privileged Parisians treated life as a spectacle in which they were both actors and spectators. The Cours-la-Reine promenade (C 3), built in the seventeenth century, was spoken of as "the theater of the universe," and soon a number of *places* were added to the city, where one went to see and be seen. Attendance trickled down the social scale in the new theaters, while outside their confines the city mimicked the staged spectacles. The city as theater, the theater as city were apparent at the Odéon. Five new access streets were cut. They debouched upon a semicircular *place* that was also residential and became the foyer of the new theater. One of the five, the rue de l'Odéon, was the first street in Paris to have sidewalks. Yet another indication of the democratization of the city: one need not attend the theater in a coach with liveried drivers but could arrive on foot. This was also the first *place* in Paris not devoted to the cult of the monarch.

The new theater occupied a novel urban space, unencumbered by Voltaire's detested Gothic clutter. The philosopher had wanted significant portions of Old Paris cut away so that the existing buildings and *places*, churches, bridges, and châteaux he admired, virtually all dating from the Age of Louis XIV, might be appreciated as they deserved and as good taste demanded. The Bourbons had bequeathed two cities. They had planted the seeds of a new city amid the old, leaving the latter intact. Voltaire's preferred solution would

have been to eliminate medieval Paris. The more practical and difficult challenge would be to integrate the two.

In the beginning was the island, the present-day Ile de la Cité (E-
F 4). At first the cradle, now the museum of Paris, the Ile would prove
durable and fruitful in evoking metaphors for the birth and nurture of
a remarkable urban civilization. Here the *Parisii*, a branch of the
Senon Gauls, had made their settlements for perhaps a hundred years
before Roman annalists or generals recorded their existence in the
first century before the Christian era. Through subsequent centuries
successors occupied the island, recycling the building materials,
strengthening the walls, appropriating the sacred sites.

No other place in the world of similar size—some twenty acres in
a bend of the Seine—is so rich an urban text. Virtually every age of
Paris has left its imprint and artifacts. Remnants of the first wall
erected on the Ile de la Cité, around A.D. 250, have been found
and a museum built under the *parvis*, or plaza of Notre Dame. The
great cathedral itself, the most stunning and familiar medieval
building in the city, occupies the site of an earlier church destroyed
by fire, it in turn built on the same spot, redolent with sacred properties, even earlier used for a pagan shrine.

The Ile proved irresistible to Gaulish kings, Roman Caesars, and
Christian counts. When Hugh Capet, count of Paris, was elected
king of France (987) and founded the Capetian dynasty, his writ ran
not much beyond the confines of the Ile de la Cité and its tentative
extensions into the surrounding region: his ostensible subjects, the
Dukes of Normandy, within a day's ride of Paris, mocked and ignored his authority. From the Ile the monarchy would eventually establish its dominance and, through force and fraud, along with the
gentler statecraft of the marriage bed and the fortuitous extinction
of dynasties, create the French nation, whose center, for centuries,
would be the Ile. Today this remains literally but not politically true:
all distances in France are measured from Notre Dame Cathedral.

Once the dreaded invasions of the Normans had abated, in the
ninth century, a long and gradual transformation of Paris began.
The city acquired a form, physiognomy, and character that would
determine her destiny. The most fundamental physical fact was that

Paris is a river city. The city spilled over from the Ile, first to the Right and then to the Left Bank, but the island remained preeminent: here the two banks were united, here was the center of the city. This first urban occupation of the land on the two banks set their still distinct personalities. The Right Bank, chiefly because of the market, became commercial and almost simultaneously administrative. The Left Bank, home of the University of Paris, became intellectual, residential, and dotted with small shops, churches, and eventually aristocratic châteaux.

In the twelfth century Paris emerged not only as a city clearly superior to her rivals but as a royal capital. The history of Paris and the history of French kings ran in tandem. Unlike nearly all other French cities, Paris had never obtained a charter of liberties that might have granted a measure of independence from the crown. However assertive local officials might have been, the city's destiny lay legally in the king's hands. This unique relationship of city and state would continue to our own day, determining the city's history by assuring the state's intervention. The long period of peace in this part of the kingdom, from about 1110 to 1170, was the precondition for the remarkable evolution of Paris, the creation of the structures and culture that would direct and mark Paris until Haussmann's intervention.[8]

By the twelfth century Paris's physiology was fixed. The king's palace was on the Ile as were his law courts. In an age when the physical presence of the monarch defined the seat of government, this was all-important. Close by was the palace of the bishop of Paris.[9] The two most powerful men and the institutions they represented were within walking distance.[10] If the bishop's authority was great and his wealth commensurate, the king slightly surpassed him and was, in the formula of the day, "supreme lord and master" of the greatest part of Paris. The city would remain the capital of the lay authority, not the church. Paris never became Rome, even for the French church.

The greatness and genesis of Paris was determined by its early structures. Philippe Auguste's (1180–1223) decision to enlarge the market, le marché des Champeaux, at the expense of the recently expelled Jews was momentous for the history of the city and of bigotry. Favored corporations received confiscated Jewish businesses and homes, while a few royal friends got expropriated morsels as well. In the now aggrandized market the king ordered two new buildings to replace the demolished Jewish houses: these were the first *halles*, or sheds, which soon became a generic word for market. The enlarged market, laid out on a grid, was walled and the gates were locked at night. The new structures gave the neighborhood— between the present-day rue du Pont-Neuf and rue de la Grande-Truanderie (E 3)—its configuration and character, which were retained until les Halles were demolished in 1969 and the entire provisioning operation moved out of Paris. Some see this as the death of Paris as a living historical entity.[11]

Around the markets gathered the multitude of merchants, workers, and hangers-on connected with provisioning, and there emerged the several associations of merchants, including the most powerful of them, the *marchands de l'eau*, those concerned with river traffic, who received from the kings the right to police the river, which led to a monopoly melding economic and political authority. Here was the origin of Paris municipal government as distinct from that of the king. The physical center of this emerging authority was also on the Ile, the *place de grève*, the plaza in front of what is now the Hôtel de Ville, where boats were beached, loaded, and unloaded.

The University of Paris took form around the same time, across the river. Early divided into faculties and nations of students, each of which had its own seal and legal identity, the University and its parts were quickly freed from the tutelage of local authorities. As an autonomous corporation the University governed itself, fixed its membership, established its own rules and regulations. The bishop of Paris had no authority over the University, which was directly attached to the distant protection and oversight of the papacy, a sure guarantee of relative, even complete independence in all but the most notorious matters. The University neighborhood, like that of les Halles on the Right Bank, was a world unto itself, with unique patterns of property ownership, population, and architecture that soon became indelible.

There remain two aspects of Philippe Auguste's work: he walled

Paris and built the first Louvre. Both left lasting urban imprints. The long peace that made possible the medieval growth and urbanization of Paris ended in the last decade of the twelfth century. The king responded to external danger with a fortified château and a military wall, which also served as a safe vantage from which to watch and intimidate an urban population already known for unruliness. Paris at the time had perhaps fifty thousand inhabitants and the new wall enclosed some five hundred acres.[12] The old Louvre, whose mass of turreted towers can be seen in the background of the *Très Riches Heures* of the duc de Berry for the month of October, was erected on the route from Vexin and was the center of the city's defenses. Machiavelli, who deeply considered such matters, would later insist that the best way to hold a conquered city was to live there oneself. Philippe Auguste needed no theoretical arguments. He lived in Paris and would hold it as all kings of his day held towns: with a citadel. His successors, whether kings, republics, or emperors, would also hold Paris best by living there, a fact that bedeviled governments of the eighteenth and nineteenth centuries.

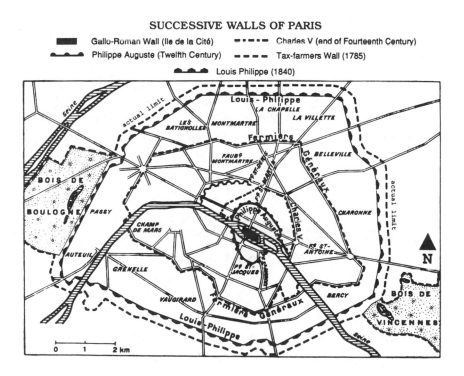

SUCCESSIVE WALLS OF PARIS

████ Gallo-Roman Wall (Ile de la Cité) ▄▀▄▀ Charles V (end of Fourteenth Century)

▄▀▄▀ Philippe Auguste (Twelfth Century) ▬ ▬ ▬ Tax-farmers Wall (1785)

▄▀▄▀ Louis Philippe (1840)

Paris would remain a walled city from this moment until the infamous wall of the Tax Farmers (1785) was torn down by the French Revolution. But the idea of the enclosed city persisted. In 1840–41, during the July Monarchy, another wall was erected. All have vanished—although a large chunk of the second Paris wall, built at the end of the fourteenth century by Charles V, can still be seen, near the Hôtel de Sens, on the Right Bank (F 4)—but the *périphérique*, a highway that today rings the city, containing Paris as surely as did any medieval wall, testifies to the durability and persistence of urban patterns.[13] The Louvre too would remain, defining Paris as clearly as Notre Dame, les Halles, the walls, or the University, although Philippe Auguste's original structure would be razed and transformed by an enormous palace begun by François I (1515–47) and not completed until Napoléon III.

Philippe Auguste left Paris the capital of his kingdom, with the monarch and the market, the Ile de la Cité, the bridges over the Seine, and the University enclosed within his walls. He had enlarged the original Ile de la Cité, and an ever-expanding system of walls would continue to envelop the growing city. Socially and politically as well, this king of large views put his stamp on the destiny of Paris. He closely associated himself and the embellishments of his capital with the bourgeoisie. The office of *prévôt*, for example, traditionally held by an important nobleman, would henceforth be occupied by an influential bourgeois. It was during his reign that the names of those important bourgeois families that would be so significant in Paris at the end of the century first emerged from obscurity to impose their identity upon the city. He even paved the streets for the first time, a challenge Haussmann would confront six centuries later. There is an attractive historical anecdote, worn smooth from reiteration. One day the king smelled the nauseating odors of the unspeakable mixture of filth, temporarily transformed from an open sewer into a street by the tramp of pedestrians. The king immediately ordered the paving.

The Paris inherited by the Bourbon kings—the dynasty originated in the seventeenth century—was essentially a medieval city in size, shape, function, and pattern. Guided by the watchful extravagance of her kings, the city had grown following the contours fixed in the Middle Ages. Indeed all governments would be constrained by the shape and direction given Paris by Philippe Auguste.

The growth of Paris, which no government could control or check, the need to feed and police an expanding population, are as fundamental to the city's history and destiny, as well as its place in the nation's history, as any buildings or physical features. The etymological derivation of words like "police" and "policy" from the Greek *politeia*—the governance of a city—provide a constant reminder. Like the growth rings of a tree the walls of Paris marked her expansion; each new circumvallation was an attempt to contain the city, which was still considered as a defensive entity composed of everything within its walls. But the medieval idea of the city as a fortress was early challenged by the very size of Paris. The city soon exceeded a population of twenty thousand, which overburdened the old structures for provisioning and required more and more surrounding countryside for support.[14]

The urbanization of Europe after 1500 demanded "the subordination of an important part of the countryside to the needs of the city and the elaboration of an extensive system of transportation."[15] Because Paris had early become a royal city, even though the medieval kings and their courts were peripatetic, the long, desperate, and brutal struggle to wrest control of the food supply from an agrarian economy controlled by peasant communities made the city central to the formation of the French nation-state. The presence and policing of the central markets in Paris fixed patterns for the intervention of the state in the city, while the problem of the location and organization of the central markets raised fundamental questions about the function and future of the city that were removed rather than solved in 1969 with the destruction of les Halles. The food demands of the capital sent its merchants and bureaucrats, both local and national, farther and farther afield to the north and west of France. Within this large and fluctuating area of supply the great city had long enjoyed priority over its rivals, including the local towns, for grain purchases. The kings regularly backed this priority.[16]

By the eighteenth century the so-called supply crowns for the Paris grain trade reached well beyond the Seine basin—deep into the provinces of Flandres to the north, Alsace-Lorraine to the east, Burgundy and the Bourbonnais to the southeast—to supply the city's three grain and flour markets.[17] And the city continued to grow, drawing more and more of the kingdom's substance, bursting its medieval constraints as the core city filled. The kings responded with edicts and sought to assure grain supplies lest the capital explode in food riots, the chief political expression for the majority of French men and women until the nineteenth century regulated the nation-state as the principal arena for political contestation. In 1528 François I became the first king to spend most of his time in Paris, proclaiming it his "*résidence habituelle*." He was determined to build himself a fit château. Thus began the other Paris Voltaire so loved, classical in inspiration and taste, ceremonial in function, monumental and geometric in aesthetic. In 1548 Henri II, François's son, issued the first of many edicts to limit the city's growth by interdicting building outside the walls. Almost immediately the monarchy itself violated the royal injunction, erecting the Tuileries palace (D-E 3).

Medieval Paris, cluttered, congested, hemmed in by walls, had grown by incorporating then urbanizing adjacent land. Surrounding forests, marshes, and monasteries, even the nearer villages, were enveloped. Unexploited space within the walls was built upon. So long as there was vacant land the city's expansion was a process of accretion and encroachment. There was no need to destroy what already existed. Gradually land disappeared as king and court settled down in Paris.

During the second half of his reign François had built magnificently near Paris, at Fontainebleau, St. Germain-en-Laye, and Villers Cotterets (in the present Bois de Boulogne). He also sold off substantial tracts of royal holdings within the walls (in the north and east of the city) and opened them to development by the nobility. Here was another strategy for holding the capital: implanting the nobility therein. But the most important of François's acts binding the Valois kings to Paris, reaffirming the city's primacy in the realm, was the new Louvre, which he was determined to build on the site of the old Louvre. This decision was the first large-scale project—and note it was taken by the central government, not local elites—calling for significant demolition.

François's Louvre was not a military château but a royal residence that formed no part of the city's defenses. In 1546, the year before his death, the king chose Pierre Lescot as his architect, a position Lescot would hold until his own death in 1578. The Louvre would become the largest palace in Christendom, a structure so formidable and centrally placed that it would affect the urbanization of Paris and the flow of traffic, as it still does. After François and Lescot many would have a hand in that stupendous project: Catherine de Medici, Henri IV, Louis XIII, Louis XIV, Napoléon I, Napoléon III, and their architects, as well as a long list composed of the most renowned plastic artists. Virtually every architect of stature sought the Louvre commission. Even the great Bernini was invited from Italy to consult; his plans were rejected. Then in 1564 Catherine de Medici embarked upon another great royal palace, the Tuileries, to the west of the Louvre, beyond the walls of the city, which would be eventually linked to the latter by Napoléon III: a new city was rising alongside the old.

Medieval Paris remained, its importance and mystique undiminished. The Renaissance kings and their successors still conceived of their capital in terms of the original core from whence it originated. In the new bird's-eye-view maps of the day Paris is depicted as an irregular geometric form dotted with important public buildings and dominated by church spires. Even the most characteristic views

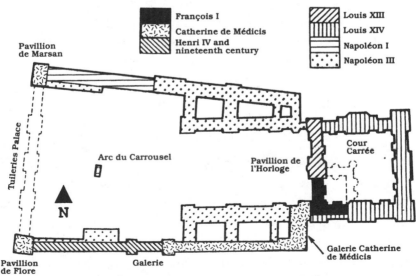

STAGES IN THE CONSTRUCTION OF THE LOUVRE

across the Seine were fleeting at best. The banks and bridges were lined with buildings. The visual relief was upwards to turrets and dormers, and the church towers that rose to heaven. The viewer's gaze was forcibly vertical. The perspective of an imagined vantage above the city gives a sense of more rational order than existed at ground level. In Léonard Gaultier's 1611 map, the Ile de la Cité is in the center and, with the exception of the Louvre, ecclesiastical buildings dominate. Gaultier saw Paris as a medieval city—although he straightened a number of streets—despite the implantation of many new buildings. Paris continued to be described as tripartite, as it had been in Philippe Auguste's day: "la Ville, Cité et Université de Paris" (the city itself, the administrative center, and the University).

Even the greatest of French kings, and one of the greatest builders of the species, Henri IV, found himself constrained by medieval Paris. He entered the city on March 22, 1594, after nearly thirty years of murderous civil war, set in grim relief by the massacre of Protestants on St. Bartholomew's Day (August 23–24, 1572), a slaughter he had escaped only by a hasty conversion to Catholicism. Henri was determined to live in his capital, heal the wounds of religious strife, and embellish the city that now, perhaps more than ever, had come to represent the kingdom and, he hoped, would soon represent his single, stable, centralized government. He embarked on a brilliant and ambitious building program.[18] Henri provided the pattern for the next three centuries of urban design, oepning the way to French urban classicism.[19] For the next eight decades—until Louis XIV moved his court and concerns to Versailles—the first three Bourbon kings lavished care and money on their capital, building a classical city alongside the original medieval city.

Marie de Medici, Henri IV's second queen and long associated with his urban projects—her influence gave Paris an Italianate aspect—honored her assassinated husband with a bronze equestrian statue on the Pont-Neuf, one of his most important projects and the scene of his murder. He was stabbed by a Catholic fanatic, Ravaillac (May 14, 1610), as he descended from his coach, which was hopelessly stalled in traffic. The statue was long delayed, but when finally erected (1614) was the first such statue of a French king put in a public place. Significantly, Henri gazes toward the Ile de la Cité. Westward, at the bronze king's back, lay a new Paris in embryo.

Between Philippe Auguste and Haussmann no person had so indelibly put his mark and personality on Paris as Henri IV. He built bridges and palaces, churches and convents, gardens and quays, promenades and streets. He revitalized old *quartiers* and created new ones. He made the Ile de la Cité the judicial center of his kingdom. He attracted private capital to his vast urban schemes by giving entrepreneurs undeveloped urban land in exchange for their investment in bridges and residential projects. His friends and cronies followed suit, as did his two wives (Margot and Marie de Medici), his son and grandson and their queens (Louis XIII and XIV, Anne of Austria and Maria Theresa), and the powerful cardinals (Richelieu and Mazarin) who respectively served them as first ministers. They all built town residences, some as magnificent as Richelieu's Palais-Royal (E 3) or Marie de Medici's Luxembourg Palace (D-E 4), most more modest, as the duc de Sully's *hôtel*. Henri's reign not only marked the end of the civil wars but coincided with a resurgence of Catholic feeling and energy, visible in Paris in the mushrooming of new and sumptuous churches, several of them crowned with superb domes. The ambitions of church and state momentarily harmonized, and Henri gave a good deal of his own money—as did his queens—to ecclesiastical building.[20]

It is not so much the number of Henri's projects as their originality, individually and as part of a grand urban vision, and the fact that they were built in Old Paris, that characterizes his importance. The Pont-Neuf (E 4), already begun when Henri came to power, was transformed into the largest and most singular of the Paris bridges. It was the only bridge without houses, the first to have a pedestrian walk and to be decorated with sculpture: 381 carved satirical heads of important court figures. The bridge instantly became a major promenade and three important streets were cut on the Left Bank (the rue Dauphine being the most significant) to continue the rectilinear bridge and open new land to development. All who bought and built here had to agree to erect in a similar style.

The Place Royale (the present Place des Vosges [F 3–4]) is a square—all Henri's projects would be geometric forms—of about 140 meters each side, containing thirty pavilions or row houses, with the larger and more elaborate residences of the king and queen facing each other across the square. "It was as though the setting for a royal tournament or pageant, with king and queen in pavilions of honor, had been turned into permanent architectural form."[21] This is the first and largest uniform residential square in Europe, built in a combination of inexpensive red brick and cut stone; it was the last significant project done in eastern Paris until Haussmann. The Place Royale reflected both hierarchy and order in the city as in the state. The king expected those closest to him would live here, although he himself officially resided at the Louvre, which he significantly enlarged and decorated. Paris was steadily moving westward, a trickle and soon a regular flow that the king's heavy investment in the older neighborhoods could not stop.

The Place Dauphine, on the Ile de la Cité, was conceived even before the Place Royale was completed. An isosceles triangle with a base of 60 meters and a height of 90, all the houses built here would also be uniform, of red brick with stone highlighting. Unlike the Place Royale most of the owners were neither noble nor of the highest rank but men of commerce or *rentiers*. Thirty-two houses were built, with private capital, but, alas, unlike the Place Royale, little today remains: two heavily restored houses and only two of the triangle's sides, whose houses have suffered serious to fatal reworking.

The third of Henri's *places* was never built. The Place de France was to symbolize the unity of the kingdom despite its regional diversity. Semicircular in shape, it was to have a diameter of 156 meters. From this semicircle would radiate a series of streets carrying the names of French provinces, a representation of all roads leading to the capital, and because these were to be official buildings, the home of the crown's administration, the provinces would find their logical terminus in the monarchy. This was the first example of street names taken from geography and a prescient foreshadowing of the railroad law of 1841 that made Paris the nation's railhead. Henri's three *places* share so many common characteristics that they can be considered as three aspects of an urban strategy for dominating Paris.[22] Henri's urbanization is the Renaissance equivalent of Philippe Auguste's walled citadel. Holding Paris was never far from the minds of the kings.

Henri combined two styles, usually associated with Italian and Flemish cities, conjoining political and urban ideas with aesthetic values, as have all rulers who have laid hands on Paris. Around a geometric core he grouped houses whose scale and relative austerity related to Flemish taste, but they were designed with the classical rigor associated with Italy. Realized in simple materials, they were comfortable and unostentatious. These *places*, basically rejecting the elaborations of the new Baroque style, inclined more toward a logical, rational conception of building and urban space that we usually call classical and represent the most original contributions of European urbanization in the first half of the seventeenth century.

Henri's work was continued after his death. New neighborhoods to the west were opened—the *quartier* Richelieu (today the neighborhood around the Bibliothèque Nationale and the Bourse), the *quartier* St. Honoré (the neighborhood bordering the Tuileries gardens)—as well as the Ile St. Louis (F 4), the small island adjacent to the Ile de la Cité. The Tuileries and its magnificent gardens, designed by André Le Nôtre, whose masterpiece would be the Versailles gardens, put the royal imprimatur on the movement westward, expressed the new taste for large gardens, and further aggrandized the already sprawling royal palace. So too did the gradual emergence of what would become the faubourg St. Germain (C-D 4), to be celebrated, by authors from Mercier to Balzac to Proust, as the most elegant aristocratic neighborhood in Paris. Land in western Paris, especially on the Left Bank, was less expensive; new bridges, particularly the Pont Royal, now made it accessible; and the châteaux of queens Margot and Marie de Medici, among others, made the area fashionable. As one moved south of the river on the Left Bank there were the convents with their new domed churches: the Val-de-Grâce (E 5) and Port-Royal, and neighboring religious houses were beginning to sell off their land to developers. The walls of Paris had become meaningless. When Louis XIV finally tore them down, creating the first boulevards, Paris became an open city.

The great domed churches of the Sorbonne (E 4) and St. Paul (F

4) were built, the Louvre received the attentions of two more kings and their architects, Louis Le Vau's elegant Collège des Quatre Nations (then thought the most elegant new building in Paris, today the home of the Institut [D-4]) was the first classical building on the Left Bank riverfront, and the Parisian skyline now had a series of magnificent domes to compete with the old medieval towers. Louis XIII doubled the bridges across the Seine from five to ten and Richelieu and Mazarin both built great palaces befitting their importance. Marie de Medici built the boulevard Cours-la-Reine in western Paris in imitation of Henri's *cours* Le Mail in eastern Paris (the present Boulevard Morland [F 4]), and erected an equestrian statue of Louis XIII in the Place Royale, another addition to the royal cult.

The next Bourbon, Louis XIV, had an acutely developed sense of grandeur. What he lacked in originality was compensated by vigorous, or stubbornly held, ideas, attention to detail, unquestioned faith in his own taste, a good eye for talent, and a highly evolved conception of the monarchy, which included the city as a theatrical representation of the king's greatness. Paris had to wait for the long reign of Louis XIV to receive the necessary endowments of a ceremonial city, fit for the theater of absolutism he would enact until abandoning his capital for Versailles.

The great king never liked Paris. He had heard the menacing shouts of the riotous Frondeurs when a boy, which he never forgot or forgave. He returned to Paris only four times once he moved to Versailles in the 1680s. He was the first of the kings to hold Paris from afar. His conquest of urban space was as purposeful as that of his grandfather, Henri IV, but on a much larger scale: the king's physical absence was, ironically enough, complemented by a grand stone presence.

Louis's personal rule (1660–1715) began traditionally enough with plans to complete the Louvre-Tuileries. He added Claude Perrault's austere and stunning colonnaded facade to the eastern end of the Louvre, some said to still the incessant promptings of Colbert, his first minister. The monarchy, soon to abandon Paris for Versailles, eighteen miles to the west, still looked eastward in Paris. Louis's most ambitious scheme had been first broached by Mazarin: a great ceremonial road linking the château at Vincennes to the port St. Antoine, where the Bastille stood. Louis even had Perrault begin an immense triumphal arch that would stand between the château and the prison. This was to be a grand and intimidating entry into the royal capital. Ambassadors and dignitaries, generals and aristocrats would enter Paris from the east, traverse the old city, and be received at the Louvre-Tuileries. There was even talk of connecting the triumphal road to the Tuileries by cutting a street across Paris. Louis was intrigued at the conception yet balked at the vast urban confiscations and demolition necessary along the faubourg St. Antoine, not to mention the question of the Bastille, even then a problem for the monarchy. The plan remained incomplete. Had it been realized Paris might well have been permanently oriented to the east. Louis built only the cours de Vincennes, a broad roadway planted with four ranks of trees, which ran from the château to the Place du Trône, laid out in the form of a star (today the Place de la Nation [G 4]), but he stopped short at the ninety-foot walls of the Bastille. His triumphal way did not enter the city nor require extensive property confiscation and demolition.

After Louis XIV there were a few urban projects of significance, but with the exception of the Place Louis XV (present Place de la Concorde [D 3]), yet another altar to the royal cult, and the Ecole Militaire (C 4), the important changes in Paris were not the result of monarchical building. The new aristocratic *quartier* of the Chaussée d'Antin (now the neighborhood of the big department stores) gave work to a younger generation of architects and a new, more intimate sensibility in domestic design, but it also was a centrifugal expansion of the city, under the sponsorship not of the king but of his cousin, the duc d'Orléans, arguably more important for Parisian history in this decade than his cousin at Versailles. But if the last two Bourbons before the French Revolution did little building, the royal regulations of 1783–84 reveal serious urban thought. Building owners now had to submit their plans to a bureau that would become, in the nineteenth century, the basis for building permits. Haussmann would elaborate and exploit this administrative machinery. For the first time, mass domestic construction came under the control of the authorities. Architects and their clients had to conform.[23]

The Ecole Militaire, with its enormous drill field, the Champ-de-Mars, was the most significant royal undertaking of the age. Land for the project came from the purchase of only two parcels on the Left Bank—to find so much land across the river was out of the question—but even the Left Bank was filling up. First the walls had hindered urban growth, then central density had pushed Paris beyond several defensive extensions, then the walls came down and Paris spilled to west and south and north.[24]

By mid-eighteenth century, a growing Paris was being surrounded by institutional blocks set into open spaces, new barriers to expansion. The aristocratic faubourg St. Germain was bounded on the west by Louis XIV's majestic veterans' hospital and hospice, Les Invalides (C 4). When Louis XV built the Ecole Militaire he added yet another obstacle to westward expansion. What little space remained in Old Paris was quickly exploited. Germain Soufflot gave Paris yet another wonderful dome, that atop the church of St. Geneviève (now the Panthéon [E 4]), located on one of the highest spots in Paris and visible from surprisingly diverse vantages. The sheer size of Soufflot's dome was made possible, after his death, by incorporating some ironwork into his designated stone. And the elegant Halle aux Bleds, the new grain market, was built adjacent to les Halles (E 3), showing another precocious use of iron and stone that foreshadowed much nineteenth-century engineering.

By the 1780s the history of Parisian development had little to do with the king. More and more the city government, although royally appointed, grappled with local matters. Most of the new streets were cut by private individuals using their own capital. The Palais-Royal, the home of the Orleanist branch of the royal family—the château had been fundamentally reworked recently by the architect Victor Louis—became the center for a new generation of architects seeking commissions. Domestic building had clearly outstripped monumental projects. Then the absentee monarchy intruded disastrously: in 1785 a new wall was built, the wall of the Tax Farmers, to collect excise on everything entering and leaving the city. The nonmilitary wall followed the lines of Louis XIV's boulevards, which in turn followed the lines of the defensive walls the Sun King had demolished. The new wall checked the expansion of Paris and reduced the city to its dimensions of a century earlier. Claude-Nicolas Ledoux, the most inventive and original architect of the age, decorated the hated wall with more than fifty "Propylées"—one may still be seen at La Villette (F 2), another in the parc Monceau (C 2)— surely the most beautiful tax collection booths ever designed. His temples to taxation were still incomplete when his protector, Calonne, the first minister, fell from power in 1787.

In Paris before there could be rational urban order there had to be an accurate map of the city. Between the end of the seventeenth century and the revolution, growth of the city complemented the desire for accuracy and led to the registration of 132 maps and plans, including the beautiful "city portrait" commissioned by the *prévot des marchands* of Paris, Turgot. These are no longer the idealized overviews of the Renaissance encompassing the entire city in a single image but maps with a bird's-eye perspective that try to depict every detail of street and building, their relationships to one another, and the rational order of the whole. Yet it was not until the late eighteenth century that the first geometric plan of the city, whose accuracy was incontestable, was made. From 1776 until 1783, Edme Verniquet, a Burgundian architect who had a successful Paris career, worked without official support on his map, squinting in the torchlight, for he could not take accurate measurements during the day in the crowded Paris streets. His ground observations were corrected by triangulation to determine the elevations of the city. Verniquet spent thousands of his own money before he received any official help. On April 10, 1783, the first royal declaration of an urban policy was promulgated, tied, it is worth noting, to an accurate map. It insisted that the alignment of streets was "important for the public welfare," that they ought to be "sufficiently wide and free of any barriers to the free and easy passage of vehicles and pedestrians" and further asserted that overly tall buildings were "prejudicial" to clean air in a city as populous as Paris, as well as contrary to public safety, and prone to fire.[25] Verniquet's map was successfully completed, the great urban projects, directed at the old city, were not. The revolution intervened.

The Parisian geography of the revolution was familiar: the Hôtel de Ville and the Louvre-Tuileries were the seats of city and national government, respectively. The Palais-Royal remained a magnet for low-life and political agitation, les Halles continued the stomach of Paris and its grumblings were nervously watched by the new government, and the crowds who were so important to the revolution came from the neighborhoods of St. Antoine (G 3–4) and St. Marcel (F-G 5), both in eastern Paris (on the Right and Left Bank, respectively).

The revolution disrupted any plans the monarchy might have had for Paris, but it did some important demolition work, bequeathed an influential though unrealized urban vision, and put the transformation of Paris on the agenda of the future. The Bastille was demolished within a year of its fall. The long-desired road across Paris, from east to west, which would eventually become the rue de Rivoli–St. Antoine, was now possible. Many of the earlier legal obstacles to improvement or redevelopment were similarly razed. Vast tracts of land, rural and urban, had been confiscated by the revolution, first by the Civil Constitution of the Clergy (1790), which seized ecclesiastical property, and then by the Law of Suspects (1793) and subsequent legislation associated with the Terror, which seized aristocratic holdings. Much of this land was sold off to raise money for the revolution with no thought of what purpose it would eventually serve. About one-eighth of the land in Paris changed hands. The immediate result was the creation of considerable open spaces in Paris, much of it outside the line of the boulevards, which was divided into small parcels and quickly became building sites. The revolution also breached the hated tax wall. Here was a unique opportunity to transform Paris. But the revolution hadn't time to create a new city, to realize the urban dreams of the eighteenth century. What it did do was appoint a Commission of Artists, in May 1793, to advise the government on what should become of confiscated property in Paris and to propose needed urban projects.[26]

The commission met irregularly, "twice a decade [the ten-day periods in the revolutionary calendar that replaced the old, Christian week], seldom at the same hour, often with few members present, and almost never as a whole" and was dissolved in 1797. They realized little but they drew a plan of capital importance.[27] The artists proposed a number of new streets, many of which foreshadowed Haussmann's work as well as indicating precisely where radical urban surgery would be performed. An east-west thoroughfare, crossing Paris, from the Place Louis-le-Grand to where the Bastille had stood, was indicated, as well as a series of new streets through and around les Halles to make the markets accessible and unclog the core city. In both the east and west there were new streets to open these areas to further development, and on the Right Bank another series of east-west streets branched off the rue St. Denis and the rue St. Martin. Considerable surgery was proposed for the Ile de la Cité, including a street ringing the eastern end as well as another cutting across the Ile, and a bridge linking the Ile St. Louis with the Right Bank. Radiating from what is today the Place de la Bastille was a complex of streets connecting eastern Paris to the rest of the city. The dreaded and isolated faubourg St. Antoine, which had produced so many of the insurrections that fueled the revolution, was to be integrated in this manner.

On the Left Bank even more construction was proposed. The extensive street cutting suggested by the artists would have early opened the Left Bank to development. Instead it remained what it had been in the Paris of Philippe Auguste—and in a sense still remains—less commercially developed than the Right Bank. Some of this proposed development was dictated because a sizable portion of the land on the Left Bank had been in the hands of the church and the aristocracy. Even the artists, with so much confiscated land to work with, sought the path of least resistance. They proposed leaving substantial tracts of Old Paris intact, building around rather than through the core city. The problem was the atomization of property in Old Paris: it was simply too difficult, too expensive, too tedious or socially disruptive to acquire the necessary land. Instead they looked southward to the Left Bank as the new area of urban expansion and development.

In the Plan des Artistes the street was the essential instrument of urban development and rationalization, not new houses or public buildings; and streets were envisioned as straight and purposeful. The urban aesthetic of the age not only connected the public places of the capital but led the eye from one to the other in a conscious attempt to control perspective. One could now see the monumental structures of Paris not merely as a dome in the distance, rising above the urban clutter, but a dome along a rectilinear street. Domes, and public buildings generally, became street signs, landmarks, points on a journey. In embryo the plan already embraced the idea that move- ment ought to be the central organizing principle for Paris. The Plan des Artistes, although never realized, fixed the urban ideals of the eighteenth century, which remained virtually unquestioned in the nineteenth, although credit was rarely given to these revolu- tionary origins. The Plan des Artistes, the first comprehensive urban scheme for Paris, is a palimpsest. Underneath is Old Paris. The artists, as all subsequent transformers of Paris, thought in terms of preserving as much of the Old Paris as possible while rendering the city rational, which then meant accessible to traffic. Haussmann knew of the artists' work and grudgingly admitted they had had the right idea: "it [the map] shows a great many proposed new streets, to aid circulation in all neighborhoods of the city, facilitate con- struction, and to liberate the principal monuments."[28]

Napoléon might have been expected to accomplish what the Bourbon kings would not and the revolution could not. He had power, he was imperious, he was a man of the most grandiose ideas and conceptions, he was anxious to make an imperial city, and as an upstart he not only wanted to put his mark on Paris but in so doing to attach the capital to the imperial destiny. In fact Napoléon failed to transform Paris; and in his failure lie the germs of his nephew's ultimate triumph. The Napoleonic ideas that fueled so much of Louis Napoléon's political and urban thinking were as grandiose and extravagant as those of his uncle, but without the former's timidity when it came to Paris.

In his urban vision, as in so much else, the first Napoléon is the heir of the eighteenth century and the French Revolution. He re- lied upon the proposals of the Commission des Artistes for his gen- eral conceptualization, adding a few personal touches. Although a chorus of contemporary witnesses celebrated Paris in 1815, it was not, if one looked at an overall plan, significantly changed from the Paris of Louis XVI. The major difference was that Napoléon had far less reverence for Old Paris than had the monarchy or even the

Commission des Artistes. He was willing to take up the scalpel, or better yet the saber. "Paris is suffering from an aneurism of the heart," he said. In the center was the decrepit organ with no great arteries leading to it. Beyond this zone of human density, between the wall of the Tax Farmers and the boulevards of Louis XIV, were ill-defined spaces and gardens. This diagnosis called for some radical treatment. First, sharing Voltaire's aesthetic views, Napoléon wanted to see the existing monuments in a fit setting. The list of his destructions is long. On the Right Bank a number of convents disappeared (those of the Feuillants, Capucins, and Jacobins), as well as the Temple (which was replaced by a market), and St. Jacques-de-la-Boucherie (of which only a tower remains). All these structures, it is perhaps not coincidental, had served important political and symbolic functions during the revolution, as meeting places for political sects or a prison (the Temple) for the condemned king. Napoléon would tolerate no competitive shrines or monuments. He also razed, on the Left Bank, the houses on the pont St. Michel, the *collèges* of Cluny, Cardinal Lemoine, and l'Ave-Marie; and the churches of St. Marcel, St. André-des-Arts, the abbey St. Victoire, and the convent of the Grands-Augustins. This frenzy of destruction impressed and frightened contemporaries, although it was very much in keeping with the kind of demolitions undertaken by the revolution. "They announced to the residents of a neighborhood," a visitor to Paris wrote, "that they had to be gone in six weeks. They destroyed the buildings and the owners were only partly compensated. In ten years it would all be done, or so it seemed. But for the moment . . . even in the good neighborhoods there are as many houses boarded up as there are handsome new houses."[29]

The magical ten years that Voltaire imagined would be sufficient to transform Paris again appears. Perhaps it is merely a convenient figure, or figure of speech. Yet the work Voltaire imagined was on a scale that might well have been accomplished in ten years. The same may be said of Napoléon's relatively modest plans. The single major project, crossing the city from east to west, was the only proposal formidable enough to rank with Haussmann's work, and even this, the eventual rues de Rivoli–St. Antoine, was not completed by Napoléon. Most of what the earlier transformers envisioned was localized: disengaging the major monuments, building some access streets between the monuments and some others on the underbuilt Left Bank.

Napoléon's destructions were not a prelude to a new city. Only a few projects captured his imagination. He had inherited from the ancien régime the "great dream" of uniting the Louvre to the Tuileries with another gallery running parallel to that built by Henri IV. During a lunch with his architect, Pierre-François Fontaine, he dictated a note ordering the demolition of the buildings and squatter's huts that clogged the site to make way for a triumphal arch and a road linking the two palaces. After the treaty of Tilsit (1807), he returned to the scheme and decided against it. Napoléon III would complete the project. Only the arc du Carrousel was built. Fontaine's *Journal* reveals a hesitant and indecisive figure unlike the Napoléon with whom we are familiar on the battlefield or in the council chamber.

Napoléon did have an unerring sense of grandeur and its urban expression, and he read Paris better than many of her earlier masters. He saw clearly that the orientation of the capital had changed from east to west. The Champs-Elysées, previously a recreational area for the well-born, now became a grand triumphal route leading to the emperor's residence. The eastern triumphal route was permanently abandoned and the seat of government now faced westward, power was oriented toward fashionable Paris, turning its back on the east. More than symbolism was involved: Napoléon's decision reoriented the city both socially and politically, fixing, literally in stone, a long movement from east to west. Those left behind in eastern Paris would, for many years, follow a curve of historical evolution different from the western quarters of the city, and those sometimes sharp and hostile differences would have much to do with Haussmann's eventual transformations.

Napoléon was also anxious to put the imperial stamp on Paris. The original monument proposed for the empty Place de la Bastille, thrown up quickly and made of poor materials, was bizarre: a fountain in elephant shape. It fell to pieces in the 1840s and was replaced by the present July Column.[30] Not only would the monument claim the sacred ground of the site of the Bastille for the empire and further cement Napoléon's assertions to be the heir of the revolution, it would also form a pendant for the monument he planned at the other end of Paris, the Arc de Triomphe. The site for the latter was the single most impressive urban perspective in Paris, leading from the Tuileries, up the Champs-Elysées at a slight rise, to the spot where the arch stands today. Since the eighteenth century many had been aware of the prestige of the site and had sought just the right monument. Napoléon now seized the place and made it his. Work was began in 1806. Although not completed until after Napoléon's fall, it has remained his monument.

Napoléon's most daring scheme, however, was to cut a broad street from the eastern facade of the Louvre to the Place de la Bastille. This would go through the very heart of Paris, beginning with the church of St. Germain l'Auxerrois (E 3).[31] It might appear that this resurrection of Louis XIV's plan contradicted the western orientation of imperial power. In fact it did not. Napoléon did not conceive of the eastern route as a triumphal entry into the city but rather as a strategic road giving him access to the faubourg St. Antoine, the cradle of revolutionary street insurrection. Again Napoléon was prescient: subsequent governments would also regard the route from the Louvre eastward as a military road. Whether he could have carried out so vast a scheme of urban demolition is doubtful. Napoléon soon turned his attention to a more modest plan, proposed by the Commission des Artistes: a road running along the Tuileries and the Louvre, across Paris, eventually to link up with the rue St. Antoine and thus the Place de la Bastille. All the buildings along the rue de Rivoli were to be uniform and set back from the new thoroughfare by a series of arches that imposed order and elegance. The new street would be the first to give troops an easy route across Paris, and Napoléon—probably more than his nephew—was ever mindful of strategic matters. The rue de Rivoli was never completed. The Russian disaster intervened, which also brought to an end Napoléon's extravagant dreams of an enormous palace for the king of Rome, his son, where today the Palais de Chaillot stands (B-4).

Napoléon solved none of the problems of Paris. His energies were too focused upon celebrating his own glory and solidifying his usurped throne, and too often diverted by warfare, which drained away the money needed for urban transformation. With his failures may properly be dated the beginnings of the history of modern Paris. From the fall of the First Empire to the coming of the Second, from 1815 to 1853, Paris bent and finally broke under the mounting social, economic, and political pressures she had to endure.

· II ·

Haussmann Before Paris

GEORGES-EUGENE HAUSSMANN TRACED HIS LINEAGE BACK SEVEN generations and spoke of himself "as a descendant of the Lords of Andernach, near Cologne." All the Haussmanns were born and died in Tennstedt (today Bad Tennstedt) until Balthazar Haussmann moved to Colmar, in Alsace, in 1702. There he died on March 29 1736. Balthazar, a pharmacist by trade, married Marie-Madeleine Burger, the daughter of a merchant, in 1705, and thus established the Haussmanns in the cloth trade. Beginning with Balthazar's children all the Haussmanns were born in France. Christian (1716–93), also a pharmacist, was the father of Nicolas (1760–1846), and the grandfather of Haussmann.[1] Here our story begins.

Nicolas Haussmann became the director of the Versailles branch of the family business, la Maison Haussmann frères, which dealt in printed fabrics, then an administrator of the department of Seine-et-Oise, the first government servant in the family. He was elected a deputy from that department to the Legislative Assembly and then to the Convention Assembly in the French Revolution. He later was mayor of the town of Chaville, where he owned a country house. He married Catherine-Thérèse Thiénot in 1786, and their son, Nicolas-Valentin, born at Versailles on October 22, 1787, was Haussmann's father.

41

Haussmann's memories of his grandfather were clear and he wrote of him warmly as an exemplary character whose views and values were not unlike his own. "He had a broad and liberal intelligence, resolute yet calm. He had self-mastery and desired, above all, as so many others did, only the reform of the abuses and prodigalities of the ancien régime. His political program was wholly expressed in the realization of the 'immortal principles' consecrated in the Declaration of the Rights of Man and Citizen." To be descended from a man who served in the assemblies of the French Revolution, especially the Convention, the cradle not only of the First Republic but the Terror as well, caused Haussmann some embarrassment. He carefully pointed out that his grandfather, absent *en mission*, "took no part in the trial of Louis XVI." Even had he been present, "I know that he would not have voted for the king's death." Lest there be any misunderstanding, Haussmann further distanced his grandfather from the Jacobins, insisting that "he would most certainly have been the victim of his loyalty in the deplorable affair of the unfortunate General Custine"—guillotined for treason at the insistence of the Jacobins, although much of the evidence against him was circumstantial—had Robespierre not fallen on 9 Thermidor (July 27, 1794). Grandfather Haussmann had insisted, in print, that "Custine is the terror of the German aristocracy; he has the confidence of the army and the local inhabitants, and I believe myself able to assure you that he deserves your confidence. You can count on his courage, on his abilities, and on his patriotism. I believe that he will continue always to be a true republican." These were compromising, and possibly dangerous, views in 1793.[2] In a less controversial moment grandfather Haussmann was the author of a report on the *assignats*, the paper money of the revolution.[3]

"The capital act in his career," the grandson, whose own greatest work was the extension of the limits of Paris, insisted, "was the administrative organization of Belgium and its annexation to France." Grandfather Haussmann and his colleague, Philippe-Constant-Joseph Briez, created a central administration to oversee eight subsidiary administrations. Their main task, after subduing the country, was to administer the sequestered property of those who had fled, collect taxes and customs, and see that everyone was fed. They also had charge of roads, bridges, canals, agriculture, and manufacturing. They ran the country.

Unfortunately, the restored Bourbon government took a much broader view of what constituted regicide than did Haussmann or his grandfather. All those who had not specifically voted to spare the king, whatever their excuse, were considered guilty. Despite his absence during the king's trial, Grandfather Haussmann was exiled as a regicide in 1816. He took refuge in Basel. When he returned to France after the fall of the Bourbons, he sold his property in Seine-et-Oise and settled quietly in Paris, in the faubourg du Roule. Here he read Montaigne and the *Livre de la Sagesse* by Pierre Charron, and visited the masterpieces in the Louvre. "It is here [Paris], up until the time I entered the departmental administration, that I regularly came to see him, listen to him, take his advice, and where he died, full of days, in June 1846."[4]

Haussmann quoted his grandfather, always an uncanny echo of his own views, several times in his *Mémoires*. "If you had seen the men of whom you speak [Danton, Saint-Just, and Robespierre] up close, as I did, had you been involved as I was in the events of that terrible time, I like to think that you would see things differently," Haussmann remembers the old man snarling in response to the revolutionary enthusiasm of another grandson: "You call yourself a republican! Then why don't you start by changing, from top to bottom, your lazy life of a man of pleasure?" France's future lay not in more revolution but in better administration: "We cannot know . . . how rich and powerful France would become if she were well governed, especially if she were well administered!" Although he "believed sincerely in the Republic," he thought it a "philosophical form of government that did not match the French genius."[5]

On his mother's side Haussmann's ascendance was equally bound to the revolution and the shifting borders and jurisdictions of eastern France. His mother, Caroline Dentzel, the daughter of Georges-Frédéric Dentzel, was born in Landau, then a possession of the Austrian Empire, on February 23, 1789. Georges-Frédéric had what can only be called a romantic life. Born in Durkheim, July 25, 1755, he studied at Jena and came to America to fight in the War of Independence, in the Deux-Ponts regiment. Upon his return to Europe

(1786) he settled at Landau, where he married the mayor's daughter, became a pastor in the Lutheran church, and "obtained letters of nationality" in France. In the revolution he was instrumental in organizing the local national guard and attached himself to General Kellermann, who put him in charge of bilingual correspondence. He was elected a deputy to the Convention for the Bas-Rhin, and he too was absent *en mission* during Louis XVI's trial and did not vote on the king's fate.

The siege of Landau thrust Dentzel dangerously into the limelight. He himself tells the story of his adventures, when he narrowly escaped a lynching at the hands of his own troops. He landed in prison and was spared further travail only by the fall of Robespierre.[6] What actually happened in the besieged town is probably lost to history. Dentzel's version is that he was surrounded by intrigue, cut off from all communication with the Committee of Public Safety, which had sent him to Landau, and became convinced that another representative of the Convention, Jean-François-Bertrand Delmas, had parlayed, perhaps treasonously, with the enemy, with whom the Committee of Public Safety had specifically forbade negotiation. Dentzel ordered Delmas arrested. Then Dentzel was himself arrested by General Laubadère, the military commander, and Delmas was reinstated. Laubadère, an aristocrat, had two brothers who had emigrated during the revolution and were serving in the army besieging Landau. The general himself was in a precarious position: those with aristocratic ties or titles, who lost battles, were suspected of treason and, as did General Custine, might pay with their lives. The Committee of Public Safety was sometimes as dangerous to a general as to the enemy.

The soldiers, believing Dentzel a traitor, now called for his head, and he was attacked and wounded in his place of confinement by a zealous soldier. There followed long harangues with the agitated troops about Dentzel's fate. He was saved from a lynching and managed to send his version of events to Paris via a certain "citoyen Schanégans," who got to see the Committee of Public Safety. Meanwhile the reinstated Delmas again tried to parlay with the besiegers. When the siege finally lifted, Dentzel left for Paris to clear his name,[7] was imprisoned,[8] and when liberated after 9 Thermidor went on to enjoy a successful career under Napoléon. He had the reputation of being a humane commander and in 1813 was promoted to brigade general and named a baron of the empire. This is the source of Haussmann's bogus baronetcy. Dentzel retired in 1815 and died in 1820. Landau was acquired by France in 1797 with the treaties of Campoformio and Turin.

If Haussmann's paternal grandfather is presented in the *Mémoires* as a temperate, even philosophical representative of enlightened administration, his maternal grandfather, a more bellicose figure who makes fewer appearances, served as Haussmann's direct link to Bonapartism and an exemplar of the man unjustly treated, forced to redeem his reputation from slander.[9] The respective children of these two revolutionaries were married at Versailles, June 12, 1806. Haussmann's father was not quite eighteen, his mother had just turned seventeen. The union was made possible by the revolution. Merchant and minister had fought for the revolution, made military and administrative careers, deserted their prerevolutionary and provincial vocations, and come to Paris for a larger stage of action and expectation. All this was unthinkable before 1789. The alliance of the Haussmanns and the Dentzels reinforced and launched a second generation of the beneficiaries of the revolution, who would in turn enter public service as had their fathers.

Nicolas-Valentin, whose father had been forced from the mayoralty of Chaville, about halfway between Paris and Versailles, by the Restoration of the Bourbon kings in 1814–15, was himself forced into semiretirement as a *commissaire des guerres*. He was an Orleanist, supporting the cadet branch of the restored Bourbons, and contributed articles to *Le Temps*, one of the most important opposition newspapers. In 1830 he became one of the signers of the Protestation des Journalists, which precipitated the revolution and drove the Bourbons out of France.[10] Nicolas-Valentin wrote a number of brochures on political questions and military provisioning.[11] His *Lettre* on political independence and decentralization, directed to Louis-Philippe's first minister, Odilon Barrot, foreshadowed a number of his son's political ideas. Nicolas-Valentin opposed the Orleanist position of letting local elites, the "notables," make decisions, without some central "bureaucratic" restraint. Municipal elections were still heavily influenced by the local lord or property owner and seldom did enlightened men, by which he understood liberals, get elected. Enlightened centralism, Haussmann's father insisted, was "entirely impartial, having for a goal only the execution of the law and the prosperity of the region."[12]

A large part of the pamphlet was given over to a historical survey of the development and failure of local government in France. Napoléon, who had "joined to the talents of a great captain those of a capable administrator," saved France from herself. The prefects were given the power to nominate municipal counselors—which would be of fundamental importance for Haussmann in Paris—as well as the mayors of communes. The abandonment of the Napoleonic practice of strong centralization would lead "ineluctably to the political dissolution of the state." Centralization was part of the genius of France.[13] This blend of Bonapartism and Orleanism, this faith in administration, is Haussmann's family heritage: when circumstances changed, he had no difficulty dropping the encumbering Orleanist allegiance, an ease experienced by many of Haussmann's generation.

Haussmann's mother, a shadowy figure in the *Mémoires*, as are all the women in his life, is described as having "a fine and delicate nature." From her he received "a nervous constitution, demanding a great deal of care since my exceptionally rapid growth fatigued me." Her first son (and second child) was born at Paris, March 27, 1809, and baptized Georges-Eugène at the home of his parents, 55 rue du faubourg du Roule. The autobiographer characteristically added a few particulars of place: he was born in "a small townhouse (hôtel) with a court and garden which was attached to the former possession of the Farmer General Beaujon and which, as prefect of the Seine, I had demolished to build the small *place* that marks the end of the boulevard Haussmann and the commencement of the boulevard Friedland." Haussmann was not a sentimental man. "I was baptized," he inaccurately embroidered, "in the Protestant church of l'Oratoire," which was "restored by M. Baltard according to my ideas, some fifty years later."[14] Present at the ceremony, in fact but not recollection, were only his maternal grandparents, who stood as his godparents.

That he gave himself a church baptism is not especially significant, and the detail of later restoration became a habit; but making Eugène de Beauharnais his godfather is an interesting twist. In later years Haussmann enjoyed insisting he was a Bonapartist from the cradle. In his *Mémoires* he set down a tale he often told, which created a myth of Bonapartist origins. His maternal grandfather became not merely the conduit for stories about Napoléon's glory—a common enough phenomenon that passed readily into the novels of Stendhal and Zola, among others[15]—but the man who links him directly to the first Napoléon.

He was walking, Haussmann wrote, with his maternal grandfather, Baron Dentzel, in the Tuileries Garden when they came upon Napoléon. "The surprised sovereign stopped, asking with severity: 'Who is this child, General?' 'Sire, he is my grandson, a future soldier for the King of Rome. He is waiting, with me, to be received by the Viceroy of Italy [Eugène de Beauharnais], his godfather.' The Emperor laughed, then said: 'Good, good'. Then he looked intensely at me for several seconds and I held myself upright, my eyes fixed on him, my right hand in a salute, my left in my belt for I was in the uniform of a hussar of my uncle's regiment and my grandfather, of course, was in uniform. 'What,' he said, 'you already want to join the army, young man?.' 'I first want to enter the corps of the Emperor's pages,' I answered, without worrying about my audacity. I merely repeated what I had so often heard from my grandfather, who stood there clearing his throat nervously. His Majesty smiled, took me by the chin, deigned to speak to me: 'You have not chosen the worst path. Eh bien! Hurry up and grow and learn how to mount a horse, then enter the service.' 'Long live the Emperor!' I repeated as he resumed his walk." General Dentzel later recounted the episode to Eugène de Beauharnais, who said, "Perfect. It pleases me to see that my godson does not aspire to put himself in the front lines."[16]

An anecdote that foreshadows a life, gives pattern and purpose. Details of setting and dress and conversation appear concrete, but equally important details, time, for example, not to mention likelihood, are missing. Haussmann may, as a child, have seen Napoléon. He reports that grandfather Dentzel sometimes took him to Versailles to watch the fountains play and troops on parade, and to cheer the emperor and empress as they toured the grounds in an open carriage (drawn by six horses, he specifies) and "surrounded by soldiers, pages and officers, all of which exalted me to the highest pitch." But the man recollecting the actual meeting and conversation with Napoléon could not have been more than five when it took place. He had, legitimately enough, a Napoleonic connection through his maternal grandfather and his uncle, while his father had strong Bonapartist sympathies. But he felt the need to have this laying on of hands, to claim the emperor's stepson as his godfather. Recalling another Napoleonic memory in the *Mémoires*—the family maid, Jeanette, being assaulted by the invading allies in 1815—he says specifically, "I learned [it] much later."[17] Admittedly, the two memories are incomparable, but the one that does not personally involve him and has no political significance he treats as a family tradition, not an eye-witness account.

Haussmann's health was delicate as a child and his parents sent him to live with his paternal grandparents until his grandfather was expelled from France as a regicide in 1816. His robust adulthood, a blessing to which he attributed his enormous capacity for work, belies his frail childhood. Haussmann suffered from respiratory difficulties, and to ward off consumption was dressed in wool from head to foot, winter and summer. Even after his early years with his grandparents, ill health in his thirteenth and fifteenth years again interrupted his education and he returned to the country to convalesce. It is difficult to assay the impact of a sickly childhood on the adult, but surely there is some connection between his early fragility and his later obsession with cleanliness, his deep fastidiousness, manifest in his ready destruction of parts of Old Paris he thought filthy, and his equally obvious passion for sewers and a clean water supply. Urban hygiene was a concern of Haussmann's generation, but the tenacity and depth of feeling such questions evoked in him goes far beyond the norm.

Because he was too frail to attend school, his first lessons came from grandfather Haussmann, who inculcated "methodical habits, the principles of order that everywhere reigned in the house of this true sage," as well as the example of his "clear, judicious, well-regulated mind." "I owe him," Haussmann continued, "the sense of duty, . . . indefatigable perseverance" that have overcome so many obstacles and "personal disinterestedness which make me prefer a clear conscience and the proud legitimacy of an important task well done to the satisfactions that come from money and honors. . ."[18] The autobiographer traced his civil service convictions, as well as his Napoleonic origins, to childhood. He returned to his parents in Paris when he was seven years old and thought healthy enough to attend school, and they enrolled him in a *pension* at Bagneux, near Sceaux, run by an ex-Oratorian, M. Legal, who accepted some fifty pupils in his large, clean school. The theme of cleanliness runs through the *Mémoires* and is always equated with civilization. There is nowhere in Haussmann's makeup any of the romanticism or nostalgia for the old, for ruins, for decay that infected so many of his generation.

He remained with M. Legal for two years, acquiring the rudiments of Greek and Latin and demonstrating a taste for natural history. He loved to take nature walks and collect botanical specimens, butterflies, and insects. He could easily distinguish a wheat from a rye field and knew the names of all the trees and bushes of the region. M. Legal's school—the Oratorians had been the great teachers of France before the revolution drove them from their calling—Haussmann thought "exceptional." His young mind, "naturally inquisitive, opened to varied subjects" that would later stand him in good stead "in my administrative career," and he "received the impression of a systematic education."[19] Haussmann's was a practical intelligence, a powerful but manipulative mind with little interest in speculation or abstractions. He had, and would additionally acquire, strong opinions on abstract, metaphysical, aesthetic, and philosophical matters, but he had no unalloyed interest, and no originality, in such questions. It is the future prefect of the Seine that is being prepared. The *Mémoires* are the record of his journey to the most important administrative appointment in the administrative state.

At eleven (1820) he was enrolled in the best school in Paris, then called the Lycée Henri IV.[20] He went to the head of the class. He was also physically impressive, tall for his age—he became a very tall man, six feet two inches—and thought his lungs had been weakened by the disproportionate growth of his frame. He considered Henri IV "the most salubrious" school in Paris, "thanks to its great court and lovely terrace planted with large trees"—another instance of his obsession with cleanliness. When his health forced him to live at home for a time, he finished his studies as a commuting student at the collège Bourbon.[21] He "very easily" earned his *bachelier ès lettres* when he was seventeen. In addition to a solid education Haussmann made an important friendship: the duc de Chartres, the eldest son of the duc d'Orléans (who would sit on the throne as king Louis-Philippe), was his classmate. "We called him simply 'de Chartres', but without using the familiar 'you' [tu]". At table the duc and his brother, the duc de Nemours, dined with everyone else but "had their own table setting . . . for them and their preceptors, at the head of the table." "We had as a comrade, the Prince and I," Haussmann continues, "Alfred de Musset, about whom nothing announced the great poet. He was a handsome boy with blond hair, not so different from us, but less vigorous and very thin, very studied in his comportment. His manners were quite affected. He was called 'Mademoiselle de Musset'."[22]

After the lycée Haussmann entered law school (1826). The Law Faculty of the Sorbonne took him across Paris from approximately where the St. Augustin church (D 2) today stands to the *place* in front of the Panthéon (E 4). Recalling the walk, he evoked the shabbiness and squalor, the smells of the meandering little streets, "the miserable little square [of St. Michel] where, like a sewer, the waters flowed out of the rue de la Harpe." This regular walk through Old Paris was also a walk through time, from medieval to eighteenth-century Paris, from squalor to order, from Gothic to classical. When he reached his destination he stood in an impressive space dominated by Soufflot's great domed church and its complementary buildings (the law school and what is today the *mairie* of the fifth arrondissement.

The obvious emotional spring of the passage is the filth of Old Paris, for which Haussmann feels nothing but repugnance, and the irrational order of the streets of the city. The passage is most often read as a description of Old Paris. It reveals even more about Haussmann—his detestation of a chaotic world—and is only one of many such in the *Mémoires*. As he took up his several provincial administrative posts, we shall see that each of them is introduced by a similar passage describing the wretchedness of the roads of France and how difficult it is to get from one place to another.[23] The revealing psychological aspect of this habit of description is that Haussmann needed the world to be ordered, its roads straight, its itineraries rational. He found no charm in the customary, the historic, or the organic. He grew up, after his seventh year, in the Paris lovingly described by Balzac, Eugène Sue, Gérard de Nerval, and Victor Hugo, yet saw in the capital none of the energy, mystery, or charm that seduced his contemporaries. He loved Paris best after it had been cleansed and its streets straightened.

Haussmann was a student during one of the golden ages of French university life. An ironical fact for the Restoration was generally unsympathetic to lay education. The law school curriculum was not very absorbing, and Haussmann preferred to follow lectures at the Sorbonne or the Collège de France, where he heard François Villemain lecture on literature, Victor Cousin on philosophy, Joseph Gay-Lussac on physics, Jacques Thénard on chemistry, François Beudant on mineralogy, Augustin Cauchy on differential and integral calculus, and Elie de Beaumont on geology. He also occasionally went to the medical school amphitheater for lectures. He heard, however unsystematically, the best thinkers of the day.[24]

The one spiritual or aesthetic dimension of Haussmann's character as a young man was music. His was not a distinguished talent, but he had a passion for music. He says he took to music so early that he cannot remember when he learned to read notes. He played cello in a student orchestra and learned piano and organ from M. Choron, the director of the Ecole de Musique Religieuse, who also taught him harmony. From his limited training he went on to the National Conservatory and audited the counterpoint classes of M. Reicha.[25] It is here that he met Hector Berlioz. He dutifully celebrates Berlioz's genius but passes quickly to the level of anecdote. Luigi Cherubini, who taught composition at the conservatory, confronted Berlioz with a two-measure rest in one of his student compositions. "What's this?" he asked the most original French composer of his generation. "Monsieur le Directeur," Berlioz answered, "I wanted, with this silence, to produce an effect." "Ah, you believed that two measures of silence would produce a good effect on the listener?" "Yes, Monsieur." "Eh, bien, suppress everything else and the effect will be even better!"[26]

Haussmann did not, probably could not, understand the originality of Berlioz, especially his harmonic invention, which shattered many of the rules of composition. He categorized the composer as a romantic, characterized his music as "pompous, quite incorrect, bombastic rather than sonorous, seemingly inspired by certain poetry, and much admired by some."[27] A conventional contemporary judgment. But if Haussmann's musical tastes were conservative, his appreciation was sincere. He remained a passionate operagoer throughout his life, played the piano *en famille*, and went to considerable trouble and expense to insure the presence of a piano wherever he was posted. He spoke of music as "an elevated distraction of the spirit and the most agreeable of all pastimes."[28]

There is no daring, no originality, no rebelliousness in the formation of Haussmann's mind. The romanticism that seduced so many of his generation left him unmoved, as did the emerging body of socialist criticism of individualistic, capitalist society. He embraced and cherished bourgeois culture. His imagination and sympathies were limited, constrained by social and personal rectitude, but he took some pains to acquire an impressive stock of information, always with a practical goal in mind. He studied musical harmony, for example, essentially as an exercise in mathematical thinking. His formal training was in the law, but he seems to have had little interest in practicing the profession. Nor did he show any desire to follow his father into journalism. He found few attractions in the money-making professions open to his class. The family tradition of public service beckoned. But during the Restoration, with a father involved in opposition journalism, it was no easy matter to find government work. The ideological preferences of the Restoration for throne and altar were probably less galling to Haussmann—although not to his father—than the aristocratic monopoly of the state bureaucracy. Seventy percent of Restoration prefects and 40 percent of the subprefects had been nominated from the old nobility. By 1830, 45 percent of the corps was aristocratic.[29] Young job seekers without the right family connections saw the Napoleonic promise of careers open to talent disappear.

Haussmann's grandfathers had made careers as the result of a revolution. Haussmann, as much as the radical students of his generation—whether socialist, republican, Jacobin, or even romantics—was blocked by the very conventionalities he embraced. It was the unpredictable, the unexpected, the exceptional, the very uncertainties he disdained that determined Haussmann's future, in the form of the Revolution of 1830, in no small way "a revolution of frustrated careerists."[30]

· III ·

Climbing the Greasy Pole

THE HAUSSMANNS AND THE DENTZELS HAD BEEN MADE BY THE REVolution of 1789. Their children and grandchildren, the professional bourgeoisie, would form the backbone of postrevolutionary France. Haussmann, the product of Napoleonic schooling—itself a direct result of the revolution—inherited this tradition. But what the great emperor had intended by careers open to talent soon lost the heroic glamour of the militant and conquering empire, when even bureaucracy took on the sheen and glory of governing subdued Europe. After Napoléon's fall and the restoration of the Bourbons, the products of his schools, originally destined to be the elite of a world empire, had to settle for the tedium, the red tape, and the laborious advancement offered by a mundane and inglorious civil service.

Haussmann, as did so many young men of his generation, joined the bureaucracy. Careers in the church or the army, the poles of Julien Sorel's ambitions or fantasies in Stendhal's *Le Rouge et le Noir*, were not available to Haussmann: he was a Protestant, and the army had been emasculated by the allies who defeated Napoléon. Only the civil service or the liberal professions remained. Haussmann followed the traditions recently established by his family, in the Great Revolution, and chose government for his career. He would become one of the most successful public figures of his generation, his bureaucratic career a model not of precocious advancement but of tenacity, singleminded management, supple and adroit political maneuvering, opportunism, and good luck. Among the bourgeoisie who entered government service in the first years of the July Monarchy, Haussmann's success—he would hold, as prefect of the Seine, the most important appointment in the bureaucratic state—would remain both unique and remarkable: in the hothouse world of French administrative life and achievement, a Napoleonic career.

Haussmann was twenty-one in June 1830 when street fighting broke out in Paris. He had received his law degree a year earlier, had no employment, and his father was a long-standing opponent of the Bourbons. During the Restoration he described himself as a "simple observer of events" who "maintained a calm that passed for indifference."[1] But when the Bourbon throne was seriously shaken—and Haussmann's father was among those who confronted the government in July 1830, signing the petition against the July decrees that destroyed freedom of the press—Haussmann fought in the new revolution as had his forbears in 1789.

On July 29—the first of the Trois Glorieuses, the Three Glorious Days of the Revolution of 1830—Haussmann arrived, early in the morning, at the offices of *Le Temps*, the opposition newspaper to which his father was connected. He agreed to carry a message to Baron Baude and to return with his answer, thus becoming a minor actor in the uprising against Charles X, the last of the French Bourbon kings. The courier, musket slung over his shoulder, set off with a companion, Etienne Arago: "it is thus equipped that I entered the Hôtel de Ville for the first time in my life." A lifetime later, recollecting his first appearance on the historical stage, Haussmann detailed the route he followed. He descended the rue de Richelieu (where *Le Temps* was located) toward the Seine and made his way eastward to the Hôtel de Ville through the very thick of the street fighting, zigzagging through the heart of the city, for there was no direct route. Returning to *Le Temps* later, he carried another message, this time to the Théâtre français (again, he minutely describes the route), where he was wounded superficially "behind my right knee, by a bullet that I didn't feel in the heat of combat," which passed through "the fatty part of my left thigh."[2] Haussmann makes little of this exhilarating moment, and wound, in his *Mémoires*, but he characteristically noted which streets he later eliminated: "It gave me considerable satisfaction to raze . . . this rue du Rempart, running diagonally in front of the Théâtre français, where I was caught in the fighting on July 29, 1830."[3] But if the prefect razed the place of his birth as well as that of his bravery, he did not obliterate their significance. His wound was the stroke of good fortune he exploited to launch his career.

Haussmann well understood the art of self-advertisement, which he practiced, from this moment forth, with aplomb and increasing skill. He parlayed his revolutionary zeal and flesh wound into a place in the escort of the duc d'Orléans when the latter took the oath (August 9, 1830) as king of the French, after the last of the Bourbons had been driven into exile. The young hero stood, in the regiment of Colonel Bro, "not far from the duc de Chartres," his school chum who now became the duc d'Orléans and heir to the throne. These two men stood godfathers at Haussmann's bureaucratic baptismal font. On September 20 Colonel Bro testified that Haussmann "had disarmed and captured an officer of the Royal Guard whose saber he took, [and] never ceased being an example of the most unflagging perseverance and devoted courage. For six days and nights he took no rest." A commission recognized his courage, decorating Haussmann "with the special July cross with three branches, corresponding to the three days of fighting that it honors." He "easily entered public life from the first days of the July Monarchy."[4]

He knew what he wanted and was not shy about it. "I ask your Excellency to grant me the administration of a sub-prefecture," Haussmann boldly addressed Casimir-Périer, reminding him of the "dangers to which I exposed myself during the July Days," and asserting that the "satisfaction" expressed by the Royal Prince is "perhaps my best claim to the favor that I beg." In a follow-up letter he explained his social and political fitness for the appointment: "The child of parents whose industry has placed them among the most important commercial notables in Alsace, the social position of my family is a sure guarantee of my love of the social order and the maintenance of our institutions." It was not politic to linger long over one's revolutionary past, even in the July Monarchy, which was favorably disposed. More preferable was to stress one's reverence for property and social order. The letter closed with Haussmann's reiteration of his bravery in the Trois Glorieuses. The minister indicated "a polite response" in the margin. On September 16, 1830, Haussmann wrote the minister of the interior, "on the suggestion of the duc d'Orléans who is interested in his old fellow student, M. Haussmann, and recommends him to the attention of M. the Minister of the Interior."[5] This did the trick.

On May 21, 1831, by royal appointment, Haussmann was given the position of Secretary General in the prefecture of the department of Vienne. It was less than he had requested, but on the twenty-fifth he swore the oath of office.[6] At the outset of his career he felt a bit lost, out of place. Dressed, however simply, in the Parisian fashion, with reserved manners and high expectations, he did not fit easily in the provinces. He soon resigned himself to the boredom and set a strategy for ingratiating himself with the local notables while methodically determined to supplement his education with a regimen of self-improvement. Apparently all did not go smoothly in the former endeavor for he describes a duel in Poitiers fought with a student, whom he lightly wounded.[7] Otherwise his brief time in Poitiers was uneventful. The work of general secretary was not onerous and Haussmann spent time exploring the town with the fourteenth-century chronicles of Jean Froissart in hand. He located and examined old battle sites, but there is no mention of architecture—Poitiers has some interesting churches—and scarcely any of the physical appearance of the place. Using Froissart as a guidebook does not so much bespeak Haussmann's interest in medieval military history—a period and subject he cared little for—as his practical-minded desire to educate himself, to forgo no opportunity to acquire information, which he always confused with erudition and culture.

What he desired above all was to get out of Poitiers. His official dossier is filled with letters asking for a better post: Haussmann's father wrote on his son's behalf, Ferdinand Philippe d'Orléans pulled what strings he could. The prefect of Vienne, M. Boullé, wrote Haussmann in May 1832 explaining that the secretary generalship was being suppressed but assured the young man of "a position which will be appropriate and will at the same time offer you the means of using the learning and talents with which you are endowed." This turned out to be the subprefecture of Yssingeaux, in the Haute-Loire department. Haussmann pedantically recounts his "laborious journey." He had to take the Paris-Bordeaux coach as far as Angoulême, transfer for a postal service coach to Limoges (by way of La Rochefoucauld, Chabanais, and Saint-Junien). From Limoges there was a daily run to Clermont-Ferrand but it took two days to make a trip later accomplished in several hours. From Clermont-Ferrand he went to the "charming" town of Saint-Léonard, then the "monotonous landscape" of the Creuse, followed by the mountains of the Auvergne, which he much appreciated. Haussmann was always sensitive to natural beauty, perhaps the heritage of his first years spent at Chaville with his grandparents. The mountains, not the sea, engaged his imagination. He had spent five days on the road to his new post, testimony to the deplorable road system of the time.[8]

Haussmann remained only a few months in Yssingeaux (June 13, 1832–October 11, 1832), just long enough to buy a horse, which he used for social occasions and to explore the region—his account is filled with detailed geological descriptions. And he began cultivating the local notables. "Naturally," he wrote, "I concentrated my habitual relations in the bourgeois milieu; but what I had the occasion to see of legitimist society [who recognized only the departed Bourbons as the legal kings of France] caused me no sharp regrets for their standoffishness from the functionaries of the July Monarchy."[9] His next post was the subprefecture of Nérac in the Lot-et-Garonne department, where he would remain for eight years (1832–40). In a long letter explaining the political situation in Yssingeaux, written shortly before his departure, Haussmann already shows a sure grasp of local power blocks and how they could be manipulated. He also exercised his skills for self-advertisement.[10]

When the summons to Nérac arrived—a town he described, as if writing a guidebook, as the seat of the old court of Navarre, the theater of the love exploits of the young Henri IV, and famous for its terrines—"the idea passed through my head of returning to Paris and saying: I want another post." But he did not. The *Mémoires* celebrate his transformation of the place: "because of me people now go everywhere by carriage and the value of the land is considerably augmented" by the new roads.[11] Doubtless he read back his later financial formula that new streets created enhanced property values, but the passion for road building runs throughout Haussmann's administrative career. In Nérac, he says, he completed his administrative education, his apprenticeship in public life. "In leaving the place I was already ripe for the function of prefect, which I fulfilled only ten years later."[12]

In Nérac he continued isolated and lonely, until his mother and two sisters came to live with him while his father was attached to the Military Division of Constantine, organizing the Portes-de-Fer campaign in North Africa. He built them a small apartment attached to the subprefecture and with his family attended a round of parties and balls where his piano playing, hitherto kept private, was so much in demand that he feared "it might prevent people from taking me seriously during the day." He need not have worried that pleasure or lightheartedness would undermine his authority or seriousness. He worked constantly at his education, after discharging the light duties of subprefect. Haussmann needed little sleep and set a small lamp by his bed so that should he awake in the night he could read the *Mémoires sur l'histoire de France*—an enormous historical collection that he read from beginning to end in Nérac—or write down ideas that had occurred to him in the night.[13] For a man who had neglected historical studies when a student, and who never expressed much interest in the discipline, Haussmann was remarkably well read in the French past, although little of this learning found its way into his official reports or his *Mémoires*. He was driven less by intellectual curiosity than professional preparation and cultural pretention: knowing something of the French past was part of the baggage of the professional bourgeoisie, if the considerable sales of historical literature in the July Monarchy are an indication.

It is from this period that we have one of the earliest characterizations of Haussmann from someone other than a functionary putting a report into his dossier. George Sand's portrait is uncolored by politics. One of the major literary figures of the age in her own right, although her novels are now little read, Aurore Dupin (1804–76) was also the lover of Alfred de Musset and Chopin. She came to Nérac in a panic. Her daughter had been taken from her (at Nohant) by the girl's father and ensconced in Guillery, a château in Haussmann's bailiwick. As soon as she arrived in Nérac George Sand sought out the subprefect for aid and protection. Literary genius, so potent a calling card in French culture, worked its usual magic. "[Haussmann] immediately got into my carriage to go to Guillery where he had my daughter returned to me without fuss or difficulty." The subprefect would not hear of George Sand, her traveling companions, and her daughter returning to the inn, and took them back to his residence. Here they remained for two quiet days, taking leisurely walks along the lovely Beise River beside whose banks, tradition has it, the young Henri IV disported with Florette. They dined with some of her old friends "and I remember that we talked a lot of philosophy, a neutral terrain compared to politics where the young functionary would not have found any agreement with us." George Sand describes Haussmann as "a serious person, avid to engage general matters, but his exquisite politeness kept him from raising any delicate questions."[14]

Haussmann's description of the encounter forms a nice counterpoint. "She was completely astonished," he wrote, to discover "behind the walls of an old monastery in the depths of the provinces, in a tiny apartment," modest but lovely and thoughtfully appointed, he added, a young man "living intellectually a Parisian life, in the midst of the most realistic occupations." He goes on to describe himself as "a young functionary capable of holding his own on a number of philosophical, religious, political, and social questions."[15]

These first provincial appointments seem singularly unpromising. But administrative advancement in the July Monarchy was sluggish and getting a subprefecture so quickly was unusual. It is Haussmann's autobiographical impatience, doubtless a reflection of how he lived his early career, that paints his rise so bleakly. His contemporaries languished longer as secretaries and not necessarily because they lacked talent or education. Haussmann may have impressed his first superiors but what mattered was connections, especially his friendship with the duc d'Orléans.[16] But even the heir apparent could not protect Haussmann from himself. His official dossier was slowly being filled with complaints from superiors. The prefect of the Lot-et-Garonne praised him for having "given evidence in this important matter of an intelligence which has been crowned with success" but described his subordinate as difficult. Friction was more frequent than harmony. Haussmann continued bombarding Paris with his requests for advancement. His superiors, to keep him happy, because they could not otherwise accommodate his restless ambition, and because he had the patronage of the duc d'Orléans, awarded him the Legion of Honor.

The first hatchet job in his file was the work of the prefect, Brun, who deplored Haussmann's "isolated" life in Nérac, which he attributed, with mock empathy, to his youth; but standing apart from local society was not what the government expected of its subprefects, and Haussmann—a complaint to be reiterated even in the years of his greatness as prefect of the Seine—"neglected more than was necessary a conciliatory approach." The apparent ease with which he got George Sand's daughter from her estranged husband testifies to his capacity for tact, but he did not always exercise it; and Brun was out to get him. In Nérac Haussmann was an outsider disdainful of fitting in. He did not, for Brun, understand the "delicate nuances of his situation," traits that would prove innate.

Brun's first report was written in 1833, only a year after Haussmann's arrival in Nérac. His next annual report continued in the same vein. Despite Haussmann's obvious abilities, the prefect wrote, he got embroiled "a bit too much in the petty passions" of various groups and did not maintain "the perfect impartiality that one has the right to expect from an administrator." He continued to live "in isolation at Nérac." In 1836 Brun elaborated on the same theme. Haussmann's behavior sprang from "a vanity that degenerates into self-praise and an exaggerated penchant for hyperbole." His character, despite its attractive aspects had too much "self-satisfaction [amour-propre] and presumption." He continued to have little influence in Nérac because he remained "in isolation." His execution of the laws and his general administration, Brun wrote in 1839, "is partial and follows his preferences or antipathies." He is "generally disposed to substitute his own wishes and particular ideas for those of his superiors because of the excellent opinion he has of his personal merit." Insubordination was a new charge. Relations between prefect and subprefect were coming to a head. Haussmann was "a dominant character" and one "can have no confidence in the veracity of his word." He "alters the truth even in the most in-different matters" and had showed his superior "reserve and defi-ance." But, Brun added grudgingly, "he loves to work in his office" on administrative affairs.

"I take this occasion," Brun wrote the minister of the interior, "to complain particularly about something M. Haussmann has done which seems to me to undermine the administrative hierarchy." Without consulting Brun he used a trip to Paris to go to the ministry and oppose, "as strongly as he could" a project "presented by myself and approved by the general council," by producing "inexact facts" to support his insubordination. The prefect reminded his Paris supe-riors that he had repeatedly spoken of Haussmann's faults in his re-ports "which were perhaps too indulgent toward the subprefect. I submit this incident . . . without further comment."[17]

More and more frustrated, surely aware of Brun's hostility, Hauss-mann enlisted the support of the marquis de Lusignan, whose eleva-tion to the peerage had exacerbated Haussmann's difficulties with Brun. Lusignan had been the deputy for Nérac. Haussmann was now asked to recommend a replacement, one of the chief responsi-bilities of a subprefect. The government rejected his nominee. To forestall further embarrassment, perhaps even disgrace, Lusignan wrote to the minister of the interior that Haussmann should not be removed from his post except for a promotion. He received a polite explanation that Haussmann's faults were "in large part those of his years" and should not cause disgrace. Haussmann started looking for another post. He wanted the subprefecture of Libourne, the most important in the Gironde, and sent out feelers. This earned him further rebuke from Brun for ignoring the regular channels of communication. Jealousy as well was involved. The crown prince and his wife had visited Haussmann in Nérac, which was not the *chef-lieu* of the department: the prefect had been snubbed. The bu-reaucratese of Brun's reports hardly veiled Haussmann's faults. He was insubordinate, contemptuous of the chain of command, arrogant, and stood aloof from the local life of Nérac: intolerable faults in an administrative corps.

On February 19, 1840, the king signed the ordinance sending Haussmann to St. Girons as subprefect. Haussmann considered the move a disgrace and rightly so: the official he replaced, Dumont de Jumilhac, was sent to Nérac to replace Haussmann, who sulked. Petit de Bantel, the prefect of his new department, the Ariège, had to write to the minister of the interior requesting that he order Haussmann to report to St. Girons and assume his post. Haussmann apparently threatened to resign. Some compromise had to be found: whatever his personal faults one could not cashier a protégé of the duc d'Orléans. The ministry hit upon a face-saving solution. Haussmann would be sent to St. Girons, but on a special mission. The Carlist War was raging in Spain and there was not only constant border crossing in the Pyrenees passes around St. Girons but a brisk trade in contraband arms. The dangled carrot included the subprefecture of Libourne, which might soon be vacant.[18] The letter from the ministry made it clear that the appointment was both temporary and a test: "The services you perform in the department of the Ariège, you may be sure, will not escape my attention," the undersecretary of state, M. de Maleville, wrote Haussmann. "I will go to St. Girons," Haussmann responded "despite the perfectly understandable repugnance that I feel for a post that will separate me even farther from my family, and from my interests, without any compensation." He reminded Maleville that he wanted to stay no longer than his specific mission. Once completed, he boldly averred, he expected a post where "I can more conveniently await the advancement to which I am entitled" and repeated, lest the undersecretary forget, "the verbal promise that you made me, to grant me a leave until the fulfillment of your kind intentions."[19] Still Haussmann did not set out for St. Girons. On November 17, 1840, the mayor of the town sent a letter to the minister of the interior complaining of Haussmann's long absence from his post.[20] His parting shot at Brun, as he left Nérac, was a circular letter to all the mayors of his arrondissement, dated March 1, 1840. "I receive calmly the disgrace that has fallen upon me," he declared, "and which is going to close before me, prematurely, as a result of a situation that is easy to foresee, the career that I have followed for ten years with the single goal of serving the King, of being useful to my country." "I especially regret being rudely separated from you after having given more than seven years to the study of the needs of your arrondissement." He was the victim of those who tried to use him for "private interests, interests of ambition and influence," the victim of self-serving interests that would pervert the common good.[21] This ethos of selfless civil service was to inform all of Haussmann's future justifications.

Haussmann's official correspondence is surprisingly forthright, as well as contemptuous of channels of authority. He who was so thoroughly a courtier, and insisted on the most rigorous adherence to bureaucratic protocol from his staff, displayed little of it as a young man. His freedom of expression, his energy, his anger, his forwardness in soliciting advancement bespeak a man sure of himself and impatient of others; and a man who enjoyed enough protection in Paris to insulate himself from punishment. He had gotten off to a fast start in 1830, and he seemed destined to move quickly. His Protestantism had proved advantageous: Yssingeaux was a Protestant center, Nérac was the town in which Jeanne d'Albret is said to have hidden Jean Calvin. The July Monarchy, reacting against the strident Catholicism of the Restoration, offered Protestants many opportunities. Haussmann's school chum, the duc d'Orléans, had married a German Protestant princess, and Guizot, the most important minister of the regime, was Protestant. The minority was not just tolerated but advanced. Haussmann had been granted the Legion of Honor in 1837, when only twenty-eight, a precocious accomplishment in the administrative corps. Guizot himself, Haussmann said, had nominated him as a reward for working on behalf of education reform. The truth is Haussmann had never cultivated Guizot. His patron, nagged by his impatient client, was M. de Lusignan.

Earlier he had attached himself to Casimir-Périer, a banker, a tough advocate of order, and one of the leaders of the liberal opposition, whom he visited in early 1832. He was in Paris looking after his career, "sniffing the air at the Ministry," as he put it. Casimir-Périer, the president of the council, took him aside for some personal advice: "A propos [of our conversation], a young functionary should always find the wives and daughters of the deputies charming and even beautiful, when it is possible. The others as well, but I think that less necessary." "I have never forgotten this precious advice," Haussmann added.[22] Soon afterward Casimir-Périer was dead, a victim of the cholera epidemic that swept through Paris that summer.

Then, on July 13, 1842, came another devastating blow. The duc d'Orléans, around whom had gathered the liberal opposition to his father and Guizot, was killed in a freak carriage accident. "For me," Haussmann wrote, "the duc d'Orléans was not only the highest and most powerful of protectors. Since the collège Henri IV he had shown me the most amiable and consistent sympathy. Each time I was in Paris he received me graciously, asked me about my career and offered me his help. I was pleased to take his advice, but I put off using his intervention for the day when my advancement would depend on a supreme effort." "For the future of my career," he added, "the death of this kindly protector was an irreparable loss."[23] Haussmann remembered, or chose to remember, inaccurately. He had enjoyed the influence of the duc d'Orléans from the beginning of his career.

The same retrospective myopia is evident in Haussmann's account of his short time in St. Girons (February 19, 1841–November 23, 1841). The contemporary record contradicts what he remembered.[24] The town lies in a valley of the Pyrenees some 30 miles from Foix, the *chef-lieu* of the department of the Ariège, about 450 miles from Paris. If the late-19th-century photos accurately represent the town when Haussmann was in residence—and there is no record of any intervening substantial change—St. Girons was a pretty, sleepy mountain town. It seems to have changed very little in the century and a half since his subprefecture. The church now has a concrete steeple, some flood control work has been done, and the town has spread out a bit. But the center of St. Girons, with its tile-roofed houses clinging to the riverbank, its stone quays, and the mountains rising all around, looks much as it did 150 years ago. Its economy has only slightly improved with the coming of the railroads and a decent road system. St. Girons is now a national, rather than a regional, magnet for trout fishing, campers, hikers, and skiers. Haussmann thought it the end of the world and his career, despite what he had been told about the importance and delicacy of the Carlist refugee problem. Still gnawing on the bone of disgrace, he wrote to the ministry reminding them that his acceptance of the post would be seen as a victory by his enemies, and he had accepted only because his refusal would have "placed the government in an embarrassing position." "But it is urgent to put an end to the false situation in which I am, and I count, to this end, upon the loyalty of the Minister."[25] Haussmann's epistolary diplomacy had not improved.

In his usual disciplined way he explored the region, although there is no evidence that he visited the prehistoric caves, and made a thorough study of its geography, geology, economy, and history. He would later write that he derived from St. Girons his "inextinguishable" conviction of the benefits of good, safe water and adequate sewers, to which Paris owes the system Haussmann built. He related with some pride a raid and capture of gunrunners in the mountains. But there was little to keep so restless a man occupied. He was often absent, doing whatever he could to get out of St. Girons. His log of letters sent and received and reports written furnishes abundant evidence of Haussmann's cavalier understanding of residence. On September 5, 1841, he requested a leave of three months, saying he was called home "by the most urgent matters," which were not specified. The next day he assured the prefect that "the most complete tranquility reigns" in St. Girons.[26]

When he was in residence the work was routine and boring. He kept track of foreigners and regularly reported on the state of the prisons, who had died in the town, and the Maison de Santé. He oversaw what public works there were and drew up the budget for the Maison de Santé. He arranged a celebration for the tenth anniversary of the Trois Glorieuses, inaugurated a street in St. Girons, reported on the harvest, issued hunting licenses, delivered aid to combat the drought, collected information on abandoned infants.[27] He sent to the prefect the arms and ammunition taken from refugees from Don Carlos's army when they entered France. He had some repair work done on the local school and on the clock tower of the church, St. Lizier, freed some prisoners, and reported on the insane patients in the Maison de Santé.[28] The mentally ill were kept together in the asylum of St.Lizier, which intrigued Haussmann.[29]

His discontent extended to the subprefect's residence, which he pronounced "uninhabitable." The toilet needed rebuilding, the terrace had to be repaired, as well as the salon, and he wanted the government to pay his rent during the period of the rehabilitation. He also needed more money than originally appropriated for the work. The negotiations were not brought to a conclusion before Haussmann was transferred to Blaye.

More than forty years later, Haussmann remembered his exile quite differently. He celebrated his young manhood in verse. *St. Girons, une campagne administrative dans les Pyrénées* was written in Nice in 1876. The free-verse poem shows little talent but signifies the importance of these years for the author. Gendarmes, customs agents, the police "under his vigilant eye do their duty." He accompanies them into the mountains and "one would find him more often on horseback than in his office." Thus does he describe himself:

> *He was tall, a good physique, slim, and very elegant;*
> *His complexion was fair and rosy as that of an infant.*
> *His hair was ash-blond, his beard carefully trimmed,*
> *His expression was soft, veiled, and a bit sexy.*
> *And above this was the prestige of rank*
> *That was revealed by nobility of blood!*
> *How, given all this, could others not be charmed,*
> *How could they not want to be loved*
> *By a gentleman that they found so handsome!. . .*
> *Add to this that he was extremely polite,*
> *The first to present himself, the first to speak to everyone*
> *But especially to women and always to all of them,*
> *Sowing, without number, flattering words,*
> *And, when proper, lovely compliment*
> *As he had done to noble young ladies,*
> *To the women of chateaux, so proud and so beautiful.*[30]

The poem is cast as a pastoral. On a ride in the mountains this remarkable young man encounters an equally young, beautiful shepherdess. They exchange pleasantries. A stanza later they are lovers, and he carries forever "in his heart" this fleeting happiness. Fiction and fact, the mundane and the desired, are mixed into an elaborate fantasy. Behind the conventions of the form the author—sixty-seven at the writing—imagined himself to have been the swain. The setting is the mountains around St. Girons, where he often rode. The poem evokes his youth more than the subprefecture. The sexual fantasy is central. The physical description of himself is generally accurate, but he had no noble blood. His hero's personal charm is also autobiographical, if equally fanciful. He thought his conversation irresistible, supple, molded to his auditors. Most who met him complained that he talked only of himself. Finally, he had spent virtually no time in the châteaux of the mighty and had had none of the casual affairs he also alludes to in the poem.

These blurs between the actual and the imagined Haussmann are instructive. He was a wholly conventional man, anxious to order the universe by imposing rational solutions, impatient of his stalled career, banished to a beautiful but boring post. How much was remembered, how much imagined by an aging, disgraced administrator, transforming his first professional disgrace into a moment of sexual ecstasy. Banishment to St. Girons came soon after his marriage, and the happiness of his first years of married life are also entwined in the St. Girons fantasy. The mysterious shepherdess may owe a good deal to Haussmann's recollections of his new bride.

"During one of my trips to Bordeaux [in 1837]," his wife first appears in the *Mémoires*. He was presented to her family by M. Henri de Laharpe, a Protestant minister of Swiss origins whose father was a rich merchant. "The reception I received," he continued, "touched me deeply." The future Mme Haussmann—"very friendly, very gracious, and even very pretty"—had rejected other suitors to remain with her parents, who were inconsolable over the death of another daughter. In October his future brother-in-law came to Nérac for a visit. There the question of dowry was apparently settled and the contract signing was set for October 10.[31] Haussmann's father had hoped to bring his wife to the wedding, but she was too ill to attend. Instead Nicolas Haussmann arrived accompanied by Haussmann's younger sister. The marriage took place on the seventeenth and the religious part of the service was celebrated that same day in the Protestant church in the Chartrons neighborhood of Bordeaux, a lovely classical building.[32]

It was a perfectly proper marriage between the commercial and professional Protestant bourgeoisie, an eminently reasonable, advantageous, match. The bride was young and appropriately dowered, the bridegroom was of the expected age for taking a wife, and a pastor had acted as the intermediary—a nearly ideal concordance of circumstances.

Louise-Octavie de Laharpe, born in Bordeaux on February 15, 1807, into a respectable and comfortable family, brought an attractive if not extravagant dowry to the marriage. She had inherited jewelry valued at 4,000 francs, 130,000 francs in cash, and 3,000 francs for a trousseau. The couple had agreed to a contract of community property but only of those things acquired after marriage. Louise-Octavie's possessions would be considerably enhanced when her mother died (in 1862), leaving her significant property near Bordeaux.[33] "I pass over the particular circumstances that preceded, accompanied, and followed this capital act of my life," Haussmann wrote of his marriage. "They would be of no interest to my readers."[34] The few details of married life he intruded into the *Mémoires* reveal Mme Haussmann as in love with her husband, utterly devoted to him, consecrating her life to his career, and of frail health: the perfect helpmate, despite her mildly fashionable fragility.[35] He took his new bride to Paris to see the capital and be presented to his mother, and then, because she was ailing, left her with her family in Bordeaux while he hastened to return to his post. It was not until April 1839 that she joined him in Nérac. In the last days of December of that year "I brought my wife to Bordeaux, '*in a family way*' as the English say with ridiculous prudery"—Haussmann had learned some English in Nérac and asserts he could speak the language with fluency and understand it readily[36]—while he returned to his post. He was back in Bordeaux on January 12 but left on January 16: the next day, "at five in the evening, my daughter, Marie-Henriette, was born."[37] The birth of his second daughter, Fanny-Valentine (December 1, 1843), receives a single sentence, considerably less than that given to any step in his career. As with many self-absorbed men Haussmann doted on his daughters and, at least for some years, on his wife, although he gave them little of his time. He insists that he and his wife were such a loving couple that in Blaye the local residents shared the opinion of the Comtesse-Mère Duchâtel that "perfect harmony" existed between the two. As they walked, arm in arm, along the port, with their daughter between them, residents murmured "what a lovely family."[38]

On November 23, 1841, Haussmann assumed the duties of subprefect of Blaye. He had written to Léon de Maleville, the undersecretary of state for the interior, complaining that the post, in the department of the Gironde, was unworthy of his abilities and his ambition, but at least it was near Bordeaux. He now had a *bordelaise* wife, a young family, and some property in the region; and he was desperate to get out of St. Girons.

Blaye, about twenty-five miles downriver from Bordeaux, was a port and wine-growing region wholly overshadowed by Bordeaux, where Haussmann spent most of his time. His wife lived there with her parents, coming to Blaye "only on important occasions." The subprefect's quarters were modest if not inadequate—a salon, a dining room, three small bedrooms—but it was enough because the Haussmanns had an apartment at his in-laws in Bordeaux and another in their country house, at Bouscat. Besides, he was seldom in residence. "I usually left [Blaye], cane in hand, every Saturday, and sometimes on Friday, taking the boat that arrived from Bordeaux around noon, and I returned on Wednesday mornings." The journey, with numerous stops, took two and a half hours with a favorable tide, three to four hours against the current. He frequently had the company of acquaintances and looked upon the trips as does a business commuter. He did a good deal of his administrative paperwork on the boat and cultivated the friendship of landowners from the arrondissement of Lesparre, who boarded at Verdon, Pauillac, and Beychevelle, where the boat put in to port.[39] His habitual energy went into his career and playing the landed gentleman. Haussmann faced a long bureaucratic climb to satisfy his ambition, and it became even more problematical with the death of the duc d'Orléans. After 1842 he was essentially on his own, forced to find new patrons and opportunities, and perhaps disillusioned about the future of the more liberal Orleanism the crown prince had represented. His new appointment fixed him in the southwest of France, where he set about establishing himself. His gaze reached no farther than the prefecture of the Gironde, one of the more important in France because of Bordeaux's wealth. A shrewd if cynical political analyst, Haussmann read the situation (and his prospects) correctly. His timing was a bit off—although he was less impatient than he had been in Nérac—and he failed to foresee, as did virtually everyone else, the Revolution of 1848.

Bordeaux was an oligarchy dominated by the great wine growers, merchants, legal establishment, owners of refineries, arms makers, and those who supplied the navy, all of whom were allied by strong bonds of common interest that were strengthened into the rigidities of a caste by frequent intermarriage. He cultivated friends accordingly.[40] The political reflection of these economic and social interests was a strong and conservative Orleanism. Before the July Monarchy, Bordeaux had been equally conservative, its oligarchy equally self-serving. The city had welcomed the restoration of the Bourbons in 1814, even unhitching the horses of the duc d'Angoulême's carriage—"that idiot Prince," as Haussmann called him—and themselves drawing it through the streets in their enthusiasm for the restored monarchy. Napoléon and the empire, for the *Bordelais*, had meant the Continental System, with its blockades, commercial ruin, and the loss of the colonies. Under the July Monarchy the *Bordelais* wanted peace at any price and cleaved to the Orleanists, who offered monarchy without the encumbering historical baggage of absolutism, divine right pretensions, and strident opposition to the French Revolution. The "democracy" that prevailed in Bordeaux in the 1840s was little different from that of 1400. There were 2,448 electors in the nineteenth century, approximately the same number as in the Middle Ages, and they belonged to the same class.[41] A similar parochialism prevailed in intellectual life. Even the self-proclaimed advanced thinkers did not concern themselves with questions of industry, labor, and social transformation. They were sunk in provincial torpor and complacency. In religious life there was the semblance, and to some extent the reality, of toleration, because of the historical diversity of the region. The population was overwhelmingly Catholic, but there was a substantial

PARIS IN 1611. A bird's-eye view of the city by Léonard Gaultier. The wall of Charles V encloses the city, which is dominated by church spires. Notre Dame, larger than life and the center of the city, the most important building in Paris, is almost exactly in the middle of the map. The old Louvre can be seen at approximately nine o'clock. The Bastille at two o'clock. The highest point (around eleven o'clock) is Montmartre. The pattern of the streets is completely lost in the mass of buildings, the city being principally defined by its churches.

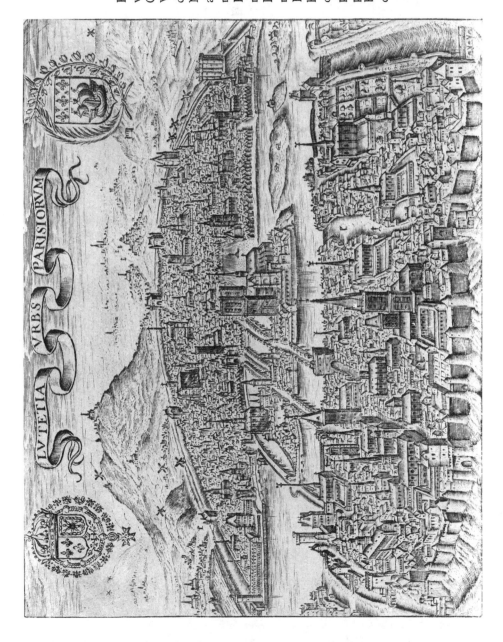

LVTETIA VRBS PARISIORVM

PLACE DES VICTOIRES. An etching from 1686. The statue depicted here, of Louis XIV crowned with the laurels of victory while standing on a pedestal adorned with six low reliefs and four carved captives representing vanquished Spain, Holland, Prussia, and Austria, was commissioned from Desjardins. It was melted down in 1792. A new equestrian statue of Louis XIV, by Desaix, was erected in 1806. It in turn was melted down in 1815 and definitively replaced with another equestrian statue, by Bosso, in 1822. The facades overlooking the square, by Mansart, fared better. The side of the square with even-numbered addresses is less damaged today, revealing the elegance of the original design. This was the last *place* and monument erected to the cult of the king.

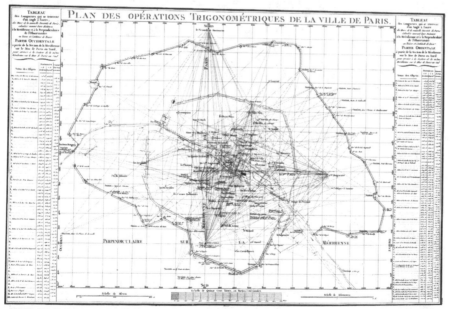

THE TRIUMPH OF GEOMETRY. Edme Verniquet made the first mathmetically accurate map of the city—begun in 1774, completed in 1791, published in 1795–96—taking his measurements at night or early morning when the streets were empty. These are Verniquet's trigonometric calculations. The meridian is drawn from l'Observatoire, in the south, to the heights of Montmartre, in the north. The black spot nearly in the center, overlaid by the filigree of lines of calculation, is Notre Dame. Haussmann's map, usually called the Deschamps plan after Eugène Deschamps, the architect he appointed to head the bureau of the Plan de Paris, was even more accurate. Measurements were made from wooden towers, and the city's topography was mapped for the first time. Verniquet's map, in seventy-two panels and based upon geometric principles, became the model of all the modern maps of Paris.

RUE DE LA REINE BLANCHE. Paris before Haussmann. Note the absence of sidewalks for pedestrians, the trough running down the center of the street—which carried all waste that didn't go into the cesspool—and the typical two- and three-story houses. This modern print made from the original photograph of Charles Marville reveals just how good are his negatives.

PLACE ST. ANDRE DES ARTS. Another Marville photograph. This *place* still exists (on the Left Bank, a block from Haussmann's Place St. Michel). Although the painted wall advertisements have disappeared, the buildings are mostly intact, conveying some of the flavor of Old Paris, which looks all the more striking for the relative scarcity of such cityscapes within the new city.

RUE DE L'ARBALETTE.
Seen in this Marville photograph from the corner where it
intersects the rue Mouffetard.
This intersection survived
haussmannization. Marville
had a sure instinct for camera
placement. He wonderfully
captures the drama of the rising street, its perspective closed
by a building yet with two visible (and enticing) streets
branching off, imparting a
sense of the complexity of the
old city. This particular part of
the fifth arrondissement is a
reminder of Old Paris. The
lower third of the rue Mouffetard remains one of the best,
oldest, and most colorful street
markets in the city.

RUE CHAMPLAIN. An oft-reproduced Marville photograph showing the "zone" of the
banlieue. Some scaffolding for the transformation of Paris can barely be seen in the background. The photograph gives an idea of the wretchedness of the shantytowns that lay
just beyond the old limits of Paris. The detail of the young man in the foreground not
only provides some perspective but adds a note of longing to the composition.

LA BIÈVRE. The river Bièvre, in the thirteenth arrondissement, has been covered over with streets and buildings. Only a plaque on a new apartment building now indicates its bed. Before Haussmann, as this Marville photograph shows, it was the site of tanneries and dye shops—Les Gobelins, where the famous tapestries are still made, is nearby, the sole reminder of the neighborhood's commercial past—and one of the foulest neighborhoods in Paris. The extreme tranquillity of Marville's composition, especially the placidity of the river, belies the activity of the craft industry as well as the polluted river and its accompanying smells, much remarked upon at the time.

THE SEINE, LOOKING EAST. A Marville photograph taken from the Pont du Carrousel. In the foreground, on the left, are the quays of the Right Bank. Behind the scaffolding along the river is Henri IV's Louvre pavilion. The bridge visible in the background is the Pont des Arts, leading directly to Louis Le Vau's Institut (the domed building on the Left Bank). In the distance (around eleven o'clock) are the towers of Notre Dame. Again, the exceptional tranquillity—a quality Marville imparted to virtually all his photographs with water, partly for technical reasons but also for aesthetic considerations—is remarkable.

INTERSECTION IN OLD PARIS. The rues Fromentel, St. Marie, Jean de Beauvais, Chabretière, and Mont de Marsan, in the fifth arrondissement. Only the rue Jean de Beauvais remains; the others were destroyed to make way for the rue des Ecoles. Marville, again choosing the most dramatic perspective, conveys the complexity of Old Paris as well as its labyrinthine charm.

BEHIND THE FACADE. Marville's photograph of the courtyard of the Maison de Hugue-Aubrio. The small sign on the shed in the court reads Boutique. It was not uncommon, as Parisians exploited every square inch of unused space in Old Paris, to turn such sheds into workshops and even retail stores. The two buildings sharing the courtyard date from different eras. That on the left appears to be early eighteenth- or late seventeenth-century. The structure at the back of the courtyard is perhaps late eighteenth- or early nineteenth-century.

LOUIS NAPOLÉON'S PLAN FOR PARIS, I. This is the earliest surviving version—and it is much more sophisticated than the original sketch—of Louis Napoléon's plans for the transformation of Paris. The emperor presented it to Friedrich Wilhelm of Prussia in 1867. The street indications were made some six years before the map obtained by Merruau, and reproduced on the following page. This version, although by no means completely accurate, is far more comprehensive. The boulevard St. Germain is shown complete, the avenues de Philippe-Auguste, Friedland, and Haussmann are marked accurately, the rue de Rennes is marked, and so too are the streets around les Halles; all are absent on the Merruau plan. But the very presence of the boulevard St. Germain, for example, indicates that the emperor conflated what he remembered of his original sketch—where St. Germain was not planned—and the actual state of Paris in 1867. The two maps, considered together, chart the emperor's rather haphazard cartographic impressions of Paris. Neither map reproduces his original sketch or adequately depicts transformed Paris.

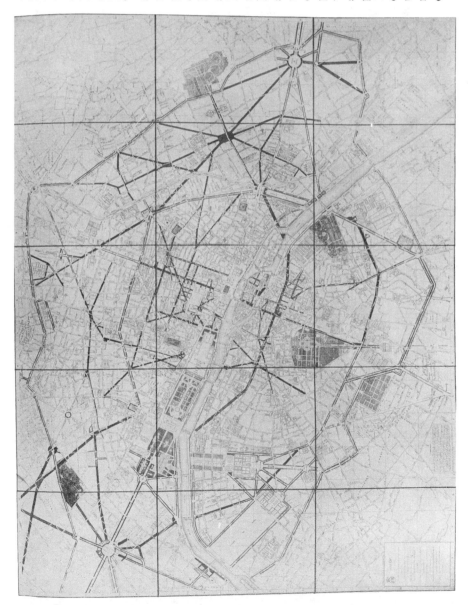

LOUIS NAPOLEON'S PLAN FOR PARIS, II. This is the map Merruau requested of the emperor in 1873, indicating the streets Louis Napoléon remembered from the sketch he showed Haussmann in 1853. Louis Napoléon used two colors to indicate (1) the streets created by his orders and at his initiative, and (2) the streets he had wanted built but that were not done during his reign. The *grande croisée* is in the center. The emperor, already dying, had forgotten a number of streets. In western Paris, for example, almost none of the streets cut in the triangle with the Etoile as its apex and the avenues des Champs-Elysées, roi de Rome (Kléber), and the Seine as its sides are indicated, nor (on the Left Bank) are the boulevards Port-Royal, Arago, and St. Marcel or the rue de Rennes. The boulevard St. Germain—proposed by Haussmann, not the emperor—is shown unfinished (as it in fact was at the time).

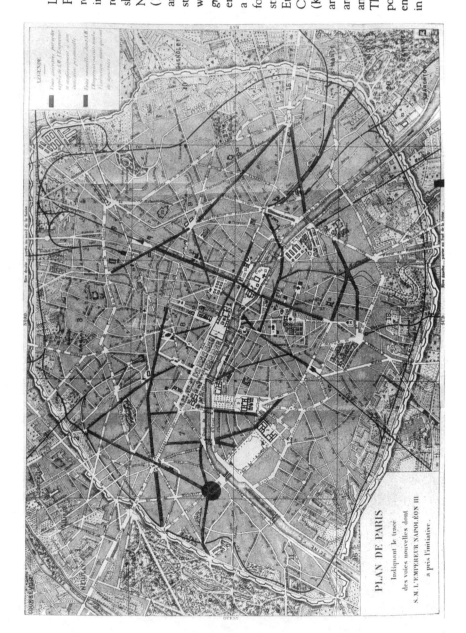

Jewish population in Bordeaux, there were more Calvinists than Lutherans, and Haussmann experienced no religious discrimination.[42] The archbishop, Monseigneur Donnet, was a prelate who socialized with the leading commercial families in the department. He was worldly, clever, practical, and ambitious.

Haussmann assiduously cultivated these self-satisfied notables and drifted toward a more conservative Orleanism than that he had imbibed from his father and apparently cherished so long as the crown prince was alive. He also developed an understanding of the self-regard of the local notables that would later make him immune to the pretensions of many Parisians. His Bordeaux friends, a number of whom he would retain for the rest of his life, came from the best society: the marquis de LaGrange and his wife, M. Guestier, a rich wine merchant—the firms's name still appears on many a bottle—Nathaniel Johnston, the American consul, who stayed on after his retirement and built an extraordinary house on the quay in Bordeaux, and the English consul, Mr. Scot. Also in his circle were Jean-Elie Gautier, a deputy from Bordeaux who became a senator and eventually one of the governors of the Banque de France, his son-in-law, Baron Travot, and the aforementioned Archbishop Donnet. For a man who was thought aloof, even antisocial in Nérac, Haussmann, did no harm to his career in Bordeaux. Although he never penetrated the old and distinguished legal culture of the city, remaining a parvenu—as he would later be in Paris—he moved easily, even gracefully in the best circles of Bordeaux.

Had Haussmann not been a functionary, had he not had the protection and friendship of the prefect, Baron Jean-André de Sers,[43] it is doubtful he could have gained entry into the best Bordeaux society. But he did, easily taking on the local coloration, imitating the tastes, and doubtless the opinions, of the notables, although he could not afford the former and did not completely share the latter. He enjoyed the theatrical representation of a landowner's life, but as a newcomer, despite a good marriage, he hadn't the means to turn theater into reality. The substance behind the scenery would not come until he became prefect of the Seine.

As any self-respecting *Bordelais*—and he liked to speak of himself as *Bordelais* by adoption—Haussmann became a connoisseur of wine. He assiduously attended the tastings of the *grands crus* held by prefect Sers and developed an excellent palate that would be responsible for his later reputation of maintaining the finest cellar in Paris. The *bon vivant* archbishop of Bordeaux was exceptionally proud of his table and his cellar, and enjoyed baffling his guests by serving them lesser-known wines or vintages from his excellent cellar. On one occasion he poured Haussmann "a very good white wine from Château d'Yquem whose sweetness betrayed its vintage (1844)" followed by a red wine "from the Médoc whose vineyard he could not recall."

> It was very easy for me, as it would have been for any *Bordelais*, to tell that it came from the 1841 harvest, easily recognizable by its very special finish. It seemed to me to be from the commune of St. Julien. But I thought this a very light St. Julien, very delicate: clearly it had to come from the neighborhood of Beychevelle . . . I said to the Bishop: 'Monseigneur, your wine merchant is a clever man. He has, I believe, provided you with a wine from St.Pierre.'"[44]

Needless to say, he was right on the mark.

Life in Blaye and Bordeaux was pleasant. The work was not taxing, Haussmann was moving in the best society, and if his career seemed again stalled, at least he was not isolated in some godforsaken town hundreds of miles from the civilization he craved. In the local archives we see Haussmann as a competent, precise, energetic, hardworking, impatient braggart. He had inherited from his predecessor dilapidated quarters in a town so completely overshadowed by Bordeaux that it was difficult to draw attention, let alone funds, to the place. His waiting room in Blaye contained an oak bookcase, three armchairs, and six side chairs. His office had two new desks, a green carpet, two pedestals for busts, two writing tables and a conference table, twelve chairs, two arm chairs, and a bookcase, most of it of mediocre quality.[45] The public buildings in Blaye had been as neglected as the official residence. There was considerable humidity damage to the Palais de Justice, which also needed new furnishings, including a new clock. The subprefect's *hôtel* was beyond hope. Haussmann's predecessors had tried to interest the prefect in the project, and at least two departmental architects had looked at the building and given estimates.[46]

The man who would condemn, raze, and rebuild whole neighborhoods in Paris became involved in a niggling dispute with a certain Mme Binaud over a wall separating her garden from that of the subprefecture. Mme Binaud wanted to sell the wall to the subprefecture. Haussmann was sure it already belonged to the government. Mme Binaud refused to produce, or have her lawyer produce, her title to the property. To needle Haussmann into buying she let the wall fall into ruin.[47] This petty struggle is a symbol of Haussmann's years in Blaye, perhaps even emblematic of all the frustrations of his mediocre bureaucratic career in the provinces.

The subprefect wanted the postal service reformed and demanded departmental funds so he could collect the fines imposed by the Council of State. He asked for more money to repair the subprefecture as well. Ten thousand francs were originally granted, but his predecessor had spent more than a third of this amount and much remained to be done. His first years, he reported, were highly successful. Council members listened to his report (1842) on the "moral and material situation of Blaye" with "sustained attention."[48] The next year they thanked the subprefect for the "zeal with which . . . he has tried to enlighten the Council on the various matters submitted to his examination. . .[and] the satisfactory results which are due to his firm and intelligent administration" and (in 1845) "the Council unanimously renew[ed] its expressions of satisfaction with M. the subprefect for the manner in which he continues to direct all the aspects of his administration."[49] But he had no patience with democracy, even when its exercise was restricted to an oligarchy. Complaints reached the minister of the interior: "M. Haussmann," reads a letter of February 28, 1846, "has alienated the . . . overwhelming majority of the mayors of the region. He has raised the resentments of a considerable number of property owners whose land he has expropriated without listening to any request . . . making promises without keeping them. We could cite, without exaggeration, twenty examples of such unforgivable actions." The notables of Blaye wanted him transferred.[50]

The minister ignored the complaints. Haussmann was too useful. One of the chief functions of any prefect and his subordinates was to assure the government a parliamentary majority. Napoléon had reformed the administrative corps of France as a political arm of the autocratic empire. Every subsequent government has wielded this admirably forged weapon for its own ends: the political control of the nation. In the 1846 elections four of the nine electoral districts of the department, including, Blaye where Haussmann had prepared the election, returned government candidates. His friend, the marquis de La Grange was easily elected.[51] "M. le sous-préfect," the minister of the interior wrote Haussmann on August 11, "I have received the several communications you have addressed to me concerning the recent election in Blaye. I am delighted to congratulate you on the zeal and the energy of which you have given proof in this important work."[52] Haussmann was a gifted political manipulator and arm twister.

The lazy life of petty provincial vexations and equally petty satisfactions, a career stagnant and perhaps permanently enmired in the swamp of bureaucratic red tape and influence peddling, might well have continued almost indefinitely. The Parisian political ferment of the late 1840s had little or no impact in Bordeaux. Life went on as usual for the local elites of Haussmann's acquaintance. Bordeaux was pleasant and easy but Haussmann still sought that elusive prefecture. Then, at the end of 1847, word came that he had been nominated. "I saw open before me the career for which all I had done was but a long apprenticeship, made almost always laborious, often painful, by circumstances; and in the future I envisioned the brilliant prospects that henceforth it would be possible for me to obtain." He had heard nothing by January 1, but the moment was approaching when the king's signature would make his appointment official. The minister of the interior had told him to prepare to go to Augoulême as prefect of the Charente.[53] Then came the Revolution of 1848.

How a nation remembers and mythologizes its history is revealing. The Revolution of 1830 is spoken of as the Trois Glorieuses, the three glorious days, and a single stirring image, Eugène Delacroix's justly famous painting *Liberty Leading the People*, has made the July rising the least ambiguous of all French revolutionary upheavals. Delacroix's heroic, bare-chested Liberty, with a musket in one hand, the tricolor in the other, a Phrygian cap on her head, accompanied by a child brandishing two pistols, rallies the populace to victory. The crowd at her back, as well as the fallen fighters at her feet, are a sociological cross section of France: soldiers and artisans, bourgeoisie and clerks. The nation in arms, led by Liberty. Delacroix endowed the street fighting with transcendence, made the defeat of the Bourbons not only a popular national event—although he indicates Paris was the battleground by the towers of Notre Dame visible in the background—but a universal triumph: a revolution led by Liberty.

The fighting began on July 27 and was over by July 29. The insurgents lost 1,800 dead and 4,500 wounded. The royal troops suffered smaller casualties. Charles X's tardy concessions were spurned by the provisional government and the last of the French Bourbons was unmolested in his melancholy flight from France. General Lafayette refused the presidency of a proposed republic on July 31. Then in a stirring and inspired moment on the balcony of the Hôtel de Ville, the old Hero of Two Worlds draped the duc d'Orléans in the tricolor, embraced him, and declared: "What the people need today is a popular monarchy surrounded by republican institutions."[54] France was launched on a new political experiment: a monarchy chosen, so to speak, by urban revolution. Thus was the July Monarchy born. Eighteen years later it too would perish in the Paris streets. But for the moment the more than six thousand barricades slowly came down, the fallen insurrectionaries were buried with all the pomp and circumstance befitting national heroes, and the bourgeois king was installed.

Haussmann's buoyant description of his own part in the fighting, the slight wound he parlayed into an appointment in the heretofore exclusive, impenetrable bureaucracy, the absence of tragedy, the relative absence of blood in his account reflects not just the satisfaction of one of the victors but the general satisfaction of his class, the professional bourgeoisie, hitherto excluded from much participation in the nation's public life. The year 1848 would be bloodier, more problematical, more ambiguous for Haussmann and for France.

There is no single image of the Revolution of 1848, no single dramatic moment, and the ultimate beneficiary, Louis Napoléon, was so unlikely, so unexpected, so inappropriate a victor that he figured in no one's calculations or even fantasies—save his own—at the time of the revolution. In addition 1848, unlike 1830, had two distinct but closely related episodes, eventually convulsed a substantial part of the country although the original fighting was confined to Paris, and proved a sharp divider in European history, demarking the old and the new.

The year 1830 had been set in motion by the promulgation of Charles X's July decrees, rescinding some of the fundamental guarantees of the 1814 charter. The year 1848 had a similar political trigger: the government crackdown on the public banquets invented in response to the July Monarchy's restrictions on political assembly and criticism. On February 23 the Parisians took to the streets and quickly the same loose coalition of discontent with the government, embracing broad class cooperation, marked the movement as it had in 1830. The National Guard, called out to restore order, fraternized with the crowd and shouted "*Vive la réform*" and "*Guizot démission.*" Popular fury fixed easily on Guizot, the first minister and arguably the most hated man in France. But the days when a monarch's misfortunes were attributed to his ministers were long past. Louis-Philippe would not survive the resignation of Guizot. That afternoon Louis-Philippe, apparently until this moment unaware or unconvinced of the extent of discontent with his foreign minister, accepted Guizot's resignation. As soon as news of the unpopular minister's departure hit the streets, a spontaneous celebration erupted. The crowds meandered triumphantly through Paris, thousands eventually demonstrating before the Ministry of Foreign Affairs, then located in the boulevard des Capucines.

Shots were fired by the soldiers guarding the ministry and several demonstrators were killed. The movement turned instantly somber and radical. The dead were put on carts and drawn throughout the city; a lugubrious and inflammatory funeral procession followed. The first barricades went up.

The next day the government collapsed before an armed populace determined to avenge their fallen comrades. The fighting

began early in the morning and was sporadic and not very purposeful until around midday, when the Tuileries was attacked. Louis-
Philippe, completely demoralized, saw himself ending "like Charles
X." He ordered all resistance halted and abdicated in favor of his
grandson, the nine-year-old Count of Paris. It was too late for concessions. Across the city, at the Hôtel de Ville, traditional center of
insurrection in Paris, another government was forming. The official
seats of power, the Tuileries and the Palais-Bourbon, where the
Chamber of Deputies sat, no longer counted. The left-wing politicians made their way to the Hôtel de Ville, where a new government was proclaimed that evening. The eleven-member provisional
government represented a compromise between the two tendencies
that divided the republicans into nonsocialist liberals and socialists
of one sort or another. All the former were attached to some variety
of French socialism. Marxist socialism played no significant part in
1848.

Rather than take a chance on an antirepublican coup d'état, as
happened in 1830, the republic was immediately proclaimed, while
the smell and smoke of gunpowder still hung in the air. Universal
suffrage, the touchstone of a republic, was simultaneously proclaimed. Within the next few days slavery was abolished in the
colonies, the death penalty in political cases was abolished, and terror was renounced. Representatives were sent to the provinces,
where word of the Paris revolution had been spread by telegraph.
Roads and transportation in midcentury France were so wretched
that these apostles of the republic did not reach their destinations
for days. Olliver arrived in Marseilles on February 29; Chevallier did
not reach Bordeaux until March 7. In the wealthy environs of western Paris there were foreshadowings of the violent problems the
new republic would soon face. Louis-Philippe's château, in Neuilly,
was sacked, as was Baron Rothschild's in Surenses. In the provinces
there were isolated incidences of antigovernment violence. Some
tax booths in the larger towns were burnt. In Lyons a few convents
that had been selling the work of their dependents—orphans and
old people—below the market price of artisan labor were attacked.
At Limoges the porcelain workers, already on strike, smashed some
machinery. In a number of villages there were even more ominous

attacks. Forest land, both public and private, was seized by peasants deeply resentful of being deprived of access to resources they believed traditionally theirs. In Alsace Jews were attacked as usurers speculating in land.

In retrospect these isolated incidents foreshadowed the great peasant insurrection of 1851, the largest upheaval in French history. But for the most part the end of the July Monarchy, accomplished by a few days of street fighting in Paris, was peacefully received in the provinces. Bordeaux, where Haussmann was, experienced no violence, even though the new representative of the republic did not arrive till more than a week after the fall of the monarchy.

In Paris, for the moment, the broad and significant agreements between the liberal republicans and the socialist republicans held them together. They differed on which flag was to fly over the republic and on the issue of national workshops to guarantee jobs to the hoards of unemployed concentrated in Paris and driven to the wall by the combination of an industrial and agricultural crisis. But they agreed on the centrality of "liberty" and "equality." The mood in the capital was joyous and carefree. "Because business was suspended," wrote Flaubert in *L'Education sentimentale*, his great novel of 1848,

> the boredom and the street-scene drove everyone outside. The informality of dress softened the difference in social rank, hatred was hidden, hope was manifest, the crowd was filled with good feelings. Pride in having won their rights lit up faces. There was the gaity of a carnival, the expectation of sleeping under the stars. Nothing was more attractive than the appearance of Paris during these first days.

The euphoria of victory, the broad social fraternity did not last long. The nascent republic was not only dependent upon fragile and hastily made political alliances, and led by men of dubious capacity for such difficult work—the poet Lamartine, or the doctrinaire Ledru-Rollin, not to mention the merely bewildered, the inept, and the opportunists—but the social and economic problems of a society in transition were perhaps beyond legislative solution. The National Workshops, established to deal with at least 150,000 Parisian unemployed—not counting small masters working alone, whose businesses had collapsed—may stand as symbolic. "From March to May 12, when enrollments were stopped, the number of men in-cluded rose from 14,000 to about 113,000. . .Even if no men from outside Paris were admitted to the workshops—an unrealistic as-sumption—at least 40,000 unemployed Parisian workers and their families were not receiving the government dole."[55]

The wage for those in the workshops was inadequate even for an unmarried worker, and the state provided only part-time work. The trigger for the second 1848 insurrection, the bloody June Days, was the government's decision to close the Paris workshops and send those enrolled back to the provinces, where there was no work, or into the army. The announcement, on June 21, touched off angry demonstrations against the government. Demonstrations continued on the 22nd and by evening tumultuous crowds marched or roamed in eastern Paris. On the 23rd men poured into the Panthéon. The police reported shouts of "To the barricades" by 8:30 a.m. A large contingent marched to the Place de la Bastille for a rally, others pa-raded along the boulevard St. Martin. By late morning the barri-cades were being built.

The National Guard was called out, but only members from western Paris answered the summons. Shortly after 1 p.m. scattered fighting between guardsmen and insurgents broke out, soon fol-lowed by more systematic attacks on the barricades. General Cavaignac, the minister of war, was given command of the troops in Paris. He mounted a three-pronged attack against the rebellious eastern part of the city. Early on the 24th the insurrection contin-ued to spread, with some fighting reported in the suburbs of the north and east, beyond the *octroi* wall. By midday the assembly rec-ognized the collapse of civilian authority in Paris and proclaimed a state of siege. Cavaignac now had sole authority. Relentlessly the army, the National Guard, and the *garde mobile* hammered away at the barricades. It was civil war. No quarter was given by either side. Alexander Herzen, the exiled Russian revolutionary, sat petrified in his apartment with his family, listening to the soldiers shooting their prisoners.

By the morning of June 25 many parts of Paris had been subdued. Fighters from the barricades melted away, returning to their homes in the face of superior force. On the 26th the position of the insurgents was hopeless. The last center of resistance, in the neighborhoods of the Temple and the faubourg St. Antoine, gave up. The beleaguered republic, having provoked the insurrection, was able quickly to mobilize enough troops to destroy it completely. Perhaps thirty-seven thousand troops were available in Paris, and two regiments arrived by rail on June 23–24. The number of National Guardsmen who fought is unclear because so many did not answer the call, but possibly 6,000 men were available to supplement the 12,000 who came from western Paris. And perhaps 120,000 men from the provinces flocked to Paris in the course of the fighting.[56]

The number of insurgents was estimated by the authorities between 40,000 and 50,000. Tilly and Lees, who studied the uprising, reduce this to 10,000 to 15,000. At least 15,000 were arrested, but the arrests were sweeps of neighborhoods rather than an accurate roundup of those who fought. There are arrest records for 11,616 arrested, of whom 4,500 were jailed or transported.

The losses in four days of fighting were enormous. Casualties in the revolutions of July 1830 and February 1848 had been small and the governments had fallen with relative ease. For the June Days the prefect reported 1,400 dead, surely a minimum. The wounded taken to the hospital within a day or two of the fighting exceeded 1,700, and doubtless many hundreds were cared for at home to escape detection. Army and *garde mobile* casualties (708 killed and wounded, 114 killed, 475 wounded, respectively) are probably accurate. And the atrocities of the *garde mobile* were attested to by several witnesses, not the least of them Ernest Renan, who described them as "drunk with blood" and heard "incessant shooting" from the Luxembourg, where prisoners had been taken, a few days after the fighting.[57]

Bordeaux was a long way from Paris, especially in the nineteenth century, but 1848 spread quickly, engulfing Haussmann's department, altering his life and career.

Haussmann learned of the Paris revolution in Blaye. He was at the La Grange château helping the marquis's wife decide where to plant some ornamentals. It was February 26, two days after Louis-Philippe had abdicated, and a day after he insisted the news reached Bordeaux, having been delayed by atmospheric conditions hostile to the transmission of telegraphy.* The news, in fact, had reached the prefect on February 24 at 1:30 p.m., noted Antoine Gautier, the mayor and an indefatigable diarist. By 4 p.m. it was generally known. It was not the abdication itself that frightened Gautier, "but the uncertainty about the facts that led to this revolution." Some young men "sang The Marseillaise at the Theater, but all this was done in an orderly way and with a certain calm."

On the 25th Gautier went to the city hall at 10 a.m. At 1:30 came another extraordinary dispatch from Paris: "The Republican government is constituted. The nation will be called upon to sanction it. You will have immediately to take all necessary measures to assure the new government the support of the population and public tranquility." This dispatch was "a bolt of lightening . . . but [public] order was not disturbed."[58] On February 28 the republic was proclaimed in Bordeaux. The mayor, surrounded by his council, came down into the courtyard of the *mairie* and read the proclamation. At the prefecture they did the same. The National Guard heard the proclamations later that afternoon. Haussmann went immediately to his office in Blaye and took measures to assure the maintenance of order, including summoning the National Guard to his residence. The next morning he departed for Bordeaux, having designated a member of the council to act in his absence. As earlier when he left Nérac, his wife and daughters remained behind to put their household accounts in order and pack their bags—with the help of Joseph and Marianne, the Haussmanns' servants. At this

---

*The apparatus in question is the Chappé telegraph, named for its inventor, Claude Chappé. First constructed in 1794, the visual telegraph depended on a series of stations, each with two operators (one to receive and one to send). These stations formed a series of towers so situated that each was visible to those adjacent to it on both sides. Atop each tower was a single large movable beam and a shorter beam, both on pivots. These could be manipulated into 192 different positions to send semaphore messages, either straight or in code. With clear atmospheric conditions, given a message of only a few hundred characters, the system could pass on information at the rate of four hundred kilometers a day. Obviously, the system did not work in bad weather.

point Haussmann's account becomes hopelessly confused, his chronology of events mistaken. He kept no diary and made no notes from which he could later reconstruct the past. He insisted, for example, that the republic was not proclaimed for a long time in the more obscure corners of the Gironde, when it was everywhere proclaimed between March 1 and 5. His own actions are no more accurately chronicled. He wrote that he went to the prefecture where he learned Sers had not yet resigned. He interviewed the prefect's chef de cabinet, M. Dosquet, who told him M. Chevallier, the representative of the newly proclaimed republic, was in Bordeaux, where he did not, in fact, arrive until March 7, to be replaced on April 6 by Clément Thomas, who in turn was replaced on April 12 by Henri Ducos. Their definitive replacement, as prefect of the Gironde, Alexandre Eugène Neveux, arrived August 4, 1848.[59]

Haussmann remembered telling Chevallier, who offered to use his influence to keep him on as subprefect, "that I could absolutely not, without dishonor, become the representative of the policies of the republic after having served the recently overthrown July Monarchy for seventeen years." Chevallier immediately offered him the presidency of the *conseil de préfecture* of the Gironde, which both men agreed was acceptable because it was "pure administration."[60] His scruples satisfied, Haussmann then told Sers what he had done, expressing to his old patron "my extreme repugnance in participating, under whatever title it might be, in the work of a revolutionary administration."[61] Sers, he dryly noted, was more scrupulous than his protégé. Haussmann managed to have his change of function indicated as "summoned to the council of the prefecture of the Gironde," rather than by some formula connoting official disgrace, such as "removed" or "resigned" or "replaced."[62] "From Bishop I had become a Miller." Thus does he describe his fate in the 1848 revolution.

In addition to the factual errors and a general haze of confusion Haussmann leaves much unsaid. His behavior in 1848 was supple, even devious, but not out of character for an ambitious man. So plastic and accommodating a conscience was common enough in those unstable and dangerous times. Haussmann behaved better than some, worse than others; and none of his contemporaries later

flung his accommodations of 1848 in his face. He had been oppor-
tunistic in 1830, perhaps with more justification, for he welcomed
the Orleanist triumph, and he would soon again have to decide
whether he could conscientiously cleave to Louis Napoléon, the author of the coup d'état of December 2, 1851. The evidence, although not abundant, does not indicate he betrayed the July
Monarchy. He cleverly and adroitly contrived, by means unknown,
to be almost the only sitting prefect or subprefect to escape the
wholesale dismissal ordered by Ledru-Rollin and the provisional
government. This manoeuvering would not make his greatness, but
by escaping the ruin of the July Monarchy he survived to continue
his administrative ascent. Most around him were less clever. Sers
was disgraced and retired from public life. Neveux soon embraced
the republic and suffered a similar eclipse. There is no paper trail in
the archives, but it is highly probable that Haussmann had more
protection than most subprefects. The local Bordeaux historian, Albert Charles, spoke of "secret influence" and offers the dubious evidence that Haussmann's signature throughout these months was
followed by three dots, which he speculates may have been some
kind of code.[63] Haussmann, alone of the old administrators, was
able to stay on the council of the prefecture, a post of no small importance that kept him at the center of events. He could wait and
watch. What he observed was an exceptionally nervous Bordeaux
elite, anxious for stability, and a confused and pusillanimous republic that sent weak men to represent it in the Gironde.

Chevallier, Clément Thomas, and Ducos were all mastered by
events. Universal suffrage proved a burlesque in a department where
only a small elite had voted for generations. Thomas's ineffectual-
ness may serve as an example. On April 9, in a solemn ceremony, he
officially planted a tree of liberty, aping the ceremonies and symbolism being enacted in Paris. Haussmann was present for this occasion
and recorded it in his *Mémoires*. Representatives of the three reli-
gions were present: Monseigneur Donnet, Pastor Maillard, president
of the Consistory of the Reformed Church, and the grand rabbi,
Isidor. They all blessed the tree. Pastor Maillard called upon heaven
to water the sapling "and a downpour ended the ceremony." Wags
quipped "that of the three it was the Protestant Pastor who obvious-

ly had the greatest credit with the Almighty." Haussmann, who lacked the light touch, made a point of mentioning that he burned Thomas's pathetic oak in his fireplace a few years later.[64] Thomas came to a wretched end: he was shot by the Communards in 1871. Haussmann recorded this pathetic destiny, but it did not prevent him from mocking Thomas as a representative of the republic.[65]

However much he retrospectively slandered the republican officials sent to Bordeaux while celebrating his own mastery of events, at the time Haussmann ingratiated himself with the new administrators. In his Paris dossier is a long report from Henri Ducos, dated July 13, 1848. Haussmann "has given proof of his loyal and firm adherence to the new order of things," Ducos wrote. Now that revolutionary sympathies were more useful than they had been under the July Monarchy, Ducos pointed out that Haussmann's grandfather had been a *conventionnel* and the grandson "demonstrated in July 1830 that he had not forgotten his origins." He had been "completely neglected by the authorities [of the July Monarchy] who withheld advancement, despite favorable judgment on his administrative capacities, which you will find in his dossier." Ducos concluded, "I would say to you here that his place is not on the Council of the Prefecture. He deserves better than that."[66]

Ducos's replacement, Neveux, also enjoyed none of Haussmann's respect. He was unable to stem the growing antirepublican movement, the subprefects told their superior what they thought he wanted to hear, and as Haussmann saw it no one "put any obstacle in the way of the reactionary movement [that was] increasingly obvious in the department." Neveux had served only in a series of small towns as subprefect before 1848, as had Haussmann, and he made the serious political mistake of sympathizing too openly with the Bordeaux Orleanists and their now defunct cause. Haussmann had the necessary ruthlessness for political survival and success in nineteenth-century France: he was quick to abandon the restraints of ideological conviction, a characteristic common to the elites of the Gironde, which reflected the general fluidity between Orleanism and Bonapartism. With Neveux the government of one of the richest departments in the kingdom was in the hands of a timid and limited man with divided loyalties. Haussmann observed

Neveux's administration from the inside, and his rival's mistakes were not lost on him.

The first problem for the new prefect was delicate and risky: he had to nominate mayors for every town in his department to insure control at the local level. In Bordeaux itself, where those who received the most votes were all hostile to the republic, the situation was especially prickly. Neveux solved this problem by naming an absolutely obscure individual whose sole qualification for office was hatred of the socialists. His candidate, a certain M. Curé had, incidentally, placed thirty-fourth of forty candidates. He carried neither popularity nor authority.[67]

Haussmann, with his usual lack of modesty, described these errors of political judgment, the general vacillation and political drift that momentarily reigned in Bordeaux, and insinuated that the return of order was largely his doing. From his position on the prefect's council he midwifed opposition to the republic. The truth is that the notables, the rich bourgeoisie, demoralized by the revolution, slowly regained their confidence and recovered from their stupor to defend their menaced position. Gautier noted in his diary (March 12) not that democratic or socialist doctrines had some appeal in Bordeaux—for they had very little—but that the 5 percent bonds had fallen from 113 to 75 francs on the Bourse, and that treasury bonds "were worthless or were not being traded."[68] Even the most enlightened saw themselves and their privileges threatened. This became especially true after the June Days in the Paris streets. When the first news of "these terrible days" reached Bordeaux, Haussmann recollected, "the exasperation against Paris knew no bounds. For the third time in less than four months Paris gave to a peaceable France the spectacle of an insurrection, and in this case blood flowed in waves!"[69]

The newspapers—there was not a strictly republican newspaper among the four that served Bordeaux—were laced with new formulas, new images. The bourgeoisie were convinced "they will save civilization," being the "champions" of "France, Europe, the world" threatened by "barbarism," by which they meant socialism. From their previous complacency they now threw themselves into politics as they would a business deal. This was not just a bourgeois but a

Girondin counterrevolution. The *Tribune de la Gironde*, a new republican newspaper founded under the patronage of the minister of the
interior, manifested sentiments that could not have pleased Paris.
Bordeaux, along with other great regional urban centers such as
Lyons or Marseilles, had at one time been independent of Paris and
continued to think in regional terms. There appeared a lead article
on the possibility of separation from the capital and its problems.[70]

None of this was Haussmann's doing. He was not yet an important historical actor. But he did have a center-aisle seat for the 1848
revolution in Bordeaux. That he kept it throughout is a tribute to
his political acumen and dexterity. He did so by taking no risky initiatives. Despite his important friends and long residence he was,
and remained, a minor player. He was, however, offered the prefecture of Bordeaux by General Cavaignac, who had been given dictatorial powers after the June Days and before the presidential
elections. Haussmann was apparently convinced, by the summer of
1848, that the republic offered little job security. He declined the
desired post, telling Cavaignac that he did not want to "reenter the
administration before the Constitution was voted and a definitive
government installed." He added, forty years later, that there was a
growing inclination of opinion toward Louis Napoléon and he,
Haussmann, did not want to take a post "where my official duty
might be to combat it while my personal sentiments might compel
me to support his cause."[71]

His own career rather than concern for that of Louis Napoléon
shaped his decision. In politics timing is, if not everything, a great
deal. Haussmann decided to wait. If he was a Bonapartist from the
cradle, as he later loved to assert, he was a secret Bonapartist before
December 10, 1848, when Louis Napoléon was elected president.
He was indifferent to or ignorant of the embryonic Bonapartism in
Bordeaux that early declared support for Louis Napoléon in the
pages of the local *Mémorial*.[72]

Haussmann's Bonapartism was pragmatic and cautious. The enemies of the Second Republic were everywhere in the Gironde, and
Haussmann soon decided he had no future with that shaky government, for which he felt neither ideological nor personal allegiance.
Peasant property ownership was centuries-old in the department

and had been spectacularly increased by the French Revolution. It required no great political acumen, in an overwhelmingly agricultural department, to see and paint Paris as controlled by the demagogues of the Left and thus unite the bourgeoisie, great and small together, with the peasantry. The economic power of France remained in the hands of property owners, and in Bordeaux they did not even have a flirtation with republican ideas. There was neither a republican tradition nor presence in Bordeaux or the Gironde. Those sent to impose order were weak, incompetent, or halfhearted. In a very real sense the *bordelais* bourgeoisie were ripe for the plucking. They had no alternatives of their own; but they hated the republic and feared for their privileges. The social fears of the local bourgeoisie were abstract, even imaginary, but no less intense for that. Proof came with the presidential elections.

Louis Napoléon swept the nation, receiving 75 percent of the popular vote. In the Gironde he did slightly better: 78 percent. Louis Napoléon received 104,000 votes in the department. His nearest competitor, General Cavaignac, 20,500. Ledru-Rollin received 8,400 and Lamartine a mere 537. Thus did Haussmann analyze the vote: the vote for Ledru-Rollin represented the radical-socialist interest in the Gironde; General Cavaignac received not only a good many republican votes but also those who favored the status quo and who were frightened by Louis Napoléon;[73] the overwhelming vote for Louis Napoléon Haussmann explained with an anecdote. Lunching with an Orleanist wine grower he had joined in the interrogation of the man's servant who, along with his peasant friends had earlier voted for men "absolutely unknown in the region." Some proved helpful, most were not. "We don't know whom to believe. This time we want to vote for someone we know." "Well, then, my friend," said Haussmann's host, "how about General Cavaignac!" "Oh, Monsieur, that is not a happy name around here." The father of Cavaignac had been *en mission* in the Gironde during the Terror and his brutality was still remembered. Mothers told their children, in the local patois, "I'm going to give you to Cavaignac." The interrogation continued. The peasant said he would like to vote for Napoléon but was reminded that both father and son were dead. "Well, we still have the nephew," he responded.

Haussmann's host then related the fiascoes of Strasbourg and Boulogne, when Louis Napoléon had attempted ill-conceived, foolish coups: "Nevertheless, Monsieur, I want to vote for him!"[74]

There is no way of knowing to what degree Haussmann worked for Louis Napoléon's election in the Gironde, but he had remained untainted by the republic and had a reputation for efficiency. On December 20, 1848, Louis Napoléon was proclaimed president of the Second Republic and swore the oath to the constitution in the midst of the National Constituent Assembly. That same day a new ministry was named, with Léon de Maleville, Haussmann's old friend, at the interior. A few days later Haussmann received a summons to Paris; but before he could answer it Maleville was replaced by Léon Faucher, who at the beginning of January renewed the summons. Haussmann departed for the capital aware only that his future lay with Louis Napoléon.

· IV ·

Paris in Crisis

WHEN HAUSSMANN ARRIVED IN PARIS IN EARLY 1849 TO ATTACH himself to Louis Napoléon, he could easily have read in the city's physiognomy the crisis that had finally overwhelmed the capital. Even without reference to the statistical, political, and journalistic record, the city presented itself as the battleground for the nation's struggles, a reliable text of overcrowding, decrepitude, incoherence, and, most recently, class warfare. Roughly speaking the two Frances—those that were the beneficiaries and those that were the victims of the French Revolution—were faithfully reflected in Paris. The murderous June Days had further separated citizens, reinforcing and hardening old fears. The formula "*classes laborieuses, classes dangereuses*" had been reaffirmed. Even though it now seems clear that the traditional *classes laborieuses* were not the street insurrectionaries in June, the bourgeoisie didn't think so at the time. The typical insurgent in this urban civil war

> was a male worker employed in the metal, building, furniture or clothing trades. He had a wife and children and was between the ages of twenty and forty. Although he lived in eastern Paris, he probably had not been born there. In addition, our typical participant was very likely to be a member of either the National Guard or the National Workshops.[1]

Added to this myopia about changes in the workforce, the population of Paris, and their politics, was a new factor in urban insurrection. The barricades of June often received men and matériel from the suburbs. The fear of being surrounded by the social enemy further frightened the bourgeoisie. "The barbarians who threaten society," preached Saint-Marc Girardin, a deputy from the Creuse, the department that provided thousands of migrants for the Paris building trades, "are in the faubourgs of our manufacturing towns, not in the Tartary in Russia." "Every manufacturer," he continued, "lives in his factory like the colonial planter in the midst of his slaves."[2]

These complaints were not new, only more urgent because of 1848. So too were Voltaire's accusations of beautiful monuments choked in a Gothic tangle. Little had been done to Paris in the century that separated Voltaire's criticism from Haussmann's visit. Napoléon's schemes remained unrealized, like the half-finished rue de Rivoli. The projects of the July Monarchy were too scattered to change the city. And now another government, already with blood on its hands and deeply terrified of Paris, would attempt to heal the wounds of civil war.

For centuries the kings, and since 1789 republican, monarchical, and imperial governments had sought to contain the city as a precondition for maintaining order. All conceived of Paris confined—a medieval view of the city as walled and defensive—which presupposed a vibrant central core. Already by the seventeenth century this view was mistaken. The dynamic of the city was no longer centripetal. The old neighborhoods of eastern Paris were losing their charm and desirability as the rich moved westward and northward to less congested and cheaper land. Centrifugal forces were breaking the old city apart. Paris was pulling loose from its original moorings but there was no thought of abandoning the city. Even when Louis XIV left the capital for Versailles, most residents, including the aristocracy, stayed on. Paris offered more than a palace town ever could. Rather than leave, the wealthy were creating their own palaces in western Paris, imitating the royal château and its fabulous gardens.

A new Paris was growing up alongside the old. Those who could afford to do so deserted eastern Paris, so recently the site of thousands of barricades. Indeed, the geography of urban insurrection provides a reliable index of the population movement from east to west. The Trois Glorieuses in 1830 were fought largely in central Paris, from Notre Dame to the Palais-Royale. The revolution of February 1848 began on the boulevard des Capucines, one of the Grands Boulevards. The revolutionary quarters of the June Days were in eastern Paris, most notably the faubourg St. Antoine, site of a huge barricade at the corner of the rue St. Maur and the rue du faubourg du Temple (G 2). Long before the June Days the city's center of gravity and wealth had shifted, and so had the sociology of urban insurrection. The workers who lived in western Paris, where they were a small and beleaguered minority, proved more passive in June than their easten comrades. Bourgeois control, in the form of social deference and economic dependency, was compromising militancy.[3]

By the early eighteenth century the east side was already overcrowded, increasingly populated by artisans who filled the gaps left by fleeing elites. The urban core, its buildings inherited from the old Parisian bourgeoisie, had lost value as single-family dwellings. Migrants bloated central Paris, pushing outward in all directions. Urban blight was also centrifugal. The original medieval space of Paris was saturated and nearly impenetrable.[4] Its narrow streets and alleys resembled "the tortuous paths of insects in the heart of a piece of fruit."[5] Paris was a city of two- and three-story structures with only church spires and domes thrusting above the common scale. In the most densely populated neighborhoods uninhabited space vanished, appropriated by a swelling poor population living in tenements.[6]

The traditional land parcel inherited from the Middle Ages, deep and narrow, coupled to a uniform architectural scale and materials, gave the city unity and artistic beauty. Old Paris successfully absorbed the pressures of increasing population until around 1815, when they finally broke through the city's defenses. What remaining space there was in courtyards was filled up to create rabbit warrens of habitation and artisans' shops. When the horizontal space was exhausted the city climbed vertically, topping houses with additional structures of every shape and configuration, to squeeze more people in.[7] The city grew in upon itself rather than outward, creating a congested, chaotic, incoherent jumble. One had only to look at the facade of the typical Parisian town house, or *hôtel particulier*, to grasp the desire to escape the streets and the turmoil. Facing the stinking, dirty, narrow, dangerous street was a solid wall maybe fifteen feet high, pierced by a passageway for a carriage, and more often than not closed to the street with a solid wood door (the *porte cochère*) rather than open grillwork. Bankers, judges and functionaries, wealthy merchants and the aristocrats who inhabited these *hôtels* turned their backs on the street. The center of gravity for their residences was the inner garden, part of whose charm was the illusion of not being in the city. The rich and wellborn went from one *hôtel*, built between court and garden, to another, only descending from their coaches when safely inside the *porte cochère*, away from the public filth. When Balzac's hero, Eugène de Rastignac, in *Père Goriot*, arrived at a *hôtel* with mud on his boots, he was disdained by the servants. He had walked.

The only decent city streets ran parallel to the river or ringed the city. Those crossing Paris were virtually impossible to use.[8] Visitors and residents alike were as horrified by the Paris streets as Haussmann. Mrs. Trollope (in 1835) was "shocked and disgusted at every step . . . by sights and smells that may not be described."[9] Stendhal called the Parisians "barbarians" whose "streets exhale an infected odor; one cannot take a step without being covered with a black mud" that is the result of "the absurd idea of having made of your streets a general sewer."[10] The rue Lobau, which Balzac described at the beginning of *Une double Famille*, was no more than five feet wide. When it rained, "black water" filled the street, carrying with it the "refuse deposited by each house." In the summer the sun's rays "momentarily cut through the shadows, like a saber's blade, without being able to dry out the permanent dampness that reigned from the ground floor to the first floor of these dark and silent houses. The inhabitants, who in June lit their lamps at 5 p.m., never extinguished them in winter."[11]

Public space, what little there was, was equally repulsive. The Place de la Concorde, which Haussmann doubtless crossed on his way to the Elysée Palace to meet Louis Napoléon, was "a vast plain of mud in winter, and of shifting sand in summer." The western extension of the Louvre was occupied by a cluster of "closely-packed houses, booths, and mean shops."[12] The rue Doyenné, where

Balzac's Cousin Bette, the sinister heroine of his revenge novel of the same name, lived, was located here: "The continued existence of the conglomeration of houses running the length of the old Louvre is one of those reassuring defiances of common sense by which the French fondly hope to persuade Europe that Frenchmen have not much intelligence and are not to be feared."[13] Haussmann's schoolmate, Alfred de Musset, described the moral meaning of urban filth and decay:

> What sadness in these tortuous streets where everyone walks painfully . . . where thousands of anonymous persons rub elbows, this sewer where only bodies are a part of society (souls remain isolated), and where there are only prostitutes who hold out their hands as you pass! 'Corrupt yourself, corrupt yourself! Stop suffering!' This is what cities cry out to men, what is written on their walls with coal, on the pavement with mud, on bloodied faces.[14]

Paris was strangling, suffocating under a crush of internal immigration from the provinces to the capital. The first waves came from the regions around Paris, with an admixture of new arrivals from the departments of the Creuse and the Cantal, the former mostly as masons, the later as chimney sweeps. All came for work. The numbers increased with each year. The vast majority of new Parisians were born north of a line running roughly from St.Malo (in Brittany) to Geneva. The south of France continued to provide limited numbers.[15] Those who came were poor and young, and were usually buried at public expense, "leaving absolutely nothing to their heirs but poverty."[16] They flocked to central Paris in quest of cheap rents. In the present third arrondissement[17] there were 800 inhabitants to every two-and-a-half acres in 1817, 850 by 1831, and 960 by 1851. Around les Halles there were more than 1,000, which, as they then calculated, gave each inhabitant eight square meters of living space.[18] The population within the old tax-collection walls of 1785 had doubled between 1800 and midcentury, from 547,000 to 1,170,000. Of even greater future significance, the population outside the walls had more than quadrupled in the same time.[19] The barbarians were already in the city and additional hoards hammered at the gates; or so it seemed to wealthy Paris.

The old center of Paris absorbed a good deal of this new population by dividing and subdividing the existing housing until the smallest humanly habitable space, the *garnis*, or furnished room, was created. These wretched dwellings of the poor, sometimes shared in shifts, day and night, by men with contrasting schedules, were one of the features of the immiserization of the old city. By 1850 the area within the inner ring of boulevards on the Right Bank "was an almost impenetrable hive of tenements and shops." In this space, less than "twice the size of New York's Central Park, piled one above another in rooms or tiny apartments, lived more than a third of the city's . . . inhabitants. The density of the population was higher than on the lower East Side of New York in the 1930s."[20]

All the basic urban services collapsed under this burden. Water, sewers, hospitals, police, transportation, education, commerce— nothing functioned adequately. Pedestrians and carts could no longer use the same space. Complaints as well as demands and schemes for improvement issued from every quarter. Then came the ghastly cholera epidemics of 1832 and 1849, the former more deadly than the latter. The microorganism *Vibrio comma* that caused the disease had not yet been identified, nor had the fact that it was waterborne. Paris drew its drinking water from the Seine, and not always upriver from where sewage and human waste were released, and the Ourcq canal, built by Napoléon. Not only was the city's water expensive and inadequate, it was contaminated and potentially deadly.

The first epidemic killed 20,000 Parisians out of a population of 861,400.[21] "In the years of the cholera, 1832 and 1849," wrote the novelist and social reformer Eugène Sue, "the death rate on this little island [the Ile de la Cité] was exceeded in only two other quarters among the 48 into which Paris was divided."[22] Cholera struck everywhere and everyone, but "the highest number of deaths was . . . in the *quartiers* inhabited by the poorest population in the capital: 53 per thousand habitants in the Hôtel de Ville, 52 per thousand in the Cité, 42 per thousand in les Arcis,"[23] which together form a dense cluster in the center of Old Paris. Charles Merruau, the secretary-general of the Paris Municipal Council, saw the epidemics of 1832 and 1849 as an aftershock to "the revolutionary storm." But all Parisians were threatened. For the first time rich and poor had a common cause. No one was immune. Salubrity became good politics and increasingly became the language of urban transformation. *L'Edite de Paris*, a newspaper addressed to property owners, made the linkages in 1833: "Today there are more than a hundred of these impracticable streets where one sees livid and cadaverous physiognomies . . . these properties are valueless . . . even though they are all in the center of Paris and in that part of the city where land has an enormous value."[24]

The rhetoric of desired change stressed the connection between business and social improvement, but since the Revolution of 1830 urban reform had been imbued with politics. The populace remained restless and dangerous. Their anger and resentments would not be blunted unless something were done to ameliorate living conditions. The July Monarchy, born on the barricades of 1830, quickly found itself storming them. The anticlerical rioters in 1831 sacked and burned the archbishop's palace, which had shortly afterward to be demolished. The barricades went up in Paris in 1832 and 1834 in response to a government that seemed more concerned with maintaining order than meeting the demands of the poor, the artisans, the emerging proletariat. In April 1834, the massacre in the rue Transnonain testified to the profound divisions and class hatreds that attached to all urban questions and to the city itself. Any consideration of radical urban change in Paris would need to be political and strategic.

When the barricades had gone up in 1834, the minister of the interior, Adolphe Thiers, called out the troops and arrested all the republican leaders in the capital. In the early morning hours of April 14, four generals and their forty thousand troops converged on a few remaining barricades, capturing them one by one. The army reached the angle of the rues Montmorency and Transnonain around 5 p.m. Soldiers, believing a shot had been fired from the five-story building at 12 rue Transnonain, massacred the twelve inhabitants they found in the building and wounded several others. None had been armed, none had participated in any of the street fighting. The police chief, Gisquet, would later "regret" the incident. The memory of the massacre is preserved in Daumier's powerful lithograph.

Workers' misery and demographic pressure marched hand-in-hand in the 1830s and 1840s, and the government could only respond by reacting abruptly, treating unrest as a problem to be solved by force and repressive strategies. With the exception of two bills limiting female and child labor, the notables of the July Monarchy did not recognize a distinct "social question" that demanded their attention. They considered the relationships between workers and bosses as between individuals, a moral question in which the state should not intervene.[25] The urban ideas of the Orleanist notables reflected their social assumptions and fears.

The July Monarchy was committed to centralism in France. In Paris that translated into a revitalization of the original urban core from which the city had emanated. Not only did the notables own property here, property whose values had fallen sharply in recent years, but they could only conceive of Paris in traditional terms: a city with a center that must be preserved and protected. They sought to contain the city, protect it from the eastern and northern suburbs—the department of the Seine included a ring of suburbs around Paris—that the prefect Chabrol had characterized as "the cord that will strangle us one day." At the same time they wanted relief from the threat of urban violence and insurrection, they wanted salubrity, and they wanted Old Paris penetrated by streets that would allow commerce to flourish. The political ideal of a *juste milieu*, a middle way through the ideological tangles at midcentury, best articulated by Guizot, had no more obvious urban analogue than the call of landlords for some parity between development on the Right and Left Banks and the return of some urban equilibrium.

For a society so rich in literary culture—historians, novelists, poets, social theorists, critics, essayists—the July Monarchy produced surprisingly little in the way of urban planning. Certainly there was no official, coherent vision of Paris, no clear thesis to bind together the many strands of desired change. But the July Monarchy was determined to confront the urban crisis. The man chosen to synthesize the several perhaps incompatible, even incoherent urban proposals was Claude-Philibert, comte de Rambuteau, appointed prefect of the department of the Seine on June 21, 1833.

Administratively, as in every other way, Paris was unique. Because of its size, its historical importance, its immense concentration of wealth, talents, and special interests, and because the national government sat there, Paris could not be governed as were other cities, could not even have its own mayor lest his power influence national politics. Until 1834 Paris was administered under a law of 28 Pluviôse, year VIII (February 16, 1799). Unlike any other French city, Paris had two prefects: the prefect of the Seine and the prefect of Police, with constant disputes over where the jurisdiction of one ended and the other began. An appointed general council was simultaneously the deliberative body for the department of the Seine—dominated, overwhelmed by Paris—and the municipal council for the city. Both prefects deliberated with the council, although the prefect of the Seine took precedence.

The July Monarchy made the council elective: the two prefects remained. So too did the fine distinctions about their functions. The new council had thirty-six members, three from each of the twelve arrondissements into which Paris was then divided. These councilors were chosen by two groups of electors. The first, the so-called *electeurs politiques*, were those entitled to choose deputies to the National Assembly, a privilege granted men who paid more than two hundred francs in direct taxes. To this financial-political elite were added all those in Paris whose occupation or income entitled them to sit on criminal juries. There were about 2,100 such men. Approximately 17,000 Parisian men voted for their municipal government.

The law contained some additional refinements. The municipal organization of Paris consisted of a Municipal Corps "made up of the prefect of the department of the Seine, the prefect of Police, the mayors [each arrondissement had an appointed mayor], their assistants, and the councilors elected by the city of Paris." The thirty-six councilors, without this additional membership, constituted the Municipal Council of the City of Paris. "The King each year named, from the members of the Municipal Council, the president and vice-president of the Council." The council itself "could only assemble when convoked by the prefect of the Seine and could deliberate only on questions submitted to it by the prefect."[26] The Municipal Council was homogeneous, a faithful representation of the notables of the capital. The absence, however, of bureaucratic clarity in the governance of Paris meant that the personality of the prefect assumed extreme importance.

The scion of an old Burgundian family with considerable military distinction, Rambuteau, Louis-Philippe's prefect of the Seine, passed his youth with his mother, whom he adored, in the family château at Champgrenon (Saône-et-Loire). He was a studious boy and aspired to enter the Ecole Polytechnique, which his family opposed. Never formally schooled, Rambuteau made frequent orthographic errors in a language notorious for its complexities and suffered some disdain for having failed to acquire one of the fundamental adornments of an educated man.[27] For a number of years he lived the idle life expected of a young man of his class, both in Paris and Burgundy. Then he married the daughter of one of Louis XVI's former ministers, Louis, comte de Narbonne. His father-in-law had rallied to the Consulate and Napoléon and inspired his son-in-law to enter imperial service (1809). Rambuteau always spoke of his years in Napoléon's service as a "great school of government to which I owe all that I have since been able to achieve." Entirely devoted to the emperor, Rambuteau was named a prefect in 1813 and advanced steadily in the Napoleonic administration, until the defeat at Waterloo. The return of the Bourbon monarchy sent him back to his estates. He was elected, in 1827, to sit in the Chamber of Deputies with the liberal opposition, and he played an active role in overthrowing Charles X. His reward was the prefecture of the Seine.

During his long tenure, stretching nearly the length of the July Monarchy, as Haussmann's did that of the Second Empire, Rambuteau put in place all the instruments for the urban transformation that Haussmann would later appropriate. He considerably enlarged the vision of urban space, both in the treatment of space itself and in the ornamentation and regulation of buildings, and brought to bear the concerns of the public interest.[28] His own judgment on his work is in the closing lines of his *Mémoires*:

Since my time [Rambuteau died in 1869 so he saw virtually all Haussmann's work], they have built more beautiful and grander things. They have been bolder. They have also been less account-able. I left the city without debts, I did not burden the taxpayer. I proved myself stingy with the public's money and I always remind myself of the words Sully used to praise Henri IV: "The king's hearth was tended."[29]

Rambuteau's urban vision was not only constrained by monetary prudence that reflected the penuriousness of Louis-Philippe and his supporters—the king made a point of never abandoning his eco-nomic principles except when defending the financial interests of his family—but he saw the city itself as fixed in inflexible space, both vertical and horizontal. The city had been without walls since the tax farmers' barrier was destroyed in the French Revolution. Then in 1840 Paris was once again walled. In response to interna-tional tensions Adolphe Thiers successfully pushed through a royal ordinance to surround the city with a defensive system of walls and forts. The parliamentary opposition denounced the project as re-building the Bastille and thought the walls were more dangerous to Parisian freedom than to potential invaders. Indeed, the placement of the forts along the walls defied military logic except when seen from the Paris side.[30] They created a *zone* between where the city ended and the new defenses began, a kind of no-man's land. They enclosed what came to be called the *banlieue* ringing Paris and were a partial solution to the fear of what John Merriman has felicitously called "the French urban frontier."* Confining the *banlieusards* be-tween Paris and the forts proved an unsatisfactory solution. They were subject to multiple local administrations beyond the jurisdic-tion of Paris, the area became a tax-exempt haven for the poor be-cause it was outside the city's tax barrier, and a socially threatening band of poverty was penned around Paris.[31] Within the city Ram-buteau envisioned a Paris revitalized by being opened to traffic and

---

Banlieue, referring to the communes with independent administrative status sur-rounding a city, originated in how far the jurisdiction of a *ban*, or proclamation, reached. In the nineteenth century it meant an administratively discrete com-mune.

commerce, and endowed with monuments whose beauty and grandeur were best appreciated if disengaged from the encroaching urban growth.[32] He aspired to restore the historical equilibrium of the city, the relative equality, in population and social composition, between neighborhoods, that had disappeared in the previous fifty years. His ideas were the urban equivalent of the *juste milieu* the July Monarchy sought in politics. Paris proved as little susceptible to such an ideal as did the political nation. The Municipal Council, although sharing Rambuteau's general views, bickered constantly over details.

Jacques-Séraphin Lanquetin, a wine merchant and influential member, was simultaneously an outspoken proponent of urban centralism and Rambuteau's most consistent opponent. A resident and property owner on the Left Bank, Lanquetin resented the underdevelopment of his part of Paris and believed that additional development of the Right Bank, overrepresented on the Municipal Council, would drain off population. The neighborhood of the Hôtel de Ville, for example, had 47,080 inhabitants while that of the Panthéon had 91,880: both had three representatives.[33] He was also concerned that the ongoing flight of the rich from the center of Paris would create "an entirely new city" adjacent to Old Paris. He wanted the Left Bank included in calculations about the center of the city. If new, large streets were built not only would they circulate air but "the population will no longer think of leaving the neighborhoods where their habits have been formed" and those who have left may even return.[34]

The overriding problem was, as Merruau rightly insisted, the tensions between the state and the city government, which had bedeviled Paris history through the centuries and overshadowed Left and Right Bank animosities. The former sought a general plan for the city; the latter had its pet neighborhood projects and no desire to disturb familiar verities.[35] Ultimately the Parisian bourgeoisie and their parochial sense of the city won out. Much of what the Municipal Council approved was urban bypass surgery, having the modest goal of opening access to existing buildings and properties. "The urbanism of the property-owning councilors is thus a simple urbanism of rearrangement. Above all nothing was to be seriously disrupted."[36]

Old streets were aligned, small streets were opened to link even smaller streets, but the already existing urban fabric was not fundamentally altered. Rather than being able to concentrate what money was available on a few important projects, Rambuteau was forced by the jealousies of his Municipal Council to scatter funds over many neighborhoods on petty projects. He denounced these half-measures and those who voted them, but to little avail.[37] The only area in which he was able to impose his will and his fervor was in fountain building. He is responsible for the fountains in the Place de la Concorde, the Molière fountain, the charming fountain in the Place Gaillon, the lovely one in the Place St. Sulpice, and even the crocodile fountain at the entrance to the Jardin des Plantes.[38]

The July Monarchy was unable and unwilling to transform Paris. It was not that Rambuteau and others did not know what was required: new streets, on a hitherto unheard of scale, had to be cut through the city. The refusal to expropriate urban space and buildings had checked all earlier schemes for transformation and hampered the July Monarchy as well. Rather than cut into the existing city, Paris had, over the centuries, engulfed open land, whether beyond the walls or created by destroying the walls. Now that land was gone. Drastic measures could no longer be avoided. The determination of the July Monarchy to transform Paris was manifest in its legislation for land expropriation. The law of May 3, 1841, followed ten days later by a national plan for the railroads, provided the legal basis for Rambuteau's most important work. The law perfected legislation on land acquisition enacted first by Napoléon in 1810 and extended by the July Monarchy in 1833. The prefect of the Seine would now determine which properties were to be expropriated. The judiciary pronounced the expropriation, and the legislature authorized the work. There were two public hearings: one considered the general utility of the project, the other the specific proposal.

Legal nuances reflected the timidity and prudence of the Orleanists, especially when it came to tampering with private property. If any of the expropriated land was not used for public works, "its original owners, or their successors, could demand its return." The smallest usable parcels of land, if not directly necessary to the project, had to be restored to their owners. This reservation, and the lawyers' interpretation that only the minimum could be expropriated, made the government extremely careful about how much land it acquired. Most often too little was expropriated. The creation or continued existence of absurdly small and irregular bits of urban space are evidence of Orleanist reluctance to expropriate their peers. Charles Merruau tells of a property owner, Balzacian in his obsession, who successfully warded off the expropriators. On the corner of the rue Montmartre he had built a large house that he refused to give up. He eventually won in court, and the rue Notre-Dame-des-Victoires, then being built, was blocked by this obstacle. Getting from the Place de la Bourse to the rue Montmartre became "difficult and dangerous" as the carriages took a sharp turn and endangered pedestrians.[39]

Decisions by the Municipal Council were taken in stages, each a struggle. First there was the adoption in principle of the project, with an estimate of its cost. This action was not, however, sufficient for the prefect then to seek the necessary funds. The council reserved to itself a second round of voting on special allocations for each part of the project:

> It is thus, for example, that after having approved the projects which had been presented to them by M. Rambuteau for the rebuilding of the Hôtel de Ville, after having voted a certain sum for the construction of the reception room and the ceremonial stairway, the Municipal Council, still not having voted any sums for the sculptural decoration of this stairway, refused . . . to sanction the money disbursed for this work without its pre-obtained approval, and left it to the prefect or the architect to pay."[40]

The work on the Hôtel de Ville, along with the rue Rambuteau, were the prefect's most significant achievements. The decision to enlarge the seat of city government, a seemingly simple matter, touched upon all the sensibilities of the age. Cholera had devastated the neighborhood around the Hôtel de Ville and arguments about strategy and salubrity marched together. The plaza at the Hôtel de Ville had become, by the nineteenth century, a gathering place for those seeking work and functioned not only as a hiring hall for day laborers but a focal point for labor unrest. The French word for "strike," (*faire grève, être en grève*) fixed the name of the spot: the Place de Grève. So potentially dangerous a public space made the Municipal Council nervous.

"The Hôtel de Ville," wrote Merruau, "is, in reality, never neutral in political struggles. Either it is a citadel for the revolutionaries or it is one of the supports of authority."[41] There was, at the time Rambuteau and the council took up the problem, no direct route to that hot spot. The rue de Rivoli, only partially completed by Napoléon, could not carry troops far enough eastward should there be trouble. Rambuteau wanted to disengage the Hôtel de Ville from the slums that encroached and set it in the middle of an open urban space. Strategically it would be more difficult to attack, the work would cleanse a vile neighborhood, and aesthetic considerations made the project additionally attractive. Long before Haussmann arrived at the prefecture, Viollet-le-Duc and his school, under the aegis of the Historic Monuments Commission, were demanding this policy of isolation on aesthetic, not strategic, grounds.[42]

The first studies began upon Rambuteau's assumption of office (1833). The edict declaring the project in the public interest came in 1836, and acquisitions of expropriated property began the following year. The first demolitions, on the quay side of the Hôtel de Ville, started in 1838 but were not completed until 1843. It took ten years "to accomplish nothing satisfactory let alone definitive," Merruau complained, adding with some pride that only forty-nine houses had been demolished.[43] What is significant, despite the inefficiency and timidity, is the attack on central Paris: Rambuteau was willing to grapple seriously with the crisis of Old Paris.

The rue Rambuteau was the first street cut through the old center. It involved extensive expropriations and demolitions. There had long been felt a need for an adequate east-west route between the Marais and les Halles neighborhoods. Studies began in 1836–37 and the edict of public utility was pronounced on March 5, 1838. The expropriations began the following year but were not completed until 1845, even though only seventy-seven houses were involved.[44] Rambuteau had wanted a street twenty meters wide. He was granted only thirteen meters, the usual width of an important street in that age. Rambuteau was fiercely proud of his achievement: "I sought above all *percements*[45] which would create beautiful areas for building, where the construction would bring high prices. Such was the rue Rambuteau which cost nine million francs and where the buildings that border it are worth 50 million."[46] Not only was Haussmann not the first prefect of the Seine to cut into central Paris, he did not invent the theory of enhanced property values to justify urban renewal or the embellishment of new streets with elegant, uniform new buildings.

The duc de Persigny, Louis Napoléon's most vociferous and passionate adviser, one of the creators of the new Bonapartism, immediately saw the importance of the rue Rambuteau, which he celebrated in the cant of the day: "The Paris population had been excited seeing this new street running through a miserable, wretched neighborhood, to bring activity, air, light, and health; and the popularity which greeted this work was of the nature to encourage its imitation."[47] Persigny's rhetoric of progress and renewal was everywhere echoed and added to the strategic argument, the need to move troops quickly and directly to troubled urban neighborhoods. The rue Rambuteau brought air to "the neighborhoods of St. Avoye and Lombards, which held a population of workers and artisans," an "absolutely classic place for insurrections" that the new street "cut in two."[48] Yet even in their most ambitious project, the prefect and the Municipal Council had been cautious, failing to condemn enough land. The result was that there was too little space for new construction on either side of the street, which, says Merruau, was "the first cause of the modifications shortly afterwards added to the law on expropriation."[49]

Rambuteau seems to have followed the increasingly irrelevant Artists' Plan of 1794, which did not take account of the displacement of the business center to the northwest and had no provisions for the railroad network. The decision of the government, in 1841, to make Paris the hub of a national railroad system was in keeping with the centralizing views of the July Monarchy and would have profound effects on future Parisian and national development. For the present it imposed a series of new challenges upon the city, which Rambuteau did not adequately meet. A rail system radiating from Paris made even more imperative the cutting of major arteries through the city, because the railroad stations were built on the peripheries, functioning as gates to the metropolis. But if Rambuteau had no overall urban vision except the Artists' Plan, his apprenticeship at Napoléon's court made him receptive to bold initiatives. If his work appears piecemeal, this is because Haussmann's massive transformations so overshadow.

Had there been no revolution in 1848, followed by the coup d'état of Louis Napoléon and then the Second Empire, which made Haussmann prefect of the Seine, Rambuteau's work would be more celebrated for originality and boldness. All his projects, interrupted by the Revolution of 1848, were subsequently completed. Haussmann, an effective publicist for himself, took credit for them, denying his predecessor's originality.[50] In large part Rambuteau's work, even his failures, determined Haussmann's. He concentrated on cutting new streets and lining them with trees, encouraging the boulevard life that would become so characteristic of Paris. Where he could not cut new streets he straightened old ones, along the quays or the line of boulevards bequeathed by Louis XIV. Much of this work was motivated by strategic considerations. Rambuteau's prefectship followed the Revolution of 1830. The July Monarchy was at least as frightened of street insurrection as its successors had been.[51]

During Rambuteau's tenure as prefect ornamented buildings lining his new or aligned streets came into their own. The new style "marked the definitive rupture with a half-century of classicism" and signaled a "new economic and social organization." A new "urban order was being created." So successful was the new urban aesthetic that it is often difficult to distinguish buildings erected in the last years of the July Monarchy from those usually associated with Haussmann and the Second Empire.[52]

The July Monarchy had limited resources of money and imagination. Paris did not retire the debt contracted in 1814, the result of war and revolution, until 1852. There was little money for great undertakings, and the Parisian bourgeoisie, the backbone of the government, was wary of what it considered adventurism and fiscal irresponsibility. Rambuteau himself, fearful of borrowing, managed the budget of Paris as he managed that of his estates in Burgundy.[53]

It took yet another revolution and an urban civil war to liberate Paris from the restraints that had bound Rambuteau.

February 24, 1848, ended forever the torpor of the July Monarchy. By the bitterest of historical ironies a government that had itself come to power in revolution and that had no legitimacy save its dubious and dangerous heritage of descent from the French Revolution of 1789—Louis-Philippe's father had supported the revolution, as had the king himself—was now toppled in the Paris streets. There was an additional irony for the history of Paris: the July Monarchy was deeply in debt for its program of public works, a fact not unimportant in the government's dramatic collapse.

The fighting in February took place at the traditional sites of royal and municipal authority: the Hôtel de Ville and the Louvre-Tuileries. When the latter fell to the insurrectionists, they sacked the palace, carried Louis-Philippe's throne to the Place de la Bastille, and burned it. Popular Paris was immolating another French monarchy on a site that had symbolically marked the end of monarchical tyranny in 1789 and had become revolutionary holy ground in the Revolution of 1830. Those who fell in the Trois Glorieuses were buried below the column erected by the July Monarchy. There was no direct route from the Paris of the kings to the Paris of the people, from the Tuileries to the Bastille. The revolutionaries bore the detested throne through the winding streets of Old Paris, following the same route, in the opposite direction, as had their grandfathers when they attacked the Tuileries in 1792 and deposed Louis XVI.

The aeration, the cleansing, the opening up of Paris, so often urged during Rambuteau's prefecture, had had little impact on the central city. There were two cities, as Lanquetin, the Left Bank municipal councilor, had said. Central and eastern Paris lived apart in a closed circuit, a milieu characterized by different behavior, seen and feared as criminal by bourgeois Paris, and even another language, or rather languages, a cauldron of regional dialects and patois. Rambuteau's work had only shifted the miserable population around within the narrow confines of the old city. Even the traditional zone of monarchical power, the Louvre-Tuileries, was a notorious neighborhood of slums and squatters.[54] Once the euphoria of a successful revolution had dissipated and the hard realities of organizing the victory exacerbated class hatreds and urban injustices, popular Paris rose in a second revolution, the bitter and bloody insurrection in June.

Eight times since 1827 barricades had been erected in the streets of Paris, always in the eastern half of the city. On three occasions this had been the prelude to revolution. The barricades of 1848 followed the social and physical topography of the city. Not only were they erected in the slums of eastern and central Paris, but the very complexities of the urban labyrinth were cleverly used, natural barriers such as the Ourcq canal were woven into the constructed pattern. It took determined troops led by a ruthless commander in chief a week to recapture half the capital. An additional threat came from the *banlieue*. Its population growth had outstripped that of Paris during the July Monarchy, and now the insurgents of the faubourg St. Antoine—the neighborhood that had provided the crowds of the French Revolution—held out for three days partly because insurgents from the town of La Chapelle made a diversionary attack on Cavaignac's troops, while other *banlieusards* provided reinforcements.[55] The war for Paris had been fought and decided in the streets, in large part the streets of Old Paris. The participation of the *banlieue*, a new factor in Paris insurrection, meant that any permanent repression would have to include greater Paris, not merely the traditional city within the ring of boulevards created when Louis XIV pulled down the old defensive walls.

The crushing defeat inflicted on the *quarante-huitards* gave the possessing classes a generation of social peace. While eastern Paris slowly recovered from the slaughter of June, the victors pondered their triumph. Barricades and revolutions became problems to be solved. The city's future became a matter of life and death for governments. For any insurrectionists to succeed they had to occupy central Paris, including the Hôtel de Ville, and conquer or intimidate the national government, located in the Louvre-Tuileries and the Palais-Bourbon (C-D 3). This they had failed to do in June. The uprising had been successfully confined to the eastern neighborhoods. Nowhere do we see more clearly the two cities, popular and elite Paris, on opposite sides of the barricades, than in the June

Days. These bloody divisions made transformation imperative for any government that would hold the city, and emphatically underlined the political nature of urban transformation. The transformation of Paris would be dictated by the fundamental need of the government to remain in power, which meant siding with the bourgeoisie against the working class they saw as the dangerous class. "Macadam should end the revolutionary era," wrote Maxime du Camp, expressing the new urban agenda.[56] Material transformation "looked like the pre-condition of social and civil peace."[57] The cleansing of Paris, hitherto expressed in terms of bringing light, air, and salubrity to the dark corners of the old city, now took on a more belligerent tone, apparent in a petition to the Ministry of Public Works from some contractors in 1849. Salubrity had been replaced by strategy in the new political discourse: "We have to attack the old neighborhoods head on . . . we have to force the population away from the center [*à une excentricité favorable*]. . .we have to have the audacity to remake *quartiers* from top to bottom."[58] The struggle for Paris was entering a new phase. A Manichean view pitting the bourgeoisie against the workers, the elites against the poor, was now openly proclaimed. And a new urban aesthetic followed. The old ideal of an integrated city was abandoned, to be replaced by a zoned city with the dangerous neighborhoods isolated, quarantined.

The Second Republic, born on the February barricades, did not hesitate to shoot the insurgents down in June, but so dreadful a cleansing of the Paris streets was not a definitive solution. There were proposals for a new republican city to replace monarchical Paris—one such offered L'Enfant's Washington, D. C. as a model— but these remained paper projects. And the radical or socialist critique of the city, so promising in the 1840s, was yet another victim of the June Days. The initiative in city planning now passed to right-wing governments still reeling from the revolutions of 1848. The urban interventions of the provisional government established after the February Revolution were conventional: the continuation of projects or plans inherited from the July Monarchy. They prolonged the rue de Rivoli as a military route to the Hôtel de Ville and eastern Paris and briefly revived a proposal to erect a military barracks behind the Hôtel de Ville.[59] Otherwise they abandoned the projects they had originally proclaimed as essential.[60]

In fairness, the provisional government held power for only a few months, hardly adequate for urban renewal, even if those months had not been characterized by insurrection and martial law. It is the stunning election of Louis Napoléon Bonaparte as president of the Second Republic that determined the city's future. Feared and detested by the old political elites who controlled the National Assembly, distrusted by the bourgeoisie for his scandalous life and low friends, he was the very opposite of middle class: a bohemian and an adventurer. Karl Marx, describing Louis Napoléon's friends in the Society of December 10, has perfectly captured the scandal of the new president for the bourgeoisie:

> Alongside decayed *roués* with dubious means of subsistence and of dubious origin, alongside ruined and adventurous offshoots of the bourgeoisie, were vagabonds, discharged soldiers, discharged jailbirds, escaped galley slaves, swindlers, mountebanks, *lazzaroni*, pickpockets, tricksters, gamblers, *maquereaux*, brothel keepers, porters, *literati*, organ grinders, ragpickers, knife grinders, tinkers, beggars—in short, the whole indefinite, disintegrated mass, thrown hither and thither, which the French term *la bohème*.[61]

The new president played a canny political game. He tacitly supported repression without appearing its ideologue, separated himself from the ineptitudes of the assembly, and, as always, remained taciturn. Paris, at the beginning as throughout his career, absorbed his imagination and was used to proclaim his efficiency, his commitment to improvement, his social conscience. He had big plans for Paris and chose a new prefect of the Seine, Jean-Jacques Berger. Born in the Auvergne, Berger had been a deputy from his native Puy-de-Dôme and then a mayor of the old second arrondissement in Paris. A lawyer by training, he had been part of the liberal opposition during the July Monarchy and then, after the June Days, joined the party of order, although as a moderate member of that mongrel coalition. Berger was, according to Merruau, who knew him well, "endowed with a certain modest good nature which easily masked enormous ambition." He proved himself "courageous in the streets against the insurgents and, at the same time, circumspect in parliament." Like Rambuteau he was as cautious with public money as if it were his own. He readily spoke the language of business and businessmen, which had also been the language of administration since the July Monarchy: "he was thought to be the best prefect of Paris that one could have chosen under the circumstances."[62]

But Berger lacked the agility to sustain his sometimes paradoxical positions as well as the ruthlessness to make clear choices. He wanted to please Louis Napoléon while not displeasing the Municipal Commission. He was sincerely attached to Louis Napoléon but he was the enemy of spending and more often than not inclined toward the advice of the cautious councilors with whom he shared many personal friendships and affinities. He did not directly resist the energy flowing from Louis Napoléon but he did not transmit it to the councilors. He treated the city as his household, its finances as his own fortune. He wanted to take no risks, which meant avoiding debt. It was only a matter of time before these basic incompatibilities with Louis Napoléon caused rupture.[63]

Before his resignation there was some achievement, but mostly on projects either inherited from the July Monarchy, long contemplated, or imposed by the revolution. Until 1848 the bridges linking Left and Right Banks charged tolls and were private concessions. Of sixteen bridges only six were not toll bridges, and four of these linked the Ile de la Cité and the Ile St. Louis to the rest of Paris. The February revolution destroyed the collection booths and neither government nor concessionaires dared reinstate the fees. Those who were authorized by the government to collect tolls were, in an instant, deprived of 270,000 francs annually. In 1849 the government bought out the toll concessions, imposing a considerable debt on the city.[64] Communications across the river were now greatly facilitated. More significant were the related decisions to extend the rue de Rivoli, complete the disengagement of the Hôtel de Ville, and join the northern arm of the Louvre to the Tuileries; all three projects took their urgency from the still fresh memories of the June Days.

Before the national workshops were closed the government had sought some project of public utility that would simultaneously provide work and prestige. They decided upon a task long desired: the extension of the rue de Rivoli from the Louvre to the Hôtel de Ville. Nothing came of this until August 1851, just a few months before Louis Napoléon's coup d'état, when the necessary decrees were passed to extend the street. The first section of the rue de Rivoli had been built by Louis Napoléon's uncle and the nephew was obsessively sensitive to continuing the Napoleonic vision. The first Napoléon had conceived the rue de Rivoli as a strategic east-west road across Paris, and there was even more need now for such a thoroughfare. When finally completed the rue de Rivoli would run from the barracks at Courbevoie to the Place de la Bastille. It was the first major Parisian thoroughfare to have an essential strategic component and marks an important change from earlier urban projects.[65] But Napoléon had brilliantly masked his military purpose by the elegant buildings and arcaded walk he erected along that part of the rue de Rivoli paralleling the Louvre.

The other project that carried both real and symbolic prestige was the Louvre-Tuileries. Louis Napoléon aspired to complete the palace by linking up its various components, a dream that had beckoned and eluded French kings since the Renaissance. At the same time he wanted to put his stamp on the embodiment of monarchical or imperial authority in Paris. He was deeply sensitive to the importance of monuments as symbols of authority and legitimacy; and he was determined to recapture the enormous palace complex from the populace. In 1849 the slums cluttering the courtyard of the Louvre were demolished. The following year four-fifths of the budget went to completing the disengagement of the Hôtel de Ville.

All this work presupposed some changes in the laws of expropriation and condemnation. The law of April 13, 1850, provided the necessary legal muscle. Article I gave the Municipal Council the authority to appoint a commission "to investigate and outline the measures vital to the improvement of slum dwellings and their dependencies." Article II defined the nature of the commission and the subsequent articles distinguished the various causes of unsanitary conditions. But it is Article XIII that was crucial: "when this unwholesomeness is the result of external and permanent causes, and when these causes cannot be removed without basic alterations, the commune, following the forms and procedures set down by the law of April 3, 1841, may acquire the sum total of the property included within the limits of the relevant works."[66] The 1841 law, as amended on May 23, 1852, could now be used for clearing residential quarters and furnished the legal basis for Haussmann's vast condemnations. He inherited the power to acquire land without having recourse to the courts. In the decree concerning the extension of the rue de Rivoli (May 3, 1848) and soon afterward in the decree concerning the Louvre-Tuileries (October 4, 1849), clauses authorized the city to condemn and acquire "all properties which will be touched by the *percement* and to resell the portions which remain beyond the alignment [of the street] by lots for the construction of well-aerated housing." The definition of public utility was thus enormously extended to avoid the limitations that had inhibited the rue Rambuteau. The way was clear for the city of Paris to expropriate more land than was actually used and sell the excess parcels at a profit.

The pace of urban transformation was too slow for Louis Napoléon, anxious to have instantaneous evidence of his efficiency. But it is important to stress that most of his first projects, for which he took all the credit, merely continued the urban vision of the July Monarchy. The earliest indication of a new scale of urban transformation came with the boulevard de Strasbourg, decreed November 8, 1852, six days after the Second Empire was established and only after he had unhindered personal power. The rue Rambuteau was thirteen meters wide; the boulevard de Strasbourg would be thirty meters. In the decade separating the two "an entire mentality had changed."[67] A new era had begun.

· V ·

"My Combative Prefectship"

PARIS AT MIDCENTURY, WHICH HAUSSMANN DOES NOT DESCRIBE, would have been perfectly familiar to Voltaire. A number of buildings were gone, most significantly the Bastille, and several had been built—the church of Ste. Geneviève, the halle au Blé—some slums had been cleared, numerous fountains installed, the Hôtel de Ville partly disencumbered, and the rue Rambuteau, wide, straight, and adorned with elegant buildings, announced a new urban manner. But many of the new projects were unfinished, raw and partial attempts at the Paris Voltaire had imagined. He would still have bewailed the congestion and confusion: monuments choked by the urban undergrowth, vile streets, foul air, little movement, while the buildings he valued, Perrault's Louvre facade, for example, remained overwhelmed by Gothic clutter. Paris was still a medieval city.

Paris was not Haussmann's responsibility in 1849. As soon as he arrived in the capital he went to see the new minister of the interior, Léon Faucher, whom he found unimpressive: "absolutely without prestige," and who reminded him of "a sick silk worm." But Faucher was intelligent and courageous. He informed Haussmann he had been judged suited to the "new order of things begun on December 10th" with Louis Napoleon's extraordinary electoral victory, and that he himself had put Haussmann at the top of the list sent to the

115

prince-president, Louis Napoléon's preferred title since his election. Haussmann reminded the minister of the long years of stagnation he had endured in the lower administrative ranks of the July Monarchy, his advancement thwarted "by parliamentary exigencies," and how little inclined he was to relive such frustration under a new government. He concluded his remarks on the shortcomings of democracy with a now fashionable reminder that family traditions made him sympathetic to Napoléon's heir and alluded to the fact, which was not one, that Eugène de Beauharnais had been his godfather.[1]

Haussmann played the Bonapartist card with ease. His imperiousness, his impatience with fools, hierarchical formalities, and democratic procedures, his enormous energy, sense of his own worth, and contempt for deliberative bodies inclined him toward an ideology of efficiency, and obedience to a leader. He was ambitious and authoritarian. Frustrated by the complacency and timidity of the bourgeoisie, as he had observed it in Bordeaux and imagined it in Paris, to which he attributed his own stalled career under the democracies of the July Monarchy and the Second Republic, he was anxious to move ahead. He had only his wits for capital and desperately craved a great destiny. Louis Napoléon, with his grab bag of ideas—progress, efficiency, some concern for the plight of the poor and dispossessed, authoritarianism with a social conscience, all wrapped in a bundle of revived Bonapartism—appealed to Haussmann. Like a superficial, real-life Julien Sorel he had lamented the end of Napoléonic heroism and accommodated himself to whatever government was in power; but his personality harmonized with Bonapartism and a military model of command. He had been trained in Napoléon's schools, which stressed obedience and specialized expertise over individual expression, and promised a career open to talent.

Sixteen years of provincial bureaucratic service had also tempered him. He understood perfectly how one made a career, but his personality had gotten in the way. He entered the service with high connections and important patrons, only to find himself in a succession of dreary and insignificant posts. When he tried pulling strings his immediate superior, the prefect of the Lot-et-Garonne, complained bitterly, put damaging letters and reports in Haussmann's official dossier, and engineered his transfer to St. Girons. The chain of command was all-important, and Haussmann had ignored it. So too had he ignored the local notables. His gaze was fixed on Paris. He cultivated only those who could directly further his career. By the time he was appointed to Blaye he had learned to hide his disdain for the hierarchy, but he remained contemptuous of those below him—as the complaints of the Blaye notables attest—and cultivated only men who could do him some good. Bureaucracy is profoundly antidemocratic: fixing the attention of the place seeker on the few, jockeying for patronage and privilege, and ignoring the wishes of the many, except when they harmonize with the pursuit of one's career.

Now Haussmann was about to enjoy the patronage of the most important man in the state, the prince-president. He no longer needed the small fry of the administration. Although Faucher showed some surprise at his interlocutor's antidemocratic sentiments—it was still the Second Republic and imprudent to be so openly critical of a government that rested upon universal manhood suffrage—he sent Haussmann to see Jean-François-Constant Mocquard, Louis Napoléon's secretary, one of the architects of Bonapartism, and an old acquaintance of Haussmann's from his days in Nérac. French officialdom was a small world. They talked briefly before Mocquard stood up to greet the prince-president, who received them standing, in the salon of the first floor of the Elysée Palace. Louis Napoléon had a terrible head cold but he had been carefully briefed, and turned the conversation, Haussmann later related, to "my family's attachment to the imperial cause and the origin of my devotion to the memory of Prince Eugène." The prince-president congratulated Haussmann for work on his behalf in the Gironde and pressed his hand between his own—a gesture of intimacy—and said he would soon tell what post was to be his.

It was no easy matter for the prince-president to find acceptable prefects. The administrative corps had been purged by Cavaignac, and Louis Napoléon could hardly reappoint men sent packing by the provisional government. On the other hand, he had no intention of staffing the administration with men favorably disposed to

Cavaignac, Ledru-Rollin, or the republican cause. "When I learn from reliable sources," he wrote as late as March 1851, "that those who represent my authority in the provinces not only do not use their influence on my behalf but rather in a completely contrary way, then I believe that it is my right, as it is my duty, to withdraw my confidence."[2] Haussmann's career was once more to be furthered by a combination of his own efforts and fortuitous circumstances. He was the kind of man Louis Napoléon needed.

Shortly after his interview with the prince-president came an invitation to an official dinner. After coffee Louis Napoléon took Haussmann aside: "I have appointed you Prefect of the Var," he said. Haussmann was unenthusiastic. "Do you have some repugnance for this post?" asked Louis Napoléon. "None, Monseigneur, but Your Imperial Highness could hardly send me farther from Bordeaux except by sending me to Lille or Strasbourg." "The Var," Louis Napoléon responded, "is one of our worst departments. The demagogues operate there in force. They hold authority in check in Toulon, the great naval port, as well as in Draguignan, where I need an absolutely reliable prefect . . . From what I know of your past, I believe you better qualified than anyone to do, with decision and determination, everything that unforeseen complications may demand of you." "I will spare no effort to merit Your Imperial Highness's confidence," Haussmann answered. "I count on it!" responded Louis Napoléon.[3]

The next day, January 24, 1849, Haussmann received official notification of his nomination and the request to depart as soon as possible. He wrote Faucher to take a lien on the future: "My resolution to go at once to Draguignan, despite the difficulties this brusque abandonment of my interests in the Gironde will cause me," he wrote, "will prove to you, I hope, M. Minister, how desirous I am of justifying the strong vote of confidence given me, on your proposal, by the president of the Republic."[4] He had lost none of his brashness. Almost all his official letters display a combination of elaborate politeness and blunt egotism. His personality made groveling or quiet ingratiation impossible. He was at his best when forthright, and acquired a reputation for assertiveness that did not hurt his career.

Haussmann departed Paris on February 1 and reached his new post in three nights and three days of travel. His predecessor, Ayraud-Degeorge, a Cavaignac appointee, was already gone. Haussmann's wife would follow in April, with their two daughters, a governess, and their two servants, while Haussmann himself awaited the appearance of his valet, Pierre, en route from Bordeaux.[5]

The prince-president's instructions were not to propagate Bonapartism. Haussmann was charged with establishing order in the Var, which meant emasculating the advanced republicans. When Haussmann arrived the department was represented in the National Assembly by seven radical deputies and two conservatives: his specific task was to reverse the political balance of the delegation. The weapons available were several. The provision of the clubs law of Cavaignac permitted the dissolution of all social organizations suspected of political activity, which drove the government's opponents into illegal activity or nearly clandestine meetings. Public meetings were forbidden and prefects were authorized to close bars and cafes where republicans were reputed to assemble.

The republic had been easily installed in the Var in 1848. Sending Haussmann thence was sending him into a typically radical department hostile to Louis Napoléon, whom they had opposed in the December 10 election. The Var was a fief of Ledru-Rollin, the radical republican politician, and would be the site of the single largest republican insurrection of 1851 against the coup d'état of December 2.[6] Indeed, it is the insurrection, the largest provincial uprising in nineteenth-century France, that provides the context for judging Haussmann's repressive work in the department. Almost 100,000 citizens from nearly 900 communes participated in some form of protest against Louis Napoléon's seizure of power. Some 70,000 of these rose in armed rebellion. "As measured by the scale of protest and repression, the transition from the Second Republic to the Second Empire was the most serious political upheaval in the French provinces between the Terror of the 1790s and the Resistance movement of the Second World War."[7] The Var contributed more than six thousand participants, in 68 communes.[8] Furthermore, because the insurrection was "a crisis in the political modernization rather than the economic development of nineteenth-century

France," the uprising was "the outcome of a prolonged struggle between agents of the central bureaucracy and well-organized Republican militants."[9] Haussmann was, briefly, the agent of rationalized, central authority forcibly imposed.

The traditional radicalism of the Var had two strengths at the time of Haussmann's appointment: a formidable and talented leader, Emile Ollivier, one of the most remarkable men of his generation, and an institutional base, the so called "chambers." Ollivier would, twenty years later, have the exquisite pleasure of removing Haussmann from office, and thus testify to the Italian adage that revenge is a dish best eaten cold.[10] In 1849 Haussmann triumphed.

Ollivier was one of the most gifted political figures of his age. His brief and flawed career, permanently compromised by his eventual attachment to the Second Empire in its last month, then cast him, and has left him, in an undeserved limbo. A brilliant public speaker whose oratory was sometimes described as "sublime," Ollivier began his career as a lawyer who defended persecuted republicans in the Var, where his father, too, had solid radical credentials. The son's powerful intelligence, systematically nourished by literature and music—he would eventually marry Liszt's daughter and participate in one of the most brilliant salons of the day—was driven by conviction and unflagging energy. He had been sent to the Var by Ledru-Rollin and the nascent Second Republic as commissioner to the department, and proved much more successful than did his counterpart sent to Bordeaux, Chevallier. Supple, widely and deeply read in European literature, cultured, a compelling public speaker and attractive personality who was passionately committed to the republican cause, Ollivier was not only a match for Haussmann but provides a sharp contrast: the bureaucrat and the ideologue, the bully and the persuader.

The chambers were a phenomenon of the Midi and Provence. A combination of private club, cafe, reading room, and local cultural center, they attracted workers, artisans, and farmers in the evenings to play cards, drink, smoke, talk, and argue politics. Originally religious in character, these loose associations dated back centuries in the region and often continued to bear the name of the patron saint of their original foundation. The chambers had evolved over the years from penitential burial societies, to freemason lodges, to Jacobin clubs.[11] In the nineteenth century they had become gathering places for those involved either in cash crop agriculture or craft production for expanding markets (such as the cork makers), the two groups from which the insurrectionaries of 1851 would be recruited.[12] For Haussmann and Louis Napoléon, not mistakenly, they were a hotbed of radicalism. The new prefect estimated there were nine hundred chambers with some twenty-eight thousand members.[13] Under the guise of private, social gatherings the chambers invited outside speakers who recruited for social democracy and plotted revolution.

Employing methods both harsh and of dubious legality, he set about breaking the chambers. Communications between Draguignan, the *chef-lieu* of the Var, and Paris were slow and difficult. The telegraph between Draguignan and Toulon was costly and depended upon good weather. The post was hopeless in any emergency. Haussmann was essentially on his own. And unlike in Paris, where there was a separate prefect for the police, he wielded police power in the Var. He began by cleaning house. First he created a reliable council. The appointees of February 1848, all of them sincere democrats, were still in place. He relieved them of their posts and reinstated their predecessors from the July Monarchy. One replacement, Noyon, was an authoritarian in politics. Another, Anglès, was a Legitimist strongly connected to the clerical interest. Haussmann, who sought alliances against the republicans, found them both useful. He got rid of the republicans, all appointed by Cavaignac, demanding the resignation of any subprefect who owed his office to the general. Using a law of July 1848 directed against political clubs, he closed twenty-three of the chambers and judicially harassed others.[14] He informed those remaining open that any reading of newspapers aloud, any political discussion, any invitations to nonmembers would bring immediate cloture.

In the elections of May 13 and 14, 1849, the "red party"—thus did Haussmann indiscriminately refer to social democrats and republicans—lost all chance of regaining its earlier majority, which, according to Haussmann, provoked them to violence. When news of a Paris political crisis reached Draguignan the radicals marched on the prefecture, which they found defended by gendarmes summoned during the night. His bootmaker, Haussmann sneers, was the spokesperson for the demonstrators, demanding he turn the prefecture over to the "Delegates of the People." Haussmann later recorded his impromptu harangue:

> Even if there were 10,000 of you, I have 100 resolute men to each of whom would be given 100 cartridges, a total of 10,000: one for each of you! I would begin by opening fire, as you deserve; but those cowards, who dare not come forward themselves have sent you, deserve even more. Go and tell them that if your party carries the day in Paris and in the rest of France it will be necessary for me to turn over my position to the prefect of the new government. But barring that, if you try to take the Prefecture by force you will pay dearly.[15]

The demonstrators broke up and straggled home.

Haussmann's next heroic deed came when he was transporting some prisoners from St. Tropez. A crowd surrounded the escort demanding their release. Someone in the crowd cried out "Death to the prefect." "I took a few steps into the middle of this crowd . . . and crossing my arms, looking around, I said: 'Who speaks of putting the prefect to death? Let him step forward, this so-called republican. Here I am alone. Let him dare publicly to raise his hand against the representative of the law.'" "The *sang-froid* of an unarmed man, who resolutely stands up to danger," Haussmann added, "always intimidates a crowd, especially when that man is a head taller than those surrounding him, and his glance and voice are far-reaching."[16] In the 1850 elections for the Var five conservatives were returned, and two "rouge."

Haussmann was momentarily successful, but the great uprising in 1851 proves his methods had no lasting impact. Only the crushing repression of the insurrection ended radicalism in the Var. But Haussmann's part in the assault on social democracy reveals a good deal about him. His penchant for force, his authoritarianism, his arbitrariness, his bluntness, his contempt for democratic institutions and legal guarantees is clear, as is his relish for intimidation and coercion.[17] He systematically used the courts as an arm of the police, deliberately blurring the distinction between the two. He preferred the gendarmerie, a branch of the Ministry of the Interior and thus under civil authority, to the soldiers. The army, he liked to say, had only two weapons; the gendarmerie had three: the saber, the rifle, *and* the *procès-verbal*, a police interrogation that formed the basis for any trial. "A redoubtable weapon . . . even for this scum who were the *clubistes* of Draguignan and its environs."[18] He knew "how every good *Provençal* fears a court case . . . even if there is the almost certain prospect of acquittal,"[19] and he systematically used it to intimidate dissidents. In March 1850 he sent a man before the court for having incited others to vote "against the rich," and he brought charges of defamation against the authors of a tract that accused the conservative candidates of being "partisans of the reign of the Jesuits, of the return to feudal rights." These two cases led the prosecuting attorney of the republic to remark, "M. the Prefect of the Var has a very personal way of conceiving of the collaboration of the justice system with the administration."[20] The procureur général of Aix also complained: Haussmann had used the justices of the peace to close clubs and chambers ordered shut by administrative, not judicial, order. Haussmann appealed to the minister of the interior, who warned him that he must not use judicial officers as policemen. Haussmann was "a prefect of the Empire before the Empire."[21]

Haussmann's autobiographical celebration of his confrontation with Ollivier and his cowboy methods in transferring prisoners is misleading. He says in his *Mémoires* (I, 365) that the judiciary had issued an expulsion order against the brilliant agitator for his participation in an illegal club meeting. Ollivier, he continued, rather than go to court, had fled, although he surely would have been acquitted. Ollivier categorically denied this version: "There was no expulsion order against me but rather a police summons for having opened one of the closed clubs," he wrote. "I appeared . . . and I was acquitted April 13, 1850." He cites in support the newspaper account of the episode in the *Démocratie du Var*.[22] Ollivier, did leave the Var, but by his own choice. He did not take the road of exile but went to Marseilles, where he had a significant following.

Haussmann's account of confronting an angry crowd on the road from St. Tropez is similarly self-serving. Rather than his autobiographical heroics, it seems the prisoners themselves (Mathieu, a lawyer, and Pons, a pharmacist) harangued the crowd not to take the law into their own hands by interfering with the procession.[23] It appears that what Haussmann did, remembering the episode nearly forty years later, was to confuse Mathieu, a small-fry radical whom he did hound into flight, and Ollivier, who beat him in the courts. The faulty recollection is revealing. By the time he came to write his *Mémoires* he had been driven from the prefectship of the Seine by Ollivier, his bête noire. The revenge he could not take in the present, he imagined in the past.[24]

The pattern of exaggeration coupled with sloppiness can be followed in his official correspondence.[25] Haussmann systematically magnified the difficulties he faced in order to magnify his merit, as he systematically exaggerated his personal bravery. These autobiographical feats of personal heroism, in an otherwise unadventurous life, are closely related to the amorous young aristocrat he imagined in his vapid poetry about his months in the Ariège. Haussmann celebrated, or invented, his military virtues, which had lain dormant since the time when as a little boy he saluted Napoléon and declared his intention to enter the imperial service. When he attached himself to Louis Napoléon he created a pedigree for his Bonapartism that stretched back to his earliest childhood. He became, after 1848, a Bonapartist from the cradle and additionally imagined, by exaggeration, a swashbuckling self.

On May 11, 1850, Haussmann was appointed prefect of the Yonne. "In calling me . . . to a department thought more important than the Var," he wrote in a circular letter to his subordinates, "M. the President of the Republic attaches to my services a value that imposes upon me the sacrifice of all personal considerations."[26] It was not a position he desired: yet another minor department. He had been scheduled to go to Metz, which would have been a substantial step up the administrative ladder. The department of the Yonne was "hardly worth the difficulty and annoyance of moving" except that it was close to Paris (Auxerre, the *chef-lieu*, was less than one hundred miles southeast of the capital).[27] Haussmann had become a useful and reliable troubleshooter for Louis Napoléon. The Yonne was a Bonapartist department that had twice voted for Louis Napoléon when he stood for election to the assemblies of the Second Republic, as well as voting for him for president. But now he was concerned that the socialists, the "rouges," were making inroads, while his difficulties with the Legislative Assembly made that canny politician anxious to assure his support outside Paris. He again personally asked Haussmann to go to the Yonne. "I put the interests of my career in the hands of Your Imperial Highness," Haussmann told the prince-president, "begging him always, as now, to subordinate them to the higher needs of your service."[28] In fact he was deeply disappointed.

The department of the Yonne presents a slightly different example than the Var, although it too, despite electoral support for Louis Napoléon, rose in insurrection in 1851.[29] As in the Var the impetus for opposition to the coup d'état, in the form of encouragement, came from the bourgeois republicans: in the provinces as in Paris they were never won over by the usurper. Conservative notables, prefects, and magistrates alike all believed that democracy was dangerously linked to popular "passion." They were simultaneously "completely convinced that the principal danger came from the encouragement and the direction given to these passions by the members of the traditional political class: the bourgeoisie."[30]

In the Yonne the towns of Auxerre and Joigny furnished a predominately bourgeois elite who provided "ideological patronage and the nucleus for . . . organization."[31] The other important towns—Sens, Tonnerre, Avallon—were capitals of conservative agricultural areas. Militant republicanism began in the cities in 1848. The political clubs had disappeared during the summer of 1849, but Haussmann's arrival, in May 1850, intensified repression, which the democrats spoke of as a "white terror."

Haussmann left Paris convinced that the crisis of the Second Republic had begun and he was committed to Louis Napoléon. "'War! Eh bien! So be it,' I said to myself. 'If I have to renew the struggle against disorder, the future doubtless holds better.'"[32] His first official proclamation (May 22, 1850) was openly Bonapartist. The Yonne, in the aftermath of the Revolution of 1848, "in an almost unanimous movement, turned to the bearer of a name which awakened imperishable memories of glory, but which, at the same time, recalled another epoch when France, long agitated by the revolutionary torment, exhausted by anarchy, saw flourish once again, in the shadow of popular power, the empire of laws, the respect for authority, the veneration for holy things, and saw reborn, as if by magic, security, confidence, public prosperity." The stakes were now even higher: "It is a question of winning or losing the cause of civilization," of preserving a "regular society" or giving the country over "to some adventure in the unreal realm of utopias, of philosophical experiments." He closed on a familiar, and self-assured, note: "The department of the Yonne might miss . . . the capable administrators who have preceded me here, but the department has never before been put in surer or more devoted hands than mine."[33]

Haussmann struck quickly in Auxerre and Joigny, dissolving fraternal organizations—the Cercle Industriel and the Masonic Lodge—as well as the National Guards. He turned up the pressure with a notorious "almanac hunt," strictly "enforcing the laws regulating hawking and peddling and by carrying out thorough household searches."[34] If there remained any doubt that this repression was only a passing show of force, it vanished on June 14–15 when he quashed labor unrest among the railroad workers. All along the line then being built a revolt broke out. Haussmann at once arrested the leaders and work resumed on the afternoon of the 15th.

His months as prefect of the Var reveal the *préfet à poinge*, the iron-fisted administrator. His months in the Yonne provide a unique private record of the prefect at work in his letters addressed to Louis Frémy, the secretary of the Ministry of the Interior and representative of the Yonne to the Legislative Assembly.[35] Frémy would become a strong Haussmann supporter during the transformation of Paris, and although Haussmann's letters are sometimes disingenuous and circumspect, he confided in the secretary, considering him both a protector and a friend.[36] The letters are mostly reports on his administrative work, but some speculate on politics generally and others discuss, with Haussmann's usual bluntness, his career. All present a portrait of a competent, energetic, ambitious, ruthless man much taken with himself.

The new prefect's instructions from the prince-president were clear if general: secure the department of the Yonne for the Bonapartist cause. Formally this meant assuring the election of deputies sympathetic to Louis Napoléon, but managing elections was only one aspect of a comprehensive program of control. Haussmann requested 40–50 troops to station at St. Fargeau to intimidate the nearby towns.[37] He encouraged the establishment of antisocialist associations and dismissed any subordinate who did not give complete and immediate obedience.[38] He invited a certain M. Ferrier, a journalist from Toulon, to come to the Yonne and edit a government newspaper in Joigny. Shortly afterward he took legal action against the printer of another newspaper, *L'Union républicaine*, which he wanted "to kill," and alerted Frémy that he preferred the case come before a Paris court, where the editor lived, for there was a better chance of getting both men condemned in the capital.[39]

Haussmann understood the role of propaganda in politics and always sought to control the press. He also understood Louis Napoléon's rural strength and how it had to be managed. "If the name of *Louis Napoléon* [his italics] is not literally printed on the petitions . . . one can not accomplish much in the countryside." At issue was the all-important question of revising the constitution. The Second Republic, so recently rid of the monarchy and fearing a strong executive—a fear that intensified with the election of Louis Napoléon—drafted a constitution that allowed the president only a single term. Louis Napoléon, with the probability of yet another overwhelming popular vote, wanted to succeed himself but could do so only if the limiting clause were removed. National politics in 1850–51 turned on revision, which increasingly embittered relations between the Legislative Assembly and the prince-president. When the struggle to revise failed, Louis Napoléon—whose only legal option was to retire from politics—seized power in a coup d'état. In the meantime he inaugurated a petition drive throughout the country in favor of revision. Haussmann collected about thirty-six thousand signatures and assured Frémy that the Yonne was solidly Bonapartist.[40]

Petitioning and winning elections involved different strategies. "Whoever draws up the list of electors wins the election," was Haussmann's axiom, and he instructed his mayors to impress upon their citizens "the gravity of their choices." His zeal sometimes carried him over the line separating suasion from intimidation, legal from illegal, a distinction about which he was none too scrupulous. In Sens he forced the municipal council to resign: "Now I find myself faced with the gravest embarrassment," he wrote Frémy. There existed an administrative decree that new lists of electors could not be substituted for old ones. Haussmann needed this ruling set aside: "If it is not . . . I will be obliged to make use of the lists according to the [old] decree of 1848 and we will be beaten."[41]

Haussmann proposed gerrymandering the town of Auxerre into nine electoral districts, each choosing three councilors: "We expect success on this condition." A week later he was awaiting "with completely understandable impatience the decree which will divide Auxerre into nine electoral districts." Without it "we could very well be defeated." He urged Frémy, "as a service rendered to the nation, above all, and then as a personal service [to me] to . . . press for the decree." The next day he again wrote, arguing that the gerrymandering had the additional advantage of controlling "isolated, undisciplined" votes, as he euphemistically put it. On March 2, with the decree in hand, he was able to write: "We have obtained our goal and without difficulty, because we no longer have adversaries; the 'rouges' have abandoned the party." The "fractioning of the city has completely routed them." Rather than face sure defeat "they have resolved to abstain" from the election.[42]

Next he turned his attention to Joigny: "I have called for the dissolution of the municipal council and have forbidden the subprefect to [make public]. . .the division of the city into sections." He asked Frémy not to alert the town: "I want the dissolution and the division to fall like two bombs on our adversaries." He planned to go in person to Joigny to direct the election. On April 20, 1851, he wrote Frémy: "The dissolution of the council of Joigny has been published this morning. The provisional municipal council has been able to take power at the same time . . . Voilà, the war is begun." Joigny was gerrymandered into three sections, "assuring us the majority in two." "Our adversaries . . . will find themselves in the minority on the municipal council, even though they are in the majority in the Commune."[43] He immediately wrote the minister of the interior: "This outcome [in Joigny] completes what we have previously accomplished, first at Sens, then at Auxerre. The three principal towns of the Yonne, which were in the hands of the 'rouges' less than a year ago, and which seemed forever the property of socialism, are today reconquered for the cause of order, and furnish three arguments without reply in favor of the efficacy of the law of May 31st [1850]," which removed from the electoral roles nearly a third of the ten million eligible voters by imposing strict domicile regulations.[44] The law did not eliminate universal manhood suffrage, proclaimed by the Second Republic, but was a serious attack on the principle. As Haussmann enforced it—along with many of Louis Napoléon's prefects—universal manhood suffrage excluded the working class, who were prone to "rouge" sympathies. Using an image he would later employ often to describe the Paris proletariat, Haussmann welcomed the law as "a precious guarantee against the invasion of the electoral lists of cities and great commercial and industrial centers by a floating population of workers, subject, in general, to the worst influences."[45]

All did not run smoothly for Haussmann. He complained bitterly of an official rebuke. He had rushed to the town of Ligny to confront an unruly crowd. Without waiting for the troops—he even left his escort of eight gendarmes at the gate—he forced his way into the middle of the crowd. He stared them down, harangued them about the prince-president, whose supporters they had always been, and announced that there would be, the following day, a complete investigation into the disturbance. So there was, and ten men were then arrested.[46] "I received from M. the Minister of the Interior," he complained, "in response to my report of these troubles at Ligny, a dispatch whose contents much surprised me, to say the least." "I don't ask praise for my conduct in this affair," he continued disingenuously, "because I do not consider it a great merit to do my duty." What he got, however, was criticism. The mere handful of arrests, the minister admonished, gave "impunity" to the "multitude of delinquents" and compromised repression. Even worse, the prefect was accused of speaking "a conciliatory language" to the crowd. "I would have preferred," Faucher's reprimand continued, "that faced with a population that violently resisted you would have used more severe language."[47] You will note, Haussmann bristled to

Frémy, that "not a single phrase of my letter spoke a conciliatory language." Rather, he extracted "an absolute, unconditional obedience to the rule of law. . . . I fear there are some ill-disposed toward me at the Ministry."[48] His official response to Faucher replaced anger with wounded pride: "until now none of my superiors had believed it necessary to recommend firmness to me."[49]

Although so close to the capital, Haussmann was unable to visit at will. He complained to Frémy about the obligations that held him in Auxerre—the elections, boring social commitments, visits from his sister and father, and a steady flow of dinner guests. Everyone except "the fine Legitimist flower who hold themselves aloof" came to the prefect's table, not least because he had an excellent cook.[50] In addition a ministerial circular, in early 1851, had made it virtually impossible for prefects and subprefects to leave their posts, even for a day, without authorization from Paris. Haussmann was unable to "sniff the air" of the ministry, to feel viscerally the complexities of Paris politics. It was a difficult situation for any prefect, intensified in his case by his dependence on Louis Napoléon, still an unknown quantity for the recent convert.

Haussmann's Bonapartist sentiments were unambiguous. "I understand the word 'political' in a different sense than what our parliamentary habits have given it. For me, as you know, the truly political is to govern the country well, to speak moderately and to do a great deal." The leaders in the assembly must have a plan "that we don't suspect, because one cannot think that it gives them pleasure in exposing us to a socialist cataclysm." Haussmann did not believe the revision of the constitution would pass because the Left would never agree to it. The only response then would be another 18 Brumaire (the date of Napoléon I's coup d'état in 1799) or, "God preserve us, a Socialist seizure of power." "But," he speculated, "the President would never do it!" His imagined reluctance could only lead to an eventual Legitimist plot or anarchy.[51]

Haussmann was not a notable political seer, but on the impossibility of an armed seizure of power he was with the majority of his compatriots. It is impossible to know how long the prince-president contemplated a coup d'état, but his lifelong conviction that his destiny was to be emperor of France and his two failed attempts years earlier suggest deep designs. The constitutional struggle made it clear to all that should revision fail, there would be some violent solution imposed, if not by Louis Napoléon then by the Legitimists or even the Socialists.

Wedged between reports on his work and analyses of national politics are letters that reveal Haussmann's astonishing level of energy and accomplishment. His interest in asylums for the mentally ill, aroused in St. Girons, remained, and he had been trying to get a loan for some needed work on the local institution. "I look every day in the *Moniteur*," he wrote Frémy, to see whether the loan project had been presented to the assembly, "but in vain." He also pestered his correspondent about the condition of his official residence, which was too small. He got the necessary funds for renovations and reported that "the grand salon has been restored and we will inaugurate the famous stairway with a grand ball."[52] These two projects were the only building he did during his brief tenure in the Yonne. He also tried to find a position for his father, forced out of his job as a military adviser in 1848, yet who refused to take assistance from his children. Haussmann wrote Frémy that his father, then sixty-two, was quite vigorous: "As soon as you will have seen him you will think him as youthful as I, although I am twenty years younger. But when you have read some of his writing you will recognize in him a natural writer." Faucher was looking for someone to write on behalf of his policies and Haussmann asked his correspondent to remind the minister of the interior that he had known Haussmann senior when he was one of the founders of *Le Temps*.[53]

Far more insistent was the theme of his own promotion. His indefatigable careerism was always introduced by some formulaic protestation: "I swear . . . that I find it repugnant to put myself forward," or "You know that I am not ambitious for the great appointments," or he will go where he is sent, "as a soldier goes into battle, without hesitation, without emotion." First he wanted Metz, then Lyons, the second city in France, then he heard a rumor that he might be offered the police prefecture of Paris. At the end of November came definitive news: Haussmann was appointed prefect of the Gironde on the 26th. He wrote to Frémy: "I am completely surprised by what has happened. . . . I have never cast my eye upon

Gironde, and I had no desire to return there before the end of my administrative career. . . . But since it appears useful that I make this sacrifice for the public good, I will do it."[54] Haussmann's epistolary surprise, even disappointment, at getting the Bordeaux appointment rather than Lyons was perhaps offset by the fact that Louis Napoléon twice visited the Yonne and during these visits had private conversations with his prefect.

In August 1850 Louis Napoléon passed through the Yonne on his way to Lyons. Haussmann feared the "numerous hoards of railroad workers," housed temporarily along the line they were building, would disturb the prince-president's visit. He took careful precautions not only to avoid embarrassment but to provide evidence of his successful repression. Louis Napoléon was to travel by train from Paris to Tonnerre, where his carriage would wait. Haussmann organized an escort for the presidential party between Tonnerre and Dijon. Everything went off splendidly. Haussmann joined Louis Napoléon in Montereau, just outside the Yonne, and rode with him. At Joigny the greeting was warm and enthusiastic. Cries of "Vive Napoléon! Vive l'Empereur!" drowned out those of "Vive la République!" At Tonnerre the reception was even better. "The Prince seemed enchanted," wrote Haussmann. As he passed Louis Napoléon into the care of the prefect of the Côte-d'Or department, the prince pumped Haussmann's hand warmly, "expressing to me his warmest satisfaction."[55]

More important was the prince-president's second visit to the department, this time to inaugurate the trunk line between Tonnerre and Dijon. Political figures love to be celebrated as the authors of progress. Louis Napoléon was especially keen on associating himself with improvement, modernization, and efficiency. Haussmann saw the visit as a chance to solicit the appointment he thought he deserved. Should the minister give him "a first-class post," Haussmann would have the time "to prove that I am not a fifth-class [prefect], which is the level of my post here."[56] Frémy accompanied Louis Napoléon on his second visit to the Yonne and Haussmann reminded his friend of his desire to move on, or rather up. The reception Haussmann prepared was designed to impress the prince-president with his prefect's accomplishments and capabilities.

Louis Napoléon arrived in Sens on May 31, 1851. The procession from the train station to the archiepiscopal palace, led by troops sent from Paris and the dragoons from Joigny, was accomplished "with all possible solemnity." The following day, a Sunday, Louis Napoléon heard mass and then reviewed the troops, many of whom cried "Vive l'Empereur!" He returned to his railroad car and "seemed to be sleeping, lying back on the couch of his salon car, his eyes closed." Around the dozing prince-president his entourage, including Haussmann, were discussing politics. Haussmann, in his *Mémoires*, quotes a long monologue he delivered on the state of the nation and, his favorite topic, himself. He was not "a political man," he responded to a question from Frémy about his own views, but "a man of action who, for two-and-a-half years, has practiced a militant administration for which he had hardly been prepared." The cliché he twice used was "to take the bull by the horns." "Of course," he commented, "this is not the parliamentary way of doing things, but it works." He then sketched a scenario for establishing Louis Napoléon in power, which included proscriptions and exile of all the "rouges" and utopians, an appeal to the nation, and coercion of the parliamentary opposition. Dupin, the president of the assembly, interjected that "it is a long way from the dream to the reality," to which Haussmann responded: "M. President, I have seen realities that pass all fantasies: witness December 10th."

The prince's eyes had been open during this monologue, the autobiographer insisted, and fixed on him. At the point when the prefect described what should be done with opposition leaders of the assembly, he graced Haussmann with a half-smile—"which nothing has effaced from my memory." "I pretended not to have seen anything," he continued, "but from that instant I knew, without doubt, what would be the solution to the conflict that concerned everyone."[57] The train rolled on to Tonnerre, where the reception was exuberant. The gendarmes could hardly restrain the crowd that pressed around the presidential car. When Haussmann departed he had a short interview with Louis Napoléon. "You fully justify the mission that I have given you in the Yonne," the prince-president told him," and "cause me to place the highest value on your administrative abilities. When the moment arrives . . . I count on your devotion." "Monseigneur," Haussmann answered, "you have it without reserve."[58] The prince-president continued on to Dijon and a famous speech: "Whatever the duties the country imposes on me, it will find me determined to follow its will." The response in Paris to Louis Napoléon's provocative words was heated, not to say violent.

Haussmann's rhetorical domination of the band of visiting Bonapartists, and the faint smile of acknowledgment from Louis Napoléon, deserve some skepticism. The prefect's words seem overly frank and familiar, even given the composition of the prince-president's entourage. Haussmann was an outsider, however useful, and not privy to Louis Napoléon's inner circle. The possibility of a coup was the talk of Paris salons, but Louis Napoléon said nothing about it, and Morny, who planned the action, was equally discreet. Louis Napoléon's tour of the provinces was to test the waters, to gauge for himself the depth and quality of his popular support. He had no need of Haussmann's political advice, nor would it have been welcome. Haussmann's performance is as carefully staged in the telling as all his other arrangements in the Yonne. Another biographical detail to flesh out the self-portrait of a Bonapartist from the cradle. This presentation of self as the dedicated, blunt, efficient (because) authoritarian civil servant is psychologically important and accurate. It will be henceforth regularly and pridefully asserted.

·VI·

"This Province I Have
So Loved"

BORDEAUX! FOR SO MANY YEARS HIS AMBITION HAD REACHED NO
higher. He knew the city and its elite, his family was there, he had
land nearby, he had spent the better part of his career in the area.
He had served his apprenticeship and now came his reward. He returned to Bordeaux as a conqueror. His predecessor and rival,
Neveux, was peremptorily dismissed, despite eventually rallying to
the Bonapartist cause. "Administrative necessities," the minister of
the interior dryly informed him, demanded his removal: "I regret to
announce to you that the President of the Republic wants to reas-
sign the prefecture which you have held and to appoint M. Haussmann, prefect of the Yonne, as your successor."[1]

The move was not popular. The General Council of Bordeaux
expressed regrets and sympathy: "We cannot dissimulate that we
have viewed with melancholy astonishment how little weight has
been given to the wishes of the Council."[2] Antoine Gautier noted in
his diary (November 29, 1851): "It is all too true, M. Neveux is no
longer prefect of the Gironde and that he has no immediate employment. . . . I am deeply saddened and pained."[3] It was the end of
the Orleanist hegemony in Bordeaux. Haussmann was summoned
to Paris and saw Louis Napoléon on December 1.

It was the eve of the coup d'état. The date fixed for the long

135

expected blow took everyone by surprise, but it was so obvious. Ever sensitive to his uncle's career and precepts, Louis Napoléon chose December 2, the anniversary of the Battle of Austerlitz, his uncle's greatest victory, not November 9–10, the date of Napoléon's coup d'état in 1799. The deliberate symbolism was excellent. The prince-president, whom Haussmann found at the Elysée Palace surrounded by people, was cooler than a conspirator had any right to be. He asked whether Mme Haussmann was unhappy about the Bordeaux appointment, and after a few moments of polite small talk turned to more serious matters. "I cannot tell you here and now why I am sending you to Bordeaux," the prince-president confided, "but I want you to go there immediately. Go tomorrow morning, early, as early as possible, to find the minister of the interior for your instructions and depart immediately afterwards. . . . Go to the Minister even before daybreak," Louis Napoléon added, " that will be even better." He then pressed Haussmann's hand "in a way I knew well, that reserved for important circumstances."[4] Before leaving the Elysée Haussmann had himself introduced to M. de Thorigny, the minister of the interior. He explained he would see him in the morning to receive instructions, to which Thorigny responded that he had none to give. The minister was not in on whatever was afoot. Haussmann, realizing his error, quickly changed the subject, muttered some inconsequential remarks, and left the palace perplexed.[5]

At 5 a.m. Haussmann set out by coach from his hotel for the ministry. He noticed troops in the Place de la Concorde but could not explain their presence. At the ministry, in the rue Grenelle (D 4), the *porte-cochère* was open, the courtyard brilliantly lit, with a fully armed battalion of infantry on duty. He crossed to the vestibule, was recognized, and was asked whether he had come to speak to the minister. "Precisely," he answered. "But which one," the usher inquired. "What do you mean which one?" "Do you want to see M. de Thorigny or M. le comte de Morny?" "Announce me to M. le comte de Morny." The doors opened and he confronted Morny for the first time, Louis Napoléon's illegitimate half-brother, one of the creators of the new Bonapartism and the strategist of the coup. Haussmann was among the very first to greet Morny as minister of the interior, a significant bit of good fortune for his career. The new minister inquired, "with elegance and great tranquility": "M. Haussmann, are you with us?" "I don't know what you are referring to, M. le comte," he answered, "but I belong to the Prince. Use me without hesitation."[6] The count then explained the pending seizure of power and allowed Haussmann to read the prince's proclamation that the coup d'état was in the name of the people, the only sovereign. Haussmann did not hesitate.

Nor did he dawdle. He never looked back. He would later defend the hundreds of arrests of unsympathetic deputies and gloss over the shootings on the boulevard des Capucines. He himself would prove a vigorous, even zealous director of the subsequent repression in the provinces, lamenting Louis Napoléon's eventual pardon of hundreds of his opponents. And he would defend the coup d'état with the enthusiasm of a convert.

"I leave this evening at 7 by the baggage train for Bordeaux," he wrote to Frémy that afternoon. "The circumstances that cause me to rush my trip in so unexpected a manner do not leave me a moment to go and shake your hand."[7] By the time Haussmann arrived in Bordeaux Louis Napoléon controlled Paris, but the disgraced Neveux remained at his post, scrupulously inactive, awaiting his replacement. The General Council was hostile, and the local commander, General d'Arbouville, had strong Orleanist sympathies that he did not mask. Bordeaux remained calm. At 12:30 d'Arbouville fetched the mayor, Antoine Gautier, and accompanied him to the prefecture. The news had just come by telegraph that Louis Napoléon had dissolved the National Assembly. Gautier and d'Arbouville, without any explanation, without officially announcing the news, put the department under martial law. The prefecture and the city hall were to be occupied by regulars, and a regiment of artillerymen was ordered to the Quinconces (an immense plaza almost in the center of town). The *Tribune*, the only newspaper with republican leanings, was shut down. At nine that evening Gautier went home, his preparations for the morrow completed. "Thus was the great work begun," he concluded his diary entry. December 3 passed without difficulties. Details of the coup and its aftermath trickled in throughout the day and Gautier judged that both the Parisians and the army were pleased by events. "M. Haussmann arrived," he noted. "He gave us a great many details. He took over the administration of the department immediately."[8]

The voice of authority, punctuated with threats, replaced the cautious measures of the old elite. Having dictated his first decree, Haussmann walked from the prefecture across the city—carefully detailing his route—and arrived at his in-laws' without "seeing a cat."[9]

> . . .the powers that I hold from the government are sufficiently broad to assure the maintenance of the tranquility of the department. . . .
>
> From wherever aggression may come the energy that I can use to suppress it should certainly prevent a recurrence. . . .
>
> Troublemakers can expect no tolerance from me.[10]

There followed a series of proclamations in the same vein. He banned the sale of gunpowder and lead for shot. On January 20 he informed all the mayors that a subscription for the families of soldiers killed or wounded in the coup d'état had been opened in Paris. Because "the army has powerfully contributed to saving the country from anarchy," it is "fit that the public take the initiative in coming to the aid of the noble victims of insurrection."[11] At the first meeting of the General Council he badgered them into supporting a fawning address to Louis Napoléon: "In the name of the populations of which it is the organ, the Council thanks you, Prince, for the great act of public safety. . . . Happy for the present, France puts herself in your care for the future."[12]

"My sudden arrival and the firmness of my attitude," wrote Haussmann of his vigor, "had caused the tendency to refuse cooperation, momentarily shown by the Orleanist coteries which dominated the prefecture, to vanish." He likened his action in Bordeaux to that of Louis Napoléon in Paris: "Thanks to the quick repression of troubles in Paris, still more, perhaps, thanks to the promptness of my decisions, Bordeaux came to rediscover its habitual calm and order."[13] Louis Napoléon had sent Haussmann to Bordeaux to hold the city, whose wealth and dominance of southwestern France, as well as an Orleanist past, made it strategically important. The city would probably have continued orderly even without Haussmann: the notables were as frightened of the "rouges" as Louis Napoléon.

Just before the coup Gautier noted in his diary: "In Bordeaux as in Paris everyone is turning to Bonaparte. He alone offers guarantees of order and stability."[14] The traditional elites of the city, who had no sympathy for the Second Republic, welcomed a conservative, albeit authoritarian, turn in Paris. The Orleanism of the town easily grafted itself onto that part of Louis Napoléon's program that spoke of peace, tranquility, and commerce. Haussmann's bluster was probably unnecessary; but Morny always erred on the side of caution and preferred the sure results of coercion to the less predictable effects of suasion. Haussmann was the man for the job.

Once Bordeaux was secure he set out to destroy any opposition that remained and to prepare the elections. The habits acquired and approved in the departments of the Var and the Yonne continued. Haussmann does not tell us precisely what instructions he received from Morny, but his behavior makes it likely he was encouraged to be ruthless in suppressing dissent. The mopping up that followed the coup d'état was brutal. There were more than 26,000 arrests in France. Mixed commissions, composed of the prefect, a general, and a public prosecutor, were established in February 1852, in each department. They purged and punished on a scale that "far exceeded any other police measures against political activity in the French provinces during the nineteenth century."[15] Of those arrested, 11,609 were set free but 9,530 were exiled to Algeria, 2,804 were interned, and 5,108 were placed under police surveillance.

These official figures do not tell the whole story. It is "virtually impossible to calculate the total number of men arrested during the four months [December 2, 1851–March 27, 1852] of exceptional police powers."[16] Many who were arrested or placed in preventive detention were released and no record was made, neither by the courts nor by the mixed commissions. In the Gironde the statistics are 500 men detained of whom 74 were punished: 5 transported to French Guiana and 22 to Algeria, 20 were expelled from France, 9 were internally exiled, and 18 were interned. Haussmann vigorously pursued enemies both important and insignificant. The Bordeaux Mixed Commission was relentless.

In 1890 a certain Emile Riffaud published an attack on Haussmann's account of his work on the Mixed Commission in the *Mémoires*, particularly the prefect's treatment of Emile Crugy, the publisher and owner of the *Courrier de la Gironde*, who had been sent to internal exile in Vannes (Brittany) to live under police surveillance. Riffaud accused Haussmann of having "surpassed his mandate" and characterized the *Mémoires* as "history in the manner of Alexandre Dumas the elder." Crugy was exiled, the polemicist insisted, for a nonexistent pamphlet protesting the confiscation of lands belonging to the Orleans family. It was all a pretext for suppressing a newspaper unenthusiastic about the coup d'état. The choice of Vannes rather than some other town closer to Bordeaux was an act of cruelty.[17]

Louis Napoléon's confiscation of all the property of the Orleans family (January 23, 1852) was also unprecedented. He had long hated the family that had imprisoned him and forbidden the Bonapartes to enter France. Now he had his revenge. Haussmann, the former protégé of the duc d'Orléans, himself the scion of a family that was more Orleanist than Bonapartist, concluded that the confiscations were legal and necessary.[18] As prefect of Bordeaux he relentlessly persecuted those who expressed, or were thought likely to express, sympathy for the Orleans family or questioned the legality of the decrees. Those Riffaud defended were the victims of Haussmann's ire. Once he had cast his lot with the Bonapartists, he cut all ties with Orleanism.

Haussmann showed himself pitiless during the hearings conducted by the Mixed Commission and protested subsequently against all acts of indulgence. Louis Napoléon, who always maintained he had not sanctioned the severe repression that followed the coup, granted a number of pardons on various occasions, not least of which when he married Eugénie de Montijo. In April 1852 Haussmann opposed the pardon of the mayor of Blaye, and in June he had to justify himself to the minister of the interior against the accusation of having too rigorously used the Mixed Commission to take vengeance against those who had opposed him when he was subprefect of Blaye. In July he opposed leniency toward a man transported to Algeria, and he conducted a vendetta against the former deputy, Henri Galos, whom Louis Napoléon wanted to pardon, insisting his exile from Bordeaux "was absolutely indispensable." In a letter to the head of police he lamented "the excessive kindness of the chief of state."[19]

Bordeaux was not as dangerous as had been the Var and the Yonne. There were no republican traditions, no "rouges," and no opposition leader of stature, let alone an Emile Ollivier. The city and the department find only a marginal place in Ted Margadant's history of the insurrection of 1851. At best there was sympathy for the Orleanist cause among the elite, but they were unorganized and unwilling to resist Paris. The level of repression sprang from Haussmann, not the circumstances. He enjoyed wielding power, and his conviction that order and obedience were necessary to the well-governed state, and best achieved by a show of force, made him a formidable policeman. He had gambled on Louis Napoléon's future and won. Now he played the victor in the Gironde. Even Antoine Gautier, favorably disposed to Haussmann, remarked on the pomposity and triumphal aspect of the prefect's tour of his department in 1852, where he was "received like a prince of the blood."[20] Haussmann's version, in a letter to the minister of the interior, is self-congratulatory: "In the twenty-two years that I have been in departmental administration I have never seen a prefect greeted as I came to be greeted in the different cantons of the Gironde."[21] His tour of the department was meant to attract attention in Paris, hence the unaccustomed pomp. The state, and the prefect, needed to be visible and intimidating. Haussmann, with his innate sense of the dramatic, exploited the moment. Louis Napoléon wanted his representatives to manifest the authority he himself embodied. The *préfet à poigne* became the type of the Second Empire.

The immediate challenge was the plebiscite of December 21, a nationwide referendum on the coup d'état. Haussmann's job was to carry Bordeaux. And he did: 123,110 voters approved, 15,232 voted disapproved, and 28,485 abstained. The numbers surpassed those for the election of Louis Napoléon as president: "it was the justification for sending me to the Gironde and at the same time the complete accomplishment of the special mission that I had received."[22] But there was much more to be done. It was not enough to break the potential resistance in the Gironde, nor to win the momentary adherence of voters who were not Bonapartists. What most mattered was to build a Bonapartist party. As he put it, "gradually attach to his person [Louis Napoléon] the sympathies of the more or less important classes as well as the popular masses (already completely won over to the Empire)."[23] The instrument for building such support would be the elections, beginning with those to the new Legislative Corps, scheduled for February 29, 1852. Haussmann explained the importance of the elections, and the new version of democracy, to his subprefects and mayors. "Since the chief of state is himself elected," the Legislative Corps is to "fortify the authority delegated to the President of the Republic by the country." To create a "harmony as complete as possible" between the two independent powers is "perfectly correct and can be openly avowed."[24]

Nothing was left to chance. Haussmann carefully sifted potential candidates seeking still-scarce Bonapartists. He persuaded three men to run: Baron Travot (the son-in-law of Gautier), Colonel Thiéron (an important local landowner), and General Grouchy. The first two were married to cousins of Mme Haussmann. He then applied pressure, using all the machinery of local government. School teachers were given permission to campaign for his candidates: those who refused were dismissed. A total of 177,871 electors were eligible to vote in the Gironde, but only 54 percent, or 95,918, cast votes. The official candidates received 89,211 votes. Haussmann was bitter about the abstentions, which "served only to demonstrate once again the resentment and the impotence of the Orleanist faction."[25]

The next round of elections (July 31–August 1, 1852) was for the Bordeaux General Council and the various arrondissement councils. Haussmann was even more intrusive. He chose the candidates and, as he wrote the minister of the interior, "I have thus cut through a mass of difficulties. In most of the cantons there will only be a single candidate, the one the administration has presented."[26] Should they choose other candidates "under the pretext of making a better choice," this will be "not only an act of indiscipline but even one of hostility."[27] For the General Council of Bordeaux he excluded all "members of the current council who had not signed the addresses sent to the Prince to invite him to come to Bordeaux to receive the hospitality of the city."[28] Haussmann understood perfectly the minor art of provincial social humiliation.

In Bordeaux, with its strong Orleanist traditions and long memory of how the blockade of Napoléon I had undermined business and commerce, it was not enough to intimidate the "rouges." He had to win over the elites, who were unaccustomed to being pushed around. There was resentment about the Mixed Commission, resentment about shutting down newspapers, resentments about Haussmann's imperiousness. The sullen passivity, inertia, and indifference of the notables was manifest in their abstention from elections. Haussmann was tenacious. His instincts often led him to prefer confrontation, but he was also capable of diplomacy. Gradually he seduced important individuals, not least among them Archbishop Donnet. Haussmann convinced the worldly and ambitious prelate that adherence to Louis Napoléon could bring him a cardinal's hat.

Events in Paris impinged on Haussmann's career. Once the decree confiscating Orleanist property had been promulgated, Louis Napoléon replaced Morny at the Ministry of the Interior with the duc de Persigny, another of the inner circle but far less abrasive than Morny. The appointment of the generous, chivalric Persigny announced Louis Napoléon's desire for reconciliation after the coup d'état. On May 2, 1852, the new minister summoned the prefect to Paris. The prince-president greeted Haussmann warmly, as did Persigny, who would become his patron. The two men took to each other.

Haussmann had expected—wrongly, it turned out—that the summons to Paris was to announce his promotion to an even more important post. In fact, it was to inform him of Louis Napoléon's planned tour of the Midi and southwest of France, starting in Bordeaux. Haussmann quickly grasped the significance of the visit. Not only must the prince-president be received with grandeur, but the visit would give Haussmann the opportunity to display the wonders he had worked in Bordeaux. It is doubtful that Haussmann knew any better than anyone else when or how Louis Napoléon planned to reinstate the empire (which was done on December 2, 1852). But his imagination was inflamed by the chance to present Bordeaux as Bonapartist.

If Louis Napoléon were to arrive by the newly completed rail line, he would enter Bordeaux from its least attractive side. The area around the still unfinished Bastide station was strewn with debris from construction, and some streets leading into the center of town, still unfinished, were piled with rubble from demolished houses. Here was no fit setting for a triumphal procession. The itinerary must be changed. Louis Napoléon must visit Bordeaux last, on his way back to Paris. Then he could arrive at the city by boat. He would sail the length of Bordeaux's magnificent port, under the graceful bridge, the natural gate to the city, along the extensive quay graced with row upon row of elegant stone buildings erected by the marquis de Tourny in the eighteenth century. Bordeaux's waterfront was stunning for beauty and bustle. "The reception at Bordeaux," he told Persigny, "must be reserved as the *bouquet* of the imperialist demonstration that will be aroused everywhere by the appearance of the Prince." Haussmann's suggestion prevailed.

He returned to Bordeaux to prepare the pageant. His gift for pomp and procession would have full expression. The prince-president would arrive on October 7 and remain in Bordeaux until his departure on the 10th. The night of the 9th would be an important banquet where Louis Napoléon would address the guests. The rest of the itinerary was up to Haussmann. He advised the mayors of the pending visit and told them, "His Imperial Highness will be received at his disembarkment on the vertical quay at the Quinconces, by the mayor and the municipal corps of Bordeaux, surrounded by the mayors, their assistants, and deputations from all the communes of the department." "I do not doubt," he continued, "that all the communes will vie with each other to give the savior of France a reception worthy of him." He then addressed his wishes to the citizenry. "The inhabitants will be invited to decorate and illuminate the facades of their houses on the 7, 8, and 9 of October." "In conformity with the wishes of His Imperial Highness special distributions of aid to the indigent will be made on the occasion of his visit to Bordeaux."[29]

In a series of administrative decrees the prefect detailed the itinerary and orchestrated the visit.[30] A steamboat, contributed by M. Lubbert, the director of the company, waited upriver at Agen for the Prince's 7 a.m. departure. Louis Napoléon's party consisted of General Roguet, his first aide-de-camp and head of the military household; Lieutenant Colonel Fleury, another aide-de-camp and the premier ecuyer, or stable master; and Mocquard, the Chef de Cabinet. They were joined at Bordeaux by four ministers: General Saint-Arnaud, M. Ducos, M. Drouyn de Lhuys (minister of foreign affairs), and M. Magne (minister of public works).

The previous evening Haussmann and his entourage had arrived in Le Réole, where they joined the visitors. The boat trip terminated in Bordeaux, at the vertical quay of the Quinconces, with its two stately and elaborate light beacons, between 2 and 3 p.m. The ships in the harbor were anchored in six ranks, three on each side of the river, leaving a passage fifty meters wide between them, through which sailed the prince's party. All movement in the harbor ceased as soon as the prince's boat came into view, and the anchored ships fired salvos of greeting, complemented by the shore batteries. All the town bells were rung.

At his debarkation the prince was met by the mayor of Bordeaux, the municipal corps, and "a vast awning bearing the colors and emblems of His Imperial Highness." Waiting officialdom, including deputations from all the 544 communes of the department to the number of some 20,000—each official with his sash of office and wearing as a boutonniere a bronze medal struck for the occasion, bearing on the obverse the prince's profile and on the reverse *Voyage du Midi—Bordeaux—7, 8, 9, et 10 octobre 1852*—were disposed by rank, each behind a banner of identification. The prince passed through these lines to a waiting carriage. His formal entry into the city was on horseback. He rode to the cathedral where Cardinal-Archbishop Donnet, who had his reward, received him. A *Domine Salvum* was chanted, followed by the benediction of the Holy Sacrament. Then on to the municipal palace—the former Hôtel de Rohan, a splendid eighteenth-century château—where he stayed during the visit. Next Haussmann detailed the composition of the cortege that would accompany the prince along the route he had determined, the obvious and grandest one in Bordeaux, following

the boulevards and *places* built by the marquis de Tourny and foreshadowing the pageants Haussmann would arrange in transformed
Paris.[31]

That night he planned a dinner for sixty in the Hôtel de Rohan,
followed by a "Venetian" night in the gardens, accompanied by a
concert. All the public boulevards and the route followed by the
prince were ordered illuminated. The next day there was a morning
visit to the St. André Hospital, and at noon the prince, again on
horseback—he was a superb horseman and perhaps Haussmann
liked the image of a savior on a white charger—retraced his processional route of the previous evening, this time to review the troops
at the Quinconces. After his return to the Hôtel de Rohan, again
on horseback, he made some additional visits. At 7 p.m. was another dinner for sixty guests, followed by a ball in the Grand Theater—
the masterpiece of Victor Louis, who was also the architect of the
prefect's palace in Bordeaux and had remodeled the Palais-Royal in
Paris—given by the city. Again Bordeaux was ordered illuminated.

The next day was an excursion downriver, weather permitting. At
2 p.m. the prince went, by carriage this time, to the shipyards to attend the launching of a 2,200-ton vessel, christened the *Louis
Napoléon*, whose armament had been a gift of M. Montané, a
deputy from Bordeaux. Then at 3 p.m. Louis Napoléon attended a
carousel given by the thirteenth regiment of mounted horse in the
public garden, yet another of Tourny's improvements. Afterward
the prince returned to the Hôtel de Rohan. At 7 p.m. was another
dinner, at the Bourse—one of the important buildings in Bordeaux,
the work of Jacques Gabriel—hosted by the chamber of commerce.
Here, for the first time, the prince spoke. Then another ball at the
Grand Theater, this one given by the city for the "working-class
population." On the 10th, his day of departure, the prince attended
mass and left at noon for Angoulême by train. Again Haussmann
carefully detailed the route, this time to minimize the possibility of
seeing the mess of incomplete construction.

These elaborate preparations stand in sharp contrast with the
arrangements made in 1839 for the visit of Ferdinand-Philippe
d'Orléans, one of the sons of the king, which was the last time Bordeaux had entertained so important a visitor. Ferdinand-Philippe's

visit, described in the memoirs of the then prefect of the Gironde, Baron Sers, is marked by timidity, reserve, and a decided lack of pageantry, even though Ferdinand-Philippe was the heir to the throne and this was an Orleanist city.[32] Politics had changed and Haussmann, unlike his predecessor, understood the urban spectacle as a political act, a representation of the power and authority of the state and the prince. So too had the French Revolution and Napoléon; but it took the Second Empire and Haussmann's gifts to restore the phenomenon.

Haussmann's *Mémoires* add a number of picturesque and personal details to the bare bones of official decrees, but so closely follow them that it appears he consulted his orders when writing this section. Boarding the prince's ship to sail with him to Bordeaux, Haussmann presented the members of his council to Louis Napoléon and called his guest "Sire" inadvertently. Louis Napoléon was officially still the president of the republic. The slip, he says, surprised so few that it went virtually unnoticed, and the prince smiled. The day was perfect for the sail to Bordeaux, and as they passed the bridge and entered the harbor the prince grabbed Haussmann's arm and exclaimed: "How beautiful!" When they arrived at the Quinconces the prince, who had remained silent, said: "Here is a capital!" All along the prince's route windows were open and women waved handkerchiefs and threw bouquets of flowers.

Recording his memory of the events of the 8th, Haussmann recollected a scene of his prince and himself. The two were contemplating the Gironde, which is a tidal river. "I have asked myself," Haussmann mused to the prince, "whether the habit of watching the currents of this beautiful river, watching its level rise and fall a certain number of meters four times in every 24-hour period, did not have something to do with the facility of a great many Bordelais to follow political fluctuations, which also have rapid and violent alterations. Is it for this reason that the masses here instinctively approve the need for stable institutions giving a preponderant authority to the chief of state which would permit him to control the changing tides of opinion?" "The paradoxical expression of my premises," Haussmann adds, "made my august interlocutor smile."[33]

The highlight of the visit was the dinner given by the chamber of commerce at the opera house. Some 180 privileged invitees were seated at table and another 800 spectators stood in the gallery observing the scene. Alphand again was the designer. Haussmann carefully described his elaborate centerpiece, but it was the prince's speech that most mattered. After accepting a toast from the president of the chamber of commerce, Louis Napoléon articulated his famous formula: "The Empire is peace!" A brilliant inspiration: paradoxical, memorable, and designed to relieve the central anxiety of a commercial city. Haussmann telegraphed Persigny that the speech was "a great event".[34] It is not unlikely that Louis Napoléon was inspired to utter this formula publicly for the first time—doubtless it had long been in his mind—by the grandeur, enthusiasm, and careful pageantry Haussmann had arranged.

The next morning, after a religious service, Haussmann boarded the train with Louis Napoléon and accompanied the prince-president as far as the first station in the department of the Charente, where the prefect, M. Rivière, joined the train. As he bid Louis Napoléon adieu the prince told him, "I could not be more pleased with my visit and with what I have been able to see of Bordeaux, of the situation that you have known how to handle in this difficult place, and of the services you have rendered me. When the prince is satisfied," he added, laughing at his own witticism, "the prefect can be tranquil."[35] The allusion was to another aphorism in the famous chamber of commerce speech: "When France is satisfied, Europe is tranquil." In January Haussmann was made a commander in the Legion of Honor.

"Finally," Haussmann wrote in his *Mémoires*, "in October 1852 Bordeaux appearing to have a fundamental change of heart and logic, received the nephew, the accepted inheritor of the throne of Napoléon I, with enthusiasm, because the prince came and said solemnly to them: 'The Emperor is peace!'"[36] The autobiographer, for once, is too matter-of-fact. What an accomplishment it was, even though the ground had been long and carefully cultivated before Louis Napoléon cast the imperial seed. Haussmann was right to insist Bordeaux be the *bouquet* of Louis Napoléon's southern tour. By bringing Bordeaux into the imperial camp Haussmann had brought not only one of the important cities of France over to the prince, but he had converted a notable Orleanist stronghold to the imperial cause. The triumphal procession through the city, the brilliant mobilization of all classes of society into a single enthusiastic reception—this was a piece of political theater Louis Napoléon could scarcely have imagined. The achievement far surpassed political troubleshooting in the Var and the Yonne. In a sense it announced the new era of imperial politics where force and fraud would be disguised as celebration and consensus. Haussmann's gifts were not lost on Louis Napoléon. Six months after the Bordeaux triumph, when the names of five prefects selected by Persigny were sent to Louis Napoléon for his choice of a prefect of Seine, the emperor did not hesitate.

"I came to Paris without illusions about what lay in store for me," Haussmann recollected to the Senate. "I came with no other ambition than not to disappoint the Emperor's expectations."[37] He came also with definite notions about the design, function, and nature of cities. In nearly a dozen years of living in and around Bordeaux, he had absorbed the urban ideas of the marquis de Tourny, the intendant of the old province of Guienne, where "the genius of a great administrator had succeeded in making [Bordeaux] so beautiful!"

Louis-Urbain Aubert, marquis de Tourny, was born in Paris, May 16, 1695. His father, Léon-Urbain, recently ennobled, had cleverly amassed a fortune during the reign of Louis XIV. He used his new wealth to buy himself not only a succession of government offices— a common practice of the day—but to found an aristocratic family. His most brilliant purchase, the marquisat of Tourny, in Normandy (near Les Andelys),[38] carried with it a title, which would pass to Louis-Urbain, who also inherited a considerable fortune, but not his father's gift for finance and speculation. The future intendant's precocious intelligence was exercised in improving the family estate, which his father had treated only as an investment in prestige. In less than a single generation the Auberts had passed from business to aristocracy.

Tourny became a lawyer in the Parlement of Paris and at nineteen purchased a councillorship. The combination of personal ability, a considerable fortune, and a father to whom many were beholden and indebted, assured a brilliant career.[39] In 1730 the young marquis was appointed intendant of Limoges, where he distinguished himself by his administrative skills, ambitious building program, humane and effective response to famine in the province, and imperiousness. In the town of Limoges he first demonstrated his obsession with urban modernization: he cut several important new streets, erected public sheds as a means of cleaning up the revolting neighborhood inhabited by the butchers,[40] and created the *quartier* Tourny, the new center of the city. In 1740 he was named intendant of the adjacent province of Guienne, whose capital was Bordeaux.[41]

His years in the Limousin were punctuated by political, parochial struggles. His ability to offend and enrage local elites Tourny brought to Guienne, whose vested interests proved more formidable and had national reverberations. His accomplishments, although left incomplete at his fall, were remarkable. A bare list is impressive. He reconstructed the old port of Salinières and built a new port and new quays on the Garonne, whose banks he adorned with more than three hundred symmetrical houses. He built a new animal market and opened a drawing school. He razed the old ramparts and filled in the moat, liberating an enormous amount of land, replacing the fortifications with planted boulevards (called *cours*) ringing Bordeaux, thus urbanizing the land separating the city from the surrounding villages, incorporating the nearer suburbs into the city, and preparing the way for future expansion. He erected two outstanding buildings, the Bourse and the Hôtel de la Douane, designed by the great architect Jacques Gabriel and executed by his even more gifted son, Jacques-Ange. He began constructing the monumental decorative gates for the new city (Aquitaine, Dijeaux, Dauphine, and Berri), accompanying them with *places*—the Place Dauphine (today the Place Gambetta) being the most important—replaced two of the old entry gates, and added a new boulevard. He linked Bordeaux's first public gardens to the city's new focal point by an imposing boulevard. Tourny thought of Paris as his model.

After a bitter struggle with the Dominicans over some land bordering their convent, the intendant built the Allées de Tourny, an elegant concentration of uniform facades facing a tree-lined promenade (which he called "my Champs-Elysées") on land that had been the glacis of the old citadel. He built a mint and accompanying streets to connect it to the city. And, finally, in 1754, a year before his fall, he embarked upon "the most extensive, the most widely useful plan for the embellishment of Bordeaux . . . the long file of houses fronting the river, whose uniform facades give to this city a prospect that is unique in France."[42]

In sum, he was responsible for seven fountains, two public promenades, ten new "*grandes rues*" (in addition to six *cours,* or planted boulevards), nine gates, three hundred houses along the quays, considerable rehabilitation work on the intendant's residence, including a garden and three new streets making it what many considered the finest building in Bordeaux, until the great theater was built (1772–80), and several markets, recognizable by their mansard roofs and arcades decorated with carved stone heads. All his work reflected a uniform conception and was done in stone, a good deal of it ornamentally carved,[43] which gave the central city the aspect it preserves of homogeneity, solidity, prosperity, and elegance. Virtually all Tourny's work was intact during Haussmann's years in Bordeaux, although by 1830 all vestiges of the fortified city were gone. Bordeaux had been transformed from a walled medieval town with three major *châteaux forts* into a pacific, commercial city, symbolically expressed in the Aquitaine gate. On one side Tourny had carved the arms of the city, on the urban side the symbols of peace and agricultural prosperity, tumbling out of a cornucopia.

So successful was his work that it was faithfully continued by his successors. Only the knowledgeable *flâneur* can today distinguish the originals from derivatives. Even along the Allées de Tourny, where several buildings have had an additional story added, it is hard to tell which are the nineteenth-century enlargements. Bordeaux in a sense had no architectural nineteenth century, only a continuation of the eighteenth century. It remains an unrivaled gem of a working eighteenth-century city, its center relatively unblemished by more recent buildings.[44]

Tourny, unlike Haussmann, built largely on land previously occupied by the old walls and forts of Bordeaux. He did little demolition in the original neighborhoods. He was, however, cavalier about the architectural heritage of his province. He scrapped the doors of the old entry gates, along with parts of the battlements, and cannibalized building stone from the rampart walls of Bordeaux and surrounding villages, even plundering a part of the château of Réole, despite the protests of the community.[45] But if he did not condemn, demolish, and confiscate on so grand a scale as his disciple, he had bitter and protracted struggles over acquiring bits and pieces of land—and occasionally had to yield to a sufficiently stubborn opponent. Boulevards were his primary concern, as they were of all the city builders of the age, and would be for Haussmann. Tourny used this relatively recent instrument of urban design in the traditional way: to improve communication, define, delimit, and rationalize urban space, and to give the city not only promenades but worthy perspectives. Each of his entry gates initiated a new boulevard into the heart of the city. His most pleasing conception, which has come to be called the "Sacred Triangle," permanently defined Bordeaux. The boulevards connecting the Place Gambetta,[46] the Place de Tourny, and the Grand-Théâtre are the heart of the city.

Tourny was an administrator. Everything he did in Bordeaux had been previously attempted elsewhere in France but nowhere with the same thoroughness, on the same scale, or as part of an overall urban conception. He believed urban effect lay in the ensemble. To entice those who owned the old houses along the river to participate in the riverfront project, he offered a bribe: the government would grant sufficient land to build a new house, at the front of their original property, provided they built within three years and according to the plans of the intendant. Those who refused were forced to sell. To proclaim his intentions he had the foundations for all three hundred houses dug at once, using his own money.[47]

Elsewhere in the city he compelled all who wanted to build along the new boulevards and *cours* to adhere to strict rules. Anyone purchasing a plot of land along the Allées de Tourny had, as a condition of sale, to build a structure no higher than ten meters and conform to detailed regulations about both the facade and rear of the building. To avoid uniformity he insisted builders alter the number of stories and the type of roof. Such coercion had already been used in Paris by Louis XIV for a row of houses on the rue de la Ferronnerie and, later, in the Place des Victoires.[48] Tourny extended the experiment to his entire city.

The intendant was also fertile in finding capital for his many projects, which exceeded his budget. He invented no new financial schemes but ruthlessly used what had earlier worked in Paris. The Ile St. Louis and the Place Dauphine, among other projects of Henri IV, had involved a royal donation of land in exchange for urban development, to encourage private developers. Tourny granted land in this manner. He also played a variation on this theme, as would Haussmann. He persuaded the archbishop to donate land for development by assuring the prelate he would be amply rewarded by the enhanced land values created by urban renewal.[49] Sometimes he charged the inhabitants of a neighborhood for an improvement, as with the Augustin fountain.[50] Sometimes he paid for a project by selling off land either expropriated or owned by the municipality. He also sold materials from demolished houses to raise money. All these expedients would be later used by Haussmann.

Tourny's ambition was to build "the most beautiful city in the kingdom." Unlike so much of the urban revival of the eighteenth century that concentrated on a cluster of remarkable government buildings in the central town—as the exquisite center of Nancy built by Louis XV's father-in-law, Stanislas Leszczynski, or the town square in the smaller but exquisite center of Arras, Robespierre's natal town—Tourny attacked the entire city.[51]

Tourny's ambition was to rival the greatest city in the kingdom, to make his provincial capital at least the equal of Paris, which was then in name, but not in beauty, grandeur, or coherence, the nation's capital. The new urban elements of Paris, along with the heritage of the past, was, as Voltaire complained, compromised, even polluted, by its surroundings. In Bordeaux these same urban elements, set apart from the old city, deliberately massed for greatest impact, united by a series of boulevards, realized the ideals of the classical French city. Bordeaux foreshadowed nineteenth-century Paris. Haussmann found in his adopted *pays* a model. The urban ideas imported from Paris to create Bordeaux would be reimported by the prefect to transform the capital.

Tourny's character and comportment, like his urban ideas and achievements, were remarkably like Haussmann's: the two men, aristocrat and commoner alike, sincerely believed they were driven only by the common good. In both, egotism and the love of power masqueraded as social altruism. Where others saw obstinacy, arrogance, and contempt, Haussmann saw courage, self-esteem, and the bluntness of integrity—the essential virtues of an administrator. It was the shortsightedness, the selfishness of others that checked administrative magnanimity. The administrator was the foe of self-interest, the hammer of egotism. Enemies had to be forced to accept what was best for them. The conviction that improvement must be imposed by personally disinterested administrators enabled the two men to battle the opposition for years. Through superior abilities and force of character both had been able to hold the enemy at bay long enough so that their work could not be undone. Indeed, they had so imprinted themselves on Bordeaux and Paris that future generations would honor their memory, lament their fall, and praise their largeness of vision.

From the very beginning of his administrative career Haussmann came under the influence and spell of Tourny's urban ideas. Haussmann's first long-term appointment was subprefect of Nérac, where Tourny had built and planted two lines of *allées* along the public gardens. In Blaye, where Haussmann spent seven years, the citadel and fountain had been repaired by Tourny. The city gates at Libourne—whose subprefecture Haussmann declined, although he knew the town—as well as its port had been improved by Tourny, who had also endowed the city with several fountains and laid out *allées*, his urban hallmark. The entire province was crisscrossed by Tourny's roads.[52]

Not only had Bordeaux been the urban center of Haussmann's life for twenty years, functioning as the capital of southwestern France, exactly as Tourny had intended, but he felt a deep affection for the city. Here he married, lived, formed lifelong friendships, built a home. Paris he visited only occasionally, usually to further his career, and its filth and disorder always reawakened feelings of disgust. There is no way of knowing what Haussmann might have read or thought about the general urban crisis during his Bordeaux years, but it is fair to presume Bordeaux played a major role. It was not just his daily environment; Bordeaux became a model for organizing urban space, defining a city. Convenience, perspective, grandeur, monumentality, salubrity, regularity—these had all been achieved in Bordeaux by Tourny. And the architectural style and vocabulary of Tourny's city was innate to the realization of his urban ideas. The challenge of Paris forced Haussmann to reconsider the urban patterns inculcated by years spent in Bordeaux. The very magnitude of the undertaking forced him to rethink the problem. Although he retained all the fundamental properties of Tourny's city, Paris is not merely Bordeaux writ large—it is far more complex. The vocabulary of the two cities is the same, as are the holistic conceptualization and the aesthetic principles, but Haussmann's originality as an urbanizer goes well beyond the application of the elements of the classical city to a gigantic urban mass, accomplished by monumentalizing French classicism.

Fundamental forces and currents of the age converged in Haussmann. French classicism as the language of urban order and improvement, authoritarian bureaucracy as the tool of social progress, technical expertise as the essence of good government were animated by a strong personality and a powerful if narrow intellect. His own opportunism, hitherto largely unsuccessful, was in harmony with that of Louis Napoléon, indeed would have had no outlet without the patronage of that prince. Haussmann was competent, devoted, loyal, and compulsively ambitious when the emperor summoned him to Paris in 1853. History and psychology had conspired to forge the ideal instrument for transforming the capital.

The Paris Haussmann inherited—the reiteration cannot be avoided—was a medieval city with a decayed and decaying core, punctuated by oases of classical beauty. Haussmann was compelled to destroy on a massive scale; and he mostly destroyed medieval Paris, leaving the classical city relatively untouched. He also had no new public land in central Paris on which to build. The prefect had to connect and integrate the widely scattered classical elements of Paris and, harkening back to Voltaire's imperative, give them a fit urban setting. The classical vocabulary of Bourbon Paris, which he left untouched—boulevards, *places*, the architectural orders, axial patterns, geometric uniformity—Haussmann extended to the entire city. He enriched this vocabulary with his own sense of monumentality and Tourny's use of massed uniformity, as well as anchoring the city's new center with an opera house. Paris acquired a comfortable feeling. Virtually everywhere in the city the buildings and streets could be read, even by the architecturally illiterate. Innovation was expressed in a familiar historical vocabulary.

Paris is not only a rationalized city, a giant geometric ordering of urban space; it is a complex series of separate systems tied together into a single, systematic whole. Haussmann retained the notion that different neighborhoods would have different functions, but he elaborately connected these neighborhoods to one another, rather than attempting to tie them all to the old core of the city. Haussmann abandoned the organizing principle that had dominated Paris for centuries. Paris is today a city of hubs, inherited, enlarged, or created by Haussmann, connected by boulevards into a single system, in turn ringed by inner and outer boulevards—and today by a *périphérique* that encircles the entire city—which are similarly connected to the hubs by boulevards. Some of these hubs (Place de l'Opéra [D 2], Place de la République [F 2–3], Place de la Bastille [G 4]) look inward to the central city, connecting its parts, neighborhood to neighborhood. Some of them (Place de la Nation [G 4]), Place Denfert-Rochereau [E 5]) look outward, connecting the city with the exterior boulevards. The three great "stars" of the west, east, and south (Place de l'Etoile, Place de la Nation, and Place d'Italie [F 5], respectively) serve both functions. The majority of the boulevards created by Haussmann connect hub to hub, and the signs today directing traffic through Paris, although not erected by Haussmann, explain his system. The arrows announce what the boulevards dictate: one moves from *place* to *place*.

Before Haussmann existing hubs were used to link the neighborhoods of the city to the old center. Haussmann accepted the idea of the city as having a center, although he relocated it in the newly created hub of the Opéra, but he rejected the notion that all the roads should lead to a single center. Nineteenth-century Paris was too large for a single center or hub leading to all corners of the city. Even a city the size of Bordeaux had two centers, the port and the "Sacred Triangle."

Haussmann was obsessed with systemization, as was Tourny. He bureaucratized his staff to handle the various aspects of the transformation of Paris, which in turn bureaucratized the city. Speaking of his Paris student days, Haussmann recalled that he had often walked "in all the neighborhoods of the city," and became "absorbed in lengthy contemplation before a map of this Paris, so disparate, which had revealed to me the weaknesses of its *réseau* of public streets."[53] His constant lament over the lack of systematic streets, in the provinces as in Paris, expresses an emotional truth: Haussmann craved order in his life, his work, and his world. For intendant and prefect alike, order and system was the essence of the city.

Haussmann's Paris is focused, visually as well as functionally. Each function is identified and defined by a major public building: transportation (railway stations), business (Tribunal de Commerce), city government (Hôtel de Ville), culture (Opéra), Old Paris (Notre Dame), new Paris (St. Augustin church). There are also a number of public monuments: the Etoile, the Place de la Bastille, the Place de la Concorde, and finally the *places* he himself sometimes endowed with monuments (Place d'Italie, Place de l'Alma, Place de la République). The purely residential parts of the city, such as areas of the fifteenth and sixteenth arrondissements, are drawn into the urban structure by the pull of already existing *places* or boulevards, although the fifteenth remains somewhat isolated, without a natural magnet such as the Etoile in the sixteenth. Tying these focal points together into a system represents "the kind of conceptual simplification by which bureaucrats such as Haussmann could come to terms with the complexities of urban life . . . by which they gained self-assurance and the optimistic conviction that the new industrialized society could actually be governed and its problems managed if not wholly resolved."[54]

Haussmann's model for systematizing Tourny's urban vision, while making it more rigidly linear, was doubtless the railroads. Although he does not say much directly about the railroads, his concern for

the several terminals in Paris and their impact on the city, his close
association with the Péreire brothers, who invested heavily in railroads, and the general enthusiasm of his age for the new technology
made him keenly conscious of the phenomenon. The miracle of the
age, railroads epitomized nineteenth-century achievement, humanity's triumph over nature as time and distance. Not only did railroads
embody most of the new technologies—iron mining, steel making,
smelting, forging, the steam engine, precision time instruments—but
they palpably transformed life. For Paris and the Parisians railroads
had a special importance: an 1841 law had made Paris the hub of the
national rail system. More clearly than in any other industrial country, a single city was at the center of a vast system, a *réseau*. Haussmann extended the system throughout Paris. At his fall he advised
his successor to complete his work: "I consider this prolongation [of
the boulevard d'Enfer—today the boulevard Raspail—to where the
rue du Bac joins the boulevard St. Germain] of capital importance
for the . . . faubourg St. Germain, the neighborhood of the Observatoire, and that surrounding the railroad of Sceaux."[55] His advice
went unheeded. Nor was his proposal to link the Odéon to the Observatoire adopted.[56] His desire to carry the rue de Rennes from the
Left to the Right Bank and link it to the grand cross, the central axis
of new Paris, was thwarted by the inconvenient placement of the Institut, but the plan has remained on the agenda of Paris planners to
this day as a logical step. The Left Bank is the least systemitized, the
most neglected by haussmannization. Virtually all the major south-
north streets dead-end in the boulevard St. Germain, without linking up with any of the few *places* he built on the southern bank of the
Seine. Crossing the river remains a problem.

Architecture, too, Haussmann absorbed in Tourny's Bordeaux,
and the architecture of haussmannization is inseparable from the
prefect's urban ideas. The parallels with Tourny are striking, although the French Revolution, the First Empire, and industrial capitalism separate the two city builders. Leaving aside the momentous
political and social results, the first two upheavals made for an im-
measurably important watershed for city planning in France, the
last for city planning across Europe. The French Revolution ren-

dered the urban crisis of the nineteenth century political, while movement and circulation, the most important outward manifestations of capitalism, are everywhere sought and celebrated, not least in the railroads that Haussmann incorporated in Paris. All was accomplished under the shadow of the urban plans and dreams of the first Napoléon. Although largely unrealized, the uncle's pronouncements became the imperatives of the nephew. "I desire that Paris might become a city of two, three, or four million inhabitants," Napoléon told Las Cases on St. Helena. "In a word," he continued, "something fabulous, colossal, unknown until our time and whose public establishments would correspond to its population. . . . if heaven had given me twenty-one years of leisure men would have looked in vain for the old Paris; they would not have found its vestiges and I would have changed the face of France."[57] Haussmann translated French classicism into a new idiom of movement, monumentality, and systematic orderliness. As with any good translation the resemblances to the original text are clear, but a new text has been created by the translator.

Monumentality would seem to be incompatible with sensible capitalism. It is not functional, glorifies abstract qualities such as individual or state vanity, and diverts capital from more productive investment. Yet in nineteenth-century cities, Paris most notably, "what had once been the peculiar privilege of the spiritual and secular masters of society became a universal indulgence."[58] Along with monumentality, both for individual structures and urban ensembles, whether governmental, cultural, or residential, went the even more contradictory aspiration for perspective. Haussmann's mania for sight lines accounts for his most elaborate urban compositions, and a few of his most peculiar and hideous buildings. He had a flair for the theatrical, and "no city anywhere has taken more seriously its duties to look and behave throughout as if the eyes of the world were on it and the honor of the nation at stake."[59]

The paradox of haussmannization from an architectural point of view is that the prefect of the Seine made a great and architecturally fascinating city yet held architects in contempt and himself commissioned no great buildings. "Architecture is nothing more than Administration,"[60] he wrote. The remarkable buildings erected while he was prefect—Hittorff's gare du Nord, Garnier's Opéra, Duc's Palais de Justice,[61] Labrouste's reading room of the Bibliothèque Nationale—were either private (as was the gare du Nord, built for the Rothschilds) or built under the aegis of jurisdictions other than the prefecture. Haussmann lamented that he had no great architects in his service, although he seems to have made no efforts to attract them, implying he did not think their work up to his standards. Hittorff and Duc did work for Haussmann: the latter on his masterpiece, the Palais de Justice, begun years before the prefect came to power, the former on a few projects. It is Hittorff who designed the *mairie* of the first arrondissement, facing the facade of the Louvre, to resemble, trait for trait, the fifteenth-century church of St. Germain-l'Auxerrois, which was already adjacent on the site. To join the old church to the new city hall, he built a tower that belongs to neither structure. This copy of a Renaissance building is a brilliant urban success: the whole composition is convincing and complements Perrault's exceptional seventeenth-century colonnade. And, of course, there are Baltard's sheds at les Halles, although there was considerable dispute at the time about whose conception it was.

Haussmann did not easily tolerate the unique. His desire for uniformity, his sense of the city as a system made him suspicious. He hedged Garnier's Opéra around with buildings, almost smothering it, forcing that exceptionally rich building into a drab urban ensemble. The great buildings he had inherited—Notre Dame, or the Invalides, or the Louvre—he left unencumbered by the cityscape, or even further enhanced their isolation, but these buildings he considered monuments, pieces of urban sculpture to be set apart. Otherwise he embedded architecture in a dense and complex urban fabric.[62] The individual building, along with the individual dwelling, had no place in his city.

He talked frequently of his cultivation of "the sentiment of art," yet there is nowhere in his writings, official or autobiographical, an extended or coherent discussion of what he understood by art or thought beautiful. All his pronouncements were general and banal. On occasion he expressed a favorable opinion about a particular new building: the Tribunal de Commerce he thought "a capital work," and the church of St. Pierre at Montrouge "a charming Romanesque church." Both were nineteenth-century imitations of earlier styles. The tribunal is now most often singled out for its eccentric dome. A better case can be made for the church.[63] His taste, his aesthetic sense, must be extrapolated from his practice.

Since Napoléon I's time French architects had been trained in either the Ecole Polytechnique or the Ecole des Beaux-Arts, both state schools. Haussmann leaned clearly to the former, with its technical emphasis. He was certain a well-organized *Service d'Architecture* would attract the best talents, and he thought beauty followed technique. His two most famous collaborators, Alphand and Belgrand, were engineers. His most successful urban work was with ensembles. If he found, by his lights, no worthy architect to embellish Paris, his pedestrian taste was well served by the artistic conservatism of the Ecole des Beaux-Arts. The eight academicians who judged the yearly *concours* were mostly elderly men, and students catered to their old-fashioned tastes. There was not only a uniformity of taste and architectural practice but "the pace of change in French architecture in the nineteenth and early twentieth century was slower than that in England or America."[64] The most gifted Beaux-Arts graduates developed their own style within this tradition, but the most original architects did not work for Haussmann. The academician majority designed in a manner that admirably fit Haussmann's bureaucratic urban conception.

Early on the prefect had requested and received laws governing building, street elevation, and height restrictions. He himself often specified building materials, according to the neighborhood and its distance from the center of the city. Within a few years the regulated city had no need of legal specifications: architects designed apartment houses that met all Haussmann's desires for uniformity, even adding some conventions of their own. There was no requirement or contractual prescription for a balcony on the second story, or a balcony built above the cornice along the top story, both of which became hallmarks of a Haussmann-era building, voluntarily incorporated by virtually all architects.[65]

The general conformity of style, whether voluntary or obligatory, gave Paris the uniform appearance Haussmann craved. It also introduced the problems of monotony and differentiation. How was one to tell a public from a private building, a more important from a less important building? The solution, the variation of detail and ornamentation, introduced a new emphasis into the Beaux-Arts tradition, originally concerned with "masses rather than detailing. . . . A Beaux-Arts building was designed from the inside out," its internal spaces to be experienced when walked through.[66]

Repetition of the major elements, subtle variation of detail is the architectural language of Haussmann's Paris and marks a return to the French Renaissance. The *cour carrée* of François I's Louvre, much studied in the schools, was an important model for the new style.[67] The same seeming paradox of repetition modified by variation in detail was evident in the design of public fixtures, the urban furniture, that assured unity and was made possible by industrialization. Consider so small a matter as street lanterns. The unobservant hardly notice the differences; but there were seventy-eight varieties of gas street lanterns put up in Paris by Haussmann, variations on seven generic types,[68] all made possible by mass production. The urban furniture in Paris is a result of industrial capitalism.

Haussmann did not so much build a more elegant city, a richer city—which he certainly did—as create a new kind of city, while integrating Old Paris into the new with his boulevards. In place of Paris as the home of the kings, the church, and the university, which had defined the city for centuries, he retained only the university. Haussmann's Paris was a city of luxury, commerce, banking, railroads, capitalism, government, administration, and pleasure, whether licit or illicit, popular or socially restricted. Its most obvious physical characteristic was the boulevard and movement. The wealthy and new west end dominated the older neighborhoods, and whatever the actual percentages of workers or artisans in the city, its overall flavor was bourgeois. Uniformity of scale and similarity of design proclaimed orderliness.

He sought to control the forces of capitalism in Paris, partly by banishing heavy, dirty industry from the city, partly by favoring an architecture that denied its modernity. Stone skins hung on iron skeletons made possible the characteristic buildings of haussmannization, which structures were made to appear from a preindustrial age. Paradoxically, Haussmann's Paris everywhere celebrated the achievements of industry, mimicking the railroad, incorporating its achievements, putting his stamp on every corner of the city with mass-produced grates and benches, gates and grillwork, lamps and railings. Despite the hue and cry raised by the Eiffel Tower, the city's most famous monument—built years after Haussmann's departure from the prefecture—it fits in Paris, a city already deeply marked by the industrial revolution.

Haussmann's utilitarian mind considered order beautiful, which kept him a stranger to the most dynamic artistic and intellectual currents of his age. A historical accident had placed him in Bordeaux as a young man. His love of that city, reinforced by his strong personal identification with the intendant Tourny, early engraved upon his mind the principles of French classicism and eighteenth-century urban design and planning. All this he brought to Paris in 1853, and forged a fruitful synthesis with the concerns of his own age, which proved wonderfully durable.

· VII ·

"A State Within the State"

"FOR NEARLY FORTY YEARS THE LOUVRE HAS BEEN CRYING FROM THE open mouths of all the gashed walls, the gaping windows, 'Strike these excrescences from my face!'" Louis Napoléon heard the cries. His eye fell upon this "outrageous eyesore . . . in the heart of Paris, facing the palace where . . . three dynasties have received the elite of France and Europe." He was impatient to get on with his urban plans, especially after his coup d'état. The new regime desperately needed prestige, to demonstrate its energy and efficiency, and to put people to work. The great unfinished palace of the French kings [D-E 3] perfectly satisfied his ambitions.

Squatters colonized the courtyard; slums lapped at the walls:

> The continued existence of the conglomeration of houses running the length of the old Louvre is one of those reassuring defiances of common sense by which the French fondly hope to persuade Europe that Frenchmen have not much intelligence and are not to be feared.

This urban heap was pierced by a single passageway, the rue de Doyenné. The houses, "submerged and darkened . . . lie wrapped in the perpetual shadow cast by the high galleries of the Louvre, blackened on this side by the north wind. The gloom, the silence, the glacial air, the hollow sunken ground level, combine to make these houses seem so many crypts, or living tombs" where "the vices of Paris, shrouded in night's mantle, move as they will."[1]

Clearing this vile slum, joining the Louvre to the Tuileries, cleansing the courtyard, putting his mark on one of the master landmarks of Paris, the very symbol of monarchical power, where so many of the dramas of his dynasty had been enacted, was irresistible to Louis Napoléon. The Louvre was not the only project he was anxious to begin, nor was it an original undertaking. Completing the palace had been on the agenda of kings for centuries; but the other significant urban improvements underway—extending the rue de Rivoli, disencumbering the Hôtel de Ville, cutting the rue des Ecoles and the northern part of the boulevard de Strasbourg—lacked the drama, the visibility, the symbolism of the Louvre-Tuileries. Louis Napoléon's problem was not finding projects but finding someone to do them.

Berger, the prefect of Seine, whose rough Auvergnat bonhomie won affection and inspired loyalty, opposed none of Louis Napoléon's objectives; but he wanted to balance the Paris budget. Each new expenditure was a struggle between the prefect and the prince-president. The latter would allow no new taxes, the former refused to borrow. Berger had to go.

It was the duc de Persigny who engineered Berger's dismissal. In his account, Berger appeared in his office—the duc was then minister of the interior—proudly announcing that his administration had four million francs in savings that could be applied to the work of transformation. Persigny's idea was to use this money not to pay directly for this or that project but to pay the interest on money borrowed for a long term. If the transformation of Paris depended on a few million francs of the Paris budget squirreled away each year, the work would never be done. Persigny advocated deficit spending. Berger was having none of it: "it is not I who will ever borrow the city into ruin,"[2] he muttered as he left.

Persigny decided not to look for Berger's successor among the politicians of the capital. He wanted a stranger "to the salon cliques of Paris, yet familiar with the way the bureaucracy works," who would accept "in all its consequences, the proposed system." He wanted "a kind of fierce wild boar with formidable defenses, capable of holding at bay the blood-thirsty pack that I foresaw unleashed."[3]

But "could I find the necessary independence of mind in a prefect habituated to bend before the omnipotence of the ministers?"[4]

He found his perfect prefect in Haussmann, whose "faults of . . . character" rather than "his remarkable intelligence" seduced Persigny:[5]

> I had before me one of the most extraordinary characters of our age. Tall, strong, vigorous, energetic, and at the same time shrewd, cunning, with a mind fertile and resourceful, this audacious man did not fear to display openly what he was.

"With obvious satisfaction . . . he revealed to me the high points of his administrative career" and "could have spoken non-stop for six hours so long as it was about his favorite subject, himself. . . . He revealed to me all the facets of his strange personality. . . . the pride of triumph lit up his face. As for myself, while this intriguing personality laid itself bare before me with a kind of brutal cynicism, I could hardly contain my intense satisfaction":

> I said to myself, here was the man to struggle against the ideas, the prejudices of the old school of economic ideas, against these treacherous, skeptical men, mostly from the Bourse and the judicial professions. Where a gentleman of the most refined intelligence, the greatest capacity, the most adroit character, the oldest nobility, would surely fail, this vigorous athlete with a stiff backbone, a thick neck, full of audacity and ability, capable of countering expedients with expedients of his own, traps with traps of his own, would certainly succeed. I enjoyed in advance the idea of turning this great feline animal loose in the middle of the pack of foxes and wolves arrayed against all the generous aspirations of the Empire.[6]

Haussmann thought he "so gained [Persigny's] esteem, conquered his confidence, that at the end [of the interview] he spoke to me of everything with an open heart" and "recognized in me a firm character, a cool and resolute mind." A man who knew "how to deal with circumstances and the necessities of the moment." "For my part," he continued, "I was seduced by his gracious, loyal, communicative nature, by his keen intelligence, both sagacious and comprehensive, and I did not hesitate, despite the singularity of the interview, which was quite surprising for a functionary of the old school, to open myself up to a chief on whom I could count completely."[7] As in all desired seductions—and both men use the word—each succumbed, convinced he had triumphed.

Haussmann received official word of his appointment as prefect of the Seine on June 24, 1853, by telegraph, after his return to Bordeaux. "I have reason to believe that my experience of departmental administration is not without value in the exceptional post to which I am called. But I belong, unreservedly, to the emperor, and as personally perilous as I judge the new situation that His Majesty assigns me, I will bring to it the complete devotion of which I have already given more than one proof."[8] On June 29 he appeared at the palace of St. Cloud to swear the oath of office before the emperor. Louis Napoléon received his new prefect warmly, telling Haussmann how happy he was to be able to confer upon him a post to which he attached "an exceptional importance under the present circumstances." Persigny read the oath: "Do you swear obedience to the constitution and fidelity to the emperor?" Placing his right hand in the emperor's clasp, he responded: "I swear it." The other new prefects were similarly sworn. There followed a state lunch, at which Haussmann met the empress for the first time and had the honor of sitting at her right hand. The emperor initiated the conversation between his wife and his new prefect: "You know, M. Haussmann had, as did you, my uncle, Prince Eugène, as his godfather."[9] "Indeed!," said the empresses. "Yes, Madame," said Haussmann, "but among the godchildren of the Prince I am much older than Your Majesty." There followed some small talk about Haussmann's family before the lunch ended and the emperor led Haussmann into his study.[10]

The fit of prince and prefect needed little adjustment and would determine the shape of Paris. Of the same generation, creatures of the French Revolution although contemptuous of democracy, committed to a centralized state and modernization—the two articles of faith were intertwined—the dreamy emperor and the industrious technocrat were about to embark on a unique and fruitful collaboration for which their lives had hardly prepared them.

PARIS IN 1739. One of the plates—there were twenty in all—of the lovely Turgot map, named for Michel-Etienne Turgot, the *prévôt des marchands* of Paris, showing the Ile de la Cité, the Pont-Neuf, a tiny portion of the Right Bank (lower left), and the Left Bank. The Place Dauphine is still intact—the base of the triangle was lopped off to make room for the new Palais de Justice—and the Bishop's Palace, which was destroyed in 1831, can be seen next to Notre Dame. The etching is especially elegant, the detail of the buildings and perspective, worked out by Louis Bretez, a professor of perspective and architecture at the Academy St.-Luc, are complex yet clear. The map maker has straightened a number of streets and presents Old Paris as far less cluttered and chaotic than it was in fact. The area depicted here was one of the most densely populated parts of the city. Turgot was as much (or more) concerned with artistic beauty as accuracy. He wrote Bretez that the geometric plans were no longer "capable of satisfying the curiosity of the king's subjects. . . ." Turgot revived the form of representation used by Gaultier (among many others from the same period).

RUE RAMBUTEAU. An anonymous photograph of the first major street without a military-strategic purpose cut through Old Paris. The church in the background is St. Eustache. Note the pedestrian sidewalks and the bourgeois refinement of the buildings—made of cut stone, with considerable masonry detail and fancy ironwork. All the elements of Haussmann's boulevards are already present but on a smaller scale. Contemporaries were excited by the light, ease of movement, and width of the new street.

OLD PLACE DU CHATELET. A photograph often attributed to Marville of Palmier's fountain and the Place du Châtelet before Haussmann's transformations. The St. Jacques tower can be seen in the background (at one o'clock). Only the fountain and the tower survive, the latter providing the most interesting view from the rebuilt *place*.

MOVING THE COLONNE DU CHATELET. An anonymous photograph, looking southeast, of Palmier's fountain being moved to the center of the completely razed *place* (April 21, 1858). The bridges visible are the Pont Notre Dame and the Pont d'Arcole. Because of the direction the St. Jacques tower cannot be seen. Note the numerous spectators in the foreground.

PLACE DU CHATELET. Seen from the Pont au Change. The wide street to the right of the column is the boulevard de Sébastopol, which becomes the boulevard de Strasbourg and leads to the gare de l'Est, forming the north-south axis of the *grande croisée*. The new *place*, to judge from its muddled form, was not conceived as a whole. Haussmann fiddled with the various elements—moving the fountain, building theaters and framing them with apartments—to create an acceptable juncture. But none of the elements harmonizes well with the others. The St. Jacques tower is just beyond the right edge of the photograph (at around 3 o'clock). Anonymous photograph.

BOULEVARD HENRI IV. Charles Marville's photograph of the boulevard being cut (the part closest to the camera is the boulevard Henri IV, which becomes the Pont de Sully). The July Column, in the Place de la Bastille, can be seen in the distance, and there is a partially wrecked church in the middle ground (around one o'clock). The visual line from the July Column to the Panthéon dome was Haussmann's most successful urban optical illusion. Marville's photographs of the *grands travaux*, compared with those he made of Old Paris, are characterized by loneliness and desolation and convey the feeling of Paris torn apart. The horses in the center of the photograph, curiously set in this field of urban destruction, add to the composition's melancholy.

THEATRE DU LUXEMBOURG. Another splendid Marville photograph, taken from the rue de Fleurus (where Gertrude Stein would have her famous apartment). The theater has disappeared. The sign on the building in the center advertises "Demolition Salvage for Sale." The scale of the houses and the theater gives a good sense of the dimensions of Paris before Haussmann. Not only were there no sidewalks for pedestrians, but no space had been set aside to accommodate threatergoers.

RUE DE RIVOLI. Marville took this photograph in 1870, probably in the early morning hours, when there was no traffic. His composition makes it look more desolate than when it was alive with commerce, people, and traffic. This stretch of the street, running alongside the Louvre (the Cour Carrée is visible in the left foreground, the beginning of the northern arm of the great château just beyond) was built by Napoléon I. He conceived of it as a strategic street across Paris, to move troops into the turbulent east end, but so prestigious and central a location demanded embellishment. The arcades lend elegance and regularity. Despite the presence of the Louvre, this is no longer Old Paris. Haussmann would extend the street but not the uniform, elegant buildings, substantially changing its character.

NIGHT WORK. It is difficult to identify precisely what part of the rue de Rivoli is being cut here—is that the Hôtel de Ville covered with scaffolding?—but this is one of the earliest uses of electric lighting in Paris on a significant scale. Haussmann could never be persuaded to replace gas lighting with electric for the streets of Paris; the change was made after his fall. He stubbornly insisted gas was preferable. He used electric lighting only for industrial applications. Again, note the spectators, and an omnibus in the lower foreground.

RUE DE RIVOLI. A photograph by Jules de Planque, looking west. The Hôtel de Ville is on the left, the St. Jacques tower is in the background. By the time Haussmann came to power the Hôtel de Ville had been disencumbered from its urban setting. The large Place de Grève can be seen on the left of the rue de Rivoli, in front of the Hôtel de Ville. The activity in the streets is typical and one of the best indications of the changes in the pace and nature of urban life created by the new boulevards, beginning with the rue Rambuteau. How different this extension looks compared with the formal, elegant stretch built by Napoléon I. This is the typical Haussmann street, and no special provisions have been made to complement the prestigious Hôtel de Ville.

AVENUE DE L'OPERA. A photograph by Marville that makes perfectly clear the enormous work of transforming Paris was done with pick and shovel. There were lithographs of this same scene, which bespeaks some popularity and fascination.

AVENUE DE L'OPERA. Another Marville view of cutting this important street, in 1876. Note the urban furniture—tree grates, street lamps, and iron tree supports—on the left, and the demolition crew atop the disappearing buildings on the right. The dog, visible on the sidewalk in the left foreground, is another of those Marville touches that gives the photograph a greater emotional impact.

THE ARCUEIL AQUEDUCT. Haussmann took pride not only in bringing an adequate and healthy water supply to Paris but doing so by building aqueducts, as had the Romans. When speaking of his sewer system he also invoked the example of the Romans. This structure carried the waters from the Vanne across the valley at Arcueil. Photograph by Auguste Hippolyte Collard (May 31, 1869).

CASCADE DU GRAND LAC. The emperor had wanted a lake in the Bois de
Boulogne resembling the Serpentine in Hyde Park, London, which proved impossible
because of the topography. Haussmann and Alphand brilliantly solved the problem by
constructing this cascade, which used circulating water. Everything, with the obvious
exception of the plants, is man-made: rocks, the grotto, the cement-lined lake bed.
The engraving is from Alphand's *Les Promenades de Paris*.

CAPTURING THE DHUIS
WATERS. These etchings, by
Peulot and Thorigny, show
the various structures built to
bring the spring waters of the
Dhuis to Paris. The upper left
is the spring itself, some hundred miles from the city. The
top center is the aqueduct as
it crosses the Marne River.
Top right is the subterranean
conduit bringing the waters
to the reservoir at Ménilmontant, one of the highest
parts of Paris (depicted under
construction in the bottom
panel). The center panel is a
cutaway of the reservoir.

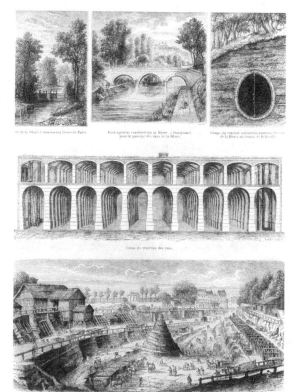

Neither had lived in Paris for a generation: the emperor barred by law, the prefect immured in the provinces. Not only did absence give each an abstract, outdated, somewhat doctrinaire awareness of the city and its problems, but their broken attachment to the capital meant neither had shared viscerally the history of Paris. Louis Napoléon and Haussmann made their plans and commanded their vast army of workers from their respective offices. Order was imposed on paper before being fixed in stone. Urban ideas arose from ratiocination rather than the "feel" of the city. In Haussmann's case the remembered impressions of his student days in Paris, in the 1820s, remained: a Procrustean bed upon which he stretched his subsequent views. For Louis Napoléon even this experience was missing. Both had acquired their ideas about urban change, modernization, and improvement from cities other than Paris: the emperor from London, the prefect from Bordeaux. For two such hard-headed realists, their urban ideas were decidedly utopian.

In addition neither had experienced 1848 in Paris. Louis Napoléon, as soon as he received word of the February revolution that drove Louis-Philippe from the throne and from France, set out for Paris. The provisional government sent him back into exile in London, where he sat out the bloody June Days. He did not return to Paris until September 24, 1848. Haussmann, of course, was wholly occupied in Bordeaux trying to stay afloat in the purge of virtually the entire prefectorial corps by the new government.

Had the two been in Paris not only would they have seen the city's crisis firsthand, they would also have experienced the euphoria of February and the fear of June in the streets. Neither saw the barricades in 1848, nor heard gunfire, nor smelled the burnt powder that hung over the city for days. Viewed from a safe distance, urban insurrection was transposed from a social to a technical problem: isolating the dangerous neighborhoods from the rest of Paris. Perhaps some of Haussmann's indifference to the very real needs and deprivations of the Paris poor stems from his absence from the capital. For him eastern Paris was not a sick city to be nursed to health. It was to be quarantined lest it infect the rest. The emperor accepted both diagnosis and treatment.

Similarly the reaction. Neither the prince-president nor his troubleshooting prefect had to deal with repression in Paris. General Cavaignac, the brutal commander who received dictatorial powers after the June Days, took care of the mopping up, as he had of the assault on the barricades. Haussmann's responsibilities in the Var and the Yonne were radically different. However harsh and dubiously legal,[11] his pacification did not include bloodletting or necessitate martial law. He was essentially a police bully and had the momentary illusion that such tactics worked. Neither the emperor nor the prefect minimized the importance of 1848, but the impact of urban revolution on the transformation of Paris was less universal than it might have been. The purely strategic urban projects of the Second Empire are surprisingly few, fortunately for Paris. What master and servant sought was not so much to punish as to strike out in a new direction, make a second Paris immune from the problems of the original city. They would implant a new city amid the old. More important than planning for some future insurrection was the massive cleansing—of politics as well as of society—inaugurated by 1848.

Louis Napoléon laid before his new prefect a map of Paris upon which he had drawn—in red, blue, yellow, and green, indicating the degree of urgency—the new streets he wanted built. He also explained how the Municipal Council of Paris had proved too cautious for his taste. Haussmann's remembered response, which fills nearly two printed pages of his *Mémoires*, deplored the obstructionist Municipal Council and contains the germs of his eventual reorganization of that body.[12] Alas, he said nothing specific about the emperor's map, thus contributing to the mystery surrounding it. Every account of Paris and Haussmann, from his day to ours, considers this map the blueprint for the transformation of Paris.[13] Yet the very existence of this map, let alone its details, raises many questions and introduces the more fundamental question—vexing, intriguing, and ultimately unanswerable—of the relative roles of Haussmann and Louis Napoléon in the transformation of Paris.

We know the emperor's map, which he showed Haussmann, signed, and gave to the prefect for his office in the Hôtel de Ville, only from description. The original has not survived and is presumed to have been destroyed in the fire at the Hôtel de Ville dur-

ing the civil war of 1871.[14] The most important verbal descriptions
of the imperial map are those of Haussmann himself and Charles
Merruau, the secretary general of the Paris prefecture, both of whom
saw the map. Berger makes no mention of it. Persigny speaks of the
emperor's passion for transforming Paris: "In fact it was he who actually traced out the major arteries that one today admires," and "he
had drawn the plan" for transforming the Bois de Boulogne into "an
English park." But he says nothing more precise about a map of
Paris.[15] The vicomte de Beaumont Vassy, when a member of the
Council of State, says he saw a number of maps in Louis Napoléon's
study. He first assumed they were "maps of the Rhine riverbanks or
of Belgium, and that Napoléon III, imitating Napoléon I, consulted
them, lying on the floor as the great man whose name he bore had
done." But upon looking more closely he discovered "that these
were maps minutely reproducing the various paths and the two lakes
newly designed for the Bois de Boulogne."[16] The emperor's motives
and urban vision are obscure. Taciturn, devious, convoluted, and
habituated to appearing enigmatic, what little he revealed is not
very helpful. But if details are unavailable, his general views of what
Paris should be are discernible. He had little precise knowledge of
the city and tended to see it whole rather than as an accumulation
of neighborhoods with their own character. He craved a ceremonial
and a salubrious city, one where progress was expressed by the free
flow of capital. Movement, circulation—and the same vocabulary
was used for business as for public hygiene—was healthy; stagnation
was unhealthy. The straight line was simultaneously the metaphor
and the instrument of urban beauty, health, and commerce.[17]

The centralized state demanded a centralized capital. Nation
building and city building marched together. Haussmann ably articulated the emperor's unspoken desires:

> Everything should have Paris for its hub: highways, the railroad, the
> telegraph, laws, decrees, decisions, orders, agents.

Paris was the "soul of France, its head and its heart."[18] "A capital,"
he insisted, "has above all the responsibility to present itself as equal
to the role it plays in the state; and when that state is France . . .
centralization is the principle of its importance."[19] Public space was

to be grand yet controlled. A potentially unruly populace had to be monitored. And the energy and stability of the empire were to be proclaimed everywhere in the city. Only the parks, for which Louis Napoléon had a passion, softened his severe rectilinear urban vision. He had long admired Hyde Park in London, fancied himself something of a landscape architect, and while in exile in Britain had laid out a portion of the grounds of Brodick Castle, in Scotland, the estate of his friend the Duke of Hamilton, who testified Louis Napoléon "was a wonderful landscape gardener."[20]

How much of this was indicated on the emperor's map? Haussmann and Merruau speak only of proposed streets indicated on a preexisting map of Paris without explaining which streets were sketched by the emperor. Both speak of additions and emendations, which make it difficult to envision the original. Haussmann says he encountered numerous problems because the emperor's new streets, drawn "on one of the maps of Paris with approximate exactitude," were left to the prefect to realize. "I had to penetrate, in effect, the inspired thought of the Sovereign" to determine which streets were to form the first *réseau* of streets to be opened. The emperor was ignorant of the topography of the city, modifications had to be made, lacunae had to be filled in, and the proposed new streets had to be coordinated with the already existing city.[21] Haussmann speaks of "the primitive plan of the emperor" to which he added a number of streets, including the seven new boulevards radiating from the Arc de Triomphe (B-C 2–3), the avenue des Gobelins (then the rue Mouffetard, F 5), and the boulevard St. Germain on the Left Bank (D-F 4), to mention only a few. With the exception of the boulevard Malesherbes (C-D 2), the street that opened up western Paris to development and already proposed by his uncle, the emperor had not indicated any major streets in the west end, where the majority of new streets would be cut. Louis Napoléon's urban vision included nothing about water supply and sewers, and his improvements were confined within the old walls of Louis XIV, the inner boulevards of modern Paris.[22] Equally traditional was his insistence on some balance between east and west Paris, which was not subsequently honored. The preponderance was given to the west, and the emperor's plans for eastern Paris were almost totally abandoned.[23] The original imperial plan was little more than a sketch of vague intentions.

New Paris was a joint effort of Louis Napoléon and Haussmann that evolved over a number of years as the work progressed. Still the emperor's plan had two important advantages: it was the first comprehensive plan since the Commission des Artistes and never before had a head of state endorsed such a massive transformation.

Haussmann began by commissioning an accurate map of Paris, the foundation of all his subsequent work. Wooden towers were erected throughout the city by the first of his administrative innovations, the department for the Plan de Paris, headed by Deschamps. Higher than the surrounding houses, these elevated platforms served as the points for triangulating the city to determine its topography. Haussmann reproduced the map in several formats. The original was kept by Deschamps's department. His own office had an engraved copy, to the scale 1/5,000, which measured nine by fifteen feet and was mounted on a rolling stand. This map, "behind the easy chair in my office, formed an enormous screen where I could, at any minute, merely by turning around, locate a detail, check on certain indications, and recognize the topographical correlations between the arrondissements and neighborhoods of Paris. Very often," he continued, "I experienced fruitful meditations studying this exact plan."[24] Each of the services engaged on the enormous work of transformation was given a copy to the same scale, and a smaller version (scale 1/20,000) was prepared for the public.

An accurate topographical map was only the first of many technical problems that had to be solved. No one knew, for example, how to measure underground water sources or how to cut a trench through sandy soil that would be large enough for the diameter of sewer pipe necessary to drain a great city. Haussmann's interest in such problems, although he was no engineer, made their solution an administrative undertaking.

Once the new maps were drawn they played a major role in Haussmann's work. He did not make a practice of visiting the various municipal projects except on ceremonial occasions, when he conducted the emperor or some visiting dignitary around a building site. His plans for the city were realized abstractly, geometrically, on a map. His working map was not a physical map of the city, with buildings and monuments depicted, but an abstract expression of the space occupied by Paris. He ordered the city, imposed his vision upon it, from his office. Remote from the turmoil and disruption he was about to create in the lives of the Parisians, Haussmann planned Paris. His deliberate distance from the work accurately expresses his view of the transformation of Paris: it was an administrative task with himself as the controlling intelligence.

Merruau has described the imperial map growing under Louis Napoléon's nurturing, with lines "successively traced, rectified, co-ordinated."[25] Two versions of the emperor's plan exist, neither of them a precise reproduction of the 1853 original. There is no way of knowing how closely these copies approximate the original. In 1867 Wilhelm I of Prussia visited Paris for the international exposition. He ostentatiously avoided discussing politics or playing any political role. His entourage was not so conspicuously circumspect: Moltke the elder carefully examined the city's defenses, which he would attack in 1870. The king himself took a keen interest in the new Paris. He visited the sewers with Haussmann and obtained from the emperor a copy of his plan for the city's transformation.[26]

The second version of the map was obtained by Charles Merruau from the dying emperor, exiled in England.[27] This map, which may well approximate how the emperor remembered his original vision, is itself more an outline than a plan, reinforcing Haussmann's insistence that he had to penetrate the inspired thought of his master.[28]

More than any details it is Napoléon's boldness in cutting streets through Paris, rather than adding to the existing urban fabric, that was a fundamental change of approach. Kings and emperors had hitherto shied away from attacking the old urban tangle in central Paris. Perhaps Louis Napoléon was inspired by John Nash's construction of Regent Street, in London, earlier in the century, the first thoroughfare cut through the city.[29] Whatever the inspiration, the emperor's ruthlessness and Haussmann's bureaucratic expertise transformed Paris into a city neither wholly foreseen nor planned. The new city was the result of the inherent logic of urban theories held by Haussmann and shared by Louis Napoléon, the constraints dictated by the historical city they inherited, the political interests of a new regime, the economic realities of adolescent capitalism, the aesthetic canons of the day, and the personalities of emperor and prefect. The elements of the new Paris—boulevards, *places*, monuments, a city conceived of as linked zones of function—determined its shape. The unfolding evolution of the city was overseen by emperor and prefect, who met regularly to discuss the great enterprise, but so incomplete or improvisatory was the imagined city that even Haussmann never made a plan of Paris that showed his urban work.[30] Paris was never completed. It remains still a work in progress, as do all living cities.

Haussmann had inherited most of the great Parisian monuments— only the Eiffel Tower (C 4) and the basilica of Sacré-Coeur (E 1) would be later added to the cityscape while Garnier's Opéra (D 2), the third of these extraordinary new monuments, was constructed under the Second Empire—as well as axial groups of streets. The principles of axial symmetry and vistas for monumental effect had been well established by the Renaissance architects: the westerly Louvre-Tuileries axis (A-D 3, along the Champs-Elysées from the Place de la Concorde to the Arc de Triomphe), the Ecole Militaire–Champ-de-Mars–Trocadéro axis (B-C 4, now punctuated by the Eiffel Tower), the group around the Invalides (C-D 4), the group around the Madeleine (D 2), and the more modest Luxembourg composition (D-E 4–5), as well as the major *places*: the Place du Trône (G 4, Nation), Place du Château d'Eau (F 2–3, République), Place de la Bastille (G 4), and the Etoile (C 2–3, Arc de Triomphe). Haussmann's historical task was to open up, interconnect, and extend the approaches to these monumental compositions with modern boulevards and to link these boulevards so one could move through the city from monument to monument. This logic of going from one monument to another transformed the *places* into traffic exchanges, and in a few cases, most notably the carrefour of the Opéra (D 2), created new urban centers. He freed public buildings from the medieval tangle and provided access between them. Haussmann's Paris was a city of movement between zones defined by function, class, and activity, and delimited by boulevards.

Haussmann honored the historical evolution of Paris while imposing upon the city a coherence it had hitherto lacked. The history of the rue Soufflot (E 4) from the eighteenth century to Haussmann's time well illustrates the continuity of his work. The street had been planned, around 1760, as the necessary urban extension of Soufflot's new domed church of Ste. Geneviève (the Panthéon) but was not approved until 24 Frimaire, year III (December 14, 1795). Napoléon I began the street and it remained a fragment for more than thirty years. The July Monarchy extended it; but it was not completed until Haussmann made it twenty-two meters wide, presenting Soufflot's Panthéon as it should be seen while drawing the somewhat isolated montagne Ste. Geneviève into the network of boulevards that united it to the entire city.[31]

Originality is often defined as a bold new conception rather than a synthesis of existing ideas. The realization of a project is thought less creative and worthy than its conceptualization. In Haussmann's age, however, the engineer rather than the poet was the hero. Haussmann built what others had only drawn or dreamed. He integrated a number of discrete projects into an overall urban fabric in a way no one before him had imagined. On these two legs his reputation and his originality stand.[32]

The relationship between emperor and prefect was close and unique. Haussmann saw Louis Napoléon almost every day—to the historian's chagrin, for there is no exchange of letters to reveal their mutual intentions, initiatives, or responsibility—although Haussmann never became a member of the inner circle of the court. He was rarely invited to private weekends at Compiègne with the emperor's intimates, and the empress did not much like him. He was something new in court life: a technocrat, rather than a courtier, who had the ruler's ear. Legally, as prefect of the Seine, Haussmann was the appointee of the emperor but was answerable to the minister of the interior as well as the Municipal Council. He was de facto the mayor of Paris, which had a mayor for each arrondissement but no elected central mayor. This centralization of the municipal government in the hands of an imperial appointee provided one of the rallying points for the opposition. Republicans especially, and a spattering of others, including Legitimists who yearned for the return of the Bourbons, embraced decentralization as a political program, running counter to the age that saw everywhere in Europe the development of strong nation-states. And it is worth noting that in class terms the bourgeoisie here was in harmony with the socialists who continued to struggle against centralization.

The national administrative entities that oversaw the work of the prefect of the Seine were the Council of State (presided over by the emperor) and the Cour des Comptes (which handled funding). The tensions between city and state provided the dialectic of Haussmann's work. His loyalties were directly to the emperor before either the city or the national legislature, an ideal arrangement for a person who, from the outset of his career, sought ways of circumventing the regular administrative hierarchy. But he was bound, especially in financial matters, to deal with the elected bodies—both the Corps Législatif and the Senate—if he wanted to issue bonds. Contemporaries knew, however, that Haussmann was one of the most important and powerful figures in France. The constitutional niceties hedging his power were not closely observed. So long as he retained the emperor's confidence, the restraint or control of the various legal entities was more apparent than real.

The transformation of Paris was the centerpiece of imperial politics and the one policy Napoléon pursued relentlessly. With very few exceptions, he consistently backed his prefect. Resistance "mostly from the Bourse and the judicial professions," the Paris bourgeoisie Persigny characterized as the "pack of foxes and wolves arrayed against all the generous aspirations of the Empire," were the enemy. Haussmann's administration was "a long struggle against the depositories of power, a series of hand-to-hand combats with a powerful coterie, incapable of itself doing anything, but jealous of letting anyone else do anything."[33] Despite their considerable monetary improvement under the Second Empire, as a class the bourgeoisie provided substantial and tenacious opposition to Louis Napoléon. The emperor never carried Paris in an election and the bourgeoisie never forgave the usurper. Not only was Louis Napoléon a bohemian and an adventurer, but the coup d'état of 1851, in Paris, had hit the bourgeoisie hard. There were 380 people killed and the "three decrees of January 9, 1852, resulted in the transportation of five members of the Legislative Assembly, the expulsion of 66 (including Hugo and Raspail) and the temporary exile of eighteen others (including Thiers, Changarnier, and Lamorcière)."[34]

Haussmann, had he pursued a private career, would doubtless have shared the hostility of his class. But he identified, rather, with the emperor and consequently found himself at the center of virtually every political storm. He was the lightning rod for economic attacks on the empire and the growing clamor for more democracy. "I understand you," said the emperor in response to Haussmann's complaints. "You are not alone in suffering from injustice, from ingratitude, and the base passions of men! It is I . . . that they wish to strike through you, who serve me with rare, absolute fidelity, without the support of any other approbation than my own. But I too am faithful, and I will be faithful to the end, to my promise of friendship that I gave you in Bordeaux."[35]

The opposition deputy Ernest Picard quipped of Haussmann's enormous power that his name had ceased being a substantive and had acquired the dignity of a verb.[36] Only by forcing some democratic limits upon the empire could Haussmann be checked, and by attacking his transformations as the result of autocratic administration his enemies could strike at the arbitrary power that lay behind the prefect. But few wished Haussmann's work undone. It was so universally praised, at least at first, that he was difficult to impede. He was not merely a bureaucrat running a government agency; he held political power as the central mayor of Paris, functioned, in many ways, as a cabinet minister, and was a senator. He was the very embodiment of the struggle between the state and the city, and brilliantly played off one against the other so neither municipality nor nation exercised clear control.

Haussmann was made a senator in 1857 because, the emperor told him, he "no longer wanted anyone to be able to say to my prefect of the Seine, in the Municipal Council or elsewhere: I am a senator and you are not."[37] It is at this time that Haussmann began calling himself "Baron," although he had no legal right to the title.

The rules fixed by Napoléon I (March 1, 1808) restricted the descent of a new title in the collateral line. "I accepted it [the title] despite myself," he wrote, "after my elevation to the Senate of the Empire, which showed itself very jealous of the distinctions of nobility belonging to its members, and never missed an occasion to qualify the titles of its members."[38] In an age of often bogus patents, few were willing to cry deceit, especially to the emperor's favorite. Louis Napoléon might have granted Haussmann a genuine patent of nobility, an offer the prefect insists he refused. Horace de' Viel-Castel, the well-informed gossip and genuine aristocrat, thought Haussmann's elevation to the Senate "a scandal" and referred to him as "a former, little-known lawyer."[39] But the title stuck: *Baron* Haussmann is the figure remembered by history. The emperor also made Haussmann a Grand'Croix, the highest rank in the Legion of Honor, "before all the dignitaries of the State, with the acclamations of an innumerable crowd [at the opening of the boulevard Voltaire, December 7, 1862], in the Place du Trône."[40] The new leaders who adhered to the empire were rewarded for their services and granted the titled stature they lacked from birth.

Haussmann's greatest ambition was to have a new ministerial post created for himself: minister of Paris. This would have obviated all the squabbling with the minister of the interior, his nominal boss. Napoléon was unwilling to take the step, despite Haussmann's threats of resignation. The emperor compromised by inviting the prefect to attend all ministerial meetings dealing with Parisian affairs and to sit with the Council of State on the same basis. "The rank of minister," Haussmann wrote, "held little attraction for me," insisting he had declined appointment earlier as minister of agriculture, commerce and public works, and had twice refused the ministry of the interior. He accepted the compromise "to spare the emperor a great many difficulties."[41] The ministers were relieved by the compromise but rankled at Haussmann's privileged position.[42]

The emperor's unwavering support of Haussmann was earned. The prefect's devotion to his master was boundless. Haussmann was not only Louis Napoléon's clever, faithful servant, he was the imperial attack dog, "the executive agent, or if you wish the delegated representative of the August Mayor" of Paris, that is to say, the emperor.[43] Those who tangled with the prefect found him tough, tenacious, blunt, and unimpressed by rank or connections. He could afford to be arrogant on the emperor's behalf. He had reached the top of the administration through his own efforts, he was a new man, beholden only to Louis Napoléon. He eagerly took on all comers, as Persigny shrewdly saw he would. Persigny had warned the prefect "to begin nothing without having had it traced on the map of Paris by the emperor's hand, without having attached the very person of the sovereign, in the most intimate way, to each of [his] acts of adminis-tration." Haussmann scrupulously followed this advice.[44]

Making Paris a modern city under the intimidating symbols of the authoritarian empire was at base a political undertaking, an exten-sion of imperial authority in stone. Haussmann's great merit was that he could "direct such vast operations . . . despite the ardent, passionate, inexplicable opposition of most of the influential mem-bers of government." The prefect's very efficiency, energy, and ad-ministrative genius, his ostentatious insistence on an expertise divorced from ideology, was central to imperial politics: the authori-ty of the empire was to derive as much from Louis Napoléon's great name as from his monopoly on technological progress, improve-ment, and administrative integrity.

Louis Napoléon spoke little and wrote less. Haussmann describes him as one of those "phlegmatics to whom the world belongs." Only once did he see Louis Napoléon in a temper. Haussmann thought his master fundamentally benevolent and never abandoned this conviction. He repeated, with obvious pride, the emperor's judg-ment, delivered from exile at the end of his life: "He [Haussmann] always gave me prudent council and sage advice. He was a Great Administrator. I did not early enough believe in his political worth."[45] Aside from Haussmann's obvious usefulness and abilities, his untempered loyalty was fundamental. The emperor honored that quality, above all others, although he was perfectly capable of abandoning anyone, however sentimental or ancient the attach-ment, should need arise. Even those he cut adrift for his own politi-cal survival he held dear on a personal level.

Qualities and characteristics less fundamental than loyalty made

Louis Napoléon comfortable with his prefect. Haussmann knew English. Although he was far less anglophile than the emperor, Louis Napoléon liked to be surrounded by those who appreciated the land and language he admired, where he had found, and would again find, refuge. Haussmann was also a new man, without significant political or personal support. He would be the emperor's man. He had not risen high enough in the administration before 1848 to be compromised by earlier allegiances. Perhaps having a parvenu in a job hitherto held by individuals of more social and political status pleased Louis Napoléon. Haussmann had no political connections in Paris, and his lack of personal charm kept him from becoming the darling of the salons, which tended to be hotbeds of anti-imperial gossip, if not worse. Haussmann was no courtier but was massively well informed, intelligent, politically astute, and fearless. In the many reported conversations between emperor and prefect in the *Mémoires*, Haussmann presents himself as deeply respectful yet familiar with his master, his conversation sometimes enlivened by wit and word play, spiced with well-placed references to Roman history and the parallels between Augustus Caesar and Louis Napoléon, who was writing his study of Julius Caesar at the time. These set pieces are too well worked to be faithful reports of actual interviews, yet the tone of familiarity, sometimes bordering on intimacy between master and servant, has an authentic ring.

We learn little about the master, for the autobiographer was his own favorite subject; but it appears Haussmann moved and maneuvered effortlessly and effectively in this world. He knew his place socially and politically but stubbornly held his ground when it came to Paris. In a few instances—as the building of the boulevard Henri IV (F-G 4)—the differences of emperor and prefect can be verified from other sources, as can Haussmann's ultimate triumph. So much was left to the prefect's discretion that Louis Napoléon may have experienced some fascination in having his musings made, literally, concrete. Certainly imperial enthusiasm, imperial celebration of his prefect expressed publicly at the inaugurations of new boulevards, orchestrated by Haussmann, were genuine and heartfelt.

In contemporary portraits of the two, the artists were careful to position emperor and prefect so that the exceptionally large servant did not physically dominate the diminutive master. It would be far-fetched to suggest that Louis Napoléon was intimidated by Haussmann, but he could not be unaware of what an imposing figure the prefect was. It may be the emperor enjoyed having Haussmann as his formidable proxy, towering over his many enemies. A Goliath to stand in for the diminutive David, to take the occasional stone in the head. Haussmann was the emperor's instrument in the politics of urban transformation—a blunt weapon, exceptionally effective in close combat.

In general Louis Napoléon confined himself to making political decisions and was willing and pleased to approve the daily realization of his desires presented to him by Haussmann. He seconded his prefect's administrative reforms, took his side in endless disputes, agreed to fundamental elaborations of his original designs for Paris, and left most of the decisions about urban embellishment to Haussmann, not to mention financing the enormous work: "as for financial questions, he left them to my care, and I did not believe it proper to burden him, then and there, with explanations overflowing with numbers, to which I would have been compelled to refer, to make him completely understand how I proposed to resolve these matters."[46] "I don't want to say that He was disinterested," Haussmann asserted, but he "gradually left me greater liberty of decision making." Yet the task would have been impossible "if I had not, in fact, been the expression, the organ, the instrument of a great idea, conceived by Him . . . whose realization he protected, at all times, with a firmness that was never slackened."[47]

There are few enough great historical collaborations. Henri IV and Sully come to mind, but both were of the same class—aristocratic companions who had, literally, been through the wars together. The relationship of Elizabeth I and Burghley, the queen and the commoner, in England, is perhaps closer to Haussmann and Louis Napoléon. The queen chose her great minister, raised him above many a scion of an old aristocratic house, and even, as an old woman, nursed him, spooning broth for her dying servant. But the differences are more significant than the similarities. The emperor and his prefect were never friends in any intimate or emotional sense. They seem to have shared nothing but transforming Paris. It was a decidedly modern collaboration: the expert summoned to implement an idea. And because Louis Napoléon thought in political terms, what he needed was not an architect, an engineer, or a city planner. He needed a bureaucrat to fashion the administrative machinery and procedures that would turn his visions into stone. Haussmann was the perfect choice. Louis Napoléon had found a servant who would not merely do his bidding but gave muscle and brawn to imperial dreams.

· VIII ·

"The Implacable Axes of a
Straight Line. . ."

THE YEAR 1848 MADE MODERN PARIS POSSIBLE. THE REVOLUTIONS had not only swept the board clean, equally toppling kings and pawns, clearing the way for the Second Empire, it was a new *point de départ*. The urgency of urban renewal infused the language of critics and reformers—the discourse of salubrity, cleansing, aerating, movement—with political meaning. Paris was sick, moribund, suffocating:

> The entire central section of Old Paris and the three arrondissements of the Left Bank [wrote the municipal councillor Victor Considérant in 1844]. . .are a sewer, as is the Cité. . .and the neighborhoods of the Gros Caillou, of St. Marcel, and the Ile St. Louis [are] atrophied because of their increasingly wretched isolation.[1]

The second wave of cholera that struck the city in 1849 grimly reiterated the diagnosis and made real the metaphor. Louis Napoléon brilliantly recognized and exploited the changed climate. He would heal the wounds inflicted by the Second Republic. The transformation of Paris would establish his authority on a more solid foundation than the dubious one of descent from an upstart, an adventurer, a conqueror. Paris itself, a new capital, would be an irrefutable argument for a healthy authoritarian regime devoted to progress.

185

First antisepsis. Louis Napoléon unflinchingly supported the massive condemnations, expropriations, and demolitions demanded by Haussmann's transformations. The emperor's urban dreams were no grander or more extensive than those of many a predecessor, but his will was firmer. Completing the Louvre-Tuileries had been considered by virtually every government since François I. Each had flinched, "checked by the necessity of demolishing a substantial neighborhood where the stables of the king, the royal riding academy, and the old hospital of the Quinze-Vingts, were located,"[2] all redolent with history. The riding academy, or Manège, had provided the makeshift home of the Convention Assembly during the French Revolution. It was here that Louis XVI was tried and condemned. Even the Restoration, anxious to purge Paris of the memory of revolution and regicide, had stayed its hand. This was also the neighborhood of the rue Doyenné, which Balzac described as "a ditch." "It was a great satisfaction for me," wrote Haussmann, "to raze all this for my debut in Paris."[3]

The enormous work of transformation had been begun by Louis Napoléon before he summoned Haussmann to power. The prefect's inaugural project, the *grande croisée*, was both symbolic and practical. The great cross was to be the north-south, east-west axes of the new city: respectively the boulevards Strasbourg-Sébastopol and Champs-Elysées–Rivoli (the former continued by the boulevard St. Michel, the later by the rue St. Antoine), and made reference to the Roman foundations of Paris as well as the city's medieval heritage. Myth and reality were loosely mingled. The rue St. Jacques (on the Left Bank) preserved a trace of the old Gallo-Roman north-south road, the *cardo*. There was no archaeological evidence of an east-west road. One had to be invented, an imagined Roman *decumanus* crossing the *cardo*. In addition, the Gallo-Roman city had been on the Left Bank while what was now needed was a great cross on the Right Bank.

Haussmann and Louis Napoléon had no need to reach back to antiquity for a pedigree, although their desire to preserve the myth that their transformations of Paris were generated by the city's original act of foundation is revealing, as is the symbolic echo of antiquity, when the first act of urban foundation was a cross cut into the earth. Haussmann preferred a more recent reference: the reign of Charles V (1364–80), when *la Grande Croisée de Paris* was first spoken of.[4] Louis XIV had wanted to build an east-west artery and the Plan des Artistes had boldly proposed such a route (from the Place de la Concorde eastward to the Place de la Bastille). The Artistes had not proposed a north-south axis, apparently unwilling to cut so drastically across Paris. The need, and the logic, of the great cross formed a long history of unrealized plans and failed nerve. Louis Napoléon did not hesitate, as had his predecessors. His map, in both Merruau's and Morizet's versions, shows the Strasbourg-Sébastopol axis, continued on the Left Bank by the boulevard St. Michel. The *grande croisée* would bind the city together: it would be "cut through the middle of the city . . . and bring its extreme limits, at the four cardinal points, into almost direct communication."[5] Paris would radiate out from the great cross as it had once radiated from the Ile de la Cité. The old moribund historical center, now replaced by an artificial great cross, would be transformed from "an

Grande Croisée

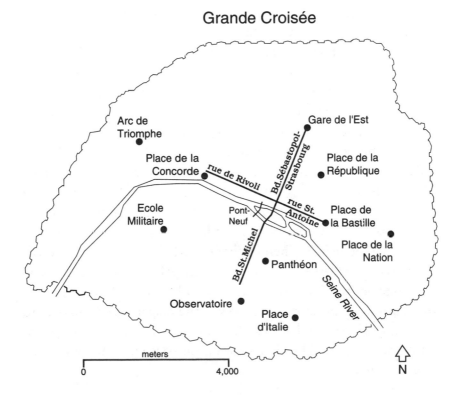

immense obstacle to general traffic movement," Haussmann explained to the General Council of the city, into "the link for all the rest."[6] In fact, he had no desire to revivify the old core of Paris, whatever he told the General Council. New Paris would take its energy from new axes, not the original city. The *grande croisée* was a new act of foundation, abstract and ahistorical. The grand cross was in conflict with two other Haussmann urban schemes: the gutting—"*éventrement*" is Haussmann's stark word[7]—of the Ile de la Cité and the creation of the carrefour of the Opéra. The old center of the city was to be destroyed and a new center created.

Haussmann's demolitions were purposeful and the emperor's urban vision broadly political, but the cliché that they were chiefly motivated by the desire to insulate Paris from insurrection underrates their achievement. The emperor authorized, and Haussmann built, some purely strategic streets. The boulevard Richard Lenoir, running north from the Place de la Bastille, was one such (G 3). The canal St. Martin, which the new street partly covered, had been one of the important popular strongholds in the June Days of 1848, holding up General Cavaignac's troops for nearly a week. "After much insomnia, brought on by anxiety, the solution came to me," Haussmann wrote. The boulevard Prince Eugène ([G 3–4], now the boulevard Voltaire) cut a strategic swath through the riotous eastern neighborhoods, but there remained the problem of the canal. Haussmann had the city buy the canal in 1861, lower it six meters, and build the boulevard Richard Lenoir over it. Not only did this destroy the natural barricade of the canal, but it provided yet another route "into the habitual center of . . . riots." Haussmann invited the emperor to visit the site. "I have rarely seen my August Sovereign enthusiastic. This time he was unreservedly enthusiastic. . . . one could, if need be, take the faubourg St. Antoine from the rear."[8] When the boulevard Voltaire was completed, the faubourg St. Antoine was encircled. Abandoned forever was the dream of the Bourbon kings to build a great triumphal entry into Paris from the east. Gone too was the emperor's original desire to endow the east end with a cluster of new boulevards. Imperial strategy, interpreted by Haussmann, was to isolate the dangerous neighborhoods.

Boulevards Richard Lenoir and Voltaire

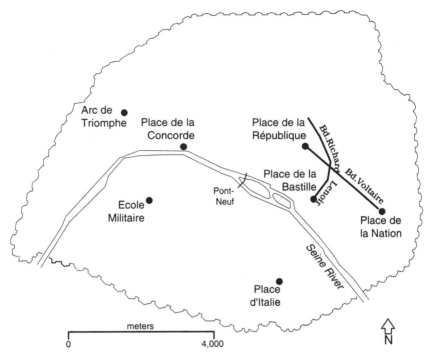

There is a similar imperial intervention concerning the rue de Mazas ([G 4], now the boulevard Diderot), which connects the Place de la Nation to the Quai de la Rapée. The street was transformed into an avenue and was to have been lined with arcaded buildings, imitating the rue de Rivoli. The arcades, expressly prohibited by the emperor, were never built: "The construction of arcades on the boulevard Mazas," he wrote Rouher on December 15, 1857, "would seriously compromise the strategic system of Paris."[9] But there are surprisingly few such directly military projects. Most of the deliberately strategic streets were cut at least a decade after the transformation of Paris began and were certainly not Louis Napoléon's first priority. The rue de Turbigo (F 3), which cut through the 1848 web of resistance around the Conservatoire des Arts et Métiers, was not completed until 1867. This street, Haussmann announced, "removed the rue Transnonain from the Paris map,"[10] obliterating any urban memory of the massacre hauntingly commemorated by Honoré Daumier. The boulevards Voltaire,

Rues Gay-Lussac, Claude Bernard, and Monge

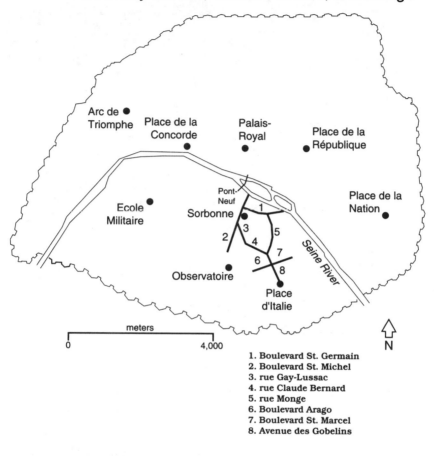

1. Boulevard St. Germain
2. Boulevard St. Michel
3. rue Gay-Lussac
4. rue Claude Bernard
5. rue Monge
6. Boulevard Arago
7. Boulevard St. Marcel
8. Avenue des Gobelins

Diderot, and Richard Lenoir were completed, respectively, in 1862, 1857, and 1863. The rues Gay-Lussac and Claude Bernard, which neutralized the montagne Ste. Geneviève on the Left Bank, were completed in 1870, while the barracks at the Place de la République, behind the Hôtel de Ville, near the Place de la Bastille, and on the rue Mouffetard (E 5), were similarly delayed. The projects that most mattered to the emperor were those that were highly visible, put thousands to work, and gave the new regime prestige: the Louvre (1857), the rue de Rivoli (1855), the Hôtel de Ville (1855), the boulevard de Strasbourg (1854), and the two Left Bank projects: the rue des Ecoles ([E-F 4], 1853) and the rue de Rennes ([D 4–5], 1853). All had been begun before the empire.

The accusation that Paris was being sacrificed to the regime's fear

of urban insurrection was tempered by the contradictory charge
that Paris was being turned into a city for sybarites. The emperor
was aware of both criticisms:

> At the present moment [he told Albert Vandam] the opponents of
> my plans have adopted the cry that I am attempting to do too much
> at once, and that this attempt is prompted by my wish to hold all
> Paris in the palm of my hand by means of broad thoroughfares, in
> which large masses of troops can move freely. . . . Another section of
> society accuses me of wishing to reduce Paris to a mere city of plea-
> sure and make it the resort of all the profligates and idlers—titled
> and untitled, rich and poor, honest and dishonest—of the whole
> world. That, according to the last-named critics, is my method for
> stifling the nation's aspirations towards a higher standard of political
> liberty.[11]

The urban plans of Haussmann and his master, the new boulevards and barracks, did not prevent the Communards, in 1871,
from holding out longer against the regular army than had the insurrectionaries of June 1848. What Haussmann's destruction of the
rabbit warren of streets in eastern Paris had done was transform barricades and urban insurrection from a cottage industry to a substantial and sophisticated undertaking, demanding larger concentrations of both force and resistance. The army was not consulted
and at exactly the same time Haussmann constructed a barracks
near the Place de la République, he was building the gardens of the
boulevard Richard Lenoir. In truth, barracks and gardens were com-
patible. Once the few strategic streets had been cut, the great
boulevards and the august perspectives could exist alongside the
habitual squalor and potential political unrest of eastern Paris: in
socioeconomic terms, "the most authoritarian public initiative and
the greatest individual liberty in questions of building" coexisted.
Imperial urban politics was to contain the working-class quarters,
not transform them, to preserve private property while assuring the
stability of the authoritarian state.[12]

Haussmann conceived of the city as a series of zones defined by
their activity and centered on some important carrefour or intersection given significance by a monument. He used the new boulevards

to define these urban zones, simultaneously delimiting and connecting them. The boulevard Richard Lenoir separated a riotous working-class neighborhood from a shabby but stable neighborhood; the boulevard de Strasbourg separated a residential from a commercial zone. Those neighborhoods that the authorities could not adequately control—the Belleville quarter (G-H 2) is an excellent example—were left to their own devices. Belleville became a zone unpenetrated by boulevards or police, unregulated by the government, a neighborhood where "unruly passions and political resentments held the upper hand."[13]

Haussmann denied that Louis Napoléon had any strategic purpose in mind when he traced the boulevard de Strasbourg, which ran, when extended by the boulevard de Sébastopol, from the gare de l'Est to the Seine. But "it cannot be denied that this was the happy consequence of all the important boulevards envisioned by His Majesty to ameliorate and cleanse the old city." Haussmann's conflation is further evidence of the transmutation of the language of hygiene into that of strategy. The prefect was obsessed with urban hygiene, which he understood in social as well as medical terms. Human vermin also needed cleansing. The rurals, who dominated the Corps Législatif of the empire, had to be assured that they were paying for the tranquility of Paris lest they withdraw "the participation of the State in the expense of these onerous undertakings."[14]

The emperor took more direct interest in the Bois de Boulogne (A-B 2–4) than in the military security of central Paris; and architecture was another of the imperial passions. An English visitor, searching for drawings and descriptions of the church of St. Vincent de Paul, then being built, was told at the Bibliothèque Nationale that Louis Napoléon had recently sent for the architect Hittorff's book and several others."[15] His most famous intervention concerns the central markets. The July Monarchy and Rambuteau had already determined to fix les Halles where Philippe-Auguste and Louis VII had originally implanted them, in the midst of the city, a decision that perpetuated medieval Paris and preserved the vitality of the old urban core. The empire and Haussmann carried the plan to completion. Designs for the market were solicited and submitted to the emperor. The first proposals were, uniformly, for stone buildings in the Beaux-Arts style, which Louis Napoléon rejected as unfit for their function. Haussmann later told his American friend, Sherard, that "it was he [the emperor]. . .who first designed with his own hands the plan of the wonderful Central Markets, which were afterwards constructed by Baltard."[16] Haussmann apparently divulged the emperor's inspiration to his friend and school chum Victor Baltard, whose designs of the famous iron and glass sheds for les Halles were ultimately adopted.

The rigidity of iron as a structural material bedeviled architects until the 1870s, when steel, the most characteristic material of industrial revolution architecture, became affordable. Baltard brilliantly solved the problem. The fragile structure of the iron supports were made supple by the use of steel cords, in the form of bars, that were suspended from pulleys. Besides the sheds at les Halles, modern both in conception and materials, the railroad stations are the only other buildings that reveal the use of new materials and methods of construction, incorporating iron into the design, revealing the sinews of construction. Iron was extensively used for strength, but one must look behind the stone facades of Second Empire buildings, which mask the new technology within.

The emperor's eclectic taste ran to historicist buildings, imitative of an earlier style. For Paris Louis Napoléon preferred a style broadly associated with the Italian Renaissance. A building should announce its function, and the emperor associated government and public buildings with French or Italian classicism. Zola described a town house on the parc Monceau as "a miniature of the new Louvre, one of those examples most characteristic of the Napoléon III style, this opulent bastard of all styles."[17] The emperor instructed Haussmann not to try and imitate the old Châtelet (the original home of the law courts in medieval Paris) in building the new Palais de Justice, but "take for a model the Loggia of Brescia, the work of Formentone and his successors, Sansovino and Palladio, which he considered, with reason, as one of the masterworks of the Renaissance."[18] If he favored bogus Renaissance for public buildings, the emperor leaned toward restorations and neomedievalism for private buildings. Haussmann shared only his master's public taste.

Arguably aesthetic considerations were more important to

Haussmann and the emperor than military strategy. Haussmann's mania for perspective, his need to have each important boulevard either connect two monuments or *places*—as the boulevard Voltaire connects the Place de la Nation and the Place de la République—or appear to connect two monuments—as the boulevard Henri IV seems to connect the Place de la Bastille, with its Column of July, and the Panthéon—involved him in some complicated urban manipulation, as well as some tough negotiations with Louis Napoléon. More often than not the emperor yielded to his prefect. "I want to say," Haussmann wrote, "that His Majesty made concessions to what He called my weaknesses [for perspective], to which a good number of our public ways bear witness."[19]

The boulevard Henri IV was to connect the Left Bank to the Right by continuing the new boulevard St. Germain—not originally proposed by Napoléon—across the Seine to the Place de la Bastille, where it would in turn be linked to half a dozen important arteries (F-G 4). There was no dispute on the usefulness of the new boulevard, but if the boulevard Henri IV crossed the Seine via a bridge parallel to all the others, it would debouch into the boulevard St. Germain with no monument to balance the Column of July. Haussmann discovered that if he built the boulevard Henri IV at a particular angle, it would have the column at one end and the Panthéon dome at the other. The new boulevard would not carry to the Panthéon, which lay atop the montagne Ste. Geneviève and could be reached from this direction only by climbing the hill via an old, winding street. But an optical illusion would be created, giving the boulevard Henri IV termini. To achieve his trompe l'oeil Haussmann had to build it obliquely across the Seine, amputating the eastern tip of the Ile St. Louis and demolishing the beautiful hôtel Bretonvilliers and its garden in the process. The emperor objected that to achieve this perspective the symmetry of the Seine bridges would be destroyed. Haussmann won the argument. The boulevard Henri IV and the pont Sully was his most successful urban illusion. The predominance of aesthetic considerations over military strategy helps explain the apparent discrepancy of purpose between street building in eastern and western Paris, and underlines Haussmann's conception of the city as a whole. In the west, where the majority of

Boulevards St. Germain and Henri IV

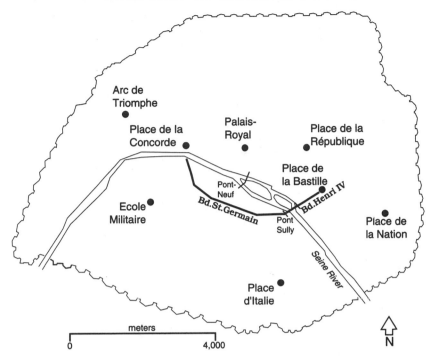

the new boulevards were built, there were no military considerations. The dangerous classes did not live in this sparsely populated area; the new neighborhoods were largely residential, with luxury shops for the wealthy inhabitants. Yet the new streets were cut with precisely the same considerations as those in the east: broad, purposeful thoroughfares connecting monuments, radiating from *places*, endowed with uniform architecture, and their perspectives closed at each end by some public structure. The boulevard Malesherbes (1862) runs northwest from the place de la Madeleine (C-D 2). To close the perspective and balance the Madeleine church at one end, Haussmann had Baltard design the church of St. Augustin at the other (D 2). St. Augustin is an eyesore: ridiculously sited, without proportion, crushed beneath an outsized dome. It fully fills an odd-shaped lot created by the intersection of four streets (the boulevards Malesherbes, Haussmann, and Friedland, and the avenue Portalis). Its dome had to be sixty meters high to be visible both from the Madeleine and the boulevard Friedland, where it joins the Arc de

Boulevards Malesherbes, Friedland, and Haussmann

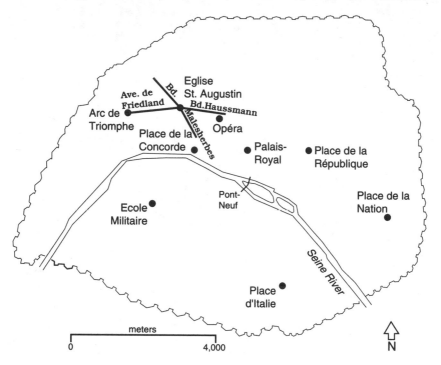

Triomphe as one of the twelve radiating streets of the Etoile. The misshapen church was dictated by the convergence of four streets and Haussmann's obsession with monuments and perspective. The irony that he erected so misshapen a building very near the spot where he was born is lost on most visitors.

Haussmann's most strenuous quest for perspective, however, is connected to the boulevard de Strasbourg. At one end of the new boulevard, which led directly to the old center of Paris, was the gare de l'Est (F 2). Haussmann devised a series of illusions for this important street. The thoroughfare had been begun before he came to power. Had his predecessors moved the street only a few meters, Haussmann lamented, the dome of the Sorbonne ([E 4], on the Left Bank) would have been visible from the boulevard de Strasbourg, providing the perspective he craved. But the July Monarchy was far more utilitarian than he.

Haussmann had to correct the oversight. As with all work in Old Paris the dense urban fabric made planning tricky. Where the rue de

Rivoli intersected the new boulevard de Sébastopol was the place du Châtelet (E 3), which Haussmann now enlarged. All the old tiny streets were destroyed, including the rue de la Vieille-Lantern, where the poet Gérard de Nerval was found hanged in 1855. "I remember . . . especially his pride in having transformed the quarter of the place du Châtelet," Sherard wrote. "'It was a sewer,' he said."[20]

Haussmann then moved Palmier's fountain to the center of the *place*, but the boulevard de Sébastopol did not bisect the enlarged *place*, so the fountain could not close the perspective. He built two theaters here, the Châtelet and the Sarah Bernhardt, to anchor the new *place*, and he linked it with the Hôtel de Ville. Queen Victoria, visiting the Universal Exposition of 1855, was persuaded to give her name to the new street. Nevertheless the place du Châtelet remains a hodgepodge, a half-baked project awaiting a final phase of development. And there was still no monument to close the perspective from the gare de l'Est.

Haussmann conceived of a domed courthouse, the only one in Paris—the Tribunal de Commerce—on the Ile de la Cité. To be visible from the gare de l'Est the dome was built absurdly off-center. Immediately he had another perspective problem. The boulevard de Strasbourg-Sébastopol, when it crossed the Seine, did not line up exactly with the pont au Change. The boulevard du Palais (1858) had, consequently, to be slightly out of line with the pont au Change; and when it crossed to the Left Bank via the pont St. Michel, there was yet another angle before it joined the place St. Michel and the boulevard St. Michel ([E 4], 1855–59), which veered eastward, further disrupting the rectilinear. To continue the illusion that his great north-south axis ran in a straight line through the center of Paris, Haussmann had the architect, Davioud, design the St. Michel fountain, which occupies a triangular space created by the convergence of the boulevard St. Michel and an unimportant street, the rue Danton. One final trompe l'oeil was needed. Looking at the place St. Michel from the Ile de la Cité, one notes that the boulevard St. Michel and the rue Danton seem of equal size and significance. In fact the former is a major new boulevard, the latter a minor little street. Haussmann emphasized the important street by the trees lining the boulevard St. Michel and the clever use of hierarchical architecture. The whole system works: the individual parts are incoherent.

The gutting of the Ile de la Cité involved no optical illusions. Here we see the complicated knotting of aesthetic, strategic, political, hygienic, and functional concerns that made Haussmann so sophisticated an urbanizer; we see as well the most extreme example of haussmannization as urban renewal by demolition.

Haussmann's treatment of the Ile de la Cité, his razing of the cradle of Paris, has been repeatedly condemned. In place of one of the densest medieval neighborhoods of Paris, containing hundreds of houses and numerous churches on a few acres of land immensely rich in Parisian history, Haussmann left only Notre Dame, the Conciergerie, the Palais de Justice (which he considerably enlarged, amputating one leg of the residential triangle of the Place Dauphine in the process), and the Ste. Chapelle. He replaced the homes of some fifteen thousand Parisians with three major structures: the Hôtel Dieu (designed by Emile Gilbert and A.-S. Diet, which replaced the original hospital of the same name, as well as the hospice des Enfants-Trouvés), the Caserne de la Cité (barracks designed by P.-V. Calliat, which eventually became the prefecture of police), and the Tribunal de Commerce, with its eccentric dome (designed by A.-N. Bailly). The parvis before Notre Dame was enlarged to forty times its original size, and a park was built behind its apse. Numerous streets were suppressed or disappeared. By the end of the century there were only five thousand residents on the Ile. This vast destruction "necessitated the expropriation of all the houses and the disappearance of the ignoble quarter that circumscribed" the old rue de la Cité and the new flower market.[21]

The Ile had suffered centuries of degradation, readily apparent in the expropriations made to build the Palais de Justice. Fifty-three renters were expelled in 1860–61, of whom twenty-four were wine merchants—generally thought a low occupation—and two keepers of houses of prostitution. The last tanners, wretched artisans working in their apartments, were driven from the Ile between 1853 and 1865.[22] The Ile was not notorious for riots and contained no strategically important buildings. In addition the infestation of the historical center of Paris by a nomadic population—Haussmann's habitual word for the poor working class—defiled the monuments. "Those who have not, as I have, walked, in every sense of the word, through the old Paris of this epoch," he declared with some pride, "cannot form for themselves an accurate idea of it, despite what has survived, for I have neglected nothing in its amelioration."[23] The medieval core of Paris had been transformed into a legal and administrative center. Once the home of king and court, bishop and hierarchy, and the thousands who clung like barnacles to Lutèce, the Ile was now not even a museum. It was a kind of midway filled with public buildings unrelated to one another by style, function, or history. Notre Dame stood like a statue to be admired, not a cathedral to be used. The Ste. Chapelle was hidden in one of the courtyards of the Palais de Justice. The old *Cité* no longer defined Paris.

The nature of this transformation, although not its excesses, derives from the same principles that guided all Haussmann's work. He disencumbered Notre Dame as the July Monarchy had the Hôtel de Ville because he shared the prevailing view that historical monuments should be set apart, as on a pedestal. The church now became a national monument, a central object in the increasingly popular cult of French historical reminiscence, whose scripture was Victor Hugo's *Notre-Dame de Paris*, published in 1831. He straightened out the streets crossing the Ile and added new bridges and buildings. He centralized the legal functions of the state.[24] The Hôtel Dieu, the new hospital, was the most ambitious, the most incongruous, and the most strenuously opposed of his projects for the Ile. Virtually everyone wanted a simple infirmary. Haussmann had grander ideas. Only in 1865—the Ile was not one of the emperor's priorities—when the demolition work began, did it become clear just what he had in mind. The logic of building a new hospital on the Ile was not so much that it would serve the neighborhood, which Haussmann had destroyed, but that it would be another public building, another monument for the transformed *Cité*. After 1870 Haussmann's Hôtel Dieu, too cumbersome for the site, was lowered by having a story removed.

Haussmann's treatment of the Ile de la Cité is an offense to modern sensibility, and many contemporaries cried out against him. No other neighborhood in Paris was so historically sacred and nowhere else did he so radically transform a neighborhood through demolition. The Ile was overcrowded, filthy, decrepit, an eyesore, potentially riotous, a disgraceful environment for the cradle of Paris, but radical haussmannization was not the only possible solution to an admitted urban problem. The true center of gravity of Paris was no longer here but to the northwest, which reflected the long leaning of the city westward. It would have been impossible to reconstitute the *Cité*, give it again its medieval importance and vigor, even if Haussmann had believed in historical restoration. The physical isolation of the Ile from Paris allowed him the opportunity, experienced nowhere else in Paris, to transform a neighborhood completely. Haussmann gave the *Cité* a new function: it became the zone of the courts and monuments (with the peculiar inclusion of the Hôtel Dieu). He made the Ile what it remains today: a passage between Right and Left Bank. Only Notre Dame and Ste. Chapelle attract those who do not have specific business on the Ile. At night, when the courts are closed, the only signs of life are around the cathedral and the hospital.

There is something personal in Haussmann's demolitions on the Ile. "I used to cross the Chaussée d'Antin," to go from his home (near St. Augustin church) to school (near the Panthéon),

> and after some detours reach the rue Montmartre and the porte St. Eustache; I crossed the square of les Halles, not then covered, amid the red umbrellas of the fishmongers; then the rue des Lavandières, rue St. Honoré, and the rue St. Denis. The Place du Châtelet was a shabby part in those days. . . . I crossed the old pont au Change . . . then I skirted the old Palais de Justice, with the shameful mass of low cabarets that used to dishonor the Cité on my left. . . . continuing my way by the pont St. Michel, I had to cross the miserable little square where, like a sewer, the waters flowed out of the rue de la Harpe, the rue de la Hachette, the rue St. André des Arts and the rue de l'Hirondelle, where at the end appeared the sign of Chardin the perfumer, like a false note.

From here, this carefully wrought passage continues, he

> launched into the meanderings of the rue de la Harpe, then had to climb the Montagne Ste. Geneviève and arrive, by the passage of the Hôtel d'Harcourt and the rue des Maçons-Sorbonne, the Place

Richelieu, the rue de Cluny and the rue des Grés, at the Place du Panthéon at the corner of the Faculty of Law.[25]

Precise and opinionated, contrasting past wretchedness with present cleanliness. One can follow his walk, street by street, on a pre-1853 Paris street map. Virtually everything he describes he himself destroyed or changed, including his house, demolished to make way for the boulevard that bears his name.

This description is informed by passionate repugnance: "shabby," "shameful," "dishonor," "miserable," "a sewer," riveted by the ironic detail of Chardin's perfume shop amid the filth and squalor. His daily walk to school engraved on his mind the foulness of central Paris. The meandering streets and old buildings held no charm for Haussmann. They were repulsive, ugly, vile, unhealthy, characteristics both political and personal for Haussmann. His fastidiousness was deep and obsessive. A sickly childhood, when he was removed from the dirty city for his health, the remembrance of weak lungs, often attributed to breathing fetid air, were perhaps painfully reawakened by his daily walk across Old Paris. He remembered his months in St. Girons as a time of purity, breathing the fresh, clean mountain air, and here it was that he became interested in clean water and the treatment of the insane. His fastidiousness was intimately related to fear—reasonable enough in virtually any French city of the early nineteenth century—a phobia that was a direct connection between filth and disease. Haussmann's was an age of concern for urban hygiene, but his own obsessions betray a personal stake in cleanliness, a deep psychological need. On the Ile de la Cité the catharsis of these childhood sensations issued in destruction.

Where he was less emotionally engaged, less obsessed by the need to cleanse and aerate, when he could look coolly at his maps and not recall the revolutions of his youth, Haussmann's work was more successful, less ruthless. He was able to preserve a good deal from the past and transform it into the needs and sensibility of the present. He saved many of the old streets and quarters of Paris from further rapid degradation, from threatened asphyxiation,[26] by integrating them into his new city. The inner quarters of Paris with their mixture of regular, large new street and narrow, irregular old streets, a complex intermingling of commercial and residential functions, "are still the most successful and agreeable parts of the city from every point of view."[27] His personal assault on the Ile de la Cité was an anomaly fueled by deep compulsions.

The fruitful weaving together of old and new is apparent in Haussmann's transformation of the urban *place*. As was the boulevard, the *place* was Italian in origin. It had emerged from the old medieval village squares and came to be decorated with statuary, most often an equestrian statue celebrating the military prowess of the ruler. An important street might lead to a *place*, but generally the two were distinct. Haussmann, with considerable ingenuity and originality, would combine them. It is useful to compare the last *place* built by the Bourbon monarchy with the Etoile.

Completed in 1685, the small, elegant, circular Place des Victoires (E 3) has as its center an equestrian statue of Louis XIV as conquering Roman hero embraced by Jules Hardouin-Mansart's elegant, curved architecture, with a false arcade, two full stories, and a double-pitched Mansard roof. The composition and detailing of the architecture are entirely classical and in this sense look forward to Haussmann's street elevations.[28] But the *place* itself looks backward to the piazzas of the Renaissance. Here, in this space lifted out of the urban hurly-burly, one may contemplate at leisure the grandeur of the king. All is made to a human scale, no large streets debouch upon the *place*. Anyone who has careened around the Place des Victoires on the Number 29 bus knows it was not designed to facilitate traffic flow.

The Etoile is completely different (B-C 2–3). The great Arc de Triomphe, designed by J. A. Raymond and J. F. T. Chalgrin to celebrate Napoléon I, had been built on what is surely the most impressive axis in Paris. Napoléon III, exceptionally sensitive to his uncle's memory in rebuilding Paris, was doubtless delighted that his prefect transformed the Etoile into the most dramatic and monumental *place* in Paris. Built on a massive scale, modeled on the triumphal arches of the Roman emperors rather than the *places* of the Renaissance, the Arc de Triomphe demanded an urban context to match its grandeur. Haussmann, with his gift for scale and monumentality, made the *place* even grander than had Napoléon's architects. To the original five streets that radiated from the Arc de Triomphe he added seven to make a twelve-armed star.[29] One of these, the present Avenue Foch, which leads to the Bois de Boulogne, was the widest, grandest street in the world (B-C 2: then named the avenue du Bois de Boulogne, originally the avenue de l'Impératrice). To accentuate the symmetry of the *place*, Haussmann located the radiating streets so that uniformly shaped building lots were created between each pair of streets. Eight of these were identical in size, and the four on the opposite side were of double size. An imperial decree required that all buildings on these lots have uniform facades set off by lawns separated from the street by identical iron fences. Haussmann built a special access street for these monumental buildings. "This lovely arrangement," he wrote, "which I am so proud of having discovered, and which I consider among the most successful works of my administration, can be seen as a whole from the top of the Arc de Triomphe, which many more tourists than Parisians visit."[30] Not only is the Etoile not removed from the urban frenzy, it adds to that frenzy. It is one of the major traffic exchanges of Paris, made for drivers, not pedestrians. There is no time to contemplate the details of the Arc de Triomphe as one drives past, surrounded on all sides by the swirling traffic. The arc must make its impression from a distance or as a gigantic presence only glimpsed. The Place des Victoires, designed for pedestrians, a kind of urban grotto, marks the end of a journey. The Etoile is part of a journey. The two *places* symbolize the differences between an eighteenth- and a nineteenth-century city: repose rather than movement, pedestrian rather than equestrian promenade, enclosed rather than open.

The Place de l'Etoile, in western Paris, is at the outer limits of the city. It is—or was until the complex of skyscrapers was built at La Défense, two miles to the west—the only perspective in Paris that was not closed. One looked down the Champs-Elysées, through the Arc de Triomphe, to infinity. The enormous scale was possible because arch and its radiating streets occupied relatively unurbanized, relatively inexpensive land. Through the arch lay open land. Haussmann's imagination had free reign for monumentality. A creation of a different order is the neighborhood of the Opéra, which was to become the new center of Paris.

The *quartier* of the Opéra (D-E 2) is Haussmann's single most important urban project, involving at least a half-dozen major new
streets, a new railroad station, and the most sumptuous and significant public building of the empire, Charles Garnier's Opéra. All the
elements of Haussmann's urbanism are here evident. As most of his
important projects, this one was contemplated long before he came
to power. Paris had needed a new opera house for years. Victor
Louis, the architect of the Grand Théâtre in Bordeaux (1773–80),
which had a profound influence on Haussmann and on theater design generally, had built two of his new auditoriums in Paris, the
Théâtre de la Comédie Française (1786–90) and the Théâtre des
Arts (1791–93), both of which would influence the new opera
house. On February 13, 1820, the duc de Berry, presumed to be the
last of the Bourbon line, was murdered at the entrance to the
Théâtre des Arts by the obscure fanatic, Louis-Pierre Louvel, who
"'wanted to exterminate the Bourbons." A posthumous child—who
would become the Bourbon pretender to the throne—was born
some months after the assassination. In the ensuing scandal the
theater, on the rue de Richelieu (near the Bibilothèque Nationale,
[E 2–3]), was demolished. The architect, François Debret, was
charged with erecting a new opera house, the city's eighth. Pressed
for time and constrained by a tight budget, he built the Salle Lepelletier (in the garden of the former Hôtel de Choiseul, on the rue Lepelletier near the boulevard des Italiens) with materials from the
demolished Théâtre des Arts. Although temporary, the Salle Lepelletier remained in use until it was destroyed by fire, on the night of
October 18–19, 1873. Through a series of urban decisions heavily
influenced by chance, Paris stumbled toward one of its most
renowned marvels.

Louis Napoléon's interest in extending the rue de Rivoli, begun
by his uncle and joining the Louvre to the Tuileries, put in relief the
need for a street linking the great palace to the city north of the
Seine. The street that would eventually become the avenue de
l'Opéra (then called the avenue Napoléon) connected the already
existing boulevards de la Madeleine, de Capucines, and des Italiens,
the original Grands Boulevards of the Right Bank that had replaced
the old ramparts, which in turn linked up with a series of boulevards

that led to the Place de la République, and eventually to the palace complex. This series of linkages would integrate the Louvre-Tuileries (and the rue de Rivoli, the east-west leg of the great cross) to the chic residential quarter that had grown up near the Grands Boulevards. The boulevards Madeleine-Capucines-Italiens were already the heart of the Parisian boulevard life that preceded the empire. The new avenue would also demand the enlargement of the rues Richelieu, St. Honoré, Echelle, and Rohan, opening up the entire *quartier* that had been originally developed in the seventeenth century (D-E 2). As the network of streets grew it formed a major urban center, the most complex of Haussmann's urban systems. It was imperative to have a center of gravity, an anchor, for this new urban core. The logic of implanting a new opera house in this neighborhood was unfolding, although this had not been the original intention.

Haussmann initiated studies of the neighborhood to determine where new streets might be cut. The project gradually became more and more ambitious. Cutting a diagonal street twenty-two meters wide (the avenue de l'Opéra) spawned additional streets. The rues Auber and Halévy were decreed in 1858 (and completed in 1862), the rue Haussmann was decreed in 1857 (this section completed 1863), the rue Lafayette was decreed in 1862 (completed 1867)— five kilometers in a straight line—and the rue du 4 Septembre (then the rue du 10 Décembre),[31] as well as some lesser streets. What was emerging was an intricate urban pattern that would eventually link up with the gare St. Lazare, the Etoile, and the Monceau plain via the boulevard Malesherbes. The insalubrious area between the Louvre-Tuileries and the boulevards Madeleine-Capucines-Italiens, which Louis Lazare described as a "labyrinth of narrow and tortuous streets, a collection of hovels whose wretched appearance can be compared to those eliminated by [the building of] the rue de Rivoli,"[32] sharpened Haussmann's appetite for additional new streets. By 1859 the carrefour that would soon embrace the new opera house was virtually completed.

On January 14, 1858, at the entrance to the Salle Lepelletier, Felice Orsini, an Italian nationalist with strong conspiratorial ties, tried to assassinate Louis Napoléon with a huge bomb. Eight were killed and 156 wounded. The emperor and the empress escaped, although the horses drawing their carriage were killed. Haussmann was in the Salle Lepelletier awaiting the emperor when the bomb exploded. Louis Napoléon, standing amid the devastation and torn bodies, directed rescue operations.[33] Another Paris opera house was cursed by a royal assassination attempt.

Haussmann, on March 13, 1858, worked out a deal between the state and the city of Paris for funds to create the rues Auber and Halévy and the place de l'Opéra, and the decrees of "public utility" were issued on November 14, 1858. The rues Scribe, Meyerbeer, and Gluck, which would complete the network of streets surrounding the future Opéra, were implicit though not included in these decrees. In July 1858, the architect Rohault de Fleury drew up a plan of the property lots of the site, along with a table for their expropriation, that outlines the complete network of streets. The definitive site was not yet fixed, but it was clear to all—not least to the ambitious architects who sketched proposals—that this would be the eventual home of the new opera house.[34]

In 1860 Haussmann made public his proposal for a new opera house site, exhibiting a "Plan of the Projected Site and Its Surroundings" (April 15–May 5), to solicit public comment and additional proposals. His appointed review commission, predictably, favored Haussmann's plan.[35] There was already a strong prejudice in favor of the neighborhood. The Grand Boulevards, planted with double rows of trees and laid out between 1685 and 1705, following Pierre Bullet's 1676 plans, had become popular promenades by the eighteenth century and were early urbanized with hotels, theaters, and cafes for fashionable society. "The elite of [the] Parisians . . . occupied the boulevard and considered it their fief," wrote Gustave Claudin, a journalist and gossip of the day. "There seemed to exist a kind of invisible moral barrier which forbade access . . . to common folk, to ordinary people, to the insignificant, who might pass by but who did not stop, all being aware that they did not belong here." The *boulevard*, Claudin specifies, "was already understood, between 1840 and 1848, [to be] the area from the rue Drouot to the new opera."[36]

The new opera house would anchor the neighborhood, fix the Grands Boulevards as the city's entertainment center, consecrate the development of the area, and encourage the further growth of prosperity. Increasing property values along the rue de la Paix indicate the flow of money into the quarter, where the elegance of the buildings had been driving rents up since the early days of the July Monarchy. This escalation accelerated in the second half of the century and proved immune to the economic cycles and fluctuations that affected so many neighborhoods in Paris. By the time the avenue de l'Opéra was opened, the rue de la Paix was already established as a luxury neighborhood. Now it became even more desirable. In 1865 rents around the new Opéra shot up to 1,000–2,500 francs a square meter. In the old *quartiers* of the east rents were 150–300 francs; in the first and second arrondissements, respectively, the average was 719 francs and 956 francs; around les Halles or the place du Théatre-Français rents were 1,200 francs.[37] The fortune of the new neighborhood was assured.[38] The gare St. Lazare (D 2), the transportation hub of the neighborhood, became the busiest and biggest railroad terminus for suburban travelers. By 1869 the *gare* was handling 13,254,000 passengers a year, more than 80 percent of them commuters, ample evidence of what the shift of Paris population and urbanization from east to west meant for the new western suburbs. The other six Paris termini together handled no more than 21,417,000 passengers.[39] Western Paris was booming. The emergence of the *quartier* as the home of the new department stores, the *grands magasins*—the Galeries Lafayette and Printemps in particular—was but another indication that Paris had a new center. The new stores abandoned the old city for the new and added the "impersonal dialogue of their display windows with the pedestrians. Like the cafés that set up their tables on the sidewalks . . . they offered the spectacle of their showcases to an anonymous public whom they hoped to make their clientele."[40]

But no building so symbolized what Paris had become after midcentury as Garnier's Opéra. The decision, taken by the emperor and Count Walewski, who replaced Fould as minister of state in 1860, to open the design of a new opera house to public competition, proved momentous. Walewski's *arrêté* of December 29, 1860, was published in the official newspaper, *Le Moniteur Universel*, the next day:

> Considering that the composition of a theater project excites, with good reason, public attention, and that it is the duty of the administration to call upon architects and to solicit all people of intelligence . . . a public competition for the redaction of an Opera project to be built in Paris is opened.[41]

There were 170 projects from which seven finalists were chosen. Charles Garnier, the ultimate winner, had not previously done a major work in Paris. He was summoned to the Tuileries to present his project to Louis Napoléon and Eugénie, who was openly hostile to the upstart who had defeated her own favorite architect, Viollet-le-Duc. "What kind of style is this?" she challenged Garnier. "It is not a style! It is neither Greek, nor Louis XVI, nor even Louis XV!" Garnier—as his widow, Louise, recounts the story—abandoned courtly decorum. "Those styles have had their day," he answered. "It is Napoléon III, yet you complain!"[42]

In the Opéra, the cliché runs, reiterating contemporary criticism, the new style is opulence, comfortable excess, a celebration of fleshy amplitude. The Opéra, wrote the journalist Ernest Chesneau in 1875, reflects a new Paris, enlarged, aerated, cleansed, transformed "with magnificence by the imperial government." It is an opera house "worthy of the grandeur, the luxury, and the arts" of the new city.[43] This architectural jewel is richly set amid elegant cafes, restaurants, hotels, shops, and apartment buildings at one end of a new and magnificent avenue that leads to a monument of immense prestige, the Louvre. The Opéra took fourteen years to build, cost thirty-three million francs, and occupied the talents of ninety artists to realize its elaborate artistic program and extravagant ornamental detail. Joining the Louvre and the Tuileries cost twenty-five millions; building les Halles, thirty-nine millions. The Opéra was easily the most costly building erected by the Second Empire. Louis Napoléon did not spend this fortune on an imperial palace for himself but on an opera house, which, along with railroad stations, were the urban extravagances of the nineteenth century, the defining structures. The emperor chose to celebrate himself and his regime not as had the kings with their châteaux, or even his uncle, with his victory arches. Paris itself was to be his monument. The Opéra was a palace for art and those who could afford it, a celebration of civilization, as a railroad station celebrated industry, science, capital, and progress. Napoléon III might reign because of peasant votes, but he declared his triumph, his modernism, his culture, the humanity of his reign, with an opera house.

Although literally supported by the new building technologies of the age, Garnier's Opéra shows none of them. All the structural iron, for example, is masked by the traditional materials of a classical building. Railroad stations and market sheds might proclaim the new industrial age: the Opéra harkened back to French classicism. The same may be said of the auditorium itself, modeled on the principles of Victor Louis's Théâtre in Bordeaux and the Salle Pelletier in Paris. But Garnier's Opéra, speaking the familiar language of French classicism, using the vocabulary of the Beaux-Arts tradition—he had won the Prix de Rome in 1848—was original. It was not a design Haussmann would have chosen, judging from the other theaters he commissioned in Paris.

Garnier had constant dealings with the city and Haussmann, but he did not work for the prefect or the city: he worked for the state. Within the general outlines of his prize-winning design the architect was free to follow his inspiration. Haussmann would have kept him on a tight leash, as he did Jean-Antoine-Gabriel Davioud, the architect of the two theaters constructed at the Place du Châtelet. The prefect insisted that the theaters imitate Louis's Théâtre de Bordeaux and be flanked by buildings housing upper-story apartments and ground-story shops. Garnier's Opéra stands isolated on its urban island, like the great historical monuments of Paris. Haussmann also constricted the budget: the larger of the two, the Théâtre du Châtelet, cost 3,379,282 francs. Davioud had to update the Bordeaux opera by abbreviating "the public entrance spaces to a blunt sequence of facade, portico, vestibule, central office with flanking pairs of rectilinear stairs, and an auditorium corridor."[44] The Davioud-Haussmann imitation is functional rather than symbolic, conceived as ornament and balance for the Place du Châtelet.

Garnier's Opéra brilliantly used the city, both indoors and out.

The Grand Escalier is an extraordinary creation. It functioned as an internal boulevard. *La sortie de l'Opéra*, the spectacle of an audience leaving the theater, brought indoors the spectacle of people promenading on the Grands Boulevards, and required similar axial vistas— "a monumental enfilade of spaces whose processional sequence could easily be read by the public."[45] The democratic-authoritarian politics of Bonapartism are also present. Everyone of whatever social rank ascended the Grand Escalier to reach his or her seat. Those who had the best seats had fewer stairs to climb, while the socially inferior continued to mount the social ladder, metaphorically and physically.[46] Of course, only those who had already arrived socially could afford the opera, and the social distinctions enacted on the Grand Escalier, as on the boulevards, were within the elite. Claudin's snobbishness about who belonged on the Grands Boulevards also pertained to the Opéra.

For those who could buy a ticket, attendance at the Opéra was itself a form of theater. The Grand Escalier was "a vast, spontaneous theater where the public performs to itself." For those both arriving and leaving, the avenue de l'Opéra provided the necessary grandeur for the procession, a triumphal yet civilian route. The widening of the avenue de l'Opéra, in the summer of 1955, destroyed some of the original illusion. The broad sidewalks, lined with trees, which lead directly to the sculpture of Orpheus strumming his lyre, were amputated. The splendid urban carpet that conducted spectators to and from the Opéra was gone, leaving only a broad, commercial street.[47]

Movement and theater, expressed under the intimidating symbolism of the authoritarian state, which determined the pace and purpose of urban mobility, is the essence of the new Paris, so sumptuously and brilliantly embodied in the new Opéra and the new *quartier* of the Opéra. It is now banks and hotels, restaurants and elegant apartments, and shortly a new commercial center dominated by the department store that declared and defined Haussmann's Paris. "The old Paris is passing," wrote Balzac, "following the kings who have passed."[48]

· IX ·

"The Vice-Emperor Is the
Prefect of the Seine"

HAUSSMANN'S LONG CLIMB TO THE PREFECTURE OF PARIS SEEMS NOT to have taught him patience or humility. But it did teach him how to get, increase, and hold power in a complicated administrative system designed to prevent so formidable an accumulation of personal preponderance. His appetite for power was voracious, early revealed, long frustrated, and probably insatiable. He waited nearly twenty years before he held and wielded significant power, and even longer for the prefecture of the Seine. Forced abstinence sharpened his desire, tightened his grip, focused his will. His amalgamation and consolidation of power as prefect of the Seine is a case study of single-minded, obsessive innovation. If Paris was a state within France, Haussmann's prefecture was very nearly an independent principality.

Haussmann inherited an administrative system that dated from the Consulate, specifically the law of 28 Pluviôse, year VIII (February 17, 1800), which created the two prefects of the Seine and their bureaucratic machinery. Napoléon was concerned—as has been every subsequent government of France—that the prefect of the Seine might become a dominant national political figure.[1] He consequently created several checks on the prefect's authority. The Council General of the Seine, the major countervailing power, "rep-

211

resented, in the constitutional order, a natural counterweight to the authority of the prefect." The body was thought "the eye of the government as the prefect was its arm," and was to monitor the administrative officer.[2] Article 17 of the pluviôse law made the Council General of the Seine the Paris Municipal Council as well.[3] In addition the law created a Council of the Prefecture, a five-member tribunal to deal with questions arising from the administration itself, and its dealing with the prefect of police, who shared administrative responsibilities with the prefect of the Seine.

The secretary general of the prefecture ran the office and served as a kind of buffer between the prefect and the general public. Between 2 and 3 p.m. each day he received, by appointment, all who had business with the prefecture. He oversaw three major departments at the Hôtel de Ville and had, among other responsibilities, to draw up the budget, convoke the Council General, keep minutes of its meetings, and maintain the archives of the prefecture and its four administrative divisions. He was also charged with the organization of religion, public instruction, hospitals, prisons, public works, canals, and water supply. These administrative counterweights did not much hinder the prefect's authority, even before Haussmann's reforms. So long as the prefect avoided financial crisis, his power to act was not dependent on the council, a loophole Haussmann brilliantly exploited; and the secretary general was a man of his own choosing.

The real checks on the prefect's power were the jurisdictional struggles with the prefect of police, the hindrances imposed by the nature and inefficiency of bureaucracy itself, and the national government of emperor, Corps Législatif, and the minister of the interior. Haussmann understood this. Nowhere is his bureaucratic brilliance more evident than in his ultimately successful manipulation of the Paris administration, which he first adjusted to fit his needs and then keep essentially independent of the authorities originally created to check its power.

Haussmann had been sounded out for the prefecture of police. He had declined "categorically."[4] He wanted only the more powerful of the two Paris prefectures. Once he had it he deeply resented sharing power. A manuscript report of 1855, "Conflit permanent entre les deux Préfectures sous les régimes," although not in Haussmann's hand, surely came from his office. The best solution, the document argued, was to abolish the dual prefecture, but "if circumstances have made the simultaneous existence of two prefects necessary, at least the jurisdiction of each of these functionaries ought to be defined." The author had precise and rigid lines in mind: "To one belongs the protection and care of persons, to the other the management of collective interests. Without this rule, so clearly recognized by the municipal law of 1855, there can only be confusion and anarchy in the administration of the city."[5] The problem was determining where one order of jurisdiction ended and another began: when, precisely did persons become the public? Louis Napoléon deftly exploited the jealousies of his two prefects as a check on the authority of each. He scrupulously balanced favors and honors: "If the Emperor granted me a favor," Haussmann wrote, shifting the blame from Louis Napoléon, "the prefect of Police did not allow him a moment's repose until he had obtained the equivalent."[6]

In 1856, the year that saw the highest bread prices during the Second Empire, there was a major struggle between the two prefects. Haussmann insisted bread prices be maintained at sixty centimes a pound so the city did not have to pay an additional subsidy. Piétri, the prefect of police, wanted the price lowered, requiring additional city support, because of the financial crisis and unemployment. Haussmann lost this confrontation,[7] but this was not the usual outcome.

There was a delightful illogicality of jurisdictions. The prefect of police was in charge of cleaning the streets, although the prefect of the Seine had charge of bridges and roads. Haussmann was convinced the former "took pleasure in caring for the macadam as badly as possible" to embarrass his administration and needle the city engineers. The employees of the prefect of police opened wide the taps that sent water down the gutters for street cleaning "without any concern for the observations of the water department which thought, with reason, that it was above all necessary to assure a supply of water for private use in the various neighborhoods."[8] The ultimate settlement of these jurisdictional squabbles and, more important, Haussmann's place in the city administration, was not entirely his own doing. Much depended on circumstances beyond his control.

The Orsini plot, which nearly blew up the emperor on his way to the opera, forced Piétri's resignation and brought a new minister of the interior. Piétri's successor, Symphor Boittelle, the former prefect of the Yonne, was distantly related to Haussmann and bent to his kinsman's will, as would Piétri's son, the last police prefect of the empire. The new minister of the interior, General Espinasse, was also far more sympathetic to the prefect than had been his predecessor. In addition, Haussmann was reaching the apogee of his power. The definitive settlement of jurisdictions came on October 10, 1859, when the emperor granted the prefect of the Seine complete control over the streets—lighting, cleaning, care of the sewers, emptying cesspools, public transportation, overseeing bakeries and butcher shops, regulating markets, provisioning the city, indeed all administrative services of the city, without exception—that had been reserved to the prefect of police by the law of 12 messidor, year VIII (June 30, 1800).[9] After six years of struggle, Haussmann was supreme. Now he aspired to remove himself from the control of the minister of the interior.

When Persigny was at the helm Haussmann was uneasy. Emile Ollivier, one of the shrewdest observers of the day, said Haussmann feared Persigny's disorderly manner and imperiousness, and "told the emperor that . . . he would go into retirement if the emperor did not create for him a clearly defined, independent position, which would remove him from the shadow of the minister of the interior and the vexations of his office. He demanded that he be given the title of minister of Paris."[10] The emperor was disposed to grant the audacious demand, but the other ministers objected. Rouher, so fecund in compromise, found the solution: Haussmann would sit with the Council of Ministers, and take part in the deliberations of the General Assembly and the meetings of the Council of State having to do with Paris. He dated the pinnacle of his career soon afterward (December 7, 1862), when Louis Napoléon decorated him with the Grand'Croix of the Legion of Honor "in front of all the branches of government."[11] The emperor's favor seemed assured. There remained only the two elective bodies, the national Corps Législatif and the Municipal Council, that might check the prefect's power.

The Corps Législatif had to approve the Paris budget each year. The first years of Haussmann's tenure presented no problems. There were no new taxes imposed, the transformation of Paris was ever before their eyes and enormously popular, the authoritarian empire was at its height and committed to the work, and the miracles of deficit spending were unquestioned. There were some in the legislature who complained, but until the early 1860s no serious hindrances were put in Haussmann's way. He believed that given regular, direct access to the Corps Législatif he "could conquer their natural sympathies and give myself a new force to use against the pygmies who succeeded to the ministry of the Interior."[12] He alone attributed his success to personal charm. Contemporaries found him charmless. It was not the lure of his personality so much as the novelty of the enterprise, a healthy economy, the popularity he shared with a still-successful emperor, and the insignificance or ineptitude of the opposition that brought Haussmann a string of triumphs. He was more feared than loved, and so long as he kept the city's debt manageable, or its size murky, the Corps Législatif did not interfere.

The corps was a nationally elected body, dominated by provincial notables who represented an overwhelmingly rural constituency. Accustomed to getting their own way, they had been sent to Paris with a long list of provincial projects. The notables had little love for Paris, although most remained attached to the emperor. Haussmann, perhaps remembering his days of administering repression in the Var, the Yonne, and Bordeaux, overestimated both his own powers and the willingness of provincial elites to be manipulated, persuaded, or bullied. During his Paris years he gradually lost his feel for provincial sensibilities. He also failed to appreciate the growing influence of a brilliant parliamentary opposition, headed by the brilliant Emile Ollivier. From about 1860, concomitant with Haussmann's growing power, the opposition increasingly took the initiative and was hostile, sometimes actively hostile, to him and his projects. Paris had been, since 19 vendémiaire, year IV (October 10, 1795), divided administratively into twelve arrondissements, which functioned as municipalities, each with its own mayor, created by Napoléon's reforms (28 pluviôse, year VIII/February 16, 1800). When the limits of Paris were extended (January 1, 1860), the city was reorganized into its present configuration of twenty arrondissements, spiraling out from the center "like a snail's shell." Under Louis-Philippe each of these arrondissements, roughly equivalent to our wards, elected three representatives to the central municipal council. Under the provisional government set up after the 1848 revolution, there had briefly been a single mayor of Paris, but the Second Republic suppressed the office to return to the system in which the prefect of the Seine was also the mayor of Paris. It is this system of an elected Assembly of Notables that Haussmann inherited. It was clear such a city government, committed to a conservative fiscal policy and opposed to borrowing, was unfit for the great work of transforming Paris.

The emperor, when he first revealed his plans to Haussmann, had thought of establishing a shadow municipal council to get around the obstructionist elected council. Haussmann's political sense was better: he wanted the official council appointed rather than subverted. The municipal law of May 5, 1855, supplemented by the law of June 16, 1859, which took into account the expansion of Paris, made the Paris city government unique in the kingdom. The Municipal Council—originally thirty-six members, expanded to sixty with the annexation—was now composed of appointees, chosen by the prefect but officially appointed by the minister of the interior. The Paris government, hand-picked by the emperor's henchman, was thus made national rather than local. The Municipal Council, presided over by the prefect, had the responsibility of voting the city's budget. There was, in addition, a body of 114 appointed councilors, which included the mayors of arrondissements—after 1855 also appointed by the prefect—as well as city functionaries, an important group of industrialists and businessmen, bankers, members of the liberal professions, property owners, and (only in 1869) a worker (a porcelain decorator). The meetings of both bodies were closed to the public, no stenographic record was kept, and the only reports issued were terse analyses of actions taken.

Haussmann's reform of the Paris administration legally destroyed

Parisian particularism. In the Rouher Papers is a six-page manuscript document, dated January 13, 1864, that presents the question
of the Paris administration in the most candid terms. The document, in a scribe's hand, carries no provenance. If it was not Haussmann's work it was almost certainly approved by him, for it
faithfully expresses his views, contains some favorite locutions—the
regular reference to the Paris population as "a floating population of
workers" or "nomads"—and appears to be a memo requested by
Rouher.

Any election of the city government, the argument runs, "in the
midst of all the . . . agitation of public opinion," would be dangerous. Paris is composed of

> a floating mass of workers who have come to the city [today], ready
> to leave tomorrow, of families whose members are dispersed
> throughout the city by their diverse places of work, of nomad
> renters who are incessantly moving from quarter to quarter, without
> knowing a fixed residence or a patrimonial place. It is an accumula-
> tion of men who are strangers to each other, who are attracted only
> by impressions and the most deplorable suggestions, who have no
> mind of their own, since they are not dominated by a strong nation-
> al feeling.

Giving them a vote in municipal elections would mean the city government would be chosen "by the lowest passions," turned over to
"the enemies of the [national] government," who would insinuate
their demagogy into the Hôtel de Ville. "This great city belongs to
France. Its administration ought not to be submitted to the chance
of a local election." It is the enlightened leaders chosen by the emperor who bring independence to Paris.[13] The anomie of the modern city, inundated by a nomadic population, makes it unfit for
democratic procedures. Immigrants outnumbered native Parisians
and treated the city as "a great consumer's market, an enormous
work place, or, simply, a rendez-vous for pleasure. It is not their
home."*

Pays (country), the word the French use to describe their natal province, has no
English equivalent.

It would be a mistake to turn the government of such a city over to "a body emanating from a local election, with its relatively narrow, egoist views, subject to the changes of caprice," which would create "a state within a state."[14] Haussmann did not conceive of the city as having neighborhoods with distinct interests: he thought only of Paris as a whole, a national capital, and rode roughshod over the pleas for local consideration. The historical coherence and integrity of particular neighborhoods was of little concern. He thought of Paris as a series of street systems integrated into a single great urban system. He himself had no roots in Paris, despite having been born there. He razed his natal neighborhood with the same businesslike indifference he showed to the slums.

Haussmann, who had "climbed . . . all the steps [in the administration]. . .without skipping a one,"[15] had the pride of a self-made man. The distaste he had acquired for the political compromises of parliamentary government, coupled with his unquestioned faith in himself and the capacity of administration to confront and solve the central problems of his age, were now to be exercised in Paris. He carefully built a personal empire that depended completely on himself, just as he depended completely on the emperor.

He did not much care for politics and its elaborate interplay of self-esteem and self-interest, persuasion and coercion, influence and leverage, ideology and ego. He understood them well enough, but all his abilities were bent to constructing a space that was free of politics, where he could reign. He consistently protested his disinterest in politics. He was prefect of the Seine, an administrative figure above the tumult of parliamentary politics. Haussmann insisted he was no more than a loyal public servant whose appointment was earned by his professional capabilities.

Urban transformation was to be the work of the expert. The prefecture of the Seine had been "so long the preserve of political personages," he declared to the Senate, that "the traditions of order and regularity, which are the glory of the French administration, were lost."[16] He wanted to restore these traditions. He was fortunate that the emperor, one of the most brilliant and adroit politicians of the age, was interested in results, not means. As Haussmann put it: "His Majesty only showed a mediocre interest in questions of administrative procedure in so far as they were not translatable into hard facts, and he had the same attitude about financial questions."[17] Haussmann was free to form the bureaucracy in his own image, and similarly free to avoid boring the emperor with administrative details, especially those related to his financial dealings.

Adolphe Thiers's accusation that Haussmann, not Rouher, was the second most powerful figure in France has much truth: Rouher had constantly to deal with a hostile Corps Législatif, Haussmann did not. The modern figure closest to Haussmann in amassing personal political power through administration, by evading institutional, legal, and constitutional controls, is Robert Moses, who built and managed the parks, bridges, highways, tunnels, wharves, and airports of New York City. All traffic flowing in and through the city came under his command.[18] Moses established his administrative kingdom in a democratic culture and, ironically enough, may have exercised more power than did Haussmann, whom he deeply admired.

Haussmann's initial meeting with his entire staff set the tone and temper of his administration. They were all assembled, in pseudomilitary order by division and bureau, in the Salle du Trône of the Hôtel de Ville. The new prefect, accompanied by Charles Merruau, the secretary general, greeted each department head, who in turn presented his staff.[19] Haussmann said a few polite words to each. Then, positioning himself "in front of one of the monumental fireplaces at the end of the [room], before the one traditionally surmounted by a portrait of the sovereign (near the entrance to the prefect's office)," he addressed them. He described his slow rise in the bureaucracy and announced he had always been and would always remain "my own personnel director. I myself intend to judge the worth of the services performed by each of you," and to reward and punish accordingly. He would not welcome recommendations, which reveal that their author has "little confidence in his own merit or in the intelligence or justice of his superiors." But he would reward "hard workers," who followed his own example. "This authoritarian speech," as Haussmann himself characterized it, "coming from a man in the fullness of his maturity, whose physical presence and resolute air matched the firmness of his words, produced a kind of magnetic effect on the auditors . . . to whom I addressed myself, and who cried out, spontaneously, Vive l'Empereur!"[20]

His physical strength, his pride in his height and physique, did indeed strike an awesome note. His imposing stature seemed an appropriate vessel for his authority. His dramatization of self, his public posturings, were a well-calibrated display of power. His physical presence and his imperious manner were doubtless more significant in asserting authority than his imagined personal charm or conversational agility.

As an administrator Haussmann was overbearing, irresistible, indefatigable, and efficient. He spoke habitually of his staff as his "militant personnel," an army whose task was "to go forth to the conquest of Old Paris." This army "would permit me to undertake ripping the quarters of the center of the city from the tangle of streets virtually impenetrable to traffic," gutting "the sordid, filthy, crowded houses which were, for the most part, but entry ways to misery and disease, and subjects of shame for a great country like France."[21] In addition to these enormous, heroic tasks, which always elicited from him the language and imagery of military conquest, were the mundane and trivial matters that crossed his desk and that he handled with the same attention and concern. It is one of the hallmarks of a great administrator that all the business of his bureaucracy be considered important. From paper clips to patronage to boulevards, Haussmann oversaw everything. His administrative capacity and stamina were remarkable.

There was a steady stream of requests for patronage, for a place or a commission in Haussmann's vast army. "I hasten to announce to Your Excellency that I have appointed M. Villeminot, whom you have kindly recommended to me, to the post of *Receveur des Halles et Marchés* for Paris," he wrote the minister of the interior. A few weeks later he acknowledged the recommendation of M. Antoine Maurin, *artiste-peintre*, who sought work. "I will not fail to place the name of this artist under the eyes of the special commission of Beaux-Arts, at the first occasion," and if he is judged capable of executing religious subjects, "I can assure you, M. le Ministre, that I will show toward this artist the interest that Your Excellency has already given him."[22]

Then there were the trivialities: complaints and demands for special consideration. "The constant traffic of carriages and omnibuses along the rue de Grenelle . . . makes this street extremely noisy," the minister of the interior wrote Haussmann. The employees of the ministry had to keep their windows closed, and still they were bothered by the noise. "The only practical way to remedy this problem," the minister continued, "appears to me to be to macadamize the rue de Grenelle [D 4] where it passes the ministry." Haussmann ordered the street paved,[23] although he disliked macadam, which was difficult to keep clean, clogged the sewers, was costly, and inefficient: "Alternately muddy and powdery, the streets must be cleaned and sprayed with extreme care."[24] Louis Napoléon, perhaps influenced by his Anglophilia, ordered this English street surfacing used in Paris. Hitherto macadam had been employed only on the highways.

A petition sent to the minister of the interior and forwarded to Haussmann concerned a certain Buzlat, a wine merchant at the port de Bercy. He complained that he had received permission to set up a table and some chairs in the public way in front of his establishment, but that now an action was being brought against him for having set up a bench with baskets of oysters he offered for sale. "It is quite true," Haussmann wrote, "that Buzlat was authorized to set up his tables and chairs in front of his establishment, but, as the authorization indicates, it was for the use of customers and not to be used as a display of whatever nature it might be. Consequently, it is my opinion that there is no more to be said about Buzlat's petition."[25]

Haussmann was a resourceful scrounger, using abandoned materials for new projects. He learned of some discarded iron gates and wrote the minister of the interior—the scrap technically belonged to the state, not the city—requesting permission to use the metal "to fence the fountain to be constructed in the Marché St. Martin."[26] When the minister of the Maison de l'Empereur et des Beaux-Arts wrote him that the steps on the pedestal of the statue of Louis XIV, in the Place des Victoires, were in bad repair, Haussmann reminded him that the monument "belonging to the state," was not in his jurisdiction.[27] Nor was the statue of Henri IV, on the Pont-Neuf, whose pedestal was similarly in need of repair.[28]

He was bombarded with requests that arrived without ministerial sponsorship. A certain enterprising Sageret wrote asking Haussmann "to designate a certain number of artists and writers who would be charged with perpetuating, by pen and etching tool, the memory of the great works executed at Paris in the past twelve years." The prefect responded that he thought it premature thus to celebrate "what the Emperor has done in Paris," but he thanked Sageret for "the sympathetic concern for my administration that informed your letter and for sending along with it the bit of verse."[29] More serious or troublesome were the requests from friends and relatives. His uncle wrote, in 1869, complaining about how much he was billed by the city for work on the public way in front of his house on the boulevard Haussmann. The prefect took refuge in bureaucratic punctiliousness: "I can only send you a copy of the report that has been submitted to me. . . . Be assured," he continued, "that I deeply regret, because of the exigencies of how things work, not to be able to give to this request a response in conformity with your desires." As for appealing a prefectorial decision, Haussmann informed him "that the file in this affair was sent to the Council of State on October 16" and was out of his hands.[30]

The heroic transformation of Paris has overshadowed Haussmann's lesser projects and responsibilities, a few of which deserve rescue from relative oblivion, to round out the picture of the administrator. The Hôtel Carnavalet, built by Pierre Lescot and Jean Bullant, and restored by François Mansart—and celebrated as the temporary home of Mme de Sévigné—was acquired by the city of Paris in 1866. Haussmann made it into a museum of the history of the city, which it has remained. His patronage supported as well the publication, in sixteen volumes, of a *Histoire général de Paris*, a collection of historical and archeological documents, for which he organized a special service at the Hôtel de Ville. Even the seal of the city was Haussmann's work:

> Originally the arms of the medieval water carriers, the seal had been appropriated by Louis XIV . . . and invested with the royal fleur-de-

lis. Rejected during the French Revolution . . . the seal was reinvoked by Baron Haussmann in 1853. It was Haussmann himself who added the banderole to the royal seal to express his hopes in the aftermath of 1848, that the Empire would not founder.[31]

It was power, not personal wealth, that drove and satisfied Haussmann. He was himself scrupulously honest, although many around him got rich off insider information. Knowing precisely where a particular street was to be cut, buying up the affected property for far less than it would bring once expropriations began, was a sure, but illegal, way to make a fortune. "From the moment the project for a new street is taken under consideration, it is important to guard against any indiscretion about the precise location of this street and the extent of expropriations it will entail."[32] But if corruption lurked everywhere in the precincts of the Hôtel de Ville, Haussmann himself took no part, probably did not wink at it, and certainly did not enrich himself. On his own testimony he refused a number of bribes, although he did not prosecute those who would corrupt him.

One case involved a relative who offered the prefect 400,000 francs—he himself would retain another 100,000 for making the contact—"in return for . . . assistance" in landing the contract for the extension of the boulevard de Strasbourg. Haussmann wrote that he showed his "relative by marriage," whom he does not name, the penal code, promised not to mention the attempted bribe, and insisted this is why "this great artery was not given to private industry, as was the [original part of] the boulevard de Strasbourg."[33] There are no contemporary charges of personal peculation. He died in debt and his château at Cestas had to be sold to pay his taxes.

His probity in an age of speculation, public and private opulence, and flexible moral standards is perfectly in character. Haussmann was a dedicated civil servant, a proud member of the new bourgeoisie who had rejected the money-making professions for public service. Different from previous generations of rich and titled men who had held his high office out of noblesse oblige, Haussmann was a new man, trained in the Napoleonic schools. He had his way to make in the bruising world so brilliantly depicted by Balzac. Among his bitterest struggles while prefect were with the old banking establishment, the landlords, and the speculators, all of whom he loathed. These were men with no civic dimension, no sense of their obligations to the common good, who, in Haussmann's view, were interested only in dining—and dining sumptuously—at the public trough. And they were the very individuals who had shut him out during his years of obscurity. The sincerity of his convictions is beyond question, reinforced by a sense of personal slight.

For all his many virtues and talents, Haussmann had a flaw that would prove his undoing. His arrogance was most often expressed through disdain or contempt, especially unmoderated when directed at those who could not hurt or hinder him. He was a bully. As the work on Paris advanced, he became reckless, convinced the emperor would continue to support him without question. He ignored the significant political changes in French politics, the ineluctable movement toward a liberal empire, which he despised, as well as the significant increase in power of the traditional elites he snubbed. Not only did his arrogance ultimately upset the delicate administrative balance he had so carefully built over the years, but it made him increasingly dependent on the Corps Législatif—whose goodwill he had not carefully cultivated—to pay the city's mounting debts. It became more and more difficult, more politically costly, for Louis Napoléon to defend his prefect. Haussmann's borrowings and financial juggling eventually caught up with him in 1869. He survived the bitter parliamentary fight over the Paris budget of that year, but the narrowness of his victory signaled the end of his career.

Haussmann blamed his fall on others, on the selfish machinations of politicians, on the greed of the speculators and landowners, on democracy. Yet his own mistakes brought him down. He had a deep contempt for democracy and thought the people's elected representatives an obstacle to good, efficient government: a collection of bumpkins he would handle, coerce, or bamboozle. But the legislature could not be indefinitely ignored and snubbed. When his own financial jugglings put him in their power, revenge against his long years of arrogance and disdain played no small part in his fall.

In the end he overreached himself. Transforming Paris was a question of money, enormous, unheard of amounts of money. For a time Haussmann was borne on the tide created by the forces of capitalism he himself had helped unshackle. But he could not continue indefinitely. His financial arrangements became increasingly devious and convoluted. If not strictly criminal, they were only marginally legal, and considered suspect even in an age of buccaneer speculation. His fiduciary legerdemain required more and more skill and agility, and seriously depleted his administrative and personal capital. From being a financial wizard he became a charlatan, mocked and satirized in the press and the legislature. Yet his reputation for administrative genius survived, as did the bureaucratic machinery he had created. And, of course, so did Paris. Haussmann's debts were not retired until 1929.

· X ·

Money

"BUILD, ALWAYS BUILD," SAID HAUSSMANN, QUOTING A REMARK OF Louis XIV to his architect, Mansard. "We will go ahead, others will pay for it."[1] It was a favorite anecdote and perfectly describes his practice in the last years of his prefectship. But at the outset all was dark and doubtful. He had arrived at the highest position in the administrative state, but the question that had bedeviled all the prefects of Seine—where would the money come from?—remained unanswered. His immediate predecessor had just been sacked for failing to solve this riddle of the sphinx.

"Ah, come in, young man," said Berger warmly, advancing with open arms to greet his successor. "I've been expecting you. I've been waiting to shake your hand."[2] The Auvergnat's easy familiarity set the tone for the first meeting of the new and departing prefect of Seine, underscoring not only their different personalities but different concerns. Berger explained the cause of the friction between the Elysée and the Hôtel de Ville and defended his conservative economic views, which caused his dismissal. He was opposed to any additional taxes on the Parisians—there had recently been a surtax on all wine entering the city—for he did not believe the populace or its representatives would stand for more exactions. As for the city budget, which he believed should be administered "as a good head of the

227

family looks after his own affairs," there was little money to spare for great public works and he did not believe in borrowing. Berger was both parsimonious and unenthusiastic about transforming Paris. The new prefect requested from his host the receipts and expenses for the city in 1852 and a copy of the 1853 budget. His social obligations fulfilled, Haussmann was "impatient to return home to study in depth and to compare the related parts of these two documents."[3]

For Haussmann there was poetry in a budget, "especially a budget for Paris," which shows "the future unveiled by a patient hand, seen in all its perspectives by a vigilant eye, and appreciated with maturity by a judgment doubtless fallible but keen and reflective."[4] The 1853 budget underestimated the expected receipts for the year and over-estimated expenses. Berger had consistently manipulated his budgets in this way to convince the Corps Législatif that Paris was poor and needed subsidies if it were to undertake any public works. The new prefect, anxious to attract private capital to his enterprises, would later do the contrary, making Paris appear a sound investment.

Haussmann shared a number of the new economic ideas of his day that are usually, although not very accurately, lumped under the heading St. Simonian, after the eccentric and influential socialist thinker, Claude-Henri, comte de St. Simon (1760–1825). Debt-financed expenditure, the argument ran, required no additional taxation and added no burden to the treasury provided the expenditures were productive and promoted the growth of economic activity. The tax rate remained stable, while expanded government revenues from economic growth and an expanding tax base not only covered interest and amortized costs but produced a profit, which in turn allowed for more long-term borrowing. Urbanization was at the heart of imperial politics: surpluses of capital and especially labor power would be absorbed through employment.

Louis Napoléon, however vague his social ideas, had been attached to public works as a means of ameliorating if not eliminating poverty. The importance of a right to work ideology in the 1848 revolution, and the dismal and deadly failure of the National Workshops designed to implement that ideology by providing employment on public works, intensified the emperor's interest in giving jobs to an unruly population. The political prestige to be gained from a public display of efficiency provided further stimulus. Louis Napoléon's first public projects were neither strictly strategic nor socially meliorating: he completed work on the Louvre-Tuileries, the Hôtel de Ville, and the rue de Rivoli.

Among the tenets of Haussmann's economic faith was "the rapid fruitfulness of all public utility projects," and its corollary, the theory of "productive expenditure." This said, the expansion of public works enhanced revenue in the form of wages and new taxes, and provided excess city income for further investment: "Could I but discover a place to put my lever to raise the heavy weight that I had to bear . . . I would be happier than Archimedes."[5] Haussmann discovered such a place: Berger's underestimation of revenue and overestimation of expenses, which provided a small surplus that could be used as seed money for borrowing. Not money to be spent directly on the various projects then underway—for which it would be a mere pittance—but money to be used to attract long-term loans that would be repaid from the profits derived from enhanced property values, which in turn meant higher direct and indirect taxes for the city. There would be no need to impose new taxes or surtaxes on already existing exactions. The emperor had specifically forbidden additional taxation, fearing the Parisian bourgeoisie, so profoundly alienated by his coup d'état, would not stand for it.[6]

Haussmann has simplified his discovery in the telling, making himself the Archimedes of urban financing. It was not merely Berger's bookkeeping that held the secret; Paris revenues were on the rise, largely owing to the emperor's building program already underway when Haussmann arrived at the Hôtel de Ville. The *octroi*, the duty paid on all goods entering the city, including building materials, had risen by more than two million francs between 1848 and 1852.[7] The dramatic increase in the Paris population, a good deal of it related to the availability of work on public projects, further swelled revenues through sheer numbers of taxpayers. The population of the capital rose from about 550,000 at the time of Napoléon's defeat at Waterloo to about a million on the eve of 1848. Economic crisis, beginning with the crop failure of 1846 and culminating in the Revolution of 1848, caused the population to stabilize for about five years. The census of 1851 listed 1,053,261 people (not counting another 200,000 in the communes of the inner suburbs). The first years of the empire brought new migrants. The majority were desperately marginal, but they had to eat and drink and so paid the *octroi* on foodstuffs entering the city. Haussmann was the beneficiary of his predecessors and circumstance, neither of which he credited.

Persigny insisted he was the author of deficit spending on municipal projects. Haussmann equally asserted originality. The autobiographical dispute is academic. Neither was the first to think of the scheme, and its realization depended upon both.[8] Deficit spending on public projects began with the railroad boom of the 1840s, and the Péreire brothers, Jacob-Emile (1800–75) and Isaac (1806–80), born at Bordeaux (an important connection for Haussmann), were central figures. The former was spoken of as "the head," the later as "the arms" of a series of financial institutions and practices that united the new capitalism with St. Simonian circles and theory. It is Emile who rushed to the bedside of James Rothschild on the morning of Louis Bonaparte's coup d'état, to tell him that everything had gone as planned. The following day the stock market soared. Both brothers had nearly identical careers: railroad financing, banking, and foreign loans. They would become the chief bankers of Paris urban renewal.

Haussmann's economic ideas rested on two principles: the empire was politically stable and prosperity was growing. All public expenditures would be productive because of inevitable economic expansion. Investment in Paris could—must—be financed over a long period. Haussmann did not have available to him the sophisticated fiduciary systems of today. Government living on debt was not only a relatively new idea, it was a terrifying one to the nineteenth-century bourgeoisie. At the outset Haussmann had to live within his means and raise the seed money for floating long-term loans without imposing new taxes or borrowing by selling bonds. Although he denied it, he followed Berger's example, squirrling away small sums from existing revenue sources. Robert Moses, in New York City nearly a century later, began in much the same way, using the tolls collected on his completed projects to borrow for future undertakings. Haussmann's milch cow was the *octroi*.

In 1847, Merruau calculated, more than 80 percent of the city's receipts came from the *octroi*.[9] The two major categories of revenue were provided by foodstuffs, especially wine, and building materials—not a very promising source of growing revenue. But Paris was in crisis, her population exploding through internal immigration. The revenue on foodstuffs grew enormously as tens of thousands came to the capital to work on the city's projects. In 1851 there were 1,053,261 inhabitants in Paris. In 1861, with the annexation of the *banlieue*, there were more than 1,696,000; and in 1872 more than 1,851,000.[10] Haussmann habitually rounded off these figures and spoke of two million Parisians. The impact of population growth on the *octroi* is most apparent in the tax paid on wine. "There is an enormous surplus value [from the wine tax]," Haussmann wrote Rouher, "that can be attributed to three causes: the increase in the population, the growth in overall wealth and well-being in Paris—to which the public works have contributed no small amount—and, finally, the large number of visitors who frequent Paris."[11]

Imperial Paris became a magnet. The urban projects were so much the subject of sight-seeing that Haussmann figured them into his financial calculations. Tourism and the tourist were not so much a new phenomenon—although the former word was borrowed, literally, from the English, only in 1841—as an increasingly significant one. A new source of urban revenue was emerging, and Haussmann was quick to see its possibilities. The universal exposition fever that gripped Europe after the sensation caused by the Crystal Palace in 1851 became a kind of tax on foreigners. Haussmann turned Paris into a vast exhibition in 1855 and again in 1867. It is impossible to know what percentage of the wine tax was derived from tourism, but the city's revenues from this tax rose dramatically.[12]

The figures on building materials entering Paris are more directly tied to the transformation and provide a useful means for tracking construction activity. Fancy cut stone (*pierre de taille*), the preferred material for luxury building, was taxed at 2 francs the cubic meter. Marble and granite, considerably more expensive but sparingly used, was 15 francs the cubic meter. Iron was 3 francs for 100 kilograms. Bricks, used in cheaper construction, were 5.75 francs per thousand, tiles 7 francs per thousand. From 1852, following the depression and the building slump of the Second Republic, there was a general rise in the importation of both cut stone and common stone, with peaks coming in 1853–54, a huge leap in 1859–60, and additional peaks in 1863 and 1868.[13] On the eve of Haussmann's fall, building activity in Paris was at its highest pitch.[14]

These figures justify Haussmann's economics and additionally explain the appearance of the new Paris.[15] Haussmann was prepared to subsidize and deficit-finance urban development provided it increased *octroi* tax revenues. He gave land to developers but insisted upon closely regulating both building style and materials.[16] His strong partiality for expensive housing for the rich had an economic as well as aesthetic and social dimensions. The disproportionate building of expensive apartments, at exactly the time when the influx into Paris was dominated by those who could afford only modest quarters, drove the *octroi*, which in turn drove future deficit financing and encouraged the gentrification of Paris. The lower middle class and the petite bourgeoisie, who would have built more simply and cheaply, and put less money in city coffers, were steadily and gradually pushed out by a haute bourgeoisie of landlords and commercial interests who could afford to look upon the buying and selling of property as a speculative activity. The old center of Paris and the newer neighborhoods to the west were filled with bourgeois housing. The horizontal segregation of Paris of which Haussmann has been accused, which sharply divided east and west Paris along economic lines, was similarly tied to his use of the *octroi*. The new financial institutions he created favored the haute bourgeoisie, who made Paris in their image, which was also his.

Haussmann both inherited and established the financial institutions that would finance the new Paris. As usual he asserted more originality than was warranted. The Crédit Mobilier, created in 1852 by Emile Péreire, was initially formed as an investment bank to stimulate the railroad industry. It was a joint-stock bank that held shares in various companies involved in developing the railroads and helped them put together the necessary financing for large-scale undertakings. Through links with a network of local branches and agencies, it attracted the savings of small customers and could also sell debt to the general public in the form of bonds, at a rate of return guaranteed by the earnings of the companies it controlled. The Péreires, brilliant but overly adventurous financial buccaneers, made much of their "democratization" of credit. They did indeed give small savers access to investment in industrial, and later real estate, enterprises. But they took too many risks and crashed in 1867, taking their entire structure down, and very nearly much of newly developed western Paris. The boulevard Malesherbes, disastrously overbuilt with expensive housing that stood vacant, was their pet project.

Their immense private fortune was not wiped out in the ruin of their financial empire. After liquidation the brothers kept more than one hundred million francs of land and buildings. Before their fall, at the outset of the transformation of Paris, so successful was the Crédit Mobilier that a number of similar institutions—including the Crédit Foncier (1861), another Péreire creation—sprang up, enormously expanding and modernizing the credit capacities of Paris. The most famous are the Crédit Industriel et Commercial (1859), the Crédit Lyonnais (1863), the Société Générale (1864), and the Banque de Paris (1869), all of which remain and define French banking.

The prefect was inventive when it came to attracting capital. He was originally driven to use state intervention to complete his massive projects because it was difficult to find enough private development companies willing, able, and resourceful enough to undertake the work. Part of the problem was that the city gave land rather than money to subsidize building: those who contracted with Haussmann had to be able to wait years to realize the enormous profits that were forthcoming because of the new values created by transformation. The city became the chief real estate speculator in Paris, while the landlords stood aghast, watching benefits they considered theirs pouring into Haussmann's coffers. This phenomenon set the stage for the counterattack of the landlords.[17] Haussmann believed in a free market, but he found real estate speculation too lucrative to abandon for abstract principle, until forced to do so.

When the law courts and the juries of expropriation, controlled by the landlords, wrested such speculation from the city, Haussmann instituted, by decree (November 14, 1858), the Caisse des Travaux de Paris, a special public works fund and the most novel of his many financial experiments. The Caisse des Travaux was an autonomous organization charged with "the special service of the treasury for the great public works of the city" and was distinct from ordinary city funding in function and operation. The Caisse des Travaux received money from the sale of materials from expropriated and demolished buildings and the sale of the parts of expropriated buildings that were not demolished and could be resold. It also administered all the expenses connected with indemnifications of displaced leasees. The caisse was empowered to issue public bonds, whose amount was fixed at one hundred million francs in 1865. It was the power to issue bonds that made the Caisse des Travaux so important.

Haussmann would brilliantly, and then recklessly, manipulate the Caisse des Travaux. Construction costs were normally paid by the builders, who would then be reimbursed by the city in as many as eight annual installments, including interest, only after the project was complete. Because the builder had to raise the necessary capital for his work when he began, he was in effect loaning money interest-free to the city, which did not have to pay until the work was completed, and then only in installments. In 1863 several of the builders ran into financial difficulties and demanded immediate repayment from the city of sums they had already advanced, although the projects were only partially complete. The city, unable to come up with the money and save the builders from financial ruin, turned to the Péreires' Crédit Foncier, which advanced the money—at the emperor's urging.

The Crédit Foncier, headed by Haussmann's old friend Frémy, bailed out the city in exchange for a letter of security from the municipality to the builder, stating the expected date of completion and a schedule of repayment. Haussmann was thus borrowing money from the Crédit Foncier through the builders, who became intermediaries, much like a dummy corporation set up to take out a loan. After the financial scare of 1863 the contractors had to deposit the cost of the project with the Caisse des Travaux as a guarantee that they could finish the projects. This gave Haussmann additional liquidity. Only those builders with considerable financial resources could work for Paris. The city had gone into the banking business, becoming a major financial speculator, gambling on the success of its own projects. Haussmann's mobilization of capital with the goal of transforming Paris made an alliance between the city and a "coterie of financial and real estate interests" who benefited enormously from a 17 percent increase in the number of housing units during the 1860s.[18]

What made the Caisse des Travaux so dangerously attractive was that its transactions could be hidden. The fund was not open to public scrutiny. The Crédit Foncier, thanks to Frémy's complicity, became the city's banker, which thus escaped any serious oversight from the Cour des Comptes or the Corps Législatif. Haussmann was neither beholden nor answerable to elected or appointed overseers. He had at his disposal a floating debt, which he used to generate liquidity. The city issued proxy bonds (*bons de délégation*) based on the amounts owed by the contractors. These proxy bonds were an additional instrument of speculation. Not only did the proxy bonds bring in money immediately, but those who held them negotiated the bonds on the market to get additional credit. The highly desirable bonds, guaranteed by the city's projects, drove interest rates on loans up to 10 percent in the boom years of the late 1860s, which in turn drove up the cost of all building.

The proxy bonds complicated Haussmann's finances by adding a parallel fiduciary system that behaved according to different rules and had a higher interest rate. Interest on normal city borrowing hovered around 5 percent.[19] The new bonds siphoned off investment capital into the bond market, and the banks were the great beneficiaries, or at least those banks that were in Haussmann's financial loop. The powerful and conservative Rothschild bank remained aloof. From Haussmann's point of view rising interest rates were not desirable, but he was powerless to control them. So long as he could continue to borrow money and issue proxy bonds without needing official approval, which would have meant opening his books to public scrutiny, he tolerated rising interest rates and passed them along through higher urban renewal costs. Indeed, rising interest rates stimulated the bond market and put additional funds in circulation: more bonds could always be issued, on the assumption that the massive building projects would continue and generate increasing wealth in the future, when the bonds fell due.

Building and borrowing was at its peak in 1868–69. The Corps Législatif learned of Haussmann's financial dealings only when he applied for his yearly budget. When the city of Paris "needs to borrow money," said the opposition leader, Picard, "it is careful to make its demand at the last possible moment. When there are details and explanations needed the city provides the barest minimum."[20] The Corps Législatif became less and less compliant, more and more suspicious and jealous of Haussmann's arrogance, secrecy, and dubious practices, but they had no choice but to ratify the mounting floating debt in each year's municipal budget. The work for which it was requested was already well underway. Refusing to honor the debt would have catastrophic results on the thousands, even tens of thousands, enmeshed in the city's financial manipulations.

In his early years Haussmann had been very careful with the Corps Législatif. To disarm the opponents of "the Emperor's program," he inflated excess city revenues by overstating his income and underestimating his expenses, the kind of bookkeeping used by all governments and their dependents at allocation time. In the beginning, opposition was sparse and isolated. The first projects, long delayed by political uncertainty, were dazzlingly successful. Haussmann and the empire reaped the rewards. Early success provided the catapult for future projects: Imperial ideology of efficiency seemed irresistible, deficit spending some wonderful alchemy. The authoritarian state, sustained by an expansion of credit, gave Haussmann carte blanche. Those who might have resisted were silent. Even to his foes he appeared some kind of magician.

The grumbling grew gradually until, in the Corps Législatif session of May 8, 1858, all the arguments against the finances of the Hôtel de Ville were voiced. Luxury building was immobilizing capital in "Parisian stone." "We are going to contribute five millions to some streets in the capital while the highway system of the kingdom gets only two millions"—a criticism especially persuasive to an assembly dominated by rural representatives. The minister Baroche responded, invoking the magic formulas of reawakened capitalism:

private construction along the new streets would be worth 420 millions in investments. "Formerly," said Nogent-St. Laurens, "we went forth to the struggle with canon and rifles. . . . today we advance with the pick-ax and the trowel."[21] For the moment there was no stopping "the Emperor's program," even had there been enough parliamentary support to do so. Haussmann's financial expedients went unexamined and unchecked.

The way it worked was simple enough, and simply infuriating to the elected representatives of the nation. So long as Haussmann had money, which he first got from the *octroi* and then from the Caisse des Travaux, he could operate without the Corps Législatif. Only a few Paris projects were funded by the state, and none of them was fully funded. The yearly national budget for Paris projects, once granted, was largely out of the control of the corps. Haussmann so mingled state and city monies that he completely obfuscated his financial arrangements. And the other aspects of urban renewal were also outside of legislative control. Declarations of public utility, which preceded confiscations, depended upon the emperor, not the Corps Législatif. Authorization for work depended on the prefect, who negotiated directly with the contractors.

Once the work was completed the Corps Législatif had little choice but to ratify the consolidation of the floating debt Haussmann had accumulated. The demographic pressures on Paris continued, driving the building programs. The deputies could not impede, let alone stop, the juggernaut Haussmann had set in motion. And he knew it. They could not refuse to honor his debts and halt all the incomplete projects, certainly bankrupting a number of builders and investors, and perhaps even the city, not to mention the intimate relationship between urban renewal and the empire itself. It was easier to pass the debt on to the future than take on Haussmann and the emperor.

The city borrowed hugely and often: 50 million francs in 1852, 75 million in 1855, 150 million in 1860, and 250 million in both 1863 and 1869. Yet even these sums, which more than doubled every five years, supplemented with additional money from other sources, did not suffice. Municipal finance had become a never-never land of fantastic liens on future revenue. Because Haussmann was banking on a future of ever-escalating real estate value—and the future offered no intrusion of reality, demanded no accounting—the day of reckoning was put off indefinitely. The first loans were relatively modest, but after 1860 the city's borrowing was of the same magnitude as the state's and surpassed the annual budgets of many a small country. The 775 million francs borrowed after 1860 "represent a sum double what had been spent on Paris from 1800 to 1853."[22] Eventually the loans would add up to 998 millions, not counting the bonds floated.[23] Haussmann's debt began to weigh noticeably on city finances in the late 1860s, at the very moment the empire was in political transition and the prefect himself was the most vulnerable. Under Haussmann the city's debt had risen from 163 million to 2,500 million francs. In 1870 the interest charges alone made up more than 44 percent of the municipal budget.[24] Only the Franco-Prussian War briefly slowed the rate of indebtedness: all urban work stopped. It resumed in 1875, ample evidence of France's financial and spiritual resiliency. Haussmann's successor and protégé, Alphand, completed most of the interrupted projects using the same financial methods as before: disguised long-term loans.[25] Urban renewal on such a scale could not be financed by more traditional means. The estimated debt Haussmann bequeathed in 1870 was 1,518,799,082, which was not fully retired until 1929.[26]

Whether this was a small enough price to pay for the glories of Paris or a fearsome and unnecessary burden imposed by a megalomaniac, whether these sums were raised by expedients that were at least dubious and eventually illegal is less interesting than the fact that it was done. Karl Marx's remark that "men make their own history, but they do not make it just as they please; but under circumstances directly encountered, given and transmitted from the past" may here serve as our text. Haussmann did not create the financial boom of the Second Empire, nor the potent and volatile forces of capitalism already released by the railroad boom, nor did he invent the speculative frenzy of the age. What he did do was facilitate and nurture the alliance between public urban intervention and private lending institutions: "the marriage of authoritarian urbanism and the new structures of capitalism" unleashed haussmannization.[27]

With singular skill he rode the sometimes treacherous waves of market fluctuations and financial instability for seventeen years. The work on Paris continued—and all the normal operating expenses of the city were regularly paid—despite the financial crisis of 1857, the absence of the emperor (he was in Italy), the Crimean War, the disastrous Mexican adventure, the American Civil War (90 percent of French cotton came from the Southern states, which also bought a sizable part of Paris craft production), the crash of the Péreire financial empire, the vulnerability of the luxury *articles de Paris*, which formed the backbone of the city's economy, the growing liberalization of the empire, Prussian belligerency on the continent, and the corrosive impact of unscrupulous speculation. Just holding things together would have been a noteworthy achievement: making Paris after his own image was exceptional.

Haussmann was a gifted economic amateur, as he was a gifted amateur engineer, architect, and city planner. His faith in the empire and its infinitely expandable wealth never wavered. He honored Louis Napoléon's prohibition against new taxes, pampered the Paris bourgeoisie, and continued to extract money from the *octroi* by expanding the tax base. The landowners benefited enormously under Haussmann's regime yet never supported the empire. It is one of the ironies of the rebuilding of Paris.

The revolt of the landowners was the first serious test of Haussmann's ingenuity at raising money. At the outset he spun millions from expropriations and demolitions. By law the city was empowered to acquire all the property within the area where work was to be done. Haussmann well recalled the rue Rambuteau, when too little property was confiscated, which compromised the street's dimensions. Haussmann wanted to raise money from each demolition and rebuilding to finance future work. He interpreted the law in such a way that the various building sites acquired by the city and improved, their value enhanced by a new street, became public property and could be sold by the city at their new market value. The laws on expropriation that Haussmann used had been enacted before his arrival at the Hôtel de Ville. The *décrets* of May 3, 1848, and October 4, 1849, extended and significantly modified the original legislation of 1841—specifically designed for railroad building—

by authorizing the city to buy all the buildings necessary to cut a new street and then "resell. . .[the land] not used in the realignments in lots for the construction of well-ventilated apartments."[28] The decree of March 26, 1852, opened the way to speculation.

Haussmann added an important and lucrative nuance to expropriation and resale: condemned buildings and parcels of land passed into the city's hands and remained there until resold. In this interim Haussmann imposed conditions and restraints on the future buyers through contracts of resale. And the practice was perfectly legal.[29] By requiring the installation of uniform iron railings, for example, Haussmann insured conformity to his urban tastes by making Paris buildings uniform, while enhancing revenues from the *octroi*, which his imposed requirements made more predictable.

The prefect had early anticipated the resistance of the landowners to his expropriations and he took steps to reduce their influence.[30] He made himself the sole member of the city planning commission and soon dominated the appointed Municipal Council, once he had adjusted its personnel, both of which had previously represented the interest of the landlords. The Council of State and the Cour de Cassation, which he could not control, continued to side with the concrete rights of the landowners against the abstract rights of "the city," an administrative entity. On December 27, 1858, the council decreed that an owner would have eight days after expropriation to reclaim from the city those portions of the property that were not necessary for the new street. The city was denied the lucrative practice of selling confiscated land. Expropriation for public utility became again a source of enrichment and speculation for the owner, whose property was now considerably more valuable because of Haussmann's new streets. The Council of State, Haussmann bitterly wrote, "thus assured the expropriated, at no expense, the benefit of increased value."[31]

Not only did the city lose a sure means of making money, but the cost of acquiring urban land increased dramatically. The expropriation juries, composed of Paris landowners, to whom appeal could be made on the amounts offered by the city, had always been more inclined toward the dispossessed, whom they perfectly represented and mirrored. Haussmann tried to avoid dealing with these juries by acquiring as much land as he could through individual arrangements between his special commission and the owner (*à l'aimable*).

The courts increasingly upheld the jury settlements, and landowners went to law. Should the location of a proposed street leak out or be stolen, as Zola imagines Aristide Saccard doing in *La Curée*, speculators and landowners would set to work "preparing all the frauds by which so many landlords and, especially unscrupulous lease-holders, have ultimately succeeded in getting exhorbitant indemnities from the overly-complacent [expropriation] juries, to the detriment of the city."[32] Haussmann wrote to a certain M. Bruyère, an *inspecteur-voyer* (one of those responsible for estimating the value of property to be expropriated): "I charge you immediately to make . . . an estimation of the value of a house on the rue St. Denis. . . . This ought to include the value of the building itself and the indemnities to be paid for the eviction of renters. I don't have to tell you to be discreet. You should submit your work to me directly."[33] Maxime du Camp, Flaubert's boyhood friend who abandoned "pure" literature for journalism, printed these oft-repeated anecdotes:

> A property owner had accepted, verbally, to sell a plot of land for 75,000 francs. A "decree of expropriation" was issued. The property owner rejected the conditions of the first sale and took his case to the courts, demanding 1,800,000 francs. He was awarded 950,000. A well-known manufacturer on the boulevard des Italiens was displaced from his business for 18 months, during which time he occupied a shop situated just across the street from the one expropriation had forced him to leave. And for this relatively easy move he received 300,000 francs. "How did you get rich?" a newly wealthy man was asked. He answered: "I was expropriated."[34]

When the city had to acquire a few house in the rue St. Martin to link existing streets to the new boulevard de Sébastopol, one shoe manufacturer received 75,000 francs compensation for the interruption of his lease,[35] more than was often paid to purchase entire properties on the side streets of Paris.

"The numerous acquisitions [of land] that the city had made in advance," Haussmann wrote, "rather than being economical mea-

sures, as was [then] supposed, have become the cause of a true disaster because of a completely new, inflexible, interpretation of the
law adopted by the cour de Cassation."[36] It was "this powerful machine," in Zola's image, whose wheels have "for fifteen years, turned
Paris on its head, making fortunes and causing ruin."[37] Not only had
Haussmann not won over the landlords by sparing them additional
taxes, he had turned them into a formidable competitor for control
of urban space. His dealings with Paris landlords were adversarial,
the courts had turned against him, and the legal battles with landlords were expensive and time consuming. The city's land speculations he considered in the public interest. Those of the landlords
were mere greed.

Driven from the real estate market by the courts and the
landowners, Haussmann went into the construction business.
When he could not find a private contractor willing or able to undertake the enormous projects he envisioned, he made them state
undertakings. The city, having mobilized the finances and done
much of the work, could then itself pocket the improvement values
on its own investment. This raised cries of outrage from the excluded speculators and developers. As had the landlords, they saw huge
profits flowing into city coffers. Haussmann successfully forged alliances between the municipality and a small group of financial and
real estate interests, assembled under the umbrella of "associated"
or "finance" capital.[38] These associations preserved the appearance
of a free market in urban renewal, or as he put it, "speculation stimulated by competition," although they were in fact a well-organized
form of monopoly competition, which Haussmann could use to
control a market otherwise wildly speculative and fluctuating. The
city could not compete successfully in a market that speculated
against its interests. The free market that had once looked so attractive as a motor driving urban renewal had become an unpredictable, even hostile environment.

In a long letter to Persigny concerning the rue Lafayette, Haussmann discussed this very question. First he had to obtain a decree of
public utility to acquire the land, which was being held up by problems with the Hôtel Laffitte, the mansion of the important banking
family of the July Monarchy. Haussmann assured Persigny that in a

matter of months he would get the necessary decree. "An important company," he wrote, had submitted a proposal for part of the project. He wanted the entire street, from the rue du faubourg Montmartre to the rue Laffitte (E-F 2), constructed by a single contractor; "but things are still not very far advanced." Should he be unable to persuade a single contractor to take on the project, it would fall to the city itself to do it, which "would delay matters."[39]

Haussmann's arrangements with the Péreire interests offers another, slightly different example. The Péreires and three other wealthy landowners gave the city all the land they owned on the Plaine de Monceau (C-D 2) in exchange for streets, sewers, and water mains. The land was ceded "without indemnity, precisely for the enormous increased value that the Plaine de Monceau owed to the cutting of the new streets, as well as others which the owners had the intelligence to undertake."[40] The land was worthless until made accessible by the boulevard Malesherbes and the several streets that formed the new system of communication opening up western Paris. The Péreires had paid 430 francs a square meter for land adjacent to the St. Augustin church, but for land farther from the growing city they paid 50 francs in the vicinity of the Parc Monceau, and 10 francs even farther to the west.[41] This is now some of the most expensive real estate in Paris.

Administration and finances were necessarily intertwined because Haussmann thought always in administrative terms. Those outside his bureaucracy never fully understood the careful and complicated relationships. During the rancorous debates on his finances in 1869, his enemies attacked the prefect and his administration without distinction. All the administrative tasks in the rebuilding of Paris were the work of specially created bureaux, headed by handpicked chiefs, the three most important being the Plan de Paris (which designated where streets were to be cut), and the departments of water and sewers, and parks and promenades (which are self-explanatory), directed, respectively, by Deschamps, Belgrand, and Alphand. Finances, however, the department that gave life to the other three, was exclusively in Haussmann's hands.

For administrative reasons the work on Paris was divided into three groups of projects, "incorrectly called '*Réseaux*'," which is the

designation in all the documents of the time as well as common par-
lance. The composition of each each *réseau* "was not determined by
any relationship between the respective streets, nor their relative
utility, nor the order in which they were built." The second *réseau*
was begun before the first was completed, as was the third. The
classification "was solely to distinguish those subventioned by the
state . . . from those the city was to undertake without any subvention."[42] Overall the state paid for a third of the first and second
réseaux but two-thirds for certain prestigious projects (the Louvre-
Tuileries, the Palais-Royal). The choice of word—in this context
réseau means a series of lines of communication serving the same
area unit, a network (the Paris subway is the "*réseau métropolitain*"),
with the clear sense of logical connection—and the order of undertaking (first, second, and third, obviously) quickly overwhelmed the
administrative distinction. Haussmann's opponents and the general
public ranked the three *réseaux* in importance and treated them accordingly. Funds were requested of the Corps Législatif in sequence,
which further fixed the idea that the first *réseau* was the most important. It was also the least expensive, some sixty to seventy million francs, and included those projects already in progress or
inherited from earlier regimes: the boulevard de Sébastopol, the disengagement of the Hôtel de Ville, the Place du Châtelet, and the
prolongation of the rue de Rivoli. The money was granted in 1855.
Opponents always harkened back to the first *réseau* as useful, essential, and not unreasonably expensive when they criticized subsequent networks. "I don't hesitate to say it," Thiers told the deputies,
"everything was good in the first *réseau*."[43]

The second *réseau*—including the prolongation of the boulevard
de Sébastopol to the Observatoire on the Left Bank (E 4–5), the
boulevard Malesherbes (C-D 2), the boulevard Voltaire (F-G 3–4),
and the new streets radiating from the Arc de Triomphe—was more
than three times as expensive as the first. The arrangement made
between the state and Paris for subvention was passed in 1858. Despite the financial crisis of 1857 the transformation of Paris was still
enormously popular—as were the emperor and his prefect. The
third *réseau* presented the greatest difficulties. Haussmann insisted
that some of the projects therein had come from the second *réseau*,

transferred to the third when the Corps Législatif voted less money than the prefect had requested. Nevertheless, the third *réseau* was almost universally seen as less important and more extravagant than the first two. In the struggle over the 1869 budget the third *réseau* was thought little more than an expensive luxury, evidence of Haussmann's megalomania. Many of the streets in the third *réseau* were a result of the annexation of the *banlieue*, while the new streets around the Opéra, as well as other projects, were in the wealthy west end, where lay the speculative interests of the Péreires and their friends. Although the third *réseau* stuck in the craw of the Corps Législatif and focused the bitter debate on haussmannization, it contained no state subventions. But by 1869 the empire was liberalizing itself, the Bonapartists had lost recent important Paris elections, and parliamentary opposition to Haussmann and his financial wheeling and dealing had reached a critical mass. Construction costs had risen enormously, along with expropriation costs. The sums that had sufficed a decade earlier were now inadequate. For a fraction of the money requested in 1869 the first (and even the second) *réseaux* had renewed the old center of Paris and made it a modern city. The third *réseau* appeared both too expensive and frivolous. Parisians and politicians alike were fed up.

· XI ·

"Lackey of a Good House"

THE CONVERGENCE OF AUTHORITARIAN URBANISM AND THE NEW
structures of capitalism unleashed haussmannization. The simultaneous convergence of "la fête impériale" and the new structures of
bureaucracy explain the shape given to Paris by its creator. Haussmann was seduced by Imperial Paris, whose charms proved irresistible to an man hitherto condemned to the provinces. Before his
summons to Paris he had carefully cultivated the local notables of
the southwest, attaching himself eventually (but not intimately) to
the bourgeoisie of Bordeaux. Suddenly, in 1853, he found himself in
Paris, instantaneously one of the most important men in France and
the head of an immense patronage network. He was no longer the
ambitious outsider trying to get a foot in the door. The titled, the
powerful, the well-connected, the sophisticated, and the greedy
were knocking on his door.

For the parvenu bureaucrat become prefect of the Seine, his own
transformation was as dramatic as that of Paris. Overnight he had
more money, more power, more attention, more of everything than
he had ever dreamed possible. He lived in one of the great buildings
of Paris, appropriately appointed and staffed, he had regular—sometimes daily—access to the emperor, he commanded a formidable
army of bureaucrats and craftsmen. He entertained queens and

czars, dined and danced with princesses and peers, and his official wine cellar, reputed the finest in Paris, was a fantasy realized, stocked with hundreds of coveted bottles he could not otherwise have possessed or drunk, let alone served abundantly. He was a great lord, newly created by the emperor.

Paris would bear the stamp of Haussmann's seduction. *La fête impériale* would be fixed in stone by this bureaucrat of genius. His brilliant elevation not only plucked him from the provinces and set him on a world stage, it surrounded him with men and women whose political views, social values, and cultural assumptions he eagerly embraced. Haussmann had never had the common touch, had never cultivated the friendship or the acquaitance of those who could do him no good in his career. He had long found popular Paris disgusting. As prefect of the Seine he now spent all his time with those who had similar views about the city and its inhabitants. With the full sympathy and encouragement of the beau monde, he neglected eastern Paris and the Left Bank, built few schools, hospitals, and little inexpensive housing, drove dirty industry (and industrial jobs) from the city, and uprooted the poor from Old Paris. He poured money into the new bourgeois neighborhoods of the western city, anchored the new urban center of gravity with a sumptuous opera house, built luxury hotels, attracted department stores to his new boulevards, overbuilt luxury apartments, and made the city convenient and salubrious for those who could afford it.

His new residence and office set the tone. For seventeen years Haussmann lived and worked in a historical monument in the center of Old Paris. The Hôtel de Ville was much more than the seat of city government and the prefect's home: it had been a museum of Parisian history since the late Middle Ages. In its rooms and precincts had been enacted most of the major scenes in the city's history, from Etienne Marcel's promulgation of the *grande ordinance* limiting royal power in the fourteenth century to the June Days, when the insurrectionaries had failed to capture the building. Haussmann had first entered the Hôtel de Ville during the Trois Glorieuses in 1830, with a musket over his shoulder. His official entrance, twenty-three years later (June 29, 1853), was considerably more dignified but perhaps no less bellicose: this time he carried the emperor's charge to transform Paris.

The Hôtel de Ville in 1853 was essentially the building conceived, although not completed, by François I. It stood upon ground long redolent of Parisian history. Etienne Marcel, the *prévôt des marchands*, had installed the city administration in a house near the Place de Grève in 1357. On this site would be enacted, through the centuries, rituals and festivals both joyous and macabre. The births of the dauphins of France were here celebrated, as were military victories. The Place de Grève had also been the site for executions since 1310. The French Revolution abandoned the Hôtel de Ville as an execution ground, separating its executions from those of the despised monarchy. After the revolution the guillotine was returned to the Place de Grève, when need arose, until 1830.

During the French Revolution, Louis XVI had come to the Hôtel de Ville on July 17, 1789, in a stunning act of submission to the Paris revolution that had just captured the Bastille. Five years later, Robespierre was captured here and led to the guillotine. The Revolution of 1830 declared itself victorious at the Hôtel, on whose balcony General Lafayette embraced Louis-Philippe, wrapped him in the tricolor flag, and proclaimed him king. In 1848, the provisional government that had chased Louis-Philippe into exile proclaimed itself on the same spot. Later, the Commune, for a little more than a month in 1871, governed Paris from the Hôtel and burned it when defeated by the troops from Versailles. Even the liberation of Paris in 1944 did not seem official until General de Gaulle arrived at the Hôtel de Ville.

François I had selected the Tuscan architect Dominique Becalor (or Bocador), often called Dominique de Cortone, to design a new town hall to replace Etienne Marcel's old house on stilts. The first stone was laid on July 15, 1533. But the work went slowly, interrupted by François's wars. In 1549 his heir, Henri II, recommenced the work with considerable modifications. In 1590 Henri IV ordered work completed. Like the Louvre the Hôtel de Ville bore the marks of many hands, a monument to changing taste, a document of Parisian history.

In the nineteenth century the Hôtel was further modified. Louis-Philippe's government undertook its enlargement and strategic disengagement from the surrounding urban tangle. The architects Goode and Lesueur were charged with building in the style of the old Hôtel. The facade was extended by two wings and the central court, doubled in depth, was complemented by two new courtyards. The work, begun in 1837, was completed in 1846, exclusive of interior decoration. Haussmann lived and worked there. With the windows open he could hear the sounds of the central markets only a few blocks away and watch the river traffic. His regular interviews with Louis Napoléon took him through the core of Paris to the Elysée Palace. Unlike most officials isolated from the heart of Paris, their offices nestled behind the walls of some magnificent town house along the Quai d'Orsay or near the Palais-Bourbon (where the Corps Législatif met), the prefect lived and worked in the midst of the city, surrounded by its sounds and sights, imbued with its history.

Upon entering the Hôtel one arrived at the central reception room, the Salle du Trône. Walking through the Salle du Trône, the prefect's office was to the right, along with that of the secretary general and their staffs. To the left was a suite of rooms designated as the apartments of the king, reserved for the sovereign when visiting the Hôtel. On the mezzanine, above his offices, was the private apartment of the prefect. The northern end of the Hôtel, bordering the rue de Rivoli, housed the offices of the prefecture, and the eastern quadrant, along the rue Lobau, contained the Salle St. Jean and the Grande Salle des Fêtes, where important public functions were held. All the public rooms were on the ground floor. In the center of the Hôtel were the three courtyards. The Cour d'Honneur, known as the Cour Louis XIV—it contained a statue of the king—was the heart of the original Renaissance building. The rooms overlooking the courtyard were reserved for the Municipal Council. At the rear of the court, on the first floor, was the meeting room, which opened on the public entertainment rooms and was connected by two galleries to the Salle du Trône. Here Haussmann conducted all his municipal business.

The newly built apartments of the prefect (1840) were lavishly decorated but of uneven quality. The fresco, painted by M. Court, depicted a group of nymphs almost completely nude. When first un-veiled the painting evoked smiles bordering on smirks. Haussmann had the figures partially clad with transparent veils, which neither satisfied the prurient nor suppressed the smirks. Several of the painted ceiling scenes were no more modest: "But neither the ex-cess of gilt ornamentation nor the liberties that the painters had taken were of a kind to displease the society of the time [when they were executed], although," Merruau delicately added, "M. de Ram-buteau only received the elite in these rooms."[1]

Haussmann did more significant work on the Hôtel than clothing nymphs. He rightly thought the Louis XIV courtyard a gem of Re-naissance art. Among his first projects was the erection of a glass and iron roof over the courtyard to protect it from the weather, an idea that had also occurred to Rambuteau, who thought it "the most beautiful stairway in Paris . . . a living Veronese."[2] Haussmann executed the plan and took credit for the original thought. At the Hôtel, as throughout Paris, he preserved the historical building but altered or violated the original aesthetic, ceaselessly elaboratating the interior decoration of the Hôtel. When he arrived the Salle des Fêtes, the Escalier d'Honneur, and the Salon des Cariatides had all been completed. In 1854 the paintings commissioned from Ingres and Delacroix, for the emperor's apartments and the Salon de la Paix, respectively, were inaugurated.[3] In 1859 Léon Coignet was commissioned to paint four panels, representing the seasons, for the Salon du Zodiaque. Adolphe Yvon, the military painter, was com-missioned in 1865 to decorate the ceiling of the Municipal Council chamber. He painted four murals: King Clovis making Paris his cap-ital, Philippe-Auguste departing for crusade in the Holy Land, François I laying the first stone of the Hôtel de Ville, and Napoléon III presenting to Haussmann the decree annexing the communes surrounding Paris.[4] Thus did Haussmann memorialize his own pre-fecture and the empire, placing himself at the pinnacle of Paris his-tory. In the prefect's office Schopen painted an allegory of the vote of December 10, 1848. The public rooms reflected his own image and achievements, correctly associated with the triumph of Louis Napoléon.

The private apartments of the prefect were lavish. Haussmann had at his personal disposal a large antechamber at the head of the central stairway for those visiting him in his apartments. There were two waiting rooms, one larger than the other. The three salons were known collectively as arcade rooms; a sixth room, the yellow room, provided access to the official dining room, which could seat fifty-two guests. When Haussmann had more invitees he converted the Salle du Trône, where he could accommodate ninety, into a dining area.[5] With his customary attention to detail, Haussmann carefully described the furnishings provided the prefect. Not only were they "absolutely complete and of the greatest comfort," but even household linen, maintained for him at public expense, was furnished. There were "several" silver table services, and "numberless" utensils and kitchen equipment "belonging to the city of Paris." Without these the "prefect would not have been able easily to maintain his position."[6]

Haussmann received fifty thousand francs annually, half the salary of the least important minister, which he found inadequate "for the expenses of my family and my private establishment." He was the first prefect of modest means, and until his elevation to the Senate he had to dip into his limited personal resources. The emperor, ever generous to those who served his regime, tried to supplement his servant's income. Appointment to the Senate gave Haussmann thirty thousand francs annually for life—which was cut off with the fall of the empire. In addition he had two carriages for his personal use—as did each minister—and a third for his family, as well as "a series of smaller privileges, much valued in Paris, such as a reserved box at the theaters." These perquisites were not paid for out of the city's budget but by the state, one of the many reminders of the prefect's dual and sometimes ambiguous role. The vehicles, Haussmann specifies, were a two-horse *coupé* and a Victoria. A larger Berlin was reserved for his family. The yearly expense for the coaches, two coachmen, and four horses was fourteen thousand francs. In addition two footmen were attached to his service but were paid from household funds.[7]

The prefect was expected to entertain lavishly and regularly. Haussmann's flair for the theatrical, for official pomp and grandeur, made his receptions notable. Lacking the personal resources of his two immediate precedessors, he had to be prudent without giving the appearance of being so. Rambuteau, a nobleman of substantial wealth, had refused to let the city pay for his receptions. He insisted upon his wife's prerogative "to open or close the door as she pleased" because she was "the mistress [of the house], not some wife whose function was to manage the prefectoral salon." Noblesse oblige had cost Rambuteau forty thousand francs a year out of pocket, "but the dignity of my functions gained thereby and I don't believe I owed any less to the first office in Paris."[8]

The professional, bourgeois civil servant saw things differently. "In this city . . . where richness is the privilege of so many families . . . in this rendevous of all luxury, of all elegance," public functionaries had no private life. Mme Haussmann was expected to be a ready, untemperamental hostess constantly in the public eye. "The wife of the prefect of the Seine, however modest she might be, could not perform the honors in their personal salon, on the mezzanine of the Hôtel de Ville, any more simply than she could those of the official salons on the first floor." Haussmann's public table "could not . . . recall that of Lucullus while my private table [was] that . . . of an anchorite." "I was not even free to regulate, with all the liberty I would have desired, the number and the menus of my family dinners and dinners with intimates. One has so many more interested relations and assiduous friends when one is more powerful, and the reputation of my cooking and of my official wine cellar imposed certain obligations on my private cooking and my private wine cellar." As prefect he had to mount a theatrical representation of his position, "played, of necessity, before an importunate public."[9] He loved the lavish life and the publicity, and regreted only his short purse.

To pay for his expensive public functions, which drove his private expenditure, Haussmann received 25,000 francs from the ministry of the interior and another 80,000 from the city of Paris. He had, in addition, access to two funds for running the regular business of governing Paris: 257,000 francs (from the state), and 200,000 francs (which was increased to 280,000 francs when Paris was extended) from the city. He had to pay the salaries of employees, heating, lighting, printing, furnishings for the various offices, indeed all the expenses, large and small, incurred in running a sizable bureaucracy.

Until 1867, the year of the Universal Exposition, Haussmann managed to remain within this budget. But in the last three years of his prefecture he ran into debt and failed to ask for an additional line of credit. He blamed himself, asserting that just as his obligations to entertain those who visited the transformed city increased—tourists flocked to the emerging urban mecca—he was preoccupied with the bitter struggle over the city's budget.

With his appointment to the prefecture of the Seine Haussmann moved in the highest circles. Provincial society, even in wealthy Bordeaux, paled. He had much to learn. Surrounded by privilege, regularly admitted to the salons of finance, commerce, industry, and government—only the intellectuals snubbed the prefect—almost daily in contact with the important men and women of his age, he was routinely invited to the celebrations of the court, to all the public functions at Compiègne or Fontainebleau, as well as to some of the more intimate receptions of the empress. Mme Haussmann had less appetite and stamina for this social round, but "it was necessary, like it or not, for us to accept, to fulfill . . . these obligations and, afterwards, to put up with the onerous consequences."[10] Their daughters, too, were part of the brilliant milieu, which further strained the Haussmann finances, especially when it came time to find them suitable mates.

Haussmann was not sought by Paris society for his charm or wit, but because he was powerful and there were fortunes to be made, even legally, from acquaintance with the person in charge of the most extraordinary patronage source in the world. Invitations to his public and semipublic affairs at the Hôtel de Ville were much in demand. He knew how to entertain *le tout Paris*, and the Hôtel de Ville was a glittering social magnet during the empire. Haussmann was so attentive and gracious to Queen Victoria when she visited in 1855 that she not only accepted the dedication of a new street but gave Mme Haussmann a magnificent brooch of diamonds and turquoise, set in chiseled gold. Count Hubner described a grand ball given on February 14, 1859, to honor the marriage of Princess Marie Clotilde and Prince Napoléon, to which there were ten thousand invitees: "I danced in the quadrille of honor, which was very lively, given the company. Prince Napoléon danced with Mme Haussmann, M. Haussmann with the princess Clotilde, myself with the princess Mathilde, and a municipal councillor with the princess Anna Murat." The baptism of the prince imperial (Louis Napoléon's heir) was marked at the Hôtel de Ville by a dinner for four hundred. The marshal de Castellane, one of the guests, described the affair as "magnificent."

> The Emperor's table was situated on a kind of stage from which Their Majesties could see all the other tables. The salons of the Hôtel de Ville were brilliantly lit. The Emperor and the Empress stayed for a long time. They appeared radiant.[11]

The magnificence of Haussmann's table matched the mise-en-scene. A dinner for the visiting Austrian emperor, Franz Joseph (October 28, 1867), cost 150,000 francs. The menu was sumptuous, the wines legendary.[12] Haussmann's cellar was especially strong in Bordeaux and he prided himself on his expertise as well as his palate. He considered nothing better than "one of the four great *châteaux*" from the legendary vintage of 1848, or better yet, a Château d'Yquem from 1846 or 1852, or a Château Laffitte from 1847 (if there was not a bottle from 1851). His collection was not left to the unsupervised care of a sommelier. Haussmann himself selected his wines, often from the vineyards of his Bordeaux friends, regularly sampled them to monitor their maturity, and served them forth as the talk of the town.

His musicales were equally famous. "No one in Paris," a contemporary testified, "knows as well as M. Haussmann how to organize a concert. *The Saturdays of Lent* concerts of the prefect of the Seine have an artistic renown that is European."[13] Haussmann himself was especially proud of this series. He rejected an invitation from a dear friend "because the Lenten concerts cannot be interrupted."[14] As he told another friend, the concerts "had become an institution" that he could not alter without "profoundly troubling my bourgeois clientele."[15] The concerts left a "brilliant and enduring memory among their habitués."[16] There is no record that he himself played the piano at any of these concerts, which were much more formal affairs than the gatherings in the provinces when he had sometimes entertained his guests from the keyboard.

The long years of intimacy with *le tout Paris*, the burden of a constant social whirl, as well as his own desire to associate with the upper classes, made Haussmann not only an adept and familiar figure in the social life of the empire but changed him. Throughout his long tenure as prefect of the Seine he continued to work extraordinarily hard, and he drove his staff to emulate his own dedication and schedule. He was one of an exceptional generation of prefects and civil servants obsessed with work and dedicated to unrelenting and honest public service. But his appetite for the pleasures of *la fête impériale*, once tasted, was never sated.

His private life, hitherto a model of bourgeois rectitude, became public and peccable. A whiff of scandal reached the Corps Législatif itself and became a part of the public record. In the midst of debate on a loan of 180 million francs for the boulevards, which included discussion of the proposed new opera (May 8, 1858), Leclerc d'Osmonville launched a bon mot witty enough to be several times repeated: "It is indiscreet that M. the prefect of the Seine should cause the Opéra to be introduced everywhere where it ought not to be." The obscurity of the jest did not escape the assembly, which broke into laughter. Haussmann had recently insulted the deputies by telling one of their number, M. Javal, a rich Jewish industrialist— Haussmann had no discernible religious prejudices, counting Jews and Catholics among his personal friends and associates—that those who voted against the loan were "idiots, imbeciles," and that "he didn't give a damn for the assembly." Leclerc d'Osmonville exacted some parliamentary revenge.

Haussmann's affair with the Opéra dancer, Francine Cellier, was the object of his quip.[17] The affair went on for some time. One of the employees of the prefecture alluded to "a certain debutante whose name and role caused some stir at the Hôtel de Ville, from 1857 to 1869."[18] Horace Viel-Castel, the journalistic concierge of the Second Empire, was less allusive than his source:

recently [he wrote on July 25, 1857], M. Haussmann, the *honorable* prefect of the Seine, was seen promenading in his coach, at Enghien, with Francine Cellier, a young dancer at the Opéra, the former mistress of the young Fronsac Baroche.[19]

The affair was also known outside official circles. In early 1860 Haussmann and his wife attended the premiere of *Le Paratonnerre*, staring Mlle Cellier. The play enjoyed some notoriety for its allusions to a "powerful protector," proclaimed by the actress in question, which "provoked unwelcome laughter from the gallery."[20]

Francine Cellier, a petite blonde, made her debut in September 1852, but her career stagnated until she attached herself to Haussmann. There is a long letter from Haussmann to an unnamed recipient on behalf of his mistress: "M. Auber has had the goodness to present to you Mlle Cellier, a dancer at the Opéra, who aspires to take declamation lessons at the Conservatory," he wrote, "in order to open for herself, if it is possible, a dramatic career. She has the good taste to desire, above all, your counsel and your lessons." "I take a genuine interest in the success of the efforts she is making . . . to create for herself, through hard work, an independent position," he continued. "I would be delighted to learn that you are able to recognize in her an ability for the theater which would offer her, in this case, a better future, and a position more in keeping with her character than the profession of ballerina." He concluded: "Allow me, therefore, Monsieur, to recommend this young artist to your kind attention. I am sure that she will be able to recommend herself to you, if she is able to find a place among your pupils."[21]

Haussmann's protection paid off. Gérard Lameyre followed Cellier's rise in the world by her increasingly expensive apartments.[22] She was living fashionably on the boulevard Malesherbes in 1877 when she disappeared from history. Her notorious alliance with Haussmann became grist for the tabloids of the day. On December 29, 1867, the satirical *Le Nain Jaune* published a slanderous article. "Each time that Mlle Cellier has taken a long lease on some apartment in Paris," they wrote, "expropriation has followed . . . and Mlle Cellier received an indemnity proportionate to the price of the rent and the length of the lease." She angrily demanded a retraction, and got it.[23]

There was another, less flagrant affair, with Mlle Marie Roze, a soprano of the Opéra-Comique.[24] She created the lead role in one of Auber's operas and sang Marguerite in Gounod's *Faust*. As her talent was more solid that Mlle Cellier's, so Haussmann's protection was less flamboyant. Music, as much as the women who performed it, drew Haussmann to the opera throughout his life. Long after he had ceased to be a public figure and a subject of gossip, he retained his box at the opera. In the inventory taken at his death is a season ticket for a loge at the opera, paid in advance.[25]

The scandal Haussmann brought upon himself did not affect his career. He lost no power and received no significant snubs from Parisian society or the government. Actively contributing to the hypocrisy of bourgeois family morality under the Second Empire carried no stigma and may even have conferred status: sexual speculators were as familiar, and as socially prominent, as their financial brethren.

Mme Haussmann suffered her husband's public infidelities. "It will be better that I remain with my husband, because I am more capable than he of remorse," she told a friend.[26] But if she endured the scandal and the pain, she did so, for a time, at her parents' home, in Bordeaux. It was the Empress Eugénie, herself the victim of her husband's incessant philandering, who reconciled the Haussmanns. Beyond the public rapprochement of the couple we can only guess at the nature of this marriage. Haussmann's career took precedence over his marriage. Externally the Haussmanns weathered the storms and temptations of the Second Empire and *la fête impériale*, but the price was not trivial. Not only his own union but those of his daughters were troubled.

Both the Haussmann daughters were married when he was prefect of the Seine. Henriette-Marie, the elder, married Camille Dollfus, a landowner, secretary to the embassy, mayor of Houeillès (Lot-et-Garonne), and a deputy, on March 27, 1861. They had two daughters. Valentine, the younger Haussmann child, first married Maurice, vicomte Pernety in 1865. This union was shortly dissolved. She then married (1891) Georges Renouard. There was a son from the first union. Finding suitable matches meant a sufficient dowry, and Haussmann had no independent wealth to draw upon. The money he and his wife had set aside for Henriette-Marie's dowry proved inadequate, given their new station in society and the social milieu in which a suitable mate was to be sought. M. Dumas, the president of the Municipal Council and a staunch supporter of Haussmann, took it upon himself to go to the emperor, in the name of the council, to ask his imperial highness to authorize a supplement to Henriette-Marie's dowry. Haussmann refused the gift, using the anecdote to celebrate the character and devotion of Dumas and his own rectitude.[27]

More serious was the scandal that attached to Valentine's name, the toll often exacted for joining the social whirl of the imperial court. "Mlle Haussmann is very pretty for those who like a good, pale complexion," wrote Mérimée, "but she is common, as is her father."[28] Much more than her sister or mother, Valentine relished *la fête impériale*, participating in the allegories staged at Compiègne and enjoying the company of the young ladies of the court. A scabrous pamphlet of the day told an elaborate story of how her father had prostituted his daughter to the emperor's lust. The child of this depraved union had been passed off as the child of the emperor's then current mistress, Marguerite Bellanger. There is no corroborative evidence.[29] Haussmann's notoriety had caused the mud slingers to bespatter his daughter. When Valentine's marriage plans were announced a quatrain made the rounds of the Paris salons.[30]

This short catalogue exhausts the stories of scandal, domestic or public, salacious or pecuniary. There were few who liked Haussmann, but even his many enemies did not begrudge him praise for his diligence, capacity for work, dedication, and honesty, and Rouher noted paradoxically that his many faults complemented his many virtues. "Everything was on a grand scale, his qualities and his faults":

> His qualities: a firm and stubborn character, unassailable probity, a prodigious capacity for work, an ability to assimilate information so highly developed that in the wink of an eye he made his own—and believed to be his own—all the ideas of his collaborators. His faults: an intolerable vanity, a taste for arbitrariness, disdain for all that was outside his pedestrian [*médiocre*] and uncultivated mind.[31]

Those who loathed and those who respected him—he did not inspire much love—did so for the reasons Rouher enumerated.

Haussmann was a philistine. Aside from his love of music, the prefect had little intellectual polish. As a young man he had worked diligently at stocking his mind with history and philosophy, although he made no mention of reading the poets and novelists either of his day or of an earlier age. But his mind was essentially manipulative, an exceptional instrument for the assimilation and application of practical and technical information. He was endowed with clarity of expression but little literary imagination, and he appears to have been completely outside of or untouched by the major intellectual currents of his age. His genius lay in administration. Now and then he quoted a historical anecdote or Voltaire's dicta on modernizing Paris, but he had little use for literary culture. The same was true of his sensitivity to the visual arts. Neither shortcoming proved a hindrance to his career. Mocked by the intellectuals with the unique exception of George Sand, who had known him as a young man and experienced his kindness, Haussmann was nevertheless ideally fit for the great task thrust upon him by Louis Napoléon.

Haussmann was a bureaucrat. The prefect seldom left his office, almost never visited a building site, did not walk about the city, and was driven by liveried coachmen to all his appointments. Paris was increasingly a series of quantifiable abstractions: the poetry of a budget, lines on a map, survey plats, tons of building materials, meters of sewer pipe, acres of garden. A stroke of his pen, a figure moved from one column to another, his signature: all set enormous forces in motion. An army of workers obeyed his commands and he saw the results of their labor only when he officiated at the ribbon-cutting. He had little tactile contact with the city. It was a series of problems to be solved, the expression of abstract ideas about the nature of an imperial capital. It was not a living organism with habits: Paris had, for Haussmann, needs but not desires, limbs and arteries, a digestive system, but no heart. Its mind was his all-knowing intelligence. From the corner office in the Hôtel de Ville he spun a vast and intricate web in which the great city was enmeshed. Both the violence and the creativity of the work of transformation was blunted for him by his bureaucratic isolation and self-satisfaction.

Haussmann's energy and capacity for administrative work were legendary. He was at his desk every morning at 6 a.m. and worked through the day, taking a frugal lunch, and on into the night if there were no social functions. There is "more time in twenty-four hours than is generally believed," he wrote. "One can accomplish many things between 6 a.m. and midnight and beyond, when one has an active body, an alert, receptive mind, an excellent memory, the ability to work rapidly and easily, and above all when one needs only a little sleep. And Sundays? Remember, there are fifty-two of them a year."[32] Virtually all the work of the prefecture passed through his hands, and he had an astonishing grasp on the details of his office. "Haussmann's predecessors had signed in advance letters that were to be sent out. The new prefect insisted that every project be submitted to him beforehand and each day he returned the files, "after having examined their contents, very often making corrections or observations denoting a close reading of each file."[33] He had at his fingertips all the projects in the city. "When he worked with his engineers and department heads he knew what was in their files without opening them," wrote Gustave Claudin.[34]

The dialectic of bureaucratic absorption, isolation, and abstraction and *la fête impériale* account for the shape and style of transformed Paris, and the destruction of Old Paris. Haussmann's detachment from the city issued in indifference—as with the destruction of the Luxembourg Gardens—or enjoyment—as with the cleansing of the courtyard of the Louvre:

> Since my youth the dilapidated condition of the Place du Carrousel, in front of the courtyard of the Tuileries, seemed to me to be a shame for France, a declaration of the impotence of her government, and I always resented it.[35]

Urban renewal is inherently destructive, and the very size of Paris meant the scale of wreckage would be unprecedented. Théophile Gautier found demolished Paris aesthetically interesting: "the shadow and the light make picturesque effects on the piles of rubble, on these accidental arrangements of stones and beams haphazardly fallen."[36] Zola, no friend to haussmannization, was also fascinated.

He has Aristide Saccard climb to the top of Montmartre to survey the city:

> When the first *réseau* will be finished then the great dance will begin. The second *réseau* will reach out everywhere to attach the *faubourgs* to the first *réseau*. The cut-up pieces will writhe in the plaster . . . from the boulevard du Temple to the gate at the Place du Trône, a gash; another gash from the Madeleine church to the Plaine de Monceau; a third gash in this direction, another in that direction, a gash here, a gash there. Wounds everywhere. Paris slashed with saber cuts, her veins opened, nourishing 100,000 demolishers and masons.[37]

Haussmann had a much more prosaic, bureaucratic appraisal of his work: "From the end of 1852 until the end of 1859 (that is, before the annexation)," he wrote, "the number of houses demolished in the original twelve arrondissements reached 4,349. Only 2,236 of these were demolished by the city after expropriation; the other 2,113 were demolished by their owners to be reconstructed by them, in whole or in part."[38] In the dense urban fabric relatively minor projects demanded considerable destruction. Haussmann razed 172 houses to unencumber the Palais-Royal.[39] Even the boulevard Malesherbes, beyond the congested center of Paris, necessitated demolition: 84 houses were sacrificed.[40]

Destruction, for Haussmann, was authority, control, and purpose, unlike the half-hearted or partial projects of earlier administrations. He spoke with no sentiment of the Ministry of Foreign Affairs, in "the former palace of the Prince de Neuchâtel . . . which, as prefect of the Seine, I had demolished and sold off in very expensive lots, for the state's profit."[41] The demolitions necessary to build the boulevard St. Germain meant the disappearance of a number of elegant private *hôtels* of the seventeenth and eighteenth centuries. Several lovely examples, however, remain in what is today the seventh arrondissement, mostly as government offices and foreign embassies, recalling the splendor of that aristocratic *quartier* so celebrated by Balzac. On the Right Bank an equally elegant aristocratic *quartier* was obliterated to make way for the boulevard Haussmann. The Chaussée d'Antin was still rural at the end of the eighteenth century when the duc d'Orléans and his friends hired the best and most fashionable architects to build their residences. A number of celebrated *hôtels* fell to Haussmann's wreckers, including that of the actress Mlle Grimard, designed by Ledoux and containing a private theater that could seat five hundred. Also lost was some of the most celebrated work of Alexandre-Théodore Brongniart, the architect of the Bourse.[42] Haussmann demolished the *hôtel* of the Queen of Sweden, which had belonged to Napoléon's marshal, Bernadotte, and at the same time tore down the house where he himself had been born. His own monument, from choice, would be a new street, not an old house. He offered these demolitions as evidence that he had not spared himself or the rich.

Throughout the seventeen years of his power a cacophony of voices was raised against his demolitions. All these criticisms formed an ever-present but unfocused Greek chorus for the dramatic transformation of Paris. Haussmann had incessantly to defend himself, but the public outcry was so diffuse, spread over so many competing interests that he could treat it with arrogance or contempt. Only with his destruction of part of the Luxembourg Gardens did the chorus of complaint seriously threaten him.

The Luxembourg Palace, the most Italianate of Paris châteaux, built by Marie de Medici between 1616 and 1623, was set amid one of the loveliest gardens in the city (D-E 4–5). Haussmann built a series of streets around the palace grounds, lopping off significant chunks of the garden. By decree (November 26, 1865) the nursery at the east and west of the gardens, a triangle between the rue d'Assas, the avenue de l'Observatoire, and the rue Auguste-Comte, was destroyed. This particular part of the grounds had been created at the time of the French Revolution, when the palace itself was used as a prison, on land that had belonged to a confiscated convent, which was demolished. Where the old convent had stood was "a forest of roses intermingled with woodland, where one could walk along narrow pathways, tasting the charms of silence while breathing the pure air."[43] "With this garden," where an earlier generation had "read the philosophy of Kant and the novels of George Sand," wrote Anatole France, "perished the noble thoughts of young men."[44] On the other side of the grounds Haussmann attacked the setting of the Medici Fountain: "The displacement of a few meters endured by the Medici Fountain, and the suppression of several plane trees in the garlanded path that leads to it, have no more compromised its excellent monumental effect than its great artistic value."[45]

Virtually no one shared the prefect's bland minimalization of the damage. His argument that the emperor had so richly endowed Paris with new parks and squares that the new city was more than adequately compensated for a few acres of the Luxembourg Gardens did not mitigate the anger. Pamphlets poured from the press and petitions circulated.[46] Haussmann defended himself in a speech to the Senate (May 1, 1861), but the attack on the Luxembourg Gardens passed into literature, political debate, and national memory. The new streets were not only ugly, they were useless, wrote Hugo. All that remained of the once lovely location was "a spot of grass and a bit of decrepit wall . . . not worth the trouble of a close look." And "in January 1871 a Prussian shell chose this corner of earth to land on, a continuation of the embellishments. M. Bismarck finished what M. Haussmann had begun."[47] Years after his fall from power, when Haussmann briefly returned to politics as a deputy for Corsica, he spoke in favor of rebuilding the Tuileries Palace, destroyed by arson during the last days of the Commune. Georges Clemenceau, shouting from his seat, interrupted the speaker: "You destroyed the Luxembourg!"[48] Even an anonymous obituary notice recalled the attack on the Luxembourg: "He unnecessarily destroyed the monuments of old Paris that had a true artistic value. These were acts of stubborn vandalism which did not even have as justification new buildings to be erected: witness the mutilation of the Luxembourg Garden."[49]

The fury over the Luxembourg Gardens endured. Haussmann had touched a raw nerve. Although he had given Parisians more parks and squares and promenades than the old city ever possessed, the loss of the Luxembourg acres, part of the city's original small patrimony of public gardens, was unforgiven. The sense of violation was profound. Haussmann could successfully appeal to progress and hygiene in justifying his destructions on the Ile de la Cité. He could not make a similar appeal with the Luxembourg. The rectilinear im-

MASSACRE AT THE RUE TRANSNONAIN. Honoré Daumier's haunting etching commemorating the massacre of innocent bystanders in the early morning hours of April 14, 1832, in the apartment at 12, rue de la Transnonain. The artist's lithograph was the most famous depiction of the scene, as well as a terrible indictment of the July Monarchy. Haussmann bragged that he eliminated the street where the army murdered the innocent residents.

RAMBUTEAU. Henry Scheffer's portrait of the comte de Rambuteau, prefect of the Seine during the July Monarchy. Scheffer's prefect is poised, elegant, self-assured: more an aristocrat than a professional bureaucrat. Indeed, it would have been unthinkable to Rambuteau to be portrayed as a mere public servant. (Haussmann was the first new man to be prefect of the Seine, wholly devoted to and dependent on administrative service for his career and identification.) A Burgundian aristocrat trained in the service of Napoléon I, Rambuteau began a number of the important projects Haussmann would complete (and take credit for). He was constrained in much that he attempted by the cautious bourgeoisie of the day, who wanted urban change but were unwilling to pay for it. The rue Rambuteau is his most successful work and evidence of his abilities as a city planner.

BERGER. An anonymous caricature of the prefect of the Seine—in full uniform— whom Haussmann replaced. Very much a transitional figure, Berger was a successful politician from the Auvergne rather than an aristocrat like Rambuteau, but not yet a professional bureaucrat. A likable, open character, Berger lacked the financial daring and ruthlessness Louis Napoléon demanded and was consequently removed from office.

HAUSSMANN "VOLEUR": A caricature, by H. Mailly, of Haussmann in the pillory. The word "*voleur*" (thief) is branded on his forehead. It refers to the city's speculations on expropriated property. A *recéleur*, in this context, is a criminal who receives stolen property. Great fortunes were made by the transformation of Paris, but Haussmann himself left office in 1870 financially no better off than when he entered in 1853. Whatever else he may have been, he was no thief. He was regularly and brutally caricatured in the press.

HAUSSMANN
Recéleur de PARIS vendu
a la Destruction.

HAUSSMANN "PREFECT": A photograph by Pierre Petit. Haussmann sat for this portrait some time in the early 1860s when Petit did a series of all the members of the Municipal Council. He is still bearded, as he was until the mid-1860s. The rosette in his buttonhole is the Légion d'honneur. In an informal yet stately pose, the bureaucrat is presented absorbed in some document but not actually working. There is no portrait or photograph of Haussmann at work. He is always depicted as a good bourgeois against some neutral background, with no specific references to what he does for a living except that it is a "profession."

LOUIS NAPOLEON. An undated photograph of the emperor by Félix Tournachon, called Nadar (1820–1910), who was arguably the most distinguished photographer of his generation. Virtually all the notable men and women of the day sat for Nadar—although Haussmann did not—who became the Yousuf Karsh of the nineteenth century. There are not many portraits of Louis Napoléon in civilian clothes. He preferred to present a military image to the public, although from the mid- or late-1860s, with the Liberal Empire a possibility, he was more often in mufti. The narrow, nearly hooded eyes were much remarked by contemporaries.

EMILE OLLIVIER. Pierre Petit's portrait of Haussmann's *bête noire*. The photograph is undated and gives little sense of the fiery republican orator. He appears distant and abstracted, much less at his ease than Haussmann was in his sitting for the same photographer. Some of his aloofness, arrogance, vanity—all three were invoked by contemporaries—is evident.

LES HALLES. The central pavilion seen from the roof of St. Eustache. This is a photograph of a colored, anonymous lithograph. In the distance, almost exactly in the center, are Notre Dame and the St. Jacques tower. The apartment houses next to the pavilions give some sense of how nicely Baltard's ingenious sheds fit into the city.

OLD AND NEW PARIS. Marville's photograph of the rues de la Tonellière (foreground) and du Contrat Social, with a market shed under construction in the background. The two streets are gone, destroyed to make way for les Halles. The photograph is far less immaculate than the preceding lithograph, and nicely shows the contrast between New and Old Paris: the modern, inexpensive building materials of iron, glass, and decorative brick, and the stucco and stone of an earlier age.

LES HALLES. Marville made dozens of photographs of the new Paris "street furniture." This one, taken of one of the sheds of les Halles, has two different *réverbères*, or street lights, a tree grate and iron support, the gates of les Halles, and even the curbstones (with sewer opening). The slatted windows of the shed were worked by Baltard's system of wires and pulleys.

THE SEWERS. Nadar designed electric lights—their glare can be seen at both ends of the tunnel— that he took into the sewers to make photographs. Because the time needed for a correct exposure was so long, he used mannequins dressed as sewermen. This photograph is of one of Haussmann's *bateaux vannes*, seen from the rear, cleaning out a passageway.

THE GRAND THEATRE. The Allées de Tourny looking toward Victor Louis's Grand Théâtre, in the center of the lithograph. This extraordinary building was the focal point of Tourny's triangle of boulevards that was, and remains, Bordeaux's center of gravity. It is very likely that Haussmann first considered using an opera house to tie together an urban center from this example. The Hôtel Saige, directly behind the Grand Théâtre—built by Victor Louis at the same time—was the prefect's residence in Bordeaux, where Haussmann lived for two years.

ST. GIRONS. This photograph of the town around 1900 gives a good sense of its charm and isolation, nestled in the Pyrenees. Haussmann said he first became aware of the blessings of a pure water supply when posted here, in disgrace, as a young bureaucrat. He attributed the robust health of the residents to their water supply.

CESTAS. The entrance to Haussmann's château. His coat of arms is carved over the central bay window, but one entered from the side bay. His study was in the wing of the house to the right; the large dining room looked out upon the gardens in the rear of the building.

CESTAS. Haussmann's study. Everything in this photograph was in the house when Haussmann owned it except the books and papers.

perative, both aesthetically and bureaucratically, took precedence over gardens. Haussmann was not hostile to city parks or gardens. Quite the contrary. He richly endowed Paris with greenery, but only within his highly disciplined and rigid aesthetic system. He sincerely thought quantity mattered more than quality. He did not see that the tradition and familiarity of the Luxembourg was irreplaceable.

Haussmann attacked, gratuitously, it seemed, the very self-image of Parisians. His new parks were not representative of some remembered pastorale existence, however mythic. The Luxembourg, with its memories, was. It was not merely a bit of the Parisian past, it carried the baggage of rural longing, a reminder not so much of Old Paris as the remembrance of another imaginative order. Old buildings and old streets could more easily be replaced by new. Old gardens could not—a reality Haussmann could not appreciate.

His urban, aesthetic, and personal priorities were well integrated and ruthlessly realized in Paris. His bureaucratic passions inclined him to more rather than less destruction. "In order to make the vast spaces at the extremities of the city, which remained unproductive, accessible and inhabitable," he wrote, "the first job was to cut streets right through the city from one side to the other, by tearing open the central districts."[50] Haussmann conceived of the city as a public, not a private, place. He thought in terms of zones of social activity, demarcated from yet accessible to each other by new streets that formed systems of communication. In his urban scheme the individual house had no place. Nor did the individual. Abstract collectivities were paramount: the city, the state, the empire, the capital. The city was for him a vast infrastructure rather than a human habitation and expression. Before these administrative priorities, individuals and their rights disappeared, absorbed into collective units.

He encouraged luxury apartment houses along his most magnificent new boulevards and avenues, not individual *hôtels*, which he demolished. Practically and technically it was easier and more profitable for the city to cut new streets than to enlarge existing ones. There were fewer expropriations and less demolition when a new street was cut, and property values were more enhanced.[51] Cutting new streets also meant that Haussmann's passion for the rectilinear could have free rein, and less care was taken about which buildings were demolished. Enlarging or aligning existing streets presumes preservation and restoration. For Haussmann only public monuments were worth preserving, and they had to be first extracted from their immediate urban environment. The character of a neighborhood, the elegance of an individual house were equally unpersuasive. Paris was to be the national capital; parochial claims carried no weight.

· XII ·

"Organs of the Large City"

PARIS UNDERGROUND WAS HAUSSMANN'S GREATEST SUCCESS. CON-
structing the city's internal organs he had no landlords to pamper,
no condemnations, no juries of expropriation, no architects, no national monuments to skirt, no neighborhood traditions to honor, no
local political bigwigs to court. The bowels of the city were not only
terra incognita, they were unowned. The engineers with whom he
worked were practical people whose concerns and choices he understood because they were so similar to his own. There was a good
deal of public contention, long and venomous, but in these bruising
confrontations Haussmann so ably marshaled the arguments of science and progress, deftly manipulating the new language of politics,
that he eventually carried the day. The Paris sewers and water supply remain, as they instantly became, the only uniformly praised aspects of haussmannization.

The Paris sewers before Haussmann were a mysterious, dim
netherworld of unspeakable filth. Jean-Paul Marat, fleeing Lafayette's
crackdown on radicals in 1791, hid out in the sewers, where he may
have contracted his horrible, agonizing skin disease that confined him
to his bathtub. By far the most famous encounter with the sewers,
however, was Victor Hugo's brilliant description of Javert's obsessed
pursuit of Jean Valjean through the sewers, a text that fixed the

imagery of underground Paris for generations. Preparing to write the extraordinary pages in part five of *Les Misérables*, the novelist had descended into the sewers to study them firsthand, accompanied by the engineer Pierre-Emmanuel Bruneseau, his cicerone in the underworld. Dark, mysterious, labyrinthine, disgusting, irrational, Hugo's sewers were also a "potent cultural symbol of moral disintegration and political disorder," unpredictable, uncivilized, an underground universe where the myriad distinctions that gave social coherence vanished. The poet identified the terror lurking in this crepuscular world of human and social waste in moral terms:

> The sewer is the conscience of the city. All things converge and confront one another there. In this ghastly place there are shadows, but there are no more secrets. Everything takes on its true shape, or at least its definitive shape. One can say this for the refuse heap—it is not a liar. . . . All the filthiness of civilization, once out of commission, falls into this pit of truth where the immense social slippage ends up.[1]

Hugo was the poet of the old Paris sewers. André-Jean-Baptiste Parent-Duchâtelet (1790–1835) their prosaic crusader. A doctor disillusioned with his profession, Parent-Duchâtelet was the first important French public health expert and the most influential reformer of his day. He studied prostitution and sewers, using a common vocabulary of sexual imagery: clandestine, sinful, irrational, filthy, diseased, vile, mysterious passageways. He put sewers and waste removal—and the water supply as well—on the public agenda. Haussmann inherited the antiquated and dangerous system painted by Hugo and deplored by Parent-Duchâtelet, and shared some of their fascination and fastidiousness. His arguments for transformation, however, were almost exclusively clinical, cast in the rhetoric of hygiene and cleanliness.

The discovery of cholera contagion as water-borne had not yet been made, but there was general agreement that the cholera epidemics of 1832 and 1849 were related to the lack of cleanliness, overcrowding, and inadequate sewers. The sewers emptied into the Seine, which provided the chief source of the city's drinking water. It had long been known that certain stretches of the river were more polluted than others. There were regulations about where water sellers might draw their supplies, but the rules were often evaded. The long manuscript, "Rapport sur la salubrité de l'eau. . .," probably commissioned by one of Haussmann's immediate predecessors, speaks to this problem.[2] The anonymous engineer examined the river "in May, June, and August, in the unfavorable conditions of a drought and a considerable fall in the water level." Seine water was "excellent at the pont d'Ivry" but altered markedly when it mixed with the waters of the Marne, "becoming more and more impure from its encounter with the Bièvre [which contained large quantities of chemical waste from the tanneries along its banks] until Chaillot," by which time "it had lost most of its primitive qualities." By the time it reached Neuilly "it was even more impure." Downstream, as the Seine neared Asnières, the water began to be cleaner, but then came the two sewer outlets (at Asnières and Clichy), and the water was not drinkable for three kilometers downriver. By exercising extreme care in drawing water from the river, the reporter concluded, Paris could be adequately and healthily supplied.[3] Opinion held that Seine water drawn from the middle of the river and well below the surface was fit to drink. The Samaritaine pump, first installed in the eighteenth century near the Pont-Neuf (E 4) for precisely this purpose, was the most important such machine in Paris.

Additional water, thought less good than that of the Seine, came from the Ourcq canal (G 1–2), created as a source by Napoléon I. "Down in La Cortille," Josépha revealed in Balzac's *Cousine Bette*, "in the rue Saint-Maur-du-Temple, I know a poor family who possess a treasure: a little girl, prettier than I was at 16!. . .She drinks water from the Ourcq, out of the town taps, because Seine water is too dear."[4]

At Haussmann's accession the water supply came from the Seine and the Ourcq, and was distributed by water carriers. Despite the fountain-building mania of Rambuteau—he endowed the city with more than 1,500, from the beautiful fountains in the Place de la Concorde (D 3), the Place St. Sulpice (D 4), the parc Louvois (E 2–3), to mere spigots—Paris was not adequately served. Even the rich depended on the water carriers for their supplies. The estimate is that only three in a hundred apartments had running water,[5] and all the water in Paris was "cold in the winter, hot in the summer, suspect at all times, and of a very mediocre quality."[6] What distribution conduits existed "in 1852 had a total length of 705,350 meters. They were mostly of a small diameter."[7] These figures do not have much meaning until we set them beside the figures for 1869, which Haussmann proudly did, dropping into his favorite idiom, statistics: "In 1869 Paris provided daily, for the private use of its inhabitants, from 24,000 to 30,000 cubic meters of well water, admirably limpid, of perfect quality, at a constant temperature, conducted [to the city] via the aqueduct of the Dhuys, while 100,000 additional cubic meters of water, even better, if possible, would soon arrive from the Vanne, also via aqueduct."[8] The *réseau* of water conduits contained 1,547 kilometers.[9] The figures for sewer building were equally dramatic. Haussmann inherited 107,430 meters of sewer line, the largest of which was 1 meter 80 centimeters in height. In suburban Paris there were only 39,300 meters. "We redid almost all the small sewers, in old and new Paris, and constructed, in the former, 217,700 meters, and in the latter, 187,975 meters of new sewer, whose smallest lines were 2 meters 30 in height . . . and as large as 4 meters." This made for a total *réseau* of 560,625 meters.[10] These achievements represented not only the most impressive and admirable engineering feats of Haussmann's urbanization but were accomplished in the teeth of bitter opposition. Ten years of acrimonious debate elapsed from his first report on the Paris water supply and the commencement of work.

The man responsible for engineering the new Paris water supply and sewers was Eugène Belgrand (1810–78). Haussmann had first met him as prefect of the Yonne when Belgrand was an *ingénieur ordinaire* for the town of Avallon. He had married "richly and honorably"—Haussmann was always careful to fix those he discussed in the social hierarchy—and had designed for the town a handsome public fountain that delivered the fresh, inexhaustible water supply he had captured by diverting a local spring. The prefect was "astonished" to discover in "this large, bald man, whose simple appearance masked his superior intelligence," a geologist and hydrologist of the first order. It was a good match: Haussmann was "an adept, or at least a curious amateur" of these two sciences. While in disgrace in St. Girons, he had been struck by the general good health of the population and attributed it, partly, to the water, drawn from several mountain streams. When he sampled the water in Avallon he sent for Belgrand and requested a report on the geology of the supply. "A mutual sympathy was established between us."[11] He later summoned Belgrand from provincial obscurity, as he himself had been summoned to greatness, and set him the engineering challenge of his generation: bringing water to and from Paris.

On August 4, 1864, the prefect submitted to the Municipal Council the learned report that would form the basis not only of Belgrand's fame but of the Paris water system. Haussmann accompanied it with his own *Mémoire sur les Eaux de Paris*—his fourth on the subject—and Mille's report on how the great cities of Britain— London, Manchester, Liverpool, Edinburgh, and Glasgow—which he had recently visited, dealt with water and sewers. This marked the last battle in "this Homeric struggle, which today is hardly believable, that I had to engage in against the fanatics of Seine water, before getting the declaration of public utility necessary to divert the water of the Dhuys to the reservoirs of Ménilmontant."[12]

The "fanatics of Seine water" made plausible enough arguments. There were no established links between disease, especially cholera, and water, they argued. If one exercised some care in drawing water from the Seine the danger of contamination was virtually eliminated. Seine water had more character, more taste than other sources, and had served Paris and its surrounding towns for centuries. All that was needed was some additional pumping capacity and stiffer regulations. The enormous expense proposed by Haussmann was unwarranted, they continued, and represented another aspect of his penchant for destructiveness and desire for novelty. Piping water via aqueducts from distant wells or rivers was foolish, expensive, and redundant when the capital had, literally in its midst, a perfectly fine water supply. The technical questions of raising the Seine supply to a sufficient height to service the newly incorporated parts of Paris could be solved by modern steam pumps. Haussmann was defending an ancient technology against opponents who posed as the defenders of the moderns against the ancients.

The declaration of public utility of the Dhuys source was issued March 11, 1862. Workers broke ground on the Ménilmontant reservoir (H 2), which was to receive the new waters, on September 1, 1862, construction of the aqueduct began in June 1863, was opened August 15, 1865, and the first waters from the Dhuys spring flowed in the Paris mains, only twenty-seven months later, on October 1, 1863. Haussmann had characteristically (and deliberately) underestimated expenses: the Dhuys aqueduct was nearly five million francs over budget.

Haussmann and Belgrand were in perfect agreement about the unsuitability of Seine water for drinking, although they ingeniously left the original system of water supply intact, using this water for street cleaning. Until very recently in Paris one could still see spigots designated "eau non potable." It was, however, no easy matter to find a suitable new supply that was ample, entered the city at sufficient elevation for distribution by gravity, was pure enough for drinking, of a constant temperature, and could feasibly be brought to Paris. Belgrand conducted a geological survey of the Seine region for a year before concluding there was no water in the immediate vicinity that would do. Aside from the problem of salubrity, Seine water was cold in the winter and hot in the summer, as noted above, and it would be difficult to filter it completely. Haussmann also opposed the river as a source by pointing out that the city's water supply had to enter above the highest point of Paris, raised with the annexations of 1860, which included the heights of Montmartre and Belleville. It would be prohibitively expensive to pump Seine water to the requisite height of at least 70 meters above sea level. In fact the eventual water source entered Paris at 108 meters above sea level.[13]

Belgrand had investigated the Loire River as a source but found that the water contained a fine sand that was virtually unfilterable, and the river, already difficult to navigate because of shallowness, could not afford to have water drawn off for Paris. The Somme-Soude valley offered the closest acceptable water, but drawing water from the Marne became so knotty a political problem that the emperor himself advised Haussmann to find another source. Belgrand finally found what he required in the old province of Champagne.

The well water from two springs, the Dhuys and the Vanne, possessed all the required properties of limpidity, salubrity, and abundance, and could be diverted to Paris. The actual engineering problem, carrying the water more than a hundred miles and having it enter the city at a height of 108 meters, was brilliantly solved by the use of an aqueduct. Haussmann, who liked to speak of Paris as "the Imperial Rome of our day," was delighted with this ancient and elegant solution, and it served him well with the emperor, an amateur of Roman history who liked to be flattered as a second Augustus Caesar.[14]

To emphasize the purity of Dhuys water Haussmann, with his theatrical flair, had constructed at the Ménilmontant reservoir a tile chamber where "all our opponents, to the great consternation of the stubborn defenders of Seine water, could easily read through five meters of this marvellously transparent liquid, the inscription of its origin: Water of the Dhuys."[15] In his *Mémoires*, Haussmann celebrated the triumph verbally but no less dramatically:

> I am myself astonished at the courage, the very audacity of which I gave proof, from the time of my arrival at the Hôtel de Ville, in being the first, and for a long time the only one, to cast doubt on the value of Seine water as drinking water. This prejudice formed an article of faith for the Paris population, usually so skeptical, and even more, an article of faith for the learned bodies, in whose midst this legend persists to this very day.[16]

His persistence, in the face of broad and respectable opposition, was a manifestation of his deep fastidiousness, along with his contempt for medieval Paris, which he not infrequently referred to as an open sewer. His personal obsession found a comfortable faith in technological progress, and his authority was enhanced by the appeal to scientific, or at least technical, arguments and opinions. Yet the intensity of Haussmann's championship of a new water supply was fired not so much by the cool conviction that comes of technical demonstration as by the need to cleanse that informed all that he did. He expressed the rational passion of the technocrat, but he was driven by deeper emotions that may be traced to a sickly childhood, when he was sent out of Paris to the cleaner, more salubrious air of the country. The association of illness with filth, which would play so large a role in his career, early took root in his being.

When it came to the issue of sewers, Haussmann had to go back to antiquity to find a precedent for what he proposed.[17] He borrowed the prestige of the Roman Empire for his own projects, which he thought superior, and hoped to win the emperor's support for an undertaking in which Louis Napoléon had shown little interest. There were no sewers or drains in the imperial sketch for the transformation of Paris, as there was no provision for a new water supply, nor any plans for improving the old sewers. The prefect, however, waxed poetic about sewers, momentarily abandoning his ideal of precise, legalistic prose. The new water system, he wrote in 1854, would require a new sewer system, and the street excavations were the perfect opportunity "to construct an urban circulatory system free of blocked arteries and fouled orifices—to correct the sluggish intestine left by the old *régime*"[18]:

> The underground galleries, organs of the large city, would function like those of the human body. Pure and fresh water, light, and heat would circulate beneath the urban skin like the diverse fluids whose movement and maintenance support life. Secretions would take place mysteriously and would maintain public health without troubling the good order of the city and without spoiling its exterior beauty.[19]

These organic images he supplemented with statistics. He had inherited 107,437 meters of sewer and left, counting the old retained system with the new, 560,625, plus 8,000 meters of collectors. There were more meters of sewer than street because several of the sections had to have double galleries. Not only did he build on a grand scale, but he did so with astonishing rapidity: in one four-and-a-half-year period he constructed 63 kilometers of sewer.[20] The length of the system, the ingenuity of its arrangement, the brilliance of the engineering, which drained the city in two directions, the great collectors—especially that at Asnières, the *cloaca maxima* of Paris, 4 meters 40 centimeters high, 5 meters 60 wide—and the size of the sewers, were all equally impressive, although it is size that captured the imagination. The old sewers were 1 meter 80 high; the smallest sewers in the new system were 2 meters 30 high and 1 meter 30 wide, the galleries were between 2 meters 40 and 3 meters 90 high, 1 meter 50 to 4 meters wide.[21] A person could easily walk through the entire system, although Haussmann would have had to bend over to make it through the smaller galleries.

The prefect was especially delighted with the system for cleaning the sewers that he devised, once he wrested control of this function from the prefect of police, in 1859. The galleries were built with a *cunette*, or channel, in the center and side paths for the sewer men, who manipulated a long-handled tool, called a *rabot*, to dam up the water in the *cunette* and then release it, flushing the gallery. Haussmann, inspired by having observed the swamps around Blaye being drained by specially designed boats when he was sous-préfet there,[22] sketched and had built sluice carts, called *wagons-vannes*, in the larger galleries and *bateaux-vannes* in the even larger collectors. The metal plates at the rear of these contraptions could be lowered, causing the sewage to back up behind them, while the strong current created by this damming would pass under the plates and through the *cunette*, washing away the sediment. The pressure of the dammed sewage water behind the cart pushed it along. Flushing was accomplished by a pierced shield, exactly the size of the sewer, fitted to the front of the cart. The water was forced through the holes, which, however, were small enough to trap solid matter, pushing it along the sewer in front of the boat.[23]

Having built a marvelous water and sewer system, Haussmann stopped short of imposing it upon the landowners, yet another instance of his pampering and a nice contrast with the accomplishments realized below and thwarted above ground. Water was available but there were no sanctions to assure its equitable or wide distribution. Each proprietor had the option of subscribing to the city water system if desired but was required to pay water rates only if a subscriber. Many landlords decided against the expense. All new buildings, and all buildings undergoing major renovation, had to be connected to the new sewer system, but only for waste water. Cesspools were handled separately. Older housing stock escaped the requirement.

Paris underground, with its spacious, well-lighted galleries, rational system, gigantic collectors—its ideal synthesis of form and function—was the result of the same urban principles that pertained above ground. Yet it was, arguably, a more perfect realization of the principles of haussmannization. To create imperial Paris much had to be compromised or sacrificed, only to be achieved through illusion, trompe l'oeil. Some of his most original ideas—the green belt around Paris, or moving the cemeteries to Méry-sur-Oise—were thwarted, the former by political opposition mounted when the emperor was absent in Italy, the latter by a very effective campaign against building a "city of the dead." Underground, Haussmann was free to let the principles of grandeur, order, rectilinearity, uniformity, and complete predictability run their course. In this netherworld the regularity achieved through administrative fiat was palpable and unimpeded. The sewers were the very essence of cleanliness, the triumph of reason over chaos, the progress of science, specifically medical science, and of enlightenment over darkness. Above ground the urban fabric stubbornly resisted the prefect's will: below ground, he could create the geometric, cleansed universe he craved.

So successful were Haussmann's sewers that they became one of the wonders of new Paris, if not of the world. During the Exposition of 1867 the sewer administration began offering public tours of what the engineers called fondly "a subterranean, second Paris," where they thoughtfully marked the streets under which visitors were passing. Even royalty made the descent. Haussmann personally conducted the Russian emperor, Alexander II, through the sewers, accompanied by the inspecter general of bridges and streets, Belgrand. Alexander visited Paris underground incognito, as "a noble foreigner." He was soon followed by the king of Portugal. Emperor and commoner took the same route, partly by boat—one of the *wagons-vannes*, without its pierced shield attached and with its metal fins raised—partly on foot. All were impressed with the tidiness and order of the system. So carefully kept were the walkways that "a lady might walk along them from the Louvre to the Place de la Concorde without fear of bespatting her dainty skirts."[24] The visit took about an hour and was highly recommended by all the contemporary guidebooks.

The underworld of Parent-Duchâtelet and Hugo, irrational and feminine according to the assumptions of the age, had been transformed into a rational, male world.[25] The whole was lit with thousands of lamps that illumined the hitherto dark and mysterious. The sewers had become underground boulevards, and, as were those overhead, they even became a fit subject for art, particularly the most modern, technological, and bourgeois art, photography. Félix Nadar took a celebrated series of photos of the sewers. In his pictures the sewers are presented as a world apart, cold, silent, austere, and peopled by another race, the sewer men in their uniforms and special boots. The bowels of the city were now exposed and no longer mysterious or terrifying.

Streets and sewers were the most dramatic and heroic aspects of haussmannization, but the parks and squares, gardens and trees that emerged during the transformation of Paris were equally characteristic, and their creator was equally proud. He invoked statistics to celebrate his accomplishment. In 1850 there were 47 acres of municipal parks. When he was forced from office, twenty years later, there were 4,500 acres.[26] He added eighteen squares to the city—an additional seven in the annexed zone—and nearly doubled the number of trees lining avenues and boulevards, with some of the grander streets given a double row of trees on each side.[27] In addition he planted trees on all public land: in the Place de la République, the Place de la Madeleine (D 2–3), the Place Malesherbes (D 2), and the Place du Théâtre-Français (E 3). This enormous accomplishment was made possible, Haussmann believed, by an "authoritarian but democratic regime." He regularly contrasted imperial efficiency with republican ineptitude. His work would have been impossible without Louis Napoléon. No republican regime—he clearly wants to contrast the Second Empire with the Second Republic that preceded it and the Third Republic that followed—would have given Haussmann the authority and autonomy he enjoyed under the emperor. The greening of Paris was a political act for Haussmann.

The prefect always insisted on the emperor's preeminent role, but if the inspiration for creating public space was the emperor's, Haussmann's translation of the wish into reality so transformed the original vision—through expansion, systematization, and hierarchical ordering—that it became his own. The emperor envisioned the Bois de Boulogne (A-B 2–5) as a kind of Hyde Park, and wanted Paris to have squares as did London. Haussmann enlarged the Bois considerably, altered Louis Napoléon's desire for a serpentine pond modeled on Hyde Park into lakes and cascades, insisted upon distributing green spaces "throughout the city," proposed the Bois de Vincennes (H 5), on the eastern periphery of Paris, as a pendant to the Bois de Boulogne, and added the parc Montsouris (E 6)and the Buttes Chaumont (G 2), Paris's old garbage dump recycled, both set in poor neighborhoods, as homologues of the posh parc Monceau (C-D 2).[28] The inspiration of a single park had become, in Haussmann's hands, an urban system.

The squares, when translated from English into French by Haussmann, ceased to be private, open (by key) only to the surrounding residents, and became public. His city was a public space rather than an agglomeration of private spaces. All these creations, from the grandest to the most humble, were fenced and gated, and the fences and gates, in their elegance or simplicity, declared a hierarchy, from the gilded portals of the parc Monceau to the simple wire gate of a neighborhood square. Davioud, the chief architect of promenades and plantations, was responsible for most of the designs that bound all the parks, squares, and boulevards together. They declared a single conception of the city and, at the same time, of the mass-productive capacity of an industrial society. Benches and wire hoops protected the grass and demarcated the gravel paths, and all were punctuated by trash receptacles, a variety of gas lamps, grates protecting tree roots, metal cages to assure uniform tree growth, individual fountains, kiosks for announcements, and an enormous variety of structures (chalets, guardhouses, gardener's sheds, restaurants). Uniformity, system, integration—the marks of Haussmann's urbanization—are evident in all the parks. And he imposed purpose as well. Haussmann's parks, with their bordered paths that kept strollers off the grass, their carefully contrived sight lines and artful geometry, largely determined how they were to be enjoyed.

The gardens Haussmann found in Paris, appendages of châteaux, were classical creations, laid out geometrically and designed for a promenade, not a picnic. These he did little to change. His taste in gardens ran to the formal French variety, perfected in the seventeenth century and traced back to the Italian Renaissance and ultimately to ancient Greece, to those, he declared, who understood "natural beauty."[29] "The art of gardens suffered a profound eclipse during the long twilight of the Middle Ages," he continued, when design "spurned" the Greek example, producing nothing very interesting for more than a dozen centuries.[30]

The art of gardening "appears to me to have attained its apogee when it learned how harmoniously to incorporate symmetrical, monumental, and sculptural elements, of an incontestable grandeur, with those of the palace they seemed to extend."[31] He dutifully acknowledged the beauties of an English garden, but his preferences diverged from those of the emperor. His tastes were derivative, even pedestrian. He wanted his gardens to imitate those of the seventeenth and eighteenth centuries. His originality as an urban gardener lay in an enlargement and generalization of two inherited traditions, the planted boulevard and formal garden, and their subjection to administration and systemization.

The Champs-Elysée, long an inner-city promenade, he replanted with chestnut trees, replacing the old elms. The chestnut, "whose beautiful early foliage and lovely bunches of spring flowers are the most magnificent of all our trees—a royal tree—which, moreover, lends itself to all uses," was his favorite.[32] Virtually all his new avenues and boulevards were planted, the larger of them with double rows of chestnuts, which not only spread trees throughout Paris but marked a sharp departure from precedent. Just as Haussmann brought the boulevard into the center of the city, so too did he bring the plantings that had lined the originally suburban boulevards. These plantings were essentially architectural: trees used to underline rectilinearity and reinforce perspective. His generous endowment of his new streets with the "royal tree" was an essential aspect of the Paris urban landscape until the 1950s, when many streets were widened to accommodate the automobile. Haussmann's chestnuts fell to the ax, completely destroying the careful proportional harmony between street and sidewalk underlined by the chestnuts that had graced the city for a century.

Haussmann's squares, unlike the Etoile, for example, function as did the eighteenth-century *place*, an area of repose. Only here, amid a nature controlled by the prefect—with often elaborate artificial lakes, rills, and rock formations, where walking on the grass was forbidden—could one escape the relentless stone and movement of the city. Every neighborhood had its squares.[33] He began building them with his very first urban project. The tower was all that remained of the church of St. Jacques la Boucherie, destroyed in the revolution. Haussmann raised it to the level of the new streets, disencumbered it from the surrounding houses, and created a handsome park in the center of Old Paris (E 3).[34]

Haussmann's interest in gardens was not only an aspect of his fastidiousness, it was abiding and genuine. At his château in Cestas, he built the first greenhouse in the region and when in residence took an avid interest in the then novel pleasure. Conservatory gardening, free of the constraints of climate and geography, domesticated Baudelaire's "vegetal irregularity" and appealed to the prefect's sense of order and control. He did not much like the contemporary taste for huge baskets of flowers or overly complicated arrangements of plants and flower beds. His gardener experienced the disappointment of his master's unenthusiastic reception of several creations: the Haussmann arms, with "*pyrèthres dorées* sitting in relief, on a red-brown background of *coleus* leaves, surround by a border of *Alternanthea*, with its tiny coral-colored flowers, punctuated by a row of that species of tiny pale gray artichokes called *Echeverria glauca*," or a decoration of the Legion of Honor, with all its details, set in a bed of tiny *sauges sanguines* in flower."[35] "These tiny masterpieces of my principal gardener," he commented, "could not fail but be imitated [in the region], heavy-handedly I must say," but "at Cestas they elicited the complacent smile of the Master, and won for the Servant a handshake in recognition of his zeal."[36]

For all the projects and undertakings that absorbed him he either created a new administrative department and appointed a special head who had his complete confidence and support—Deschamps for the *Plan de Paris*, Belgrand for water and sewers—or he himself assumed total responsibility, as with urban finances and annexation. Jean Charles Adolphe Alphand (1817–91) was appointed director of the park service in 1854 and subsequently director of public works. Alphand, allied by marriage to an important commercial family in Bordeaux, was an *ingénieur ordinaire* in that city, and had done the preparations for Haussmann's splendid reception of Louis Napoléon in 1852, decorating not only the Grand Théâtre for the great ball but the Salle de la Bourse for the banquet. Haussmann, unerring in choosing collaborators, summoned Alphand to Paris as soon as he had dismissed the "almost illiterate gardener" he had inherited from Berger's administration. At the same time he summoned Alphand he also summoned from Bordeaux the horticulturist Barillet-Deschamps, who would oversee the design and planting of lawns, trees, and shrubs. Barillet-Deschamps, whose fame would eventually earn him appointment as Ismail Pasha's gardener in Egypt, was especially fond of massed shrubbery and great baskets of flowers, a romantic embellishment Haussmann did not keenly appreciate. It is Barillet-Deschamps who established the nursery at the Bois de Boulogne, as well as that at the Bois de Vincennes, and the "magnificent greenhouses of the 'Fleuriste de la Muette,'. . .which are one of the glories, doubtless the most delicate, of the city's domaines."[37] He is also the creator of the most romantic of Paris parks, Montsouris.

Alphand had genius and played the role with Haussmann that the prefect played with Louis Napoléon: he translated his superior's grand, general ideas, intuitions, and enthusiasms into reality, elaborating them, endowing them with an aesthetic sense nourished by long familiarity with the history of gardens. Alphand's beautifully illustrated *Les Promenades de Paris* remains not only the best account of the greening of Paris but became the most widely read treatise on urban art in the nineteenth century and influenced the design of cities as diverse as Berlin, Barcelona, Vienna, and Washington.[38] He would succeed Haussmann as prefect, and when he died, on December 6, 1891, he received the funeral honors that had been withheld from his predecessor only eleven months earlier.[39]

The Bois de Boulogne is so integral to Paris it is difficult to imagine the city without this splendid park. Inspired by Louis Napoléon, created by Alphand and Haussmann, the Bois shows all three men at their best. "One day, in 1849," wrote Merruau, "[Louis Napoléon] drove through the Bois and stared intently at the long, dusty paths."

When he reached the point that is today the large lake, he told Persigny and Abbatucci, who accompanied him, "There has to be a river here, as in Hyde Park, to bring this arid promenade to life."[40] The project was dear to him and on July 13, 1852, a law was passed ceding the Bois to Paris, which would henceforth bear the expenses of maintenance and protection, with the condition that the city, within four years, embellish the Bois and these lands be used only for a park. Two million francs were simultaneously granted and work began at once. The Maréchal de Castellane noted in his diary (in 1854) that twelve hundred workers were at the task and "a magnificent lake was already completed": the Bois "is entirely transformed."[41] The enormous project was the responsibility of a certain Varé, who "without lacking some talent as a designer . . . was not up to the task." He failed to take into account the different levels of the two lakes and the consequent impossibility of turning them into a serpentine such as that at Hyde Park.[42] Haussmann took credit for solving the problem. He proposed the two lakes be separated by a broad pathway that would serve as a dike for the now famous cascade. To hold the water in the Grand Lac, and in the reservoir that was to feed the Grande Cascade, he ingeniously laid a bed of cement, which was entirely hidden by the water.[43] To make the lakes deep enough he raised their banks and then carefully landscaped them to camouflage the engineering aspects of the project.[44] During this phase of the work Alphand assumed control.

Under Alphand the work went quickly and purposefully. The Bois was completed in 1858. "In five years," Haussmann boasted, "I had been able to bring to a conclusion this undertaking . . . thanks to the active, intelligent, dedicated collaboration of my worthy assistant."[45] The second phase, the realization of the definitive project approved in 1855, included the extension of the Bois, a race course on the southern part of the Longchamps plain (half financed by the state), a dry moat around the huge park, extensive new plantings, and a series of buildings. The enormous park, containing more than two thousand acres, had seventeen entry gates. All the original straight paths were replaced by sinuous paths, some paved for carriages, some sanded for equestrians, some left as trodden earth for walkers. Channels were cut to carry water from the lakes to those parts of the Bois that had "the most picturesque vegetation," as Alphand put it. The two cascades were built, fed by a new system of water supply, the "vast lawns" around the lakes were created, trees were planted everywhere, grottoes were constructed, and the suppressed pathways planted over. Land values of parcels adjoining the Bois increased fifteenfold.[46]

Throughout the creation of the Bois de Boulogne the emperor played an active part. He made a number of visits to the park: not formal, royal inspections but purposeful trips to make sure he got what he wanted. He would descend from his carriage and drive stakes into the ground to make clear his desires.[47] Haussmann testified that Louis Napoléon personally indicated where a number of the 25,162 meters of footpath should meander.[48] The emperor's keen interest in the Bois is beyond dispute, but his essentially cosmetic concern cannot compare with Haussmann's more fundamental contribution. It was the prefect, with his sense of scale, grandeur, and perspective, who insisted upon extending the Bois to the Seine. He also incorporated a part of the Longchamps plain: "few persons know today that this plain was not always an integral part of the park."[49] He proposed opening up the Bois by knocking down the old prison wall that separated the Longchamps plain from the rest of the area, which was the subject of a witticism by Ernest Picard, the opposition deputy. "The prefect wants to aerate the Bois," he quipped, referring to one of Haussmann's favorite euphemisms for urban demolition.[50]

What had been an unkempt, neglected scraggle was transformed into one of the glories of western Paris, whose main entrance was magnificently connected to the Arc de Triomphe and the great networks of Paris by the avenue de l'Impératrice (now the avenue Foch), the grandest of all Haussmann's streets. The prefect, always partial to organic metaphors, liked to speak of the Bois de Boulogne, along with its pendant park, the Bois de Vincennes, as the lungs of the city, and insisted all his parks had "public health for [their] objective."[51] Social attractions immediately obliterated hygienic intentions. From Zola to Proust the Bois has been presented in literature as a playground for the rich. The promenade to and through the Bois became a ritual, the coaches a bewildering collection of elegant conveyances. In *Nana* Zola describes it:

The carriages arrived by the Porte de la Cascade, in an interminable, compact line. There was the large omnibus, the Pauline, which left from the boulevard des Italiens, filled with its fifty passengers, which pulled up to the right of the stands. Then came the dog carts, the Victorias, the landaus with their superb mechanisms mixed in with the sad hackney coaches pulled by nags; and the four-in-hands led by their quartet of horses, and the mail coaches, with their drivers atop and inside the servants guarding the baskets of champagne, and the flies whose enormous wheels were a marvel of steel work, and light tandems as elegant as parts of a watch, which moved to the accompaniment of bells.[52]

The physical extension of Paris, mandated by the law of June 16, 1859, and realized on January 1, 1860, more than doubled its area and added two hundred thousand inhabitants to the city. It is arguably Haussmann's most significant and visionary achievement. All previous governments had tried to limit the growth of Paris, and Napoléon I had specifically rejected annexation, as had Rambuteau. Haussmann was the first to reverse this policy. Louis Napoléon's sketch for modernizing Paris was confined within the exterior boulevards built by Louis XIV, with only the Bois de Boulogne beyond Louis-Philippe's defensive wall. Incorporating the suburban sprawl was historically, aesthetically, and strategically logical. For centuries the pattern of Parisian growth had been in roughly concentric circles, as the city spilled over its walls and then absorbed the overflow in the embrace of a new set of walls. After Louis XIV razed the walls the same pattern of urban sprawl continued. Haussmann's urban system with its rectilinear streets was, in theory, infinite. Those that connected the railroad stations to the center of the city ran, when continued by the tracks, to the whole of France. There was no reason why Haussmann's streets should not continue beyond the outer boulevards to Louis-Philippe's fortifications. His streets would thus draw the suburbs between the outer boulevards and the fortifications into the city and simultaneously exert a centrifugal force, drawing the displaced poor out of the city's center.

For strategic reasons building within 250 meters of the military wall was forbidden, but between the fortifications and the Paris tax barrier, which followed the boulevards of Louis XIV, was a haphazard collection of communes that lay outside the control of the city: this was the *banlieue*, the suburbs. None of these townships paid the *octroi*, and increasing the need for additional income was an important motive for incorporation. More important was the need to have some control over the communes, especially the crescent that embraced eastern and northeastern Paris. More rural than urban, sharply separated physically, psychologically, and socially from Paris by the tax barrier, poor and largely unurbanized, beyond the reach of even the rudimentary sanitary provisions of pre-Haussmann Paris, the suburbs also included the *zone*, a barren stretch of land adjacent to the fortifications originally reserved for defensive purposes. In the paintings and literature of the day the *zone* figured as a metaphor for desolation, poverty, misery, anomie. Rather than providing a gradual transition from the city to the country, the *zone* was a no-man's land beyond the civilized pale, marked by mud, squalor, and shantytowns.

The new military fortifications, completed in 1844, had radically altered the old Paris suburbs. Before the ramparts were built the region had been countrified, a place for vacations and excursions. Afterward the area was demarcated into a *"petite banlieue"* and the *zone*, enclosed between the tax barrier and the fortifications. This *petite banlieue* became the site for factories, especially along the Seine and the canals, and then along the rail lines, a series of fingers thrust into the countryside that fixed the patterns of suburban urbanization. In socioeconomic terms the area presented a mixed aspect: large industrial property and small parcels, which attracted a substantial artisan and working-class population in quest of cheap rent. The suburbs had been growing even more rapidly than Paris. In 1806 there were 13,000 residents, and by 1841, 114,000. By 1856 the numbers had risen to 352,000.[53] The *petite banlieue*, outside the jurisdiction of the *octroi*, became a tax-free haven for the popular classes, who left the city on weekends to partake of the cheap wine in the inns and dives that catered to them.

Political considerations shaped the question of annexation as they did all questions about Paris, in an especially urgent way after 1848. The suburbs fit the bourgeois stereotype of a "nomad" population, resentful and dangerous, ripe for red propaganda, promises, and demagoguery. Workers from La Chapelle and from the national workshops at Charenton had poured into Paris during the June Days, reinforcing the insurrectionists of the faubourg St. Antoine. The Commune of Belleville, now the nineteenth (and part of the twentieth) arrondissement, had erected a large barricade at the intersection of the *barrière* of Belleville, the rue de Tourtille, and the chaussée de Ménilmontant (G 2).[54] A village known for its wine merchants and cabarets, especially those of la Courtille, Belleville had become, by 1856, a town of 57,699 inhabitants. It attracted an increasing population of Parisian workers who sought cheaper lodgings,[55] and acquired the reputation of being a community of outcasts. "As soon as one crosses the outer boulevard," wrote a school inspector in 1856,

> one finds oneself in the middle of a population almost uniformly ignorant and ferocious, although made up of two distinct elements. First, there is the scum of Paris, those who hang out at the *barrière*. . .led to misery and brutalization by vice.

The depraved were complemented by immigrant "barbarians" who were "sunk in unspeakable mental degradation."[56] Bourgeois Paris was frightened, and their fears of a sinister and ferocious population on the borders of Paris waiting to pounce on the city weighed significantly in the decision to annex the banlieue.

Haussmann's arguments for annexation fit neatly into imperial desires to appear determined and decisive.[57] Haussmann emphasized two reasons: historical development and strategic-administrative considerations. He was seconded on the latter by the minister of the interior, Delangle, who insisted that annexation was "so natural" that it had only been "too long delayed by . . . the special interests," and was now "considered indispensable." The area in question, more than 9,300 acres, with a population of 351,189, Delangle continued, had only 68 policemen, or "one policeman for every 140 acres, or for every 5,165 inhabitants. How can there be effective surveillance with so few men?" That the population was "mostly floating, is recruited in part from workers from the provinces and foreigners, in part from those who fled central Paris," created further difficulties and engendered fear. "This mass spends the day in Paris and the night someplace else . . . passes incessantly from one commune to another, scattering and reassembling without cease." The suburbs provide a natural hiding place for "these dubious lives and suspect activities."[58] The suburbs were a social cesspool, and fear was expressed in language not much different from that used to describe the chaos and social confusions of the old sewers. The *banlieue* was a policeman's, and an administrator's, nightmare.

Haussmann's view was broader than Delangle's. Submitting the suburbs to his administrative control would, of course, fulfill his need for order, satisfy his belief that all social questions were fundamentally administrative ones, and put the entire department of the Seine under a single administration, expanding his already extensive urban empire. He noted with pride that the Paris suburbs alone were more populous that many a department of France.[59] But he also saw incorporation as part of his larger urban vision. In his *Mémoire . . . sur l'extension des limites de Paris* Haussmann put the question in the context of the history of Paris over the centuries. "The development of a city," he averred, "ordinarily results from the confluence of circumstances that are beyond prediction, beyond calculation, and which, most often, no human will can direct." He relished his place in the city's long history, especially the impingement of his own will on its course.

The history of Paris once Philippe-Auguste had been free of invasion and able to wall his capital, Haussmann lectured, was of ineluctable growth. The walls could not contain the city, despite the desires of the kings:

> One would be . . . deluded to suppose that the successive extensions of the limits of Paris had been sought in any epoch, either by the kings or by the magistrates, as a desirable occurrence. Far from seeing it as a realization of their wishes, they have always viewed it as a necessity, and have spared no pains in trying to moderate expansion. How strange![60]

Growth was "this progressive movement," equated with prosperity and improvement. The same mentality saw an infinitely expandable credit system.

Paris had no natural limits for Haussmann, either politically or spatially. The city was the capital of the empire, it was all of France. Metaphor became reality in his imagination. Walls do not a city make. The tax collectors' wall of 1785—he cites two manuscript plans drawn by the architect, Ledoux, who designed the tax collection booths—was artificial. If Paris were now allowed to extend to Louis-Philippe's fortifications the city would only occupy territory that "before 1784, was regarded as part of the city, precisely for the collection of the *octroi*."[61] Through the centuries the successive growth of Paris "is attached to the names of the five most glorious sovereigns who have ruled France . . . Philippe-Auguste, St. Louis, Henri IV, Louis XIV, and Napoléon I." Haussmann wanted to add his name to the list: it is this very moment of annexation that he had memorialized in Yvon's painting for the Hôtel de Ville. "Aside from Philippe-Auguste none of these rulers, properly speaking, was the builder of a city wall, but all have attracted the population by the excellence of their government, by the wisdom of their administration, by the splendor of their public works, and above all by the security enjoyed during their reigns."[62] This was a paean he often sang to his own reign.

His repugnance for disorder and squalor, the negation of the unquestioned virtues of "unity and firmness," provided the emotional and political springs of the argument. The suburbs "form a compact belt of *faubourgs* haphazardly built, covered with a narrow, tortuous, inextricable maze of streets where a population of nomads, without any real attachment to the land and without adequate surveillance, accumulates with prodigious rapidity."[63] More than a third of the 257 kilometers of roads and streets in the *banlieue* were neither paved nor graveled, and there were only twelve kilometers of sewer. Street lighting was wholly inadequate, there were only forty-nine schools for a population of more than 350,000, and the churches could not serve more than a twentieth of the population.[64]

Haussmann wanted to organize and regulate, reform and cleanse the suburbs. He made the same arguments for incorporation that he made for cutting new streets in Paris. And he was equally willing to manipulate the facts to achieve his goals. When he summed up the findings of the committee who had studied the problems of annexation,[65] he diluted the extent and intensity of opposition to incorporation and inflated the economic advantages. Incorporation proved neither economically nor socially advantageous in the short run. With the exception of a few residential areas the newly incorporated population was poor, imposed a heavy burden on the municipal budget, and brought no compensating sources of income. The annexation "threw Haussmann's finances into disequilibrium."[66] Even the projected benefits from the *octroi*, especially the tax on wine, did not materialize. The annexed population "was equal to a third of the original population, and the *octroi* on wine has only been augmented by a fifth."[67]

Unification and urbanization proved two distinct phenomena. The eleven years that elapsed from Haussmann's incorporation of the *banlieue* to the fall of the empire was far too brief a period to realize the benefits of annexation that would ensue decades later.[68] His incorporation of the *banlieue* made possible the eventual suburban growth of Paris, but Haussmann cannot have envisioned a development that followed World War I. The immediate results were to solidify the power of local elites—landlords, merchants, notaries, manufacturers. The petite and middle bourgeoisie were not provoked to depart central Paris for the periphery. Those who came to the suburbs to rent were overwhelmingly the working poor, driven centrifugally by the rising cost of housing. Louis Lazare, the editor of the *Revue municipale* and an opponent of haussmannization, published *Les Quartiers pauvres de Paris* in 1868 as an indictment of the prefect's annexation policy. Lazare recounted the difficulties of a poor family squeezed by Haussmann's transformations. Originally residents of the Halles neighborhood, they were driven out by demolitions and were unable to return, because rents had doubled. The family moved out of the center of Paris to suburban Belleville, and their journey to work in the city was now lengthened. When Belleville was incorporated rents were raised, and they were forced still farther from the center.[69]

The *bellevillois* saw themselves as a forcibly expelled population, driven from their homes and their city by Haussmann's transformation. Henri Rochfort, the founder of *La Lanterne*, the violent antiimperial weekly, received a standing ovation in November 1869 when he denounced the *grands travaux*: "the government thus drove the workers from the center of the city in order not to have them so near." The deep resentment of dispossession was widespread and frequently invoked by orators at the political meetings held in popular Paris in the final years of the empire. "What the administrators want," Tony Moilin told his audience in the Salle Robert, "is to destroy everything that recalls the past. They devote all their efforts to making Paris a cosmopolitan, imperial city. I am only amazed that Paris . . . which has guillotined kings, still calls itself Paris. Its real name should be Napoleonville."[70] The emotional energy of the Commune was already in place.

Those who hoped for a rapid assimilation of the suburbs to Paris, including Haussmann, were disappointed. The same speculative frenzy that had long gripped Paris was now extended to the suburbs, but unbridled speculation did little to integrate the *banlieue* into the city. "The urbanization of the near suburbs was the savage urbanism of pioneers."[71] Only years after this conquest did the outer arrondissements become Paris, and even today the scars of how the land was appropriated, by and for whom, remain. The erection of expensive housing along the new avenues, especially in western Paris, contributed to the sharp rise in rents in central Paris, which in turn stimulated the working-class exodus. The consequences were "a disproportionately middle-class Paris surrounded by a ring of working-class and industrial suburbs, surrounded in turn today by clusters of equally working-class *grands ensembles*."[72] Haussmann's incorporation of the *banlieue*, coupled to his housing policies, made the periphery home to the banished and the uprooted, a distillation of the anomie of modern city life.

Haussmann built incessantly, a fact he enjoyed savoring statistically. From 1851 till 1860 the average of houses built rose to more than 1,200, and nearly 3,600 if the near suburbs are included. After 1860 there was a further increase: more than 4,600 for the newly extended city. In financial terms, during the seventeen years of Haussmann's power, the value of buildings went from 2,577,000 to six billion francs.[73] The massive replacement and renewal of housing, as much as the boulevards, gave Paris the physiognomy it still bears.

His housing also permanently altered the physical realities of daily life for Parisians.

There had been no extensive construction from the late eighteenth century until the July Monarchy, when new apartments were built in the emerging neighborhoods around the Place St.Georges, Chaussée d'Antin, St. Lazare, and the Place de l'Europe (D-E 2). Those who could afford the rents flocked eagerly. A.-L. Lusson, writing in 1847, explained the migration by the demand "for certain conveniences . . . notably this comfortable arrangement as a whole and in detail of our apartments," which had a "combination of varying rooms . . . something very difficult to get in houses of past ages."[74] These desired apartments were "dark, oddly arranged flats, with none of the amenities subsequent generations would find indispensable: piped water, gas, central heating, water closets, bathrooms, to name a few." But these self-contained units, on a single level, with rooms for specific purposes, "marked a revolutionary advance in comfort over what had existed before."[75]

The willingness or necessity of poor and modest Parisians to live in housing that appeared to outsiders cramped, austere, often shabby, or downright nasty has a long history and would continue through the empire to our own day. An English craftsman who visited the 1867 exposition found "the general domestic condition of the French *ouvrier* greatly inferior to that of the British workman. If we speak of him with regard to his family comforts, adjudged by the English standard, 'home he has none.'" The witness singled out an eight-square-foot worker's apartment on the top floor of a building on the boulevard Richard Lenoir: "he has a little bed that turns up, and a little table that lets down, which must be done alternately each night and morning in order to make room. He has a couple of small chairs, as many basins, plates, knives, forks and tablespoons; a pot au feu, a tree planted in a tasty pot if possible, and a bird in a cage, which comprise his household goods." The *Building News*, in 1861, wrote "families are crowded worse than in any Irish hovel." Between Montmartre and La Villette was a new neighborhood with "houses built of lumps of plaster from demolitions . . . roofed with old tin trays, tin cuttings and bits of painted table-covers."[76] Victor Fournel, around the same time, seconded this English testimony and pointed the moral: "Parisian apartments combine extreme expense with extreme inconvenience," he wrote. "One does not so much live in a Paris apartment as camp out. To escape the tyranny of neighbors, landlords, and concierges, one must go into the streets to seek light, air, calm, a little repose." Fournel attributed the "anxious character, the nervous irritability which has made our people the most volatile and capricious in the world" partly to their dwellings. "I am convinced," he continued, "that the English *home*, so peaceful, and comfortable, so isolated from all the tumults of the outside world . . . plays a great role in the prosperous political and social history of that nation."[77]

Haussmann did little to alleviate the chronic overcrowding of Paris, and the mushrooming population growth, a good deal of it directly attributable to those who came to the capital to build it, worsened housing conditions.[78] As with his regulations on water supply and sewer hookup, Haussmann's regulations concerning housing seem paradoxical. Both the emperor and the prefect professed, and in some cases demonstrated, a desire to destroy the old slums. Yet they did nothing to assure that new slums would not replace the old, either in the center of Paris or on the peripheries of the city, where many of the slum dwellers moved. The new building regulations of 1859 were concerned almost exclusively with appearances. There were strict standards regulating height and facades—Haussmann added roughly one story to facades on the new streets—but landlords were free to build airless and crowded tenements behind the new fronts. The health commissioners documented the shantytowns that sprang up alongside the new construction sites. These matter-of-fact, chilling official reports are supported by contemporary witnesses and belie Haussmann's insistence that wages had kept pace with rents. Traversing Paris from the center to the fortifications, Louis Lazare counted "no fewer than 269 alleys, courtyards, dwelling houses, and shantytowns constructed without any municipal control whatsoever."[79] Although thousands had been driven from the center to the suburban semicircle around the east end of Paris, there was intense overcrowding in the notorious *chambrées* and *garnis* in the old center, and patches of poor even in the interstices of the wealthy west.

Otherwise so determined to direct the forces of capitalism, Haussmann cleaved to a strict laissez-faire policy for housing. Access to credit, which favored his coterie of developers and reinforced his policy of replacing slums with bourgeois housing, determined the market. With the revival of the economy in the 1850s Haussmann believed that the operations of a free market would meet the requirements of even the poorest Parisian: "it is best to leave to speculation, stimulated by competition, the task of recognizing the people's real needs and of satisfying them."[80] His street cutting, however, undermined or deflected the operations of the free housing market. New streets not only engulfed much land that might otherwise have held housing, but the enhanced land values created thereby led landlords to build new, more expensive housing, or to subdivide the existing housing stock to extract the most rent from their newly valuable property. Edouard Fournier noted that many displaced by the demolitions on the Ile de la Cité moved into the rue de l'Hôtel de Ville, which now became even more densely populated.[81]

The "nomads" Haussmann habitually spoke of were largely a tribe of his creation, some of them displaced by the demolitions, many newly arrived to enlist in his construction and demolition armies. The two groups did not mix. The former fled to the suburbs, the latter sought to live close to their work in the city. The thirty thousand masons from the Creuse flocked together. Seven or eight beds were set up in a single room, each bed shared by two workers. These dormitories were usually run by the wife of a mason. She made the beds, washed the sheets, and cooked a thin soup for the evening meal. Each mason furnished his own bread, saved from his afternoon meal. The rent was six francs per week.[82] These wretched rooms (garnis) were not created by the influx of workers. They had existed for years and their number did not decline even after the population was stabilized and building activity shifted away from the old center. The garnis multiplied because they were in the interest of the landlords whose decrepit, unhealthy buildings were now overvalued by the coincidence of demolition and migration. Ironically, the multiplication of garnis further added to the cost of transforming Paris. The city, in order to acquire these buildings, had to pay dearly because they had become enormously profitable to their owners as rooming houses for the workers who poured into Paris.[83]

Uncomfortable, unhealthy, expensive, the *garni* became the normal habitat for an important fraction of the population. Between 1851 and 1856 the percentage of Parisians who lived in furnished rooms outstripped the general increase of the population.[84] The opposition politicians Jules Favre, Ollivier, and Picard hammered away at the moral scandal of this new urban population. The landlords, Hippolyte Miller-Richer wrote Picard, are getting rich off the sweat of the people, "disinherited by the rising cost of living, especially in housing." They would rather "have for a tenant a criminal who pays a high rent than an honest workman who pays less" because "the morality of a renter is his money."[85] Housing shortages had become even more chronic in Paris than earlier in the century, which contributed to Friedrich Engels's famous argument, in *The Housing Question*, that the bourgeoisie has only one way of solving the housing question: by moving it around.

In fact Haussmann was not much interested in housing and, as with much else in his urbanization, left it to the coddled landowners. The accusations then made continue to reverberate. He answered his critics with statistics. Between 1853 and 1870 he had demolished 19,722 houses in Paris, and constructed or reconstructed 43,777. In the *banlieue* the corresponding numbers were 7,756 and 58,710.[86] He rejected the argument that he built only in expensive neighborhoods. The statistics, he insisted, disproved the allegation: "on the contrary, the most extensive construction and creation of housing has been in the least favored arrondissements, on the land . . . on the outskirts of the city, made accessible by cutting streets running from the center of the city to the circumference."[87] Rents had risen, which he deplored, but this rise was matched by the rise "in salaries, and gains of various kinds," because both issued from the same cause: "the development of business and public prosperity."[88]

Housing is not so accurately measured as sewer pipe. What Haussmann has left out of his figures is the numbers of Parisians competing for his new housing. He did indeed build more low-cost housing, but there were many more who needed it. Luxury housing in western Paris lay vacant while inadequate housing for the poor was built. Speculation and competition were less rational than the prefect would have desired.

Haussmann's urbanism was accomplished by regulation.[89] Those questions that did not interest him, including some of the most vexing social anxieties of his day, he did not subject to his administration, leaving them largely to the prejudices of the age via the mechanism of a free marketplace. The enormous numbers who came to Paris to escape the relentless poverty of the countryside concerned the prefect only when they became politically volatile. Otherwise they were left to fend for themselves in the midst of an emerging modern city. Housing, for those who most needed it, was only the most obvious of the urban social crises he considered of secondary importance.[90] Haussmann and his master never conceived of Paris as a worker's city, and it is highly doubtful they could have transformed it in this direction even had they had such a perspective. Haussmann's Paris was a public city. Streets, sanitation, lighting, parks are public amenities from which all might benefit equally. These are the projects that interested him, that he considered the responsibility of the state. But what was private—property above all—was not to be tampered with save for the superior demands of public necessity. The entire set of urban issues gathered under the umbrella of "social" questions Haussmann thought secondary. They fell outside the purview of administration. "The multitude," he argued, "left to its own impressions, likes great projects," which it thinks are built for its benefit. The masses enjoy "the ease of circulation, the salubrity, the embellishment of the streets, the administration of the city, the organization of municipal services" as much as "those most favored by fortune," and find satisfaction in "the sentiment of equality." They become "profoundly attached to the memory of the sovereigns who have left, by their public works, a profound trace of their reigns on the soil of our country, and, above all, on its capital."[91]

Haussmann's conceptualization of the city as a body, with lungs, bowels, arteries, considered neither the soul nor the repose of the body itself, neither the citizens nor their daily private lives. The former, immaterial and obscure, had no place in his urban physiology.

The latter would somehow be taken care of by the forces of the marketplace. Although he favored organic metaphors, he almost never talked of those who inhabited the city except in abstract, often mechanical, and always disparaging terms. The poor were nomads, the rich ungrateful. The body of Haussmann's city had a life apart from those who lived there. Indeed the citizens complicated and compromised his work. "If Voltaire," he wrote, "could enjoy the spectacle offered by today's Paris, and see all his wishes realized, he would not understand that the Parisians, his children, the inheritors of his elegant spirit, far from supporting the Administration that has brought these desires to fruition, have criticized them, opposed them, obstructed them . . . like people who hardly appreciate what has been done for them."[92]

· XIII ·

"The Vandalism of Triumph"

THE EARLY POPULAR ENTHUSIASM FOR REMAKING PARIS WAS GONE. The ingratitude of the Parisians grew steadily, as Haussmann saw it. The entire city had been a building site for nearly two decades, and there was no apparent end. The original aim, the renewal of central Paris, had been achieved. The remaining projects appeared designed to embellish only privileged, bourgeois Paris. The Left Bank thought itself neglected, neighborhoods that had been transformed complained of too much or too little. The intellectuals, generally hostile to the empire and certainly to Haussmann, had vented their criticisms in a special publication prepared for the 1867 exposition. Beside the public boosterism of the new city stood the critical voices of the most renowned writers, beginning with Hugo. Fortunes had been made, at the public expense, by those in Haussmann's coterie of bankers and contractors or who were thought to be. The whole enormous operation stank of corruption.

The enemies of the empire and the emperor easily gathered this growing chorus of criticism into an indictment of the authoritarian, centralized regime. Paris and Haussmann focused the rising opposition. The prefect was of no help to the beleaguered emperor. His insistence that he was only a technocrat, the emperor's tool, had long ago ceased to protect him from his critics, who knew the transformation of Paris was a political project. Paris and the prefect could no longer be excused from the more obvious imperial blunders. The gap between the political concessions wrung from Louis Napoléon by his enemies and his prefect's ever more obscure and imperious manipulation of the finances of urban transformation widened. Imperial politics had changed; Haussmann had not.

The emperor, since 1859 when he amnestied many of the opponents of the coup d'état, had been softening the authoritarian aspects of his regime. The commercial treaty with England (January 23, 1860), known as the Cobden-Chevalier Treaty, marked the initiation of a free-trade policy. Later that year (November 24) Louis Napoléon, his popularity shaken by the Italian war, passed a series of decrees that revived parliamentary life. He allowed political parties and empowered the legislature to reply to the address from the throne and fully report parliamentary debates. Strikes were legalized in 1864 and the fiasco of the Mexican expedition, ending in the execution of Archduke Maximilian, whom Louis Napoléon had deserted, further besmirched the reputation of the empire. The law on public meetings, passed June 18, 1868, unleashed a torrent of public criticism, and the "reunions" regularly held, especially those in the outer arrondissements, provided a platform for the profound resentments of those dispossessed by Haussmann's *grands travaux*.

Tumultuous, well-attended, increasingly radical, the reunions became a forum for attacks on the empire. Originally organized by its bourgeois critics, including the economist J.-E. Horn (nom de plume of Eduard Ignacs Einhorn, of Hungarian origin), whose *Les Finances de l'Hôtel de Ville* (1869) was highly critical of Haussmann, the reunions were quickly inundated by more threatening orators. Socialists of many convictions—followers of Prudhomme and Fourier and Blanqui—radicals and Jacobins, the Association internationale des travailleurs, all attended. The many-throated voice of the Commune was already being heard in Paris in 1868–69. The rhetoric and example of 1789 and even 1793 was increasingly employed and invoked. Edmond de Pressensé, one of the directors of the *Revue chrétienne*, spoke of the reunions as "the spring of Liberty." His auditors rejected the allusion to 1789: "No, no, not 89. 93! [the year of the Terror]."[1] Louis Napoléon was cursed as a "*buveur de sang*" (drinker of blood); property was analyzed as "founded on theft." One orator announced, using the imagery of haussmannization: "As far as I'm concerned, property has to be demolished. My own theory is to be the demolisher."[2]

The emperor and Haussmann had no friends in more traditional pockets of society. Many Legitimists, whom Louis Napoléon had cultivated, had refused to make peace with the empire for ideological reasons, out of personal resentments, or because they took the need for decentralization seriously. And his difficulties in Paris were but his provincial difficulties writ large. Louis Napoléon never had the cities solidly behind him. Bordeaux is a good example. Despite Haussmann's strenuous efforts to bring the city into the imperial camp in 1852, Bordeaux deserted the empire as soon as it became expedient to do so. Adherence was always pragmatic rather than ideological. When Haussmann returned to Bordeaux after his fall, he was an outcast. His base of power and influence had vanished with the empire.

In the midst of growing resentments and opposition, now given the means of legal expression by Louis Napoléon's attempts to prepare a liberal empire and save the throne for his son, Haussmann went about his business. Sure of the emperor's support, insulated against interference by his elaborate administrative machinery, contemptuous of his enemies, he made no efforts to change, accommodate his critics, or soften his municipal autocracy. He was beginning his sixteenth year in power, thought himself invulnerable, and was impatient to complete the great projects well underway. For someone who prided himself on his political shrewdness, Haussmann suffered from myopia. The absolute authority he exercised over his own bureaucracy did not extend much beyond the precincts of the Hôtel de Ville, his contempt for democratic procedures was increasingly out of date and a liability, the emperor's affection for his prefect was not unlimited, nor was the exasperated tolerance of his enemies. By 1869 they had had enough.

Money was more than the pretext. It was the life's blood of the despotic prefect and his Achilles heel; it was also the only aspect of the transformation of Paris in which the Corps Législatif had any authority. Haussmann's Paris was too expensive to build, a feeling and an observation that mobilized a broad band of opposition against the emperor, the prefect, and the city. The debates that opened on the Paris budget on February 22, 1869, in past years more ceremonial than real, were reminiscent of those that had plagued the July Monarchy, whose most embittered parliamentary struggles between the bourgeois king and his parliament had been over money, especially when spent on Paris. Once again the same narrow, niggling spirit, with penny-pinching raised to a political principle, infected the National Assembly. Haussmann, a generous spender of public money, could not hide his contempt.

Sprung from the same Parisian bourgeoisie as his accusers, he had chosen government service over the money-making professions. He scorned those who followed Mammon. The bourgeoisie were "imbued with the narrow ideas, the routines, of the Paris middle class," and thus, ran his syllogism, "completely hostile, in [their] very core, to our *grands travaux*."[3] In the eleven sessions given over to debate on Haussmann's financial dealings with the state, it became clear that he had misjudged the intensity of parliamentary and public anger. More than money was at stake, more than small-mindedness drove resentments.

Haussmann, who relished combat and confrontation, had never run from a good fight. He had been battling the Paris bourgeoisie for fifteen years and thought he understood them all too well. He believed he would emerge once again victorious. He believed in his own invincibility. Hadn't Rouher, Louis Napoléon's parliamentary leader and Haussmann's declared enemy, been unable to get rid of him? Hadn't the handful of anti-imperial, radical deputies railed impotently against him? He fought as he always had, while the emperor stood mutely behind his prefect, convinced Haussmann was the necessary man and perhaps realizing the prefect's fall meant the disappearance of the last prop of the authoritarian empire. Emperor and prefect would win the fight but lose the war. It was getting more and more difficult, more and more impolitic, to sustain Haussmann. The clamor was getting uncomfortably close to the throne, to the very principles of authority upon which the empire rested. In the end Haussmann had to be sacrificed. When the favorite fell Louis Napoléon discovered he had conceded more than he had intended.

Had the debates of 1869 been only about money the prefect's defense of himself and his administration, backed by the emperor's tacit support, would have again carried the day. Haussmann's arrogant yet masterful marshaling of the evidence of sums borrowed and spent, his magisterial description of Paris finances, his condescending explanation of fiduciary intricacies would have obfuscated his manipulations and lulled the deputies, while imperial support would have stifled debate. But Haussmann had grown too bold, too impatient, too obsessed, and at the same time too complacent. The prefect knew that the Corps Législatif would not assent to a new loan or new state subventions:

> So, carried away by the passion of the artist who cannot bear to see his work left unfinished, a passion similar to that of Bernard de Palissy throwing his furniture into the fire so that his kiln would not go out, [Haussmann] put himself outside all the rules and piled irregularity upon irregularity.[4]

For years there had been isolated complaints about Haussmann's handling of Paris's finances. In 1868 they were exposed in the pages of *Le Temps*, one of the opposition papers emboldened by the more liberal press laws of that year. Jules Ferry, a brilliant and ambitious republican journalist, published a series of articles between December 1867 and May 1868 that were subsequently collected in an influential pamphlet, "Les Comptes fantastiques d'Haussmann,"* which launched his career.[5]

Ferry's title was the most original part of his broadside, but its publication in an influential newspaper made city borrowing notorious. For the first time Haussmann's finances were the talk of Paris. The author's bantering irony, enlivening a dense and informed argument, was more hurtful than a dozen Senate speeches or cartoonist's caricatures. Ferry brilliantly gathered the evidence of dubious loans, bonds of questionable legality, hidden slush funds, and special

---

*The pun does not work in English. In French *contes* (tales) and *comptes* (accounts) are nearly homophones, and the cleverness comes from the play on *Les Contes fantastiques* (*The Tales of Hoffmann*) of the German writer E.T.A. Hoffmann, then enjoying a vogue in Paris.

contracts into a single, mocking public indictment. The emperor well understood the importance of public opinion, which he had jealously controlled and brilliantly manipulated for years. The newspaper attack on his prefect reaffirmed the power of the word. Haussmann had been much battered and bruised over the years, but always within the circumscribed confines of official public life and polite society. "He is a powerful *seigneur*," Ferry wrote, "one of the fundamental institutions of our day," but he was neither immune nor invulnerable to publicity that reached beyond the privileged world of officialdom.[6]

Ferry exposed the inherent contradictions in haussmannization, as well as their incompatibility with the general movement toward democracy in France. Haussmannization, he argued, "carries within itself the principle of its destruction." The final crisis would come not from without but from within:

> It is, in effect, the very essence of the economic and financial politics of M. the prefect of the Seine, never to retreat, never to remain stationary. It is not only that the building program must maintain itself, it is essential that it develop, that it grow constantly. If not, *adieu* to surplus values![7]

On a more mundane level he publicized what was by its very nature private: the financial arrangements and manipulations of a secretive state. No government would have been indifferent to Ferry's prying fluency, least of all the Second Empire.

It was no easy matter to ferret out the extent of Haussmann's manipulations, to figure out the size of the municipal debt, which remained a matter of speculation.[8] Ferry's estimates are reasonable; but it was not the raw figures of hundreds of millions of francs that aroused indignation; it was the quasi-legal means used, especially the *bons de délégations* issued by the city, and the ever-increasing cost of the work, which seemed endless, and most important, the lack of supervision and public accountability.[9] Haussmann's empire existed outside the constitutional entities that controlled government expenditure. At base the February debates were about Louis Napoléon's government, about the responsibility of its agencies, about public trust, about the destiny of the empire itself, about the deepest suspicions of the Parisian bourgeoisie for the bohemian adventurer who sat on the throne and whose court they saw as a menagerie of confidence men and schemers slopping at the public trough.

Haussmann struck a pose of indifference.[10] Ferry labeled the Paris government "an uncontrolled administration," an "irresponsible power" in the hands of "a single man, seconded by an unelected municipal council. Has the like been seen in any other place, any other time?"[11] Haussmann controlled a budget equal to that of many a medium-sized European country and Ferry monotonously reiterated that the prefect was not answerable to any legal authority, except the emperor. He raised and spent vast sums that the elected assembly was powerless to regulate, which they hardly knew about. "M. the prefect of the Seine is omnipotent. . . . he despotically administers a budget of 150 million francs. But it is impossible for him to administer it in accordance with the laws."[12]

Haussmann did not think he owed the public an accounting. The emperor had left these matters to his prefect, who felt no obligation to behave as if bound by the traditions of public accountability. He added to bureaucratic contempt for deliberative bodies a deeper autocratic arrogance. Ferry, and a growing number of his contemporaries, viewed things differently. The pamphleteer saw three possible parliamentary responses. If the deputies voted for the budget they would exonerate Haussmann for his past misdeeds and give him "a vote of confidence for the future." If they voted to control the budget in the future, they would only postpone the problem and again sanction past abuses. What Ferry wanted was a vote "to halt . . . the new round of demolitions" and "to begin the liquidation of the system as soon as possible."[13] He wanted Haussmann made accountable to the Corps Législatif. He wanted an end to the irregular, secretive, and scandalous finances of the empire. It is no surprise Ferry was close to the Rothschilds, a traditional banking family largely excluded from Haussmann's wheeling and dealing.

Paradoxically, Haussmann's great strength and single weakness was the emperor's support. Until 1869 he had had a relatively free rein, seconded and supported by the "calm tenacity" of Louis Napoléon.[14] Haussmann had originally been a lightning rod drawing criticism away from the emperor. Now he became the symbol of the embattled authoritarian empire. Ferry's articles had flushed out the prey; the proconsul's blood was in many nostrils. The emboldened opponents of the regime, for years kept at bay, gathered for the kill. It was a scene out of Zola: life imitating art.

The crowds gathered before the Palais-Bourbon on February 22 to get a seat for the forensic display over the city's treaty with the Crédit Foncier. Debate on the Paris budget promised the best theater in town. "Everyone was there, senators, counsellors of state, beautiful women," jostling one another, elbowing forward to be sure of a seat in the gallery.[15] The renowned orators of the day, from right, left, and center—Thiers, Garnier-Pagès, Picard, Ollivier, Jules Favre—were expected to speak.

Garnier-Pagès, a veteran of the revolutionary struggles of 1848, described as a cross between "Peter the Hermit preaching the Crusade and a merchant hawking his goods," launched the attack, accusing Haussmann of losing sight of his original plans. Many of the new streets had indeed cleansed "the insalubrious neighborhoods," but when they built the Trocadéro was it because this part of Paris was "choking for air"? When they opened the boulevard Haussmann, which cut through "large gardens and rich hôtels," was it to "aerate an insalubrious *neighborhood?*" No, the orator answered his rhetorical questions: "it was to satisfy a man who wanted to attach his name to a street."[16] Invoking the French Revolution, specifically the memorable night of August 4, 1789, when the nobility divested itself of feudal privileges, Garnier-Pagès insisted that it was the poor who were paying for Haussmann's embellishments of western Paris.[17] There was no budget for Paris. Rather, the city "has no fewer than six budgets: an ordinary budget, an extra-ordinary budget, a supplementary budget, a budget for special services, a budget for the *grands travaux*, and finally, a mystery budget which is neither voted on in advance nor subsequently verified: the budget of the *bons de délégation.*"[18]

Ernest Picard, a witty man whom Haussmann disparaged as "the buffoon of the regiment" of liberal deputies led by Ollivier, observed that Haussmann built straight boulevards because "bullets don't know how to take the first turn to the right."[19] The "transformation of Paris has been an anti-democratic work," Picard continued, "paid for by those who own neither *hôtels* nor houses, those who have not shared in the 600 or 800 million francs of indemnities paid [by the city]." These enormous sums might better have been used "to reduce the *octrois* [the municipal tariffs that were the foundation of Haussmann's finances], making life a bit less costly for those who work with their hands."[20] Haussmann "has created at the Hôtel de Ville the most remarkable banking house that one can find" and has generated from it more money than France had to pay to the allies following Napoléon's defeat at Waterloo.[21]

Thiers, who was no radical, took the tack that not only was Haussmann's work prohibitively expensive, but much of it was unnecessary. The prefect's budget was double that of Bavaria or Belgium, half that of Prussia. While the national budget of France increased by 50 percent, the Paris budget increased by 500 percent.[22] And what had Haussmann done with all this money? He had built "useless and luxurious" streets, "like the boulevard Prince-Eugène, for example, which cost 75 million francs. Why did we need this boulevard? They could not answer that it was to aerate the gardens it traverses or serve the interests of commerce, which were non-existent."[23] What about the Place de l'Opéra? Three great streets debouched there, but nothing had been done to improve the nearby rues Montmartre and Richelieu. On the Left Bank the rue de Rennes had been stopped short of the river, compromising its utility. "That is how they have contrived to spend 1,865 million francs on useless projects, neglecting those that are genuinely useful."[24] In the course of this speech Thiers made his famous accusation:

> They sometimes say, in speaking of M. Rouher, that he is the vice-emperor. If the title of vice-emperor belongs to anyone it is not to M. the minister of State. It belongs to M. the prefect of the Seine.[25]

Thiers's righteousness, his prestige, and his denunciation of Haussmann's prodigality were more telling than his inept and contradictory criticism of imperial urbanism.

Useless streets, bureaucratic arrogance, frivolous expenses, undemocratic procedures, secret dealings—the attack had no single theme; or rather, the theme was the empire itself. Ironically enough

Haussmann's accomplishments were celebrated even by those who loathed him, but enough was enough. The first and second *réseaux* were praised, the third was excoriated. No one wanted the transformation of Paris undone, yet none would concede, except by innuendo, that Haussmann might have proceeded otherwise. Even the dullest deputies saw that the struggle was not over money. "The Emperor did not know the details of the situation," argued Calley de Saint-Paul, invoking the old royalist apologia of a good king betrayed by bad ministers. "Certainly, if someone had said to the emperor that in order to use all this money it was necessary to break five or six laws, he would never have consented."[26] Rouher found himself in a delicious strategic position. He had long despised Haussmann and now could be rid of him, taking what appeared to him the political high road. He had only to separate the emperor who proposed from the prefect who disposed. The question was not political: "It is simply an administrative question, a matter of financial management."[27]

Rouher had a reputation for parliamentary compromise and suppleness rather than intellectual penetration or political adroitness. His skills were tenacity and simplicity. He offered the Corps Législatif, or at least the majority of its members, a chance to return to the relatively uncomplicated (and unthreatening) issues of city finance and administration. They were invited to be as splenetic as they wished about the prefect. The debate had ranged too far afield. It was prudent to focus again on Haussmann's vulnerabilities. Rouher, who was good at damage control, was delighted to give Haussmann over to the rancor of his many enemies. He extracted from the emperor—with enormous difficulty—the authorization to disavow Haussmann and thus get a favorable vote on the treaty, allowing work on Paris to go forward. The new loans would be approved, the prefect's methods deplored, with the tacit understanding that all future municipal financing would be put on a more regular basis. The vote was 185 yes, 41 no, and 38 abstentions.

Haussmann emerged from the debate, in which he could not legally participate, "simultaneously beaten and triumphant."[28] The loan was approved, the transformation of Paris would continue, and he remained prefect of Seine. It was a sloppy compromise and still left the problem of Haussmann unresolved. The prefect's response had to wait until April 13, when he defended himself before the Senate. His answer was able, his speech larded with details and statistics, his strategy well conceived. He fought tenaciously to defend his reputation. Anatole Claveau, an observant journalist who would become the "honorary head of the secretaries of the Chamber of Deputies," has left a good sketch of Haussmann in 1869. He was clean shaven—he had worn a beard, although never an imperial until the mid 1860s—and "his rosy complexion gave him the appearance of a fifty-year-old child. . . . His great height made it seem that a giant was carrying this head." "He almost never raised his voice, and his 'I want it done!' came out as a light murmur, which became a tempest, a hurricane, only if one were to resist him; he was seldom crossed." The emperor favored "a soft despotism," which perfectly fit Haussmann's manner. "His will, once expressed, became absolutely fixed, yet nothing in his person nor his language revealed the force behind it."[29] The details of physique and physiognomy apart, the manner of master and servant were remarkably similar.

In his senatorial defense Haussmann summoned only Paris as witness.[30] There was no need, he told the senators, to reiterate and defend the "*grands travaux* of Paris":

> They are everywhere. They are unavoidable. Each of you can judge the work in its ensemble and its details, recognizing the imperfections, noting the lacunae.

To accomplish this stupendous work, he continued, certain financial arrangements were necessary.[31] Those who deplored the expense, Thiers chief among them, forgot that what made Paris the great city they were pleased to celebrate were the very projects that cost so much. His enemies wanted it both ways. They embraced the great city yet insisted many of the projects were unnecessary. The work cannot be thus separated. The three *réseaux* were of a piece. Taken as a whole they were Paris. In addition it was the very projects that appeared useless that have made Paris great. Had the *banlieue* not been incorporated, for example, hundreds of millions of francs would have been saved; and Paris would have remained a city of modest size.[32] The critics wanted urban grandeur but did not want to pay for it.

As for the city's financial dealings, they were not only necessary but legal, appropriate, and based on historical precedent. When the Second Republic bought out the owners of the toll concessions on the several bridges over the Seine, the purchase was accomplished by decree, as opposed to national law, and the city, without the approval of the national government, issued bonds to pay for it. No one then questioned the legality of such bonds.[33] Besides, his administration could not be held to the same narrow standards as had those of his predecessors. The transformation of Paris was "unique in the history of administration and economics," not only for France but for the entire world. "We have succeeded," he continued, "we are almost at the end [of the work]." "We should not look back but look forward and complete the gigantic task."[34] He struck a defiant pose: "I have no reason to oppose a thorough examination of my accounts. They are, as I have said, my surest means of defense."[35] He concluded with a personal testimonial:

> The good fortune of having directed this great Parisian administration through unparalleled circumstances will be the dominant fact in my life. . . . the services to which I have, for the last sixteen years, subordinated my own interests, my personal tastes, my old friendships, even the joys of family life, constitute a capital of honor that I have amassed with jealous care, because this capital will be the clearest part of the heritage that my children will have from me.[36]

Self-righteousness and arrogance were Haussmann's customary justification, and would be so in his *Mémoires*. His defense was apt and perfectly in character. His Paris existed, undeniably magnificent. His hands were clean, and his sense of duty, personal sacrifice, and public service were beyond reproach. What more was there to say? The Parisians were ungrateful. The poor, "without religious or moral principles, half educated, greedy of pleasure," were no worse than the bourgeoisie, "who respect nothing but force," demand liberty, but take kindness for fear.[37] He made no apology, felt no regret.

In the spring of 1869 Haussmann still had the emperor's support.

Despite Rouher's parliamentary manoeuvre to disavow the prefect, Haussmann refused to think he would not once again enjoy the special relationship with Louis Napoléon that made his work possible. He believed the disavowal was nothing more than a parliamentary sleight of hand extorted by Rouher. In his defense he did not have to depend upon his own words, however heartfelt and vigorous. He spoke with the conviction of the emperor's affection. Is it not always so with the favorites of kings? They cannot imagine their own fall, nor, as we shall see, can they believe it when it happens.

The autobiographer was more bitter. Those who had attacked his budget did so, he retrospectively declared, for the narrowest personal motives. They themselves wanted a seat on the Municipal Council or hoped to place their cronies or minions. "How tedious," he lamented, "how antagonistic have been the consequences of my fidelity to the equitable principle whose application I pursued!"[38] Haussmann, who almost never mentioned men of letters, invoked the memory of Voltaire and Rousseau in his defense. "During the Restoration [of the Bourbon kings] it was to the philosophers . . . that they attributed all social disorder. This no more disturbed their glory than their repose." He asserted (and hoped) his own accomplishments would not simply transcend the jealousies of petty men:

> But I, I had to safeguard the great work that my efforts had placed in my hands. I had to prevent it from being undone. I climbed often into the breech to repulse the constant assaults; and my energetic but calm resistance, always supported by new and precise arguments, exasperated the equally energetic adversaries who accused me of stubbornness.[39]

Haussmann's misjudgment of the strength, determination, and ability of his enemies, coupled with his conviction that he occupied a special place in the emperor's heart and government, were not a mirage. Ollivier, among others, has testified to Louis Napoléon's devotion to his prefect until the very end.[40] Haussmann's fate was not decided in the February debates. He was wounded but might have recovered had it not been for the parliamentary elections that took place in May and June. The strength of the imperial opposition continued to grow and the fact that the question of Haussmann's prefectship and his handling of the budget were not directly used in the election campaign reinforces the interpretation that the 1869 debates were not fundamentally about money. Although the prefect was generally unpopular, the opposition, whether radical or republican, recognized that the question of Paris transformed would more divide than unite their constituents, while the financial questions were too intricate for campaigning. The opposition candidates stressed the more popular issue of suppressing the *octrois*, which, in fact, meant opposition to the *grands travaux*. Cutting the tax on foodstuffs and building materials brought to Paris would attack the major source of municipal income, although it was presented as a call for lowering taxes on the poor.

But if the opposition had to attack Haussmann's finances obliquely, the issue of an elected Municipal Council provided an excellent opportunity for a frontal assault in the campaigns. Implying that a democratically chosen council would not have permitted shady financial practices, the opposition could criticize Haussmann without opposing the transformation of Paris or wading in the muddy waters of financial chicanery. On the hustings, the opposition aspirants insisted they would complete the work already begun, but not begin any frivolous projects. Even Thiers, the ferocious opponent of the third *réseau* during the budget debates, now argued that the projects must be finished.[41]

The defeat of virtually all the government candidates and the selection of several radicals in the first round of voting "was like a proclamation of the republic in Paris." Emile Ollivier, who had gone over to the empire, was soundly beaten by a coalition of bourgeois and popular votes, which "symbolized the rupture between Paris and the regime."[42] Ollivier had to settle for a safe seat in his native department of the Var. The second round of voting was less radical but equally hostile to the empire. Devinck, one of Haussmann's long-time collaborators and a member of the Municipal Council, was rejected in favor of Thiers, who even received republican votes, cast by citizens who preferred almost anyone to a man so closely associated with the prefect.

Paris, traditionally hostile to the empire, was completely lost. Once again Louis Napoléon had not carried his capital. Haussmann, who had so successfully delivered the vote in the Var, the Yonne, and the Gironde, was never able to deliver Paris. His *Mémoires* are filled with bitter denunciations of the Parisians as ungrateful, greedy, and unreliable. The stubborn, persistent resistance of the Parisian electorate has to be seen as a failure of one of the central political policies of the empire. The election of 1869 cannot be construed as a vote against the transformation of Paris, but it was certainly a vote against the empire and, arguably, a vote against the methods and destruction of haussmannization. Paris continued to elude the emperor.

The complaints against the empire were not those faced by the July Monarchy. The Paris landlords—long in favor of urban renewal, long the victims of a deteriorating housing stock, static or falling rents, and paralyzed urban commerce—did not vote against the government in 1869 because there was too little state intervention in the city but because there had been too much under Haussmann. In a sense Haussmann's scorn for the landlords was justified. Ernest Picard perfectly expressed growing bourgeois resentments when he noted that the city of Paris was the greatest land speculator, shutting the landlords out.[43] Even after the landlords were regularly extracting more than generous settlements from the appropriation juries, they did not consider themselves sufficiently recompensed. Winning electors by raising property values worked far less well in Paris than had Haussmann's gerrymandering and bullying in the Var and the Yonne.

By 1869 the rhythm of expropriations seemed to be slowing. This misperception was brought about because most of the work was in sparsely urbanized western Paris. Once the bulk of the work on the central city had been completed, Haussmann's projects were less important to the landlords. The feast of renewal was over for thousands of individual owners. Since western Paris was undeveloped, much of the investment was done by banks and groups of speculators who bought up large tracts of land and built blocks of apartments—the Péreires are the best-known investors—rather than small owners of single buildings angling to be expropriated. The reality of the old quarrel between Haussmann and the Parisian landlords resulted not just from the shift of activity to the west of the city and a new group of investors, nor even from his arrogance and imperiousness. It was structural. Haussmannization rested economically and politically on the point of a pyramid and responded inadequately to the needs or desires of the Paris bourgeoisie.

In Paris, unlike the smaller cities and towns of France, where urban renewal was carried out by the local elites themselves, the intervention of the state was the problem. Paris was to be remodeled for the needs of the state, it was to be made the capital of Louis Napoléon's empire. Only occasionally were the desires of the landlords and the state in harmony. Just as Haussmann disregarded the historical integrity of Parisian neighborhoods, so he disregarded the desires of the property owners. He gave them what he mistakenly thought they needed and wanted, himself controlling the direction and degree of transformation. When the bourgeoisie complained about his projects or wrested speculative profits from the city, he was enraged. The wonderful forces of unleashed capital investment in Paris proved beyond even Haussmann's administrative genius. When the work slowed or accelerated less quickly than it had in the past, the landlords took fright, blamed the emperor, whose decided lack of bourgeois virtues already rendered him suspicious, and imagined that saturation had been reached or the empire had sold them out. Haussmann always took the heat for the fluctuations in the urban marketplace.

The early projects of haussmannization had grown familiar and were celebrated. But by 1869–70 numerous apartments in western Paris stood empty, several important projects were barely begun, the Bank of France was unhappy with the low interest rates on which haussmannization depended, there was growing resentment from certain sectors of industrial capitalism against Haussmann's policy of denying them the city, for the first time the city's budget was being roughly handled by the Corps Législatif, the third *réseau* was concentrated in western Paris, and the Left Bank had never been adequately renewed. All this local discontent smoldered in an environment of increasingly disastrous foreign policy blunders: the Italian adventures (the evacuation of French troops from Rome was begun September 15, 1864), growing tensions with Germany (most recently expressed in the Austro-Prussian War and the battle of Sadowa, July 3, 1866), and the Mexican fiasco (Archduke Maximilian was executed June 19, 1867). Louis Napoléon's coalitions were coming undone; imperial cohesiveness at home was in serious trouble.

Finally, Haussmann had simply made too many enemies, inside and outside the government. "Never was a man more the butt of Parisian malice, more the victim of gross irony, more satirized in song."[44] Jules Ferry, among many others, delighted in spreading gossip about Haussmann's peccadilloes with dancers and actresses. Had one asked "who was at that time the man in France most decried and most calumniated, everyone, with a single voice, would have answered: Haussmann!" During a debate on the proposed alteration in the course of the Loire River the deputy Eugène Pelletan reduced the Corps Législatif to guffaws by proposing that "the Loire should be diverted to Paris, if only to flush the administration of M. the prefect of the Seine."[45]

Emile Ollivier, whom Louis Napoléon would shortly ask to form a new cabinet, thus inaugurating the Liberal Empire, was an old foe and made Haussmann's dismissal one of the preconditions of his acceptance of power. Berger's youngest son, a protégé of Fould, the minister of finance, who also hated Haussmann, had never forgiven the prefect for replacing his father.[46] Rouher, of course, was a foe, while Persigny, Haussmann's one-time patron, was in retirement and Morny was dead. Frémy remained a friend, but he was compromised by the public unraveling of Haussmann's municipal finances, in which he was entangled. Throughout the February debates the defense of Haussmann mounted by deputies loyal to the government, as well as the responses of the ministers, had been feeble and ineffectual. They had no passion for the work. The great prefect was isolated.

The emperor could change political direction to save his throne, and he did so brilliantly in 1869–70, but Haussmann was trapped. He was only the emperor's creature. He had no alliances of his own, no constituency to which he might appeal, and by late 1869 almost no supporters. As Tourny before him his greatness derived from his master. Unlike Tourny he had no personal power, family prestige, or private fortune to fall back upon. Haussmann was only a bureaucrat. Once imperial support was withdrawn the servant could not stand on his own.

Haussmann had administered Paris with the same authoritarianism Louis Napoléon had used in France and was now abandoning. The prefect's fall was only a matter of time. He had done his work. He was no longer useful.

·XIV·

Haussmann After Paris

THE BLOW FELL ON JANUARY 2, 1870. THE GREAT PREFECT HAD BEEN sacked. The decree, signed by the emperor and Chevandier de Valdrôme, whose father had launched Haussmann's administrative career in 1831, appeared in the *Journal Officiel* on January 6. "What M. Rouher [at the time of Haussmann's dismissal president of the Senate] was unable to obtain despite several years of trying," wrote the daily *Le Gaulois*, "the new ministers have achieved in a few minutes."[1] The diary keepers buzzed privately. Anatole Claveau, the secretary of the Corps Législatif, seconded the newspaper: "despite his keen desire M. Rouher himself had never dared attack [Haussmann] directly."[2] "This morning," the librettist Ludovic Halévy noted, "M. Haussmann, relieved of his duties, was replaced by M. Henri Chevreau. . . .*It is a significant event*."[3] Mme Baroche added, "All the trunks are packed, all the bundles assembled. The prefect's two sons-in-law . . . have already left. They are packing up the furniture and will send it to Cestas. . . . The stunning fall of M. Haussmann is a victory for the center-left, which won in five minutes what M. Rouher was unable to get from the sovereign for five years."[4]

The emperor tried to protect his prefect. Emile Ollivier, who thought "his immorality, his scorn for rules, his reputation in public

opinion" made him an impossible colleague,[5] demanded Haussmann's dismissal before forming a new government. The prefect had
his own conditions. He had notified the emperor that he refused to
sit on any council of "the enervated Parliamentary Empire"[6] that he
always considered "the beginning of the end."[7] But Haussmann refused to resign, forcing the new government to fire him. The emper-
or's letter of dismissal arrived while the prefect was having lunch in
the Hôtel de Ville. The unimaginable had happened. Ministers had
come and gone, but Haussmann had endured. So often had Louis
Napoléon defended his prefect that he seemed impregnable. "He is
more than a great personage," Jules Ferry had written. "He is almost
one of the fundamental institutions of the age."[8]

The rituals of dismissal were played out. On January 6 Haussmann had a two-hour visit with the emperor. The following day he
said adieu to the Municipal Council as his servants finished packing
his belongings in another wing of the Hôtel de Ville. "What gives
me consolation," he told them, "after so much effort, is to fall with
the full confidence of the emperor, with the esteem and affection of
all of you gathered here, who have seen the work through, alongside
me. This satisfaction suffices to make me forget so many outrages."
"Often, in the final hour of a battle," he told his collaborators, seeking comfort in a Napoleonic metaphor, "the general falls, mortally
wounded! The army does not stop fighting. It closes ranks, wins the
victory and only turns its attention to the dead to wrap them in a
triumphant banner."[9]

He had one final theatrical moment, a perfect exit for the fallen
prefect. Haussmann had several times said he wanted to leave office
"with head held high and a firm heart."[10] On January 10 he orchestrated the exit he had imagined. Henri Chevreau, Haussmann's replacement, had not yet arrived to assume his duties. The new
minister of the interior, Chevandier de Valdrôme, assuming the new
prefect would have reached Paris, summoned all the directors of
major public services to a reception inaugurating the administration
of the Parliamentary Empire. The letter, addressed to "the Prefect of
the Seine," arrived while Haussmann was preparing to depart. He
savored the ambiguity and accepted the invitation. In full uniform,

at the head of the cortege of carriages bearing his entourage, accompanied by a detachment of Paris Guards in parade dress, Haussmann rode to the Ministry of the Interior, where his arrival caused a stir.[11] "Followed by my staff," he remembered, "I crossed the first salons, filled with a crowd that backed away from me as it would have from Banquo's ghost. The ushers, who preceded me, led me to the private salon next to the minister's office, who immediately gave the order to show me in.

"He was himself in full uniform, and surrounded by his staff, similarly dressed. Without hurry I arranged my staff in a semicircle on the other side of the room, and placing myself in the center, made a dignified bow to M. Chevandier and said to him,

> I have the honor to present the administrative personnel of the Prefecture of the Seine to Your Excellency. Profoundly devoted to the Emperor, this select personnel, above all, desires usefully to serve His Majesty. Their former chief, who is pleased to render him [the emperor] this testimony, has wanted, up to the very end, to give him the example of fulfilled duty.

The minister made no response. He advanced toward Haussmann with outstretched arms, "doubtless recalling our old relations," and said something about "the harshness of political necessities." He praised Haussmann's work, "forgetting that he had voted, in the Corps Législatif, with the systematic adversaries of the Great Work he now exalted! Completely unperturbed I responded:

> I feel myself particularly flattered by this appreciation of my career and especially my work in Paris, which, I swear, I had not expected from you.
>
> I entered the Administration during the ministry of the illustrious Casimir Périer, in 1831. Your venerable father was then one of my sponsors. I find myself especially pleased that after thirty-eight years his son, himself now a minister, would so publicly recognize that I have in no way compromised this honorable sponsorship."[12]

A bold curtain call followed before he fled Paris and his disgrace. Haussmann attended with his daughters a reception given by

Princess Mathilde. Then he took his family not to Cestas but to Nice, where he had acquired a gorgeous property on the road to Villefranche, with a stunning view of the town, the Mediterranean, and the beach. Set "amid a grove of olive trees," an old oil press had been "transformed into an elegant villa." Its gardens, laid out by Alphand, were distinguished by "an abundance of flowers, a collection of rose bushes, [and] an alley of orange trees—brought at great expense from Monaco and Menton" that led to his old friend Frémy's villa.[13] Here Haussmann licked his wounds, "majestically isolating himself in his disgrace."[14]

In June he was back in Paris and out in public. He attended the horse races at Longchamps for the Grand Prix de Paris (June 12). The emperor spotted Haussmann and sent for him. Master and former servant exchanged news, and the emperor invited his old prefect to St. Cloud the following day. After lunch the emperor led his guest into the park and "had me sit next to him, on the second bench in the alley of chestnut trees, on the left," where the trees led down in terraces to the lower park. "I want to change the Ministry," the emperor declared without preamble. Haussmann reports himself completely taken aback, unable to respond. The emperor continued: "Yes! Never did I imagine there could be such incompetence among its members." "I thought," Haussmann remembered, that Louis Napoléon, always so circumspect, had meant to say "inexperience" or "lack of aptitude," but he distinctly heard "incompetence." The emperor wanted to form another ministry "at the end of the [parliamentary] session." "Sire," Haussmann responded, "I will assist Your Majesty in this difficult work to the best of my ability," but he insisted upon some lesser position in the new government, because his convictions were "too absolute" and would create difficulties in any cabinet depending upon compromise.

"Do you think I could put together a new Cabinet with your help and not give you a position?" said the emperor. "I went from astonishment to astonishment," wrote Haussmann. "Your Majesty then intends completely changing the present orientation of His Internal Policy, to replace the Liberal Parliamentary Empire with a Liberal Authoritarian Empire?" "Yes!" the emperor answered, "forcefully accentuating this affirmation." "The experiment that I have made convinces me," the emperor continued, "that among the French power must be SINGULAR AND STRONG to be respected."[15]

The extraordinary conversation was not yet over—and Haussmann alludes to "several others" on the same subject, which he does not detail. The fallen prefect advised Louis Napoléon that what was needed was another coup d'état, "the true Administrative and Governmental Revolution," in which the emperor imagined "an important role" for Haussmann. "I want to wait for the end of the session and the departure of the deputies," the emperor added, rejecting Haussmann's advice to strike immediately.

Leaving St. Cloud Haussmann was stopped by the empress, who left him with the impression that "Her Majesty knew, more or less," her husband's intentions. Haussmann reflected grandiosely that if the new ministry had "been immediately formed, following my advice," it would have managed the complicated international situation that soon led to the disastrous Franco-Prussian War.[16]

"I never doubted that this story was pure invention," wrote Emile Ollivier. If "on the afternoon of the day he had thanked me for my abilities and my devotion, [he] had thought me an incompetent without equal, he would have been the most hypocritical of men." In fact the emperor "was courteous and just, and never did he employ against anyone words so hurtful as those put into his mouth by the former prefect." Ollivier contacted the empress, who confirmed his doubts.[17]

Haussmann's account is too self-serving and improbable, while Ollivier's concern for his own reputation rivets his concern to whether or not the interview took place. Embroidery is more probable and interesting than invention; and the embroidery is skillful and revealing.

Haussmann had never been in the emperor's inner circle. Even with Persigny and Morny, respectively, dead or in forced retirement in 1870, it is unlikely the emperor would have turned to Haussmann. The prefect was the ideal person to rebuild Paris or manipulate an election, but he lacked the subtlety, political and personal connections, and strategic sense to engineer another coup d'état. If Haussmann's story is true, the entire remarkable experiment of the Liberal Empire, Napoléon's brilliant change of policy designed to save the empire from ruin, not least because of his own foreign policy blunders, is reduced to cynicism. Ollivier's refusal to accept so crass a view is surely correct.

The interview, "on the second bench in the alley of chestnut trees, on the left," doubtless took place. But Haussmann was still reeling from the termination of his career. Meaning had not yet been metabolized. Fantasy transformed reality. The symmetry of the meeting was nearly perfect: Haussmann had been called to power at St. Cloud seventeen years earlier, very near this spot. Then, too, he and the emperor had talked of politics and plans. Now the two were no longer young. "The emperor was more than sixty [Haussmann was a year younger], his eyesight was weak, he was tired, he had not been very happy in recent years."[18] He suffered painfully from gallstones, complicated, some insisted, by a lifetime of dissipation.

Sitting amid the chestnut trees at St. Cloud, the sacked servant whose life had been given meaning and greatness by Louis Napoléon heard a call for help. He responded with affection and devotion. The intense and fruitful professional friendship of the two men is among the many incongruities of the Second Empire, one of those touching relationships that soften the annals of courts and humanize courtiers. Haussmann liked to think of himself as a member of the old imperial guard, although unlike Persigny and Morny, the disciples and advisers of Louis Napoléon's vagabond youth, he had adhered to the cause only when it was prudent to do so. Yet emotionally, if not historically, he was correct. Almost alone of the old Bonapartists, Haussmann had never been disloyal, had never sought his own grandeur, had never abandoned the imperial ideal. The bourgeois bureaucrat perfectly represented that small slice of his class who became the service aristocracy of Bonapartism. Although Haussmann had the craving, he was never fully admitted to the inner circles of power and prestige. The St. Cloud interview became the repository for years of unfulfilled longing. The emperor had finally turned to him.

The *Mémoires* are punctuated with advice: Haussmann on how to treat the republicans of the Yonne, Haussmann on the aesthetic expectations of the Parisians, Haussmann on being made a minister,

Haussmann on the character of the Bordelais. None of these remembered, elaborated, or invented conversations was in response to a national and personal crisis; none saved the regime or changed the course of history. In June 1870 the circumstances were quite different. He had been sacked, his work left unfinished; his enemy was in power and the emperor seemed to have abandoned the policies and convictions to which Haussmann had devoted his life since 1848.

St. Cloud was transformed into an epiphany and a foreshadowing. In little more than two months the empire would be swept away in the debacle of Sedan and the Franco-Prussian War. All might have been different had Louis Napoléon heeded his servant's pressing insistence on an immediate coup d'état. But if Haussmann was unable to save the emperor and the empire, his low opinion of Ollivier was given the imperial imprimatur, at least in the *Mémoires*. The emperor did not complain of his new minister's disloyalty or narcissism—this latter the frequent criticism of contemporaries—but of incompetence. The equation of authoritarianism and efficiency, the centerpiece of Haussmann's personal and political faith, was similarly reaffirmed at St. Cloud. Power must be "singular and strong," a truism for Haussmann. Even the elusive cabinet position, unobtainable in 1860, would be forthcoming, or rather offered but nobly declined.

There was magic at St. Cloud that afternoon, as Haussmann remembered it. His disgrace would be undone, his deepest political and personal faith reaffirmed and given public recognition, his enemies ruined, his love of the emperor renewed, his ambitions satisfied, his career justified. It was to have been an apotheosis. Even the empress, otherwise so unsympathetic to Haussmann, was in accord on that clear June day. But history was left to run is fatal course. Through no fault of his own Haussmann was permanently ruined.

Haussmann was a careful, calculating, we would say realistic man. He always presented himself, in life and his *Mémoires*, as unencumbered by illusions. He understood how the world worked and knew how to make his way in it. His life had been carefully reconstructed after 1848. He had cut his losses and attached himself to Louis Napoléon. Ollivier, too, had reconsidered his career and changed direction. Now Haussmann's choice had turned to ashes and Ollivier was the first minister. It was impossible for him to admit to himself that everything he had done and worked for, all the sacrifices he had made, all the loyalty he had shown, were unappreciated. His brusk refusal, after his fall, of a substantial monetary gift from Louis Napoléon is more than a fit of pique. He found it necessary to believe he would soon be back in power; the emperor's generosity seemed money for a burial.[19]

The debacle—thus do French historians refer to the military disaster that ended the empire—nine months after his sacking made his fall irreversible and wrapped Haussmann's reputation in the common obloquy of the empire. The pension of twenty thousand francs a year he expected as a *grand fonctionnaire* was reduced to the six thousand francs given to a retired prefect.[20] He was shortly in serious financial trouble and considered selling his château at Cestas. By the end of his life he had borrowed heavily and was so deeply in debt that his inheritors had to auction the estate to pay the death dues. When he came to relive autobiographically the painful days of his public death, they still seemed unreal, his dismissal unnecessary and vindictive. He attributed to Ollivier the same vengeful feelings he himself had harbored since their confrontation in the Var more than twenty years earlier. In autobiographical retrospect he was emotionally back in the world of 1870, his undiminished energies restored—he was sixty-one at the time and remarkably vigorous—plotting with the emperor to send Ollivier packing.[21]

These retrospective constructions of his life lay years in the future. In 1870 Haussmann refused to vanish into retirement. He was still a senator after his fall and attended the sessions once war was declared. On August 30 he took the floor to denounce the mayor of Châlons-sur-Marne who had surrendered his town to a small advance party of the invading Prussians. On September 3 he rose to deliver a rare improvised patriotic speech:

> If the Prussian armies had found before them all the roads, all the paths, all the trails, cut by trenches, blocked by felled trees, had they found all the forests they love to use for protection denied them by deep cleared zones, all the streets of the cities, the villages, the ham-

lets barricaded, the houses shut up, and all the inhabitants armed with hunting rifles (lacking other weapons) ready to defend, toe to toe, the national soil, their [the Prussian] advance would have been slowed by this mass uprising of the country even more than by the efforts of our heroic army of the Rhine.[22]

How redolent of Haussmann's own heroic and heavily embellished autobiographical accounts of his confrontations in the Var and the Yonne. At the time there were all too few willing to risk their necks for the empire. The next day came the news of the devastating defeat at Sedan, the emperor captured along with his army. The Imperial Senate opened its final session at 12:30. Haussmann was at his place, where he remained until the session was suspended at 3:30. Across Paris at the Hôtel de Ville a provisional government was proclaimed. Adolphe Thiers was there to ease the birth pangs. The empire was over.

Haussmann fled Paris for Cestas. There was no need but he panicked, losing his customary cool-headedness and physical courage in the face of danger. He saw the collapse of his world and ran for cover. His fears were not so farfetched. Revenge was on many minds. When he arrived in Bordeaux the nervous prefect, Larrieu, telegraphed the provisional government: "Haussmann is in Bordeaux. The people demand his arrest. Our friends are using all their influence to restrain the population. Should I arrest him? Send immediate instructions."[23] He stayed only long enough to pack his bags, then departed for Italy. He was in Nice on January 20 when the minister of the interior, Chevandier de Valdrôme, sent the prefect of the Alpes Maritime department a telegram: "Is it true that M. Haussmann is dangerously ill? Send me news." To which the prefect responded: "M. Haussmann dined yesterday at the Prefecture. He was in excellent health."[24] But the government was watching.

By the end of January he was in Rome. "I must fill my mind with many things," he wrote a friend, "in order to distract myself from uselessly rehashing a melancholy past, and from the poignant preoccupations that make the present more melancholy still. This I have been unable to do."[25] A month later, still in Rome, he wrote of the invasion of his Nice villa by "citizen Dufraisse," who searched his house and his papers "to assure himself that I had not hidden any suspect person and that I had not conspired (with Prince Napoléon!) to deliver Nice to Italy!"[26] These petty tyrannies were a taste of the treatment he would receive from the new republic. Haussmann had done so much bullying when he himself had power, he could hardly be surprised at the comeuppance now meted out.

In Italy he wandered "without a goal, from city to city, with a diplomatic passport, in a false name, which I owed to the kindness of Chevalier Negra, king Victor Emmanuel's ambassador to France." The most famous city maker in an age of urban renewal did not long meander. He was approached by a banker interested in forming a company to transform Rome after the model of Paris. The Florentine, whom Haussmann refused to name, proposed the presidency to the distinguished refugee. Haussmann declined "for many obvious reasons" but agreed "to indicate on a plan of the Eternal City . . . the possible new boulevards to be cut through the network of narrow, tortuous streets, covering [Rome's] broken terrain, which appeared to me would best ameliorate the circulation between the various neighborhoods."[27] The haussmannization of Rome! There is no way of knowing what it might have created because the map upon which he supposedly indicated his proposals has not been found.[28] The description he gives suggests that the scale envisioned by the developers—the project would not have been directly undertaken by the government—concerned only streets and circulation. Rather than telling the reader anything specific about what he thought should be done to Rome, Haussmann used the anecdote to reiterate that he left office with "clean hands. . .[and] empty pockets."[29] Economic hardship, along with all the other wounds inflicted by his dismissal, would rankle for the rest of his life.

The Franco-Prussian War and the Commune—the two gigantic events of the year for himself, the empire, and Paris—are overlooked in his *Mémoires*, where he narrowly confined himself to his rise to power and the transformation of Paris, both of which were over. The city he had built suffered two separate artillery bombardments and the extensive fires that lit the ghastly slaughter of "The Bloody Week" that destroyed the Commune. He says not a word about these catastrophes.

When he first fled Paris, in January 1870, Haussmann had left the capital a "vast building site of demolitions momentarily abandoned." There were dead-end streets, boulevards whose projected termini were not reached, a "chaos of obstacles to disperse, and pestilential lanes to demolish."[30] But the city's modern physiognomy was set and most of his unfinished projects well underway. The logic of Haussmann's planning was sufficient eventually to assure the constructions he envisioned, but he had no reason to believe in January that his work would be carried to term. As it turned out virtually all his projects were completed, some soon after his fall, others decades later.[31] But first "The Terrible Year" intervened and Haussmann again fled to Italy. His second flight from France was no more necessary than his first. But he was cut adrift, bewildered by personal and political ruin. All he could think of was running from more disaster. He made no attempt to join the scattered and disgraced Bonapartists, nor to attach himself to the hated but triumphant republic. He was waiting for the dust to settle. In the meantime he restlessly kept moving. Although less purposeful than his behavior in 1848, when the July Monarchy fell, these months are reminiscent of that earlier trauma.

Haussmann viewed the end of the empire, the war, and the Commune from exile in Naples. "I have stayed here for nearly a month," he wrote his old friend Frémy, during his second Italian visit—"the saddest trip to Italy you can imagine." "Had I believed, when I left Nice, that the war might last so long, I would have remained at the risk of everything, which my family fears more than I, or I would have returned to Cestas, despite their contrary advice." It was a feeble explanation. His daughter and grandson were at Cestas with his wife, who endured "hardships the poor woman never knew, which are especially difficult to bear in a place where her family enjoyed such high standing." Money, uncertainty, the possibility of personal danger should he return to France, and the siege of Paris preyed on his mind; but no more than the social humiliation of his wife and, by implication, himself. Haussmann was a broken man.

Frémy remained in Nice. Although seemingly more vulnerable to vengeance for his part in the empire, and especially its financial duplicity, he took no special precautions. Haussmann assured his old friend he would rush to "shake his hand" as soon as he was assured that order was reestablished in the town. The war had destroyed his already frail finances: "all my resources are gone." He was strapped for cash yet could not sell the Nice property, which he was in the process of fixing up when the war broke out. The work remained unfinished and he owed the workers money. He considered selling Cestas and some property in the Lot-et-Garonne, liquidating all his assets to raise enough cash to invest in "some promising enterprise." He had borrowed twenty-five thousand francs to get through "this wretched time and pay for the useless expenses of these inopportune travels that I have undertaken to calm the fears of my family." He had gone through the money and was negotiating another loan in Italy. "I still don't know if I will succeed in completing on time all the formalities they demand of me." Even if he did, "the conditions of the loan are very onerous." He would prefer a loan on the wine harvest at Cestas or one from a French bank on the Nice property. He needed 200,000 francs to tide him over until his friends were able to find him some work "worthy of my intelligence and of my time."[32]

On January 5, 1871, the bombardment of the southern front of besieged Paris began. The French government surrendered (January 28), parliamentary elections were held, and the National Assembly, which gathered in Bordeaux, submitted to a humiliating peace (March 1, signed May 10 at Frankfurt) that included substantial territorial cessions and the victorious Prussian Army marching up the Champs-Elysées. Bismarck had insisted. Following the ritual the Parisians scrubbed the defiled street. Radical Paris, which had endured an agonizing siege, refused to recognize the peace. On March 18 the Commune was proclaimed. Its final bloody suppression, in which more than twenty-five thousand Communards were slaughtered, was accompanied by massive destruction in Paris. Haussmann was in no personal danger, but it was a good time to be out of Paris and France. His sole surviving letter from the time of the Commune, addressed to Frémy, is dated Nice, May 24, 1871. He was gloomy about his own financial circumstances, optimistic about the defeat of the Communards. "I think," he wrote his friend, "that the taking of Paris . . . will doubtless be over by this evening." He sent condolences on Frémy's stables, lost to fire—probably set by artillery duels—and assured him that the loss could be "happily repaired, thanks to insurance." The Commune revealed to Haussmann the "powerful organization and menacing audacity of international socialism," and he hoped the experience of these national calamities would "benefit everyone." The lesson to be learned was that a continuation of the authoritarian empire ("the power founded on the constitution of 1852") would have saved society. He always blamed Ollivier and the Liberal Empire for the war and the Commune.

His own circumstances he described as "a question of existence." But he refused to let any "false vanity prevent me from accepting some small role, since it cannot be a great one, that you will find the means of assuring me in the affairs that you and your friends direct." With such help he could live modestly "in obscurity." A humiliating prospect. "After 38 years of public life," he lamented, "I have to begin working once more to assure for myself and my wife an existence sheltered from cruel embarrassment!" He planned to return shortly to Paris, stopping in Cestas to put his affairs in order and to find in the capital "employment worthy of my time and work."[33]

When he reached Paris the city lay in ruins, the emperor was in exile, the Third Republic was in power, and Emile Ollivier was gone from office, permanently as it turned out. It was small consolation that Ollivier's career had been even more thoroughly ruined by the disastrous Franco-Prussian War and its aftermath than had his own. The republican government would have nothing to do with the former prefect, but a few of those who had battened during Haussmann's administration found work for him. On September 3, 1871, he became a director of the Crédit Mobilier and in 1873 he was promoted to administrator. In 1874 he became president of the administrative council of the Magasins Généraux. While the republic set about repairing the devastations of war and Commune and completing a number of his projects, Haussmann traveled to Constantinople in early 1873 on behalf of the Crédit Mobilier. Part of the city had been burned in June 1870 and Haussmann was to assess the costs and feasibility of rebuilding. Nothing came of his three-month consultation. The possible haussmannization of Constantinople, as of Rome, remains only imagined. During these years in commercial administration he employed his keen practical intelligence on the possibility of establishing a rapid river communication system from Marseilles to Le Havre. He was intrigued by Ferdinand de Lesseps's Suez Canal, as he was by most innovations, although he remained resolutely opposed to electric lighting in Paris, insisting gas was more reliable. His canal project came to naught. On January 9, 1873, *La Liberté* published the news of Louis Napoléon's death in England. Haussmann went at once to the home of his old enemy, Rouher, to pay his respects to the memory of his late master. Once again the *Mémoires* are silent, as they are for most of his life after his fall. One of Haussmann's biographers says he went to England for the funeral, filling one of the 124 reserved places in St. Mary's Church, and was present at the burial in Camden Place.[34] For the remainder of his days he punctiliously attended memorial services for the emperor on the anniversary of his death, going for the last time, in full prefect's uniform, just days before his own death on January 11, 1891.

After 1870 Haussmann divided his time between Cestas and Paris. The land and château, some ten miles outside Bordeaux, had been inherited by his wife in 1862. The original building, which Haussmann would completely transform, had been erected by Elie-Antoine Dumas, a counsellor at the Parlement of Bordeaux, in 1778. Built in "the chartreuse style,"[35] the country house sat upon 182 acres to which Haussmann added another 19, including another house in 1864, when he purchased an adjoining property, and later still an additional 90 acres of woods.[36] "I had decided, in agreement with my wife," Haussmann wrote, to restore the château, not as a seigneurial residence, as the Bordelais taunted with exaggeration, but "a house where I might honorably fix my residence, my principal home, and lead a sufficiently generous life at less expense than in a Paris town house."[37]

Cestas was, and remains, a substantial country house. Not one of the grand châteaux of a very wealthy region, it nevertheless still conveys, despite a robbery in the mid-1970s that stripped virtually everything movable from the house—including the doorknobs—

HOTEL DE VILLE ENLARGED. One of Rambuteau's most successful projects was the enlargement of the Hôtel de Ville (begun in 1836), which more than doubled the square footage of the building. The original Hôtel was essentially the center section, framed by the two elevated sections with peaked roofs. Both wings were added by Rambuteau. This etching, with the Pont d'Arcole (now replaced) in the foreground, was made soon after the work was completed. The Place de Grève is the large plaza adjacent to the bridge. Note that the entire building stands free of the rest of the neighborhood. Three streets and numerous houses were destroyed to expand and liberate the Hôtel.

HOTEL DE VILLE IN RUINS. Collard's photograph of the facade of the Hôtel de Ville. In the fire of 1871 much of the documentation for Haussmann's work and administration perished. The ruins were razed and a new Hôtel de Ville built. Although mimicking the original, the present Hôtel is a late-nineteenth-century building.

GRANDS BOULEVARDS. A print from the 1840s depicting the boulevard des Italiens. In the top panel the old opera house in rue Drouet is just to the left of center. In the center panel the Café Anglais is the arcaded building just to the right of center. The artist has not represented the wretchedness of the public way.

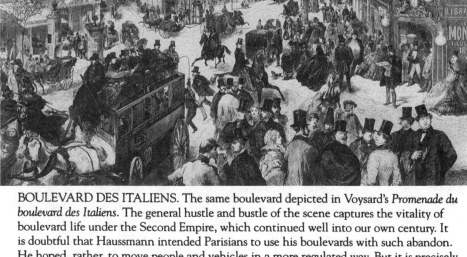

BOULEVARD DES ITALIENS. The same boulevard depicted in Voysard's *Promenade du boulevard des Italiens*. The general hustle and bustle of the scene captures the vitality of boulevard life under the Second Empire, which continued well into our own century. It is doubtful that Haussmann intended Parisians to use his boulevards with such abandon. He hoped, rather, to move people and vehicles in a more regulated way. But it is precisely the disorder and vitality of the boulevards that became so typical of urban life, as the Parisians successfully defied Haussmann's streets. The apartment houses, built of cut stone and embellished with ornate ironwork, with a commercial ground floor, are typical of the era and location. The Morris columns, for public announcements, punctuate the boulevard.

THE GRAND HOTEL. One of the first and most famous of the luxury hotels in Paris, built at the Place de l'Opéra, opened in 1862. The Café de la Paix, identifiable by its awning, faces the boulevard des Capucines and the *place*. Some al fresco diners are at the tables. In this café Baudelaire said "all history and mythology were exploited in the service of gluttony."

AVENUE DE L'OPÉRA. A photograph, by Fiorillo, of the most famous street and building of New Paris. The photograph may well have been taken from the Louvre. Garnier's Opéra dominates the great avenue yet seems hemmed in. Although the building itself stands alone in the urban fabric, as if on a cement island, the site created by Haussmann is not generous enough for Garnier's sumptuous design. The apartment houses lining the avenue are the same vintage as the Opéra, and were luxurious, as befitted the new center of the new Paris. This is the same urban scene painted by Pissarro reproduced on the dust jacket. The Théâtre Français is immediately to the right of the fountain in the foreground.

THE OPERA UNDER CONSTRUCTION. One of a splendid series of photographs made by Hyacinthe César Delmaet and Louis Emile Durandelle of every phase of the construction of Garnier's masterpiece. This is the eastern side of the building. Note the sumptuous ornamentation. The Opéra was the single most expensive structure built during the Second Empire, the gravitational center of the new *quartier* that Haussmann constructed to replace the old center on the Ile de la Cité.

BOULEVARD PROMENADE. An anonymous painting of boulevard life. Again, it is the animation of those in the streets that is arresting. Some of the thousands of chestnut trees Haussmann planted along the new boulevards can be seen. Their modest size indicates recent planting. A large Morris column is nearly in the center of the painting, which hangs in the Carnavalet Museum.

HAUSSMANN'S DREARINESS. Arguably the most familiar painting ever executed of Haussmann's Paris. The view is from the rue de Turin looking toward the rue de Moscou. Gustave Caillebotte calculated his perspective not only according to the formulas of the Renaissance painters but also used a camera fitted with a wide-angle lens. The distortions give his canvas its power and make it nearly impossible to figure out, from ground level, precisely where he stood. Unlike so many paintings of boulevard life as vital and intensely social, Caillebotte's boulevard is somber, his strollers self-absorbed and isolated. He deliberately chose one of the boulevards away from the center of the new city to emphasize the bleakness of parts of Haussmann's Paris.

DISMAL PARIS. An anonymous photograph of the angle of the boulevard Haussmann (in the foreground) and the avenue de Messine. The apartment house is elegant if a bit overblown, but the urban setting is bleak. Any number of intersections in western Paris have this same barren aspect. The boulevard life that swirled around the Opéra and the Grands Boulevards did not reach into these new, more distant, residential neighborhoods. Note the paving stones being set. It is near this undistinguished intersection that Lon Cogné's statue of Haussmann was finally erected in 1989.

ST. AUGUSTIN. The church (built 1860–68), seen in this photograph from the boulevard Malesherbes, has none of the charm and inventiveness of Baltard's sheds at les
Halles, although its technical use of iron (all hidden) is as virtuosic. Here Baltard was
constrained to build a church on a ridiculously narrow, irregular site created by the intersections of new streets, with a dome high enough to be seen from the Etoile. The result,
although an engineering feat, is a disproportionate church stuck incongruously in the
middle of an intersection. Haussmann was born very near this spot.

EGLISE DE LA TRINITE. Another of
Haussmann's churches used to complete a
cityscape. Designed by Théodore Ballu
(built 1860–67), this Renaissance pastiche
with overdone decoration closes the perspective of the Chaussée d'Antin (looking
north). The street was famous in the eighteenth century as a neighborhood of gorgeous town houses, the most elaborate of
them commissioned by the duc d'Orléans.
Those exquisite examples of domestic
architecture were knocked down to be
replaced by quite ordinary apartment
buildings. The Chaussée d'Antin is today
a commercial street leading to and from
the *grands magasins*. Marville has made the
church ghostly.

_Votre maison me fait l'effet de devoir être d'un bon produit .
_ Je crois bien ... j'ai fait deux SOUS-SOLS ...... et quand par hazard un de ces logements sera vacant j'y cultiverai des champignons

PARIS LANDLORDS. From Daumier's series "Locataires et Propriétaires." "Your house," one is telling the other, "looks as if it is going to be a good product." "I believe so," the other responds. "I have built two basements . . . when, by chance, one of these apartments should be vacant I will grow mushrooms there."

HAUSSMANN LAMPOONED. "The hailstorms of March . . . (On the rumor circulating of M. Haussmann's disgrace)," is the caption. The figure foolishly riding his bucket—trowel, paint can, and paint brush flying—is Haussmann. Jules Ferry's famous articles on the prefect's financial legerdemain had already been published, and Haussmann was in the midst of the financial fight of his life with the Corps Législatif.

HAUSSMANN IN HIS GLORY. A formal, anonymous photograph, with the prefect, in formal attire, wearing a couple of his numerous decorations. The photograph is the equivalent of a painted portrait. Haussmann looks out at us serene, self-confident, and a bit aloof. The portrait probably dates from the mid-1860s, when Haussmann shaved his beard. His coat of arms, or so it seems, pompously appears in the upper left corner. Compare this with Petit's portrait, made around the same time, where the prefect is presented as a good, professional bourgeois, without any suggestions of aristocracy.

HAUSSMANN AT THE END. This etching, made from a photograph of Haussmann by Eugène Pitrou, was published with the prefect's obituary in *L'Illustration* on January 17, 1891. The newspaper artist, a certain Hiriat, has accomplished the aging by deepening the lines in the photograph, making Haussmann nearly bald, and changing his cravat and coat. It is quite convincing and melancholy.

some of the pomp and grandeur of scale that was so central to Haussmann's taste.[38]

Built of the handsome white stone of the region, it sits well back from the road. One approaches along a broad, straight, tree-lined gravel path and enters the château itself from a modest ballustraded terrace with two equally modest, symmetrical curved stairways of several stone risers, each decorated by sculpted female figures holding a lamp aloft. Haussmann's coat of arms is carved into a stone medallion above the central entry. The hall—from which radiate two enormous vestibules as well as Haussmann's study, from which he could enter his small bedroom and an equally small room containing a piano, two salons (one for music, the other for receptions), the billiard room, the dining room, Mme Haussmann's sitting room, the toilets, and a grand staircase—was adorned with busts of the prefect and his wife, as well as those of the emperor and empress, his arms again carved into one of the lintels.[39] Painted coy nymphs in the prurient style of the empire peer from panels and above doors. The kitchen was in the basement.

The stone staircase, handsomely railed with ironwork, leads to the bedrooms on the second floor, and another to the maids' and servants' rooms under the mansard roof. The windows on the first landing, facing the front of the château, are interestingly decorated with roundels made by placing photographic negatives between a sandwich of glass. The light passing through these images of houses and places—one appears to be the Nice house—creates a curious effect and offers evidence of Haussmann's fascination with modern technologies, although he himself did no photography.[40]

The formal rooms on the first floor, especially the dining room, which looks out onto the grounds and garden at the rear of the château—no longer maintained as they were in Haussmann's day, when he employed a full-time gardener—are the most impressive in the house. The oval dining room, heavily draped, with an elaborately sculpted plaster ceiling and a ponderous chandelier, could seat forty-eight guests at the enormous table. The large salon, with an equally ornate ceiling and mythological figures painted over the doors, could also accommodate dozens of guests. In retirement the Haussmanns continued to entertain.

The outbuildings at Cestas have disappeared or are in ruins, and the vineyards have returned to nature. In Haussmann's day there was a greenhouse for this serious amateur of tropical plants and orchids, an orangery where he often received guests, a gardener's house, stables, substantial vineyards, a winepress and cellar, a small house for the cellar master, fields for cows, a house for the steward, and a *château d'eau*, which furnished water to the estate and the house using an ingenious hydraulic system installed in the old mill on the property. The waterworks tower is extant, the machinery, rusted and broken, can still be seen. Between 1862 and 1867 Cestas "was completely restored by Baltard." Every year "from 1873 until 1886, there were repairs or new work" on the estate.[41]

Haussmann put considerable sums into Cestas, more than 600,000 francs, excluding architect's fees, which he thought much too high.[42] It proved far easier to spend public monies than his own. Haussmann considered Baltard ungrateful for the work on Paris the prefect had sent his way, and especially for having rescued his unsuccessful plans for les Halles by encouraging the architect to design iron and glass sheds, thus assuring his reputation. Haussmann's relationships with architects were always strained. In retirement he continued to impose his own views and taste and resent artistic independence. Cestas confirms the impressions made by Paris: the classical traditions of the eighteenth century modified by the taste of the nineteenth, which meant grandeur achieved through enlargement and opulent ornamentation. Despite its traditional appearance Cestas is technologically advanced. The plumbing is excellent, although too much elaboration and ornamentation has been attached to Cestas, like too much jewelry overpowering an essentially simple gown. Cestas is not a hideous building, but it has no grace or proportion or elegance. It is solid, imposing, large, overstated, displaying the elements of style without being stylish. Cestas appears in none of the local guidebooks.

Haussmann's nervous energy, consecrated to Paris for seventeen years, could hardly be satisfied by country life. At Cestas, aside from puttering in his greenhouse, he laid out the gardens with Alphand, designed the hydraulic water system himself, and was a passionate vinologist, making a red *graves* that was thought quite drinkable. But he needed money to sustain the expensive life he craved. He had no investments save Cestas, which absorbed more money than it produced, his pension was inadequate, and he had no savings. His private papers reveal not only a restless imagination but someone looking to make his fortune, drawn to schemes that promised but did not deliver huge rewards. He was thoroughly bourgeois, and now that he was deprived of a regular and generous income from public service may even have regretted his rejection of the money-making professions. His few surviving letters from the period are punctuated by monetary worries and fret that his standing in society has been compromised.

He dabbled with obtaining a patent for the inventor of a solar-powered motor, and corresponded with a manufacturer of salad oil, a mining company, and a group hoping to establish a factory at Passy to make electrical apparati. He was involved in obtaining a patent for a process to generate electricity using coal.[43] None of these projects bore fruit.

In 1876 he stood for election to the National Assembly for Paris and lost. Yet another rejection by the detested Third Republic, another grudge against democracy and the ungrateful Parisians. The following year he stood for a much safer seat, that of Corsica (Ajaccio), where he opposed Jérôme Napoléon—known as Plonplon (he was the son of Napoléon I's youngest brother)—a brilliant but mercurial character who had never clearly established a political position. There was no republican candidate. "I consider it a very great honor," Haussmann wrote his political supporters, "to represent the island which has given the Napoleonic dynasty to France and which has still an inextinguishable fidelity to the imperial cause. . . . A stranger to Corsica until now, I have no other personal claim to her confidence than the absolute devotion with which I have served the Emperor Napoléon III [who had no connection with the island]."[44] Apparently this was enough. Supported by the local administration, Napoléon III's son, the clergy, and the pope—an alliance of forces that had often, under the empire, carried local elections—he was elected with nearly double the vote given Plonplon.

Bent with age—he was in his sixty-ninth year when he assumed his seat—without political connections or influence, sent thence by constituents who hardly knew him, Haussmann cut a sad figure in the Chamber of Deputies. He attracted, "like a great ruin, the most sympathetic curiosity and the most sincere respect." His fall and the end of the empire seemed to have sapped his political passion as well as the malice of his enemies. He went and shook Jules Ferry's hand, a magnanimous gesture that now had little meaning.[45] He spoke little in the assembly, although these were the years when Paris was often on the agenda. The devastations of the Commune were rebuilt, several of his own projects were brought to completion, and at least one major building, Davioud's Trocadéro Palace, for the 1878 exposition, was built. The Vendôme column was rebuilt in 1875 and the Ministry of Finance was moved into the newly repaired rue de Rivoli wing of the Louvre. A design for the new Hôtel de Ville was selected by competition in 1872. It reflected, despite its general faithfulness to the original Renaissance building, the nineteenth-century penchant for high relief, sumptuous ornamentation, and dramatic roof lines. The avenue de l'Opéra, completion of the boulevards St. Germain and Henri IV, and the Sully bridge were all debated in these years, while Haussmann sat silently in the Chamber of Deputies. When the Freycinet railroad plan, to create hundreds of miles of track, was discussed in 1879, Haussmann diligently represented the interests of his constituents: he was instrumental in having the Ajaccio-Bastia line built on Corsica. Otherwise he was a mute figure, an imperial ghost.

By far his most interesting parliamentary intervention came on July 29, 1879, breaking his self-imposed nine-year silence on Paris. A special commission had unanimously recommended clearing away the gutted walls of the Tuileries Palace. What remained after the Commune fire was, however, salvageable and several proposals were made for its restoration. Haussmann went to the rostrum to argue for rebuilding and proposed using the restored palace as a museum of modern art. The substantial ruins of the seventeenth-century building were "shocking to our patriotism." Razing the Tuileries would complete the work of the Commune and deprive the country

of a "priceless masterpiece of French Renaissance architecture."
The disappearance of the palace would destroy "the idea of the creator of the Tuileries garden, who has obviously coordinated all his
plans to the existence of this structure and the perspectives it offered him." "It's you who ruined the Luxembourg gardens,"
Clemenceau shouted at the speaker. Unperturbed, Haussmann continued, explaining that for the damaged parts of the Louvre new
stones had been made using impressions taken from the originals.
The same could be done for the Tuileries.[46]

His reasonable plea carried little weight in the Chamber of
Deputies, and even less on the reorganized Municipal Council, now
dominated by the radical republicans. Both were hostile to preserving an imperial symbol. The entire history of Bonapartism had un-
folded in the Tuileries. Under the windows of the palace—where
Louis XVI had been defeated and captured on August 10, 1792—
Napoléon's troops had gathered in 1799 when he seized power. Both
uncle and nephew had lived in this palace, where their heirs had
been born. The Salle des Maréchaux and the Galerie de Diane had
served for many of the celebrations of the two empires. More than
any newly awakened sentiment for Old Paris, these remembered
facts dictated Haussmann's intervention, as well as the rejection of
his proposal. In 1882, a year after Haussmann had left the chamber,
the year in which a final amnesty was granted to the Communards,
the city razed the Tuileries. That same year, on July 14, the new
Hôtel de Ville was inaugurated. Haussmann was not invited to the
ceremony.

In 1885, again itching to reenter politics, Haussmann, in his sev-
enty-seventh year, stood for election in Bordeaux as the president of
the Conservative Alliance of the Gironde. His bid failed. Only now
was he finally forced to leave unquenched his thirst for politics and
power. When Robert Sherard first arrived in Paris, in 1883, "Haussmann was one of those celebrities who had disappeared":

> Most people fancied that he was dead: he went nowhere; his name
> never appeared in the gazettes. He was living in retirement in the
> heart of Paris, a disappointed, lonely, and unhappy old man. . . . It
> was only when the announcement appeared that his Mémoires were

to be published—this was one year before his death [1890]—that people realized that the architect of modern Paris was still living in their midst.[47]

Sherard was right if not exactly accurate. In 1888 Haussmann contributed to *Le Figaro* a letter on the municipal organization of Paris, then being debated. "I believe," he wrote in perfect harmony with his long-held views,

> that Paris belongs to France and not to Parisians by birth or by choice . . . and especially not to the floating population of the furnished rooms who compromise the signification of the vote by the weight of their unintelligent votes. . . . I believe that . . . the central power, which represents the nation, ought to be armed at Paris with the necessary authority to make the general interest of the country prevail over all others.[48]

That same year he spoke to a gathering of Bonapartists in the Salle Wagram (August 15). "I am, in effect, a veteran, perhaps the oldest in the Napoleonic army which, thanks to God, still numbers millions of soldiers." He repeated a familiar and favorite conceit:

> an imperialist since birth, connected to Prince Eugène (the very model of fidelity), a child of the regime of the Great Emperor. I saw him myself; I approached him; he spoke to me with kindness. I was devoted from that moment to his service! With such memories how could I abandon my convictions, even for a day.[49]

In 1889 he sent another letter to *Le Figaro* on the differences between royalists and Bonapartists. This was his last public utterance until his *Mémoires* appeared.

Unable to get elected, even in Bordeaux, Haussmann played no further direct role in the nation's public life. He entered into correspondence with Victor Napoléon, the son of Plonplon, who had wrenched from his father's inept hands the leadership of the Bonapartist party after the death of the prince imperial, Louis Napoléon's son, killed in action on June 1, 1879, fighting in South Africa. Haussmann had yet another funeral to attend at Camden Place (in July).

The correspondence, initiated by Victor Napoléon, lasted from October 1885 until July 1890.[50] The young heir of a now despised inheritance—he was twenty-three when he first wrote Haussmann—treated the old man, one of the last living links to Napoléon III, with deference and kindness. Haussmann, in turn, seems to have been flattered by the attention and enjoyed his new role of avuncular adviser, which he had never had in the heyday of Bonapartism. Victor Napoléon had asked the old prefect to form an imperial committee in the Gironde. Haussmann responded, lamenting his lack of influence and means, and his age: "Ah, if only I was twenty years younger!"[51] He wrote a friend a few months later: "I'm afraid I don't have much prestige at Bordeaux, where they are completely devoted to the cult of the Golden Calf."[52] His brilliant manoeuvering of the city and the region into the imperialist camp in 1852 had proved only expedient and superficial. Land had remained in the hands of the old Orleanist elites, who readily deserted the empire and snubbed Haussmann after 1870. None of his political architecture lasted. Bordeaux reverted to its pre-Bonapartist traditions, the Yonne retained its republican sentiments, as did the Var, which in addition gave the nation Emile Ollivier. Haussmann's political ambitions came to little. His permanent mark on France lay elsewhere.

His twilight political credo, hardened into a formula, was simple. "I was present at the Napoleonic sunrise in 1848," he wrote Victor Napoléon. "So unforseen, so spontaneous, I knew that the moment had arrived. . .[that] the magical name of Napoléon would suffice, as in the past, to insure the triumph of the cause to which I wholeheartedly gave myself."[53] Imperialism—he preferred this designation to Bonapartism—was not monarchy: "It is a democracy whose authoritarian form assures stability, whose chief receives from the People an indispensable title that allows him to treat on equal footing with the most powerful sovereigns, but whose strong constitution does not permit him to compromise the imprescriptible and inalienable rights of the Nation."[54] The coup d'état of December 2 became in this scheme "nothing else but . . . an appeal to the national sovereignty." The violence inflicted on the nation was the responsibility of those who, outvoted, "had recourse to violence to make their opinion prevail."[55] His one bit of practical political advice was to tell

Victor Napoléon that General Boulanger—a would-be Bonaparte with republican pretensions who failed to seize power in 1889—was a useful, even a providential "broom" to sweep away the republic and prepare the ground for a real Bonaparte; but he could not be trusted to abandon his own ambitions once his destructive work was finished.[56]

The darkness of Haussmann's last years is lit only by these sad and formal letters written to a virtual stranger whose only claim on Haussmann's affection was his name. Old age is a kind of loneliness. Haussmann's was intensified: death deprived him not only of friends and family but of his world. The death of the empire at Sedan, the emperor's death shortly afterward, the fires of the Commune, the triumph of the republic, the success or mere political survival of his enemies, the utter neglect he suffered, accompanied by the official and unofficial villifications of his vanquishers, embittered his final years. The elegiac temper was foreign to this *homme dur*, but there was innate melancholy in his occasional reflective moments:

> When I recall, while each day traversing the *quartiers* of Paris that I have transformed, the amount of labor expended and torments endured by me during the seventeen years of my combative prefectship, I feel a pride that is not without some admixture of sadness, when I reflect on my present life. While the present generation reaps all the benefits of the colossal work of which I was the chief architect—and even sometimes admires it—I myself preserve as the reward for so much effort only the honor of having faithfully served my country in a post that was as difficult as it was important.[57]

The blows of the human condition grimly punctuated his retirement. His father died in 1876—his mother had died in 1869—and his sister, Caroline, in 1885. Then, on March 5, 1890, came the death of his older daughter, Henriette-Marie. She was fifty-one. "If you only go to the church," he wrote a family friend, "you will do as much as my wife, whose health permits her no more." "The service," he specified, "will be tomorrow, precisely at noon, in the Temple of the Redemption. . . . only the family will assemble at the funeral home, leaving for the church at 11:45."[58] His wife of fifty-two years died nine months later, December 24, 1890. Haussmann survived her by only a few weeks.

"I was rising to go," wrote Sherard of his last visit with Haussmann, shortly before the prefect's death, "when a most violent fit of coughing seized him." His servant hurried in, ministered to his master, and the paroxysm subsided. "I remember the last words he said to me," in response to a future meeting:

> Another day, *mon ami?* Shall we ever meet again? I may be carried off at any moment by one of those *crises* which you have just witnessed. May it be so. I look forward with confidence to death, and my only hope is that death may find me standing (*debout*) as it found all the strong men of my generation. I shall leave this life, if not with an erect head as formerly, at least with a firm heart.[59]

On January 9, 1891, he dragged himself to St. Augustin to attend a memorial mass for Louis Napoléon. The next day, his uniform heavy with a selection of his numerous decorations, he attended the funeral of Grand Duke Nicolas of Leuchtenberg, a member of the Russian imperial family. It was bitterly cold as the cortege moved slowly to the Russian Orthodox church in the tiny rue Daru (C 2).

The next day, Sunday, he invited old friends over to dinner. After the meal they moved to his study to talk. The baron was in a good mood, conversing easily. Between 10 and 11 p.m. he felt ill. Then he felt his chest tightening, which brought on one of his increasingly frequent coughing fits. They sent for doctors Humbert or Noblet, his regular physicians, neither of whom was at home. His friend Mme Bize summoned a certain Dr. Toupet, who arrived around 11:15. Haussmann was still in his study, fully dressed, slumped in his favorite chair. Dr. Toupet listened carefully to his heavily congested lungs and sent the old man to bed. Around 11:30 Haussmann breathed his last.

Le Figaro for January 12 printed a brief notice:

> The former prefect of the Seine held one of the most important places throughout the Empire. We trace here, in a few lines, his brilliant career, marked by devotion, honor, work, and loyalty. . . . Death overtook him in his tracks [*debout*]. . .in the midst of activity,

as he himself wished, and he departed this world as he departed public life, his head held high, his heart firm, confident in the justice of God if not that of men.[60]

The following day *Le Figaro* suggested Haussmann receive a state funeral. The justice of men was withheld.

"You are invited," read the funeral announcement, "to attend the procession, the service, and the burial of M. Georges-Eugène Haussmann, Senator of the Empire, former prefect of the Seine, member of the Institute, Grand-Croix of the Legion of Honor, etc., etc.—who died in his eighty-second year, on January 11, 1891, at his apartment, 12 rue Boissy d'Anglas, which will be held on Thursday, January 15, precisely at noon, in the Church of the Redemption, rue Chauchat." After the simple ceremony at the funeral home the body was transferred to a plain hearse, behind which marched three masters of ceremony bearing his various decorations on cushions.

The funeral cortege followed another Haussmann itinerary—from the Place de la Concorde, up the rue de Rivoli, the rue Castiglione, the rue de la Paix, the Grands Boulevards, and the rue LePeletier—to the church, where the coffin was placed on a catafalque. The pastor, M. Lods, pronounced the eulogy. The procession to Père Lachaise cemetery was followed by more than two hundred mourners. The exiles Victor Napoléon and the empress both sent representatives; the government of the Third Republic snubbed Haussmann in death as in life.[61] Haussmann was laid to rest in the family plot in Père Lachaise. Some years later the city took over the maintenance of the grave and monument—a small, unadorned stone structure typical of the cemetery—and marked it by a small plaque.

The visitor's book at Haussmann's apartment was signed by a group of mourners who had distinguished themselves under the empire. The faithful Alphand, elected to fill Haussmann's place in the Académie des Beaux-Arts nearly a year later, spoke, as was the tradition, of his predecessor.[62] His eulogy is devoid of personal detail, biographical intimacy, the expected warmth of a close friend who had worked with Haussmann for many years. It is the great administrator rather than the man who is celebrated. "In the different posts [he held], as later in Paris," Alphand told the academy, "Haussmann showed exceptional talent for an administrator, an ability rich in resources, a robust firmness of character, indefatigable activity, and an extraordinary capacity for work." The height of his power and prestige was "the Universal Exposition of 1867," when, "more powerful than a minister," he "received at the Hôtel de Ville, in a series of memorable celebrations, all the sovereigns of Europe." This was precisely the tone Haussmann himself used throughout his *Mémoires* to present himself, and the characteristics singled out for praise by Alphand were equally those Haussmann had emphasized.

Alphand, who met almost daily with the great prefect for more than fifteen years, told the academy this engendered "the keenest feelings of esteem and reciprocal affection, I would almost say friendship, were it not for the age difference that separated us."[63] But it was more than a difference in age. Haussmann might inspire respect, but he rarely engendered friendship. The same warmth lacking between the prefect and the emperor was lacking in all Haussmann's dealings with his staff, however durable. He had no instinct for personal affection; he generated no warmth. The official, administrative tone of the *Mémoires* is a faithful reflection of their author. Haussmann had the good fortune to be remembered by those who had worked with him as he desired to be remembered: hardworking, loyal, able, a great administrator, a Paris bourgeois who gave his life to government. He well understood, as did all those, friend and foe alike, that his achievement was extraordinary and could never be taken from him. "I am quite simply a parvenu Parisian, determined to make a name for himself, even a controversial name, in his beloved natal city,"[64] he wrote with the defiant candor that perfectly expressed his bluntness, tenacity, egotism, self-confidence, and ambition. He did indeed make a controversial name for himself. He made Paris—"this great and difficult work . . . for which I was the devoted instrument, from 1853 to 1870, and for which I remain the responsible editor, in a country where everything is personified."[65]

·XV·

Paris After Haussmann

THE GERMAN BOMBARDMENT OF BESIEGED PARIS BEGAN ALMOST EX-
actly a year after Haussmann's fall (January 5, 1871). The guns fired
for twenty-three consecutive days, sending between two hundred
and five hundred shells daily into Paris. An estimated six thousand
to seven thousand shells fell during the bombardment, mostly on
the Left Bank.[1] There was no military reason for the attack, which
launched the cynical excuse that has become a cliché: an attack on
civilian morale hastens peace. In the first days the Germans used in-
cendiary shells, which had proved so devastating against Strasbourg. But Paris, built largely in stone, was less vulnerable. About
fifty fires were started by the bombardment, only three of which
were significant. Destruction of houses was confined to a few
streets—the rue Monge (E-F 4–5), one of Haussmann's creations,
suffered much—and a number of public buildings were hit.[2] By far
the greater devastation came during the Commune.

The insurrection of March 18, 1871, was unlike any that had preceded. Barricades, which had defined urban fighting throughout the
nineteenth century, were erected but played a minor role. The day
began with a massive and bloodless assault on the artillery park on
the heights of Montmartre (E 1). There 171 cannons, silent since

the surrender to Prussia, were seized. "Bad news from Montmartre," read the telegram that reached the Hôtel de Ville some hours later. "Troops have refused to act. Heights, cannons, prisoners recaptured by insurgents."[3] It was to prove the decisive confrontation and had passed without a fight. The only fighting was at the Place Pigalle, at the base of the butte where the artillery was stored, and it lasted no more than twenty minutes. By 11 a.m. the insurrectionists were masters of Paris, although no one knew it.[4] Troops of the regular army melted away or mingled with the insurrectionists, to the despair of those officers determined to obey orders and control Paris. Throughout the remainder of the day the rebellious battalions, unopposed and swept along by a "human torrent," occupied all the administrative offices and government buildings without firing a shot. They found them empty. Around 9:30 p.m. the mayor, Jules Ferry, fled the Hôtel de Ville. It was occupied at 11 p.m. and the red flag run up the pole. Paris was in the hands of the Commune.

There had been two executions. Generals Clément Thomas and Claude-Martin Lecomte were both captured by chance in the neighborhood of Montmartre in the afternoon. Thomas, a bystander in civilian dress, was recognized by a national guardsman. Haussmann had known him in Bordeaux, as an interim representative sent by the Second Republic. The general was detested as one of the "assassins of the people" during the June Days. Now, more than twenty years later, men who had fought Thomas denounced him and demanded his death. An old man stepped up to the frightened prisoner and quoted the words of his cruel wit: "Pass me those scum on the end of a bayonette!" He had remembered the general saying this to his troops after capturing the rue Ste. Avoye.

Lecomte, one of the generals on duty in Paris whose troops had been unwilling to fire on the insurrectionists, was captured with his advisers returning from an inspection tour. They were separately detained, and when Thomas was brought to where Lecomte was being held, a massacre was set in motion. The crowd would not listen to Lecomte's pleas that he be taken before some authoritative body. They forced the building where he was being held and dragged him into the street, where they took an impromptu vote. "Let everyone who thinks the generals should die raise his hand." The verdict was unanimous. The generals were shot on the spot.[5]

The insurrectionists had poured into central Paris from the peripheral arrondissements and the *banlieue*, where Haussmann's *grands travaux* had banished them, descending on Old Paris along Haussmann's boulevards intended for radically different use. This image of the dispossessed reclaiming their city struck contemporaries as profoundly symbolic. Transformed Paris was not negligible among the causes of the Commune. Purely military considerations had not dictated the boulevard system, but Haussmann's two cities, neatly divided by the boulevards Strasbourg-Sébastopol, as well as the distinction between outer and inner arrondissements, gave geographical definition to more fundamental separations and antagonisms. The new city, to those forced from it, was an expression of the exploitation of labor, the rapacity of capitalism, the tyranny of the empire, ideas much in the mouths of orators at the reunions, where "all the currents of revolutionary socialism met to prepare the final blows of the battering ram for an increasingly feeble Empire."[6] "When the people take control back into their own hands," one orator had said, "we will see how rich communism is: the Hôtel the Ville, the *octrois*, the patents, the boulevards of M. Haussmann, all this belongs to communism."[7]

The life of the Paris Commune, until its formal proclamation on March 26, was reminiscent of a great urban festival. The image and symbolism of the dispossessed reclaiming their city remains apposite. The end of the Commune, the savagery of Bloody Week (May 21–28, 1871), is shocking even by twentieth-century standards. The vengeance taken by the Versaillais is the class hatreds of the June Days gone berserk. The atrocities committed by the Communards and the Versaillais—those assembled around Adolph Thiers at Versailles—are equally chilling, but the latter so far outnumber the former, the fighting and the killing were so one-sided, cold-blooded, methodical, and often sadistic that an evenhanded assessment of blame appears pedantically moralistic.

The bitterness of civil war was intensified by class war. Paris, whose every monument and neighborhood was laden with the unavoidable symbolism of a rich and violent past, became a killing ground. "The killing has been atrocious," Zola wrote:

> Our soldiers . . . have paraded an implacable justice through the streets. Any man found armed was shot. The bodies were strewn everywhere, thrown in corners, decomposing with an alarming rapidity. . . . For six days Paris was nothing but an enormous cemetery.[8]

In the presence of such slaughter it seems trivial to speak of the destruction of streets and buildings, which did not begin seriously until the Versailles troops entered the city to launch Bloody Week.

When the Versaillais—an umbrella term for a motley assemblage of the bourgeoisie who had fled Paris, returning soldiers from the defeated French armies, and in the most general political terms those who represented every conviction except revolutionary socialism, whose spokesperson was Thiers—felt themselves strong enough, they attacked Paris. The capital endured another bombardment, as destructive as the still-remembered Prussian shelling. It began on April 7 at 6 p.m. Most of the damage, ironically enough, was confined to the new neighborhoods of western Paris. The Place de la Concorde suffered heavily, as did the buildings of the Corps Législatif just across the river. So too did the great streets radiating from the Arc de Triomphe (itself miraculously untouched)—especially avenues Foch and Grande Armée—and the western *portes* (St. Cloud [B 5], d'Auteuil [B 5], Maillot [B 3]). None of this damage from artillery exchanges extended east of the Place de la Concorde. The massive destruction of Paris was to be inflicted by more primitive weapons.

There had been three highly visible and symbolic acts of revolutionary vandalism committed by the Communards before the assault of the Versaillais. Napoleon's column in the Place Vendôme (D 3), topped by a statue of the conqueror in Roman dress, was pulled to the ground.[9] The house of Adolphe Thiers, in the Place St. Georges (E 2), was destroyed, its remarkable library and equally remarkable collection of antique bronzes dispersed.[10] And the Expiatory Chapel, erected by the Restoration to expunge the guillotining of Louis XVI, destined for demolition, was only narrowly saved by the deliberate dilatoriness of a certain Libmann, charged with the work.[11] The invasion of the Versaillais troops triggered the most spectacular phase of vandalism, both revolutionary and counterrevolutionary. Karl Marx links Haussmann's work to the vandalism of Bloody Week:

> If the acts of the Paris working men were vandalism, it was the vandalism of defense in despair, not the vandalism of triumph, like that which the Christians perpetrated upon the nearly priceless art treasures of heathen antiquity; and even that vandalism has been justified by the historian as an unavoidable and comparatively trifling concomitant to the titanic struggle between a new society arising and an old one breaking down. It was still less the vandalism of Haussmann, razing Paris to make place for the Paris of the sightseer![12]

The frightened and vengeful bourgeoisie were as determined as their enemy to destroy.

On the night of May 23–24,

> Immense clouds of smoke, somber and almost black at first, mounted into the sky, then fell back to the city, which they seemed to cover with an impenetrable dome. Soon great licks of red flame lit up the clouds. Flame replaced smoke, and the city that had so often been called the light of the world, burned like a torch.[13]

The destruction was massive, the greatest ever sustained by the city in its long history. Public and private buildings alike were fired. The arsons had a certain logic as revenge, as Götterdämmerung. Among the most important monuments destroyed were the Tuileries and the Pavillon du Louvre (which contained the library), the Prefecture of Police, part of the Palais de Justice, the Hôtel de Ville, the Conseil d'Etat and the Cour des Comptes, the Palais de la Légion d'Honneur, the *mairies* of the fourth and twelfth arrondissements, the manufactory of Gobelins tapestries, the docks at la Villette, and the Ministry of Finance (on the rue de Rivoli).[14] Destruction of private buildings was especially intense in the rue de Lille (22), the rue de la Roquette (14), the rue de Rivoli (13), and the boulevard Voltaire (9).[15]

Once the invasion of the Versaillais began, the burning of Paris was largely the work of the Communards. "*At least three-quarters of the fires of the Commune—including the most serious ones—were indisputably set by the communards*," concludes a recent historian of the subject.[16] Some of these fires were set on orders from the Committee of Public Safety, the governing body of the Commune. Others resulted from deliberations at a high level—most likely in the National Guard. The majority of the houses, on the other hand, were burned on individual initiative, for a variety of reasons—insurance fraud and vengeance among them—or set by the bombardment. A good deal of the fighting was street by street, barricade by barricade, as it had been in 1830, 1832, and 1848, which also accounted for fires, sometimes set to retard the advance of the Versaillais, sometimes set to drive the Communards from their positions. Street fighting had not been eliminated by Haussmann: it took the Versaillais about as long to clear the barricaded boulevards as it had taken the army to clear the twisting inner-city streets in earlier insurrections.

Haussmann's Paris, with some notable exceptions, was not systematically destroyed. Most of the destruction in the haussmannized west was randomly inflicted by Versaillais shelling. The Communards seemed little concerned with destroying apartment houses in bourgeois Paris. Their ire was reserved for public buildings. What Paris most regrettably lost in Bloody Week was not Haussmann's work but a good part of her classical heritage that had escaped his wreckers. The *hôtels* along the quays and those in the rue de Lille were a significant part of this increasingly precious patrimony, as was the manufactory des Gobelins and the Hôtel de Ville. The *mairies*, along with the warehouses, were Haussmann's work, as were the barracks, the Château d'Eau, la Villette, and the Prefecture of Police. The sewers and water supply—although there was some talk of dynamiting the former—were untouched, while Haussmann's hospitals and schools were mostly spared, except for the random artillery shell. What the buildings were, what they represented, was more important than whether Haussmann had built them.

The decision to rebuild and restore what had been ravaged by war and civil war assured the triumph and perpetuation of haussmannization. Of monuments destroyed, only the Tuileries Palace was not restored. Paradoxically, it is to the Third Republic that we owe the preservation of imperial Paris.

The best view of Paris is from the Buttes Montmartre. Zola's Aristide Saccard took his wife, Angèle, to a restaurant there. From their table at the window they looked over "this ocean of houses with roofs of a bluish tint." The sight stimulated Saccard. He ordered a bottle of Burgundy with dessert. The wine further excited him. He looked amorously at Angèle, then at "this living, throbbing sea" below "from which came the profound voice of the masses." It was autumn, the city lay under a soft and tender gray sky. The setting sun, through a light cloud cover, threw "a fine powder of gold, a thin tint of rose, over the right bank." It was like some "enchanted corner of a city in the *Thousand and One Nights*, with emerald trees, sapphire roofs, ruby weather-vanes. . . .'Oh, look,' said Saccard, laughing like a child, 'it's raining twenty-franc pieces on Paris'."
His imagination soared, inspired by the fairyland below. He spread his hand over the city, his fingers splayed to indicate how Paris would be sectioned. He switched metaphors:

> Yes, yes, I meant what I said. More than one neighborhood is going to be melted down and gold will stick to the fingers of the men who heat and stir the pot. This great innocent Paris! Look how immense it is and how peacefully it sleeps!

The *grande croisée* had already cut the city into quarters. The other slices, so many sabre cuts laying bare the open veins of the city, will nourish "a hundred thousand wreckers and masons."[17]

Saccard's vision, his sexual energy deflected to the rape of Paris, brutally and memorably fixes Haussmann's work. The prefect had cut the city into sections and the very slashes—the boulevards—redefined urban life, fixed its contours, and indelibly marked Paris. The word *boulevardier* entered the language as a noun in 1866 and as an adjective in 1877, designating one who frequented the Grands Boulevards for pleasure, not transportation. Haussmann did not have chiefly in mind the creation of *la vie boulevardière*, but it became his most memorable cultural achievement.

It is difficult for us to imagine the vitality and attraction of boulevard life in Paris now that its century-long heyday is past. So many of Haussmann's streets now seem bleak stretches of uniform buildings, serried ranks of sameness, hot in summer, cold in winter, always unfriendly. His carrefours are hostile, inconvenient, and dangerous to pedestrians; his sidewalks are either too narrow for comfort or made so by the spillage of commerce onto the public way; and the noise is as insufferable as the automobile fumes. The hundreds of boulevard cafés are nearly identical in decor and food. The best restaurants avoid these thoroughfares. Only the store windows, which have lost much of their attraction, relieve the monotony. Parisians and visitors alike reject Haussmann's most important and influential accomplishment to seek the charms of Paris in its side streets, the nooks and crannies he left undisturbed and thought uninteresting and unhealthy. The Goncourt brothers, who loathed Haussmann's streets, have been vindicated by history. "These new boulevards," they lamented in 1860, "without sinuousness, without the unexpected perspective, implacably straight, which no longer express the world of Balzac," make one think "of some American Babylon of the future."[18] The cranky aesthetes were echoed by the stolid Sherard:

> The Paris that I loved was the Paris that had not been Haussmanised. I used to hunt out in midnight rambles such narrow streets, such gabled roofs, such memories of a more romantic age as the city could still afford. I still feel at times a revolt, and this is common with most Parisians, at the mournful monotony of the architecture which he imposed.[19]

However, most Parisians and visitors from the 1860s until at least the 1930s did not share Sherard's views, let alone those of the Goncourts and many intellectuals. George Sand was unique. She liked the boulevards, where one could walk "for a long time, hands in pocket, without getting lost, without having constantly to ask directions. . . . it's a blessing to follow a wide sidewalk."[20] On Haussmann's boulevards an elegant, sophisticated, vital, cosmopolitan, uniquely Parisian life was lived. The compelling urban theater of Belle Epoque Paris was played on his remarkable stage. Indeed, the preeminence of the boulevards, of an extroverted, outdoor, theatrical urban life was not seriously challenged until after World War II. The French, wrote Philip Gilbert Hamerton, "have invented the *street*."[21] French life seemed to burst the bounds of mere buildings, "to blur the distinctions between indoors and out."[22] The boulevards were the perfect urban representation of French egalitarianism, with its mixture of classes. They were the envy of the world, the boulevardier the quintessential Parisian, and urbanite.

The coming of the automobile, the simultaneous disappearance of the trees, the sacrifice of footway to roadway, and significant population shifts have rendered Haussmann's boulevards less attractive and more harrowing, while the growth of Paris and its suburbs has put unbearable pressure on public spaces.[23] But if the boulevardier has become virtually extinct, we can get some idea of what the boulevards des Italiens and Capucines were like a century ago from the dense and vibrant crowds along stretches of the boulevards St. Michel, St. Germain, and du Montparnasse. These still vibrant Left Bank arteries, however reminiscent of nineteenth-century boulevard life, are quite different. The throngs are more bohemian than bourgeois, generally young, and hardly fashionable.

Haussmann did not invent boulevard life—he generalized it, exaggerated it, made it monumental. Boulevard life existed during the Restoration. If a date helps, then 1821, when the opera house in the rue Le Peletier opened, is a beginning. Street activity, stimulated by the theaters, the Chinese baths (at the angle of the rue de la Michodière)—where one could take a bath and read all the new books—and the gaming tables at Fracasti's (at the corner of the rue de Richelieu), was confined to a few blocks. "The space in question," wrote Haussmann's former classmate, Alfred de Musset, "is not large. A rifle shot would carry from one end of it to the other. . . . Yet this dirty, dusty strip of street is one of the rare points on the surface of the globe where pleasure of every kind can be had for the asking."[24] The July Monarchy, Balzac's Paris, continued to use this neighborhood for its pleasures. The Grands Boulevards were the haunt of a small, largely masculine elite, whose doings and indulgences were shared and recorded by novelists and journalists. But the very foulness of the Paris street demanded endurance, agility, and considerable tolerance for physical discomfort. The English essayist Hazlitt attributed the characteristic gait of the Paris bon vivant—"that light, jerking, fidgeting trip on which they pride themselves"—to navigating the slippery, slimy paving stones.[25] Later boulevard life, made familiar by the Impressionist painters, by the literature, the theater, and the opera of the Belle Epoque, did not exist before Haussmann. There was no need for a new word to describe those who frequented the boulevards until Haussmann built or planned the familiar Grands Boulevards, and specifically defined as planted with trees and not owing their origin to any military wall: to wit, the boulevards Henri IV (F 4), Sébastopol, Magenta (F 2), Voltaire (G 3–4), Haussmann (C-D 2), Malesherbes (C-D 2), on the Right Bank, and St. Germain (D-F 4), St. Michel (E 4–5), Arago (E-F 5), and Raspail (D 5), on the Left.

The wretchedness of the pre-Haussmann streets as well as their relative isolation from the rest of Paris made boulevard life an acquired taste. "For people accustomed to the splendors of life," asked Balzac in 1834, "is there anything more ignoble than the tumult, the mud, the cries, the bad odor, the narrowness of populous streets?"[26] The majority of the Paris streets, shunned by the bourgeoisie, were given over by default to the amusements and needs of the popular classes. The hurly-burly as well as the manners and habits of those who thronged the streets made them more than a distasteful inconvenience for the bourgeoisie. The streets belonged to the people, to the entertainers, hawkers of nostrums, musicians, cardsharpers, and more dubious users of public space, who catered to popular pleasures. All these had to be dislodged, banished from the center of Paris for boulevard life to become widespread and bourgeois.

The streets had to be cleansed culturally as well as physically. The permanent "fair" of the popular streets was either domesticated for the bourgeoisie, who now flocked outdoors to enjoy boulevard life, or exiled eastward, often beyond the city to the *banlieue*. Popular street celebrations were forcefully supplanted by celebrations of industry, progress, and commerce itself, which were ultimately moved to more permanent settings as expositions. The streets gradually became bourgeois theater. The metamorphosis of celebrations of the Fall of the Bastille offers an example. The street balls that had originally marked the fête from its proclamation as the national holiday in the 1880s were, inexorably, moved farther and farther from the center of Paris. Today only a few survive. July 14 is now officially celebrated by a gigantic military parade down the Champs-Elysées.

It took eighteen years of deliberate imperial policy to wrest the streets from the Parisian sansculottes and impose a bourgeois culture on the city. Louis Napoléon's coup d'état began with a fusillade on the boulevard des Capucines. Paris had to be first subdued by gunfire and then conquered by social remodeling. The emperor occupied his capital by the purposeful and forceful intrusion of the state. The bourgeoisie never forgave the bohemian adventurer the massacre on the boulevards. Haussmann's proconsulat, charged with the grand strategy of imposing political hegemony, went well beyond the historical cliché of creating clear fields of fire and unencumbered space for cavalry charges that has attached to his work. He began by cutting the city up, as Saccard rhapsodized. With the opening of the boulevard de Strasbourg in 1853, "a new frontier was marked out in Paris; and rarely, for more than a century, did anyone live to the east of it who could afford not to do so."[27] The new center of the city was west of this artery, around the carrefour Richelieu-Drouot (E 2), very near the Bourse, where the boulevard des Italiens intersects the boulevard Haussmann. The prefect riveted this new urban center—typically bourgeois, with its expensive housing, banks, commerce, theaters, hotels, restaurants—with the new Opéra, the focal point for several important new streets. The original Grands Boulevards he transformed profoundly, stripping them of the intimate and charming character they had preserved from the eighteenth century. Luxury hotels and pompous apartment houses were built for the new inhabitants and those who visited Paris, which now proclaimed itself an international city of pleasure.

The Grand Hotel (D 2), completed in 1857 above the Café de la Paix—both of which have recently been restored to their original overstuffed grandeur—was among the first of its species. Along with a few other similar establishments it replaced the vile public accommodations Balzac described when Lucien de Rubempré and Madame de Bargeton arrived in the city. Hero and heroine found only "one of those ignoble rooms which are the disgrace of Paris, where—for all its pretensions to elegance—there is not one hotel where the wealthy traveler can feel at home. Lucien could not recognize his Louise in that cold room, where the sun never penetrated, the curtains were worn out, the polished floor stank of poverty and the furniture was dilapidated, in bad taste, and probably bought at second-hand."[28] The Grand Hotel was the new face of Paris: in the Café de la Paix, said Baudelaire, "all history and mythology were exploited in the service of gluttony." The public rooms were glittering, the food and wine were supreme, the Opéra was just across the street, the *grands magasins* just around the corner. The boulevards had been sanitized and gentrified, and the hotel guest left sumptuous accommodations to become "part of a continuous street entertainment that was the envy of every other city in the world."[29]

Only a few blocks away from the carrefour of the Opéra, the boulevard that bore Haussmann's name made possible the new urban phenomenon, the department store, symbiosis of boulevard and business, of the transformations wrought by maturing capitalism. Again haussmannization did not create department stores, but it was the precondition. The new streets, tying the several neighborhoods of the city together, made possible an intense intraurban circulation. All retailing depends on public access, but department stores need an easy, regular, and considerable flow of bourgeois customers. So extensive a concentration of merchandise cannot survive without a vast and wealthy clientele. The department stores in Paris that sprang up during the empire—Au Bon Marché, Au Louvre, Galeries Lafayette, Printemps—were built along the new boulevards, the last two adjacent on the boulevard Haussmann. They were uniquely Parisian: no other city in France could offer a sufficient concentration of rich customers to sustain this new type of commerce. The *grands magasins* were not a part of Haussmann's urban plans, but their emergence further assured the success of his boulevards, added a powerful commercial institution to street life, and more solidly anchored his new urban center. Galeries Lafayette and Printemps are probably more responsible for making the ninth arrondissement the center of Haussmann's Paris than the Opéra. The department store provided a more egalitarian theater, a more successful integration of business and pleasure.

Architecturally the *grands magasins* were among the most remarkable and modern buildings in Paris. The Louvre, Bon Marché and Printemps each occupied a full city block, were as isolated from the surrounding city as any historical monument, were built celebrating the new materials of iron and glass, and employed expensive materials—statuary, wrought iron grillwork, and multichrome mosaics—to dazzle the pedestrian, who now became a potential customer. The Opéra itself "could scarcely match" the opulence of these commercial palaces.[30] The metaphor of a city, a microcosm of Paris, both industrial town and consumer's paradise, occurred to many, linking the emergence of the new city and the new commerce.[31]

A number of small shops were crushed by the *grands magasins*, victims of a centralized metropolis: Zola's bankrupt silk merchant, Robineau, or the draper Baudu in *Au Bonheur des dames*. A number of these small merchants, bypassed by the boulevards, isolated from the commercial traffic drawn by the department stores along the boulevards, driven to the wall by the *grands magasins*, turned to the right and the "politics of resentment." But as Philip Nord, the historian of the phenomenon, points out, a perhaps equal number of *boutiquiers* benefited from the proximity of the *grands magasins* and thrived.[32]

The prefect's conception was to move citizens purposefully through the city, from one hub or monument to another. The presence of the *grands magasins* turned the boulevards, now tightly packed with shops that invaded the sidewalks, into rendezvous for social and commercial intercourse. Zola depicts them as scintillating palaces designed to seduce bourgeois women, inculcate in them, by the very opulence of their displays, a taste for luxury. The *grands magasins* served also to distinguish the new from the old city: the government, or at least the law courts and the police, were on the Ile de la Cité; the *grands magasins* were one of the defining aspects of transformed, bourgeois Paris. Commercialization of the boulevards also played a strategic role. The St. Martin and St. Denis gates, where barricades had gone up in 1851 against Louis Napoléon's coup d'état, were effectively neutralized by commercial penetration.[33]

In the nineteenth century, street improvement was "a panacea for every urban problem."[34] Haussmann's great strength and major weakness was administration, reducing decisions to uniform routine: his boulevards were in this sense bureaucratic. Congestion, both of movement and as an organic metaphor, was the bane of Old Paris. Haussmann sought to alleviate it with his customary thoroughness. If one boulevard was good, two, or two hundred, were that much better; he built them everywhere, injecting "the vitality of the *Grands Boulevards* into decaying and even moribund sections of the older city."[35] Inoculation did not everywhere prevent infection. The visitor's guides to the Second Empire lamented the lack of street animation on the boulevards when they passed beyond the *portes* St. Denis and St. Martin. Even within the city limits there were long, melancholy stretches of nearly empty boulevards.

The same boulevards that transformed urban life by creating public space deliberately drew the poor away from the new city, away from the gaze of the bourgeoisie and the increasing numbers of tourists who flooded Haussmann's city, become a mecca for sightseers. Bourgeois boulevard life stopped at the city's old borders. Haussmann's work had not so much suppressed, or even ameliorated, misery as displaced it. Indigence in the thirteenth arrondissement (roughly F-G 5)—which had more of the new boulevards than most of its Left Bank neighborhoods—increased from 8,105 in 1861 to 13,760 in 1867.[36] Before Haussmann poverty and misery had been at the core of Paris, integrated into the city. Haussmann banished misery and its accompanying unsightliness and disease, denying shelter and, with the exception of the Hôtel Dieu, moving medical care out of the city's center. The working poor would be housed and cared for, but only in the outer arrondissements. The destitute would have to fend for themselves, somewhere beyond the neighborhoods of the notables and the prefect.

Those who could not find refuge within the city, where much of the traditional housing of the chronically miserable had been destroyed, moved to the *banlieue*.[37] The faubourgs filled with a marginal or semimarginal population, denied the city by the disappearance of neighborhoods of affordable housing, even though Haussmann had left many of the working-class *quartiers* nearly intact. The banished wretched did not now even totally disappear. They sometimes turned up, unexpectedly, wrenchingly, in the very heart of the new city. Baudelaire, who was generally favorable to Haussmann's work,[38] tells of one such encounter in "The Eyes of the Poor," in his *Petits Poèmes en prose*. Two lovers gaze into each other's eyes across a table (probably at the Café de la Paix) littered with "glasses and decanters, all so much bigger than our thirst," when a man with a tired face and a grizzled beard, holding a small child by the hand and carrying an even smaller one, suddenly appeared. "They were all in rags. Their three faces were strikingly serious, with their three pairs of eyes fixed on the new café":

> The father's eyes seemed to be saying, "What a beautiful sight—how beautiful it all is—it's as though all the gold in our poor world has been spread over those walls." The little boy's eyes were saying, "How beautiful, beautiful—but this is a house where only people who are not like us are allowed in." As for the smallest of the trio, his eyes were too hypnotized to express anything but a mindless, deeply felt joy.

The poet was lost in the eyes of his beloved, when she remarked "I just can't stand those people, with their eyes as wide open as gates. Could you not ask the head-waiter to see them off?"[39]

The new industrial working class were also denied the city. Haussmann compulsively administered an earlier urban fear. Napoléon's first prefect, Frochot, remembered the dominance of the artisans, the sansculottes, in the French Revolution:

> Is it good politics for a wise administration to seek to multiply manufacturing in Paris, and thus to add a large number of workers who are so easily stirred up . . . in a city already so plagued by the germs of fermentation?[40]

His successor during the Restoration, Chabrol, reiterated the warning: "take care," he wrote the prefect of police, "not to allow the city of Paris to be blockaded by a belt of factories. This would be the rope that would one day strangle the city.[41] Haussmann, too, was determined to keep Paris free of large-scale industry. An added detraction was the pollution it created. For all his interest in technology, his abiding faith in capitalism, Haussmann checked the invasion of heavy, dirty industry into Paris.

Arguing for annexation of the *banlieue*, he wrote: "It is not essential for Paris that it have, at its gates or in its environs, factories that manufacture . . . products of every kind for the world market."[42] Haussmann was expressing the views of Louis Napoléon, which he had made his own. The emperor had written Rouher as soon as he learned that one of the railroad companies proposed building its workshops in Paris: "we must delay the plan by any means." He did not want any additional industry in Paris, even if connected to the railroads, which he actively supported. The railroad stations on the periphery of the city were to draw the poor away from the center.[43] Master and servant may well have remembered that the railroad workers of La Chapelle had been in the thick of the fighting in the June Days. Imperial Paris was to be dominated by court, commerce, and the bourgeoisie.

The new Paris, reflected in the emphasis on the bourgeois west, would, however, continue the artisan traditions of the city. Haussmann was committed to quality artisan production by individuals or in small workshops, long characteristic of Paris. Large-scale textile manufacturing, which had become increasingly important in Paris, was forced from the capital. By 1847 much of the cloth manufacturing had been sent to the provinces. Bordeaux became the center for producing rough shirts destined for the African trade: Paris remained famous for the *chemise de Paris*, a fine, elegant shirt. The garment industry itself remained, its workrooms still obvious along the rue de Turenne (F 3). Paris also became the home for the best furniture makers in France, for jewelers, watchmakers, glove makers, hat makers, luggage makers—to abbreviate a long list—and all the shops that sold these fine wares. Because of the nature of craft industry they were scattered throughout the city, but the major concentrations continued to be in Old Paris. The rue du faubourg St. Antoine (G 4) remains the furniture center of the nation. Wealthy Parisians had the convenience of the artisans on whom they depended for their luxuries. As late as the Commune of 1871 the militant Paris workers were mostly artisans, as they had been in the French Revolution. But Paris had ceased to be the vanguard of worker protest.[44] Limoges, the porcelain manufactory of France, in the southwest of the country, became known as the Red City.

P.-L. Roederer's famous, overworked observation that Paris was divided vertically, the rich on the lower, the poor on the upper floors, was true, even in the late eighteenth century when he made it, only for the neighborhoods of the petite and middle bourgeoisie. The notables had always lived horizontally apart from their social inferiors. The old monarchy and its nineteenth-century successors had tried to maintain some social equilibrium in Paris, whether horizontal or vertical. Haussmann abandoned this policy. Critics have indicted the prefect for encouraging immigration to the west.[45] In truth, he was unable to check, let alone reverse, the movement that had been an aspect of Paris's history for centuries. His administrative thoroughness hastened the process and the boulevard de Strasbourg put an urban barrier between the two cities. By 1870 Paris was characterized by a degree of social segregation far greater than it had been when he came to power. Rich and poor were geographically isolated from each other. Western Paris of the elites concentrated yet another significant population, domestic servants. The law of 1859, allowing an additional twenty meters of height to construction on the new boulevards for servants' quarters—the notorious *chambres de bonnes*—not only altered the appearance of Paris but separated servants and family, proletarianizing domestic service by degrading its status.[46] The overwhelming number of servants' quarters were built in western Paris. There are no reliable figures, but the majority were for women, introducing another demographic distinction into the city.

Haussmann favored expensive housing, but he would have preferred that it be less concentrated in the west of Paris. His attempts at dispersal failed. He could not direct capitalist speculation, let alone hobble greed. Many of the luxury buildings the Péreires created along the boulevard Malesherbes lay vacant for years. Paris could not absorb so much middle-class housing. From 1860, when the extensive work in western Paris began, to the present, the consequences of remodeling the city remain clear: the officially egalitarian culture of France was modified, in Paris, by sharp social segregation, easily observed at street level. Housing stock in the west was and remains more substantial, apartments are larger, expensive restaurants more prevalent, luxury shops everywhere apparent, theaters, department stores, corporate headquarters all concentrated here, and pedestrians are less diversified.

If the uncontrollable forces of speculation and corruption often thwarted Haussmann's careful plans, he was remarkably successful in realizing his—and the emperor's—overall vision. During the empire Paris was made a national city. Haussmann disregarded historical neighborhood variations within the capital, replaced the unique with the formulaic, and made apparently irreversible the long history of national centralization. His concentration of power in his own hands, through the organic administrative law of 1855 and its several amendments, gave his bureaucracy all the authority it needed. This same urge toward centralization was manifested in the design of Paris itself. In place of traditional centers of neighborhood gravity he built city halls to anchor each arrondissement, arbitrarily locating them to complement the new boulevards, reshaping entire *quartiers* to conform to the rational abstractions of administrative order. In the ten arrondissements incorporated in 1860 only one new city hall, in the Batignolles neighborhood, was built on the site of its original *mairie*.[47] He favored those neighborhoods that held important national monuments or government buildings, reinforcing the overarching principle of Paris as a national city, a government town. The new imperial capital also meant that a sizable part of the population were civil servants of one sort or another. The garrison for the city, including the firemen, numbered between 40,000 and 50,000. In addition there were 33,000 public functionaries, to whose number should be added another 15,000 to 20,000 office workers who sustained and supported them.[48] Paris became on a gigantic scale what it had not been since the first Bourbon kings: a court town.

Haussmann's urban patterns sometimes fixed inherited trends—like the movement from east to west—and sometimes froze or arrested urban development—such as his neglect of the Left Bank. His work was well done and durable. About 60 percent of the buildings and streets of Paris in 1970 had been built in Haussmann's time.[49] Paris has enjoyed until quite recently a century of relative urban stability. After Haussmann's wrenching rebuilding, its streets, housing stock, public life, and population—the fundamental mold for Parisian life—remained long unaltered. "Even we, the Parisians," wrote Marcel Cornu in 1972, "in our penchants and our aesthetic inclinations, remain under the spell of haussmannism. It has conditioned us. We are saturated with it. The remodeled Paris of the Second Empire has been our primary school of urbanism. . . . the urban environment is, above all, a product of haussmannism."[50] The prefect's taste was deplored by many of his contemporaries, including most of the writers and artists, as philistine. The testimony of several has already been cited. Prosper Mérimée mocked him. "You know," he wrote a friend, "that his ignorance in questions of art is complete. For him all that is involved is to know if the painting will *ornament*; this is his expression."[51] Viollet-le-Duc was similarly critical, and in print. J.-E. Horn, an economist and journalist, characterized the buildings approved by Haussmann as "half palace, half barracks,"[52] while Zola called the architectural spawn of the Second Empire "this opulent bastard of all styles."[53] Haussmann's reputation for bad taste, formed as part of the Third Republic's revulsion for Napoléon III and his times, has endured despite dissenting voices. "To the eyes of the stroller in Paris," wrote Charles Lortsch in 1913, "buildings can be classed into two categories: old buildings, characterized by a great uniformity of type, a perfect sobriety of lines and of decoration, by the measured proportions of their attics, which shelter only one floor; and new buildings, startling in their whiteness, which clash with the first."[54] Tastes change and increasingly Second Empire architecture is valued as exemplary simplicity and unity. Where many once saw only monotony or a senseless jumble of styles, eclecticism run amok—and these diametrical criticisms indicate how complex and controversial is Haussmann's Paris—a growing number now see endless if subtle variation, within a wonderful, dense harmony.[55]

The durability and beauty of Haussmann's Paris is paradoxical. Singly there is not much to admire in the extensive building projects of the Second Empire. With the exception of a few buildings over which he had no control—Garnier's Opéra, Hittorff's gare du Nord among them—Haussmann did not endow the city with great architecture. It may be that cities are not best made by great architects. The very uniformity of aesthetics and scale he imposed upon Paris gave the city harmony and proportion, qualities all too lacking in most urban landscapes. Haussmann's somewhat bureaucratic harmony is now being sacrificed to skyscrapers and high-rise apartments.

The confusing patterns of this map, like one spider web set upon another, convey in their very density the nature of Haussmann's work. The underlying pattern of streets—and by no means are all the Paris streets de-

HAUSSMANN'S BOULEVARDS

RÉPUBLIQUE

BOULEVARDS

SÉBASTOPOL

DS

BASTILLE

ERMAIN

PANTHÉON

NATION

ITALIE

BOULEVARDS

Seine River

N

picted—Haussmann inherited. He implanted within this historical network the new system of boulevards here indicated by thick lines.

Victor Hugo, no friend of the prefect, modern architecture, or the empire, put his finger on the genius of Haussmann's Paris: "Beneath the visible Paris the old Paris can be seen, like the old text between the lines of the new."[56] Paris is a great palimpsest. Too much is made of Haussmann as modernizer, and we loose sight of how much of Old Paris he preserved. Neither the eighteenth nor the nineteenth centuries thought, as our century does, of razing entire sections of the city to build it anew. Even the prefect's depredations on the Ile de la Cité or the montagne Ste. Geneviève were more restrained than modern urban renewal, a term that has become in our day a euphemism for razing whole neighborhoods. It was not current in Haussmann's age. Transformation or embellishment were his preferred terms; and what he meant was implanting the new amid the old. Les Halles is the touchstone.

There had been markets in the center of Paris since the time of Philippe-Auguste. The original site, within walking distance of the Hôtel de Ville, the Louvre, and the Ile de la Cité, was already *Le Ventre de Paris*, the belly of Paris—the title of Zola's novel about les Halles—when Napoléon decided to enlarge the ancient *halles* and keep the markets in the city center. The decrees of February 24 and May 19, 1811, designated the area between the church of St. Eustache and the rues St. Denis and de la Ferronnerie as les Halles (E 3). In 1847 Rambuteau made a capital decision: to maintain les Halles and enlarge the markets even further. Haussmann continued Rambuteau's work: Louis Napoléon was delighted with the reaffirmation of his uncle's urban vision.

The decision was a stunning reversal of the strategy of the boulevards and the incorporation of the *banlieue*. The outward explosion of the city was balanced by les Halles. The new streets built by Haussmann to serve the markets—the stretch of the rue de Rivoli from the Louvre to the Hôtel de Ville, and the rues Berger, des Halles, du Pont Neuf, Pierre Lescot, and Turbigo—unlike the majority of his *percées*, were designed only to bring traffic and people into the city's old core and move them around it. The reintegration of the heart of Paris and the strengthening of its interior structure, "this reversal of the direction of energy," a modern city planner has noted, "is one of the most dramatic in any city."[57] "The Belly of

Paris" is a literal metaphor: the heart has seemed the more appropriate organ to many.[58]

Les Halles is the sharpest and most creative juxtaposition of old and new Paris, popular and bourgeois Paris, and it is just west of Strasbourg-Sébastopol, the old city colonizing the new. Haussmann's evident desire was to transform Paris into a bourgeois city, not least by ridding the capital of a part of its industrial base and proletariat. He harried heavy industry, dirty industry, and even some light industry. His huge and purposeful cuts into the urban body and the commercialization of the boulevards forced the working poor and the destitute out of Old Paris. Simultaneously, les Halles implanted an enclave of the old popular culture in the very center of the new city.

The same paradox of old and new is evident in Baltard's glass and iron pavilions at les Halles. Louis Napoléon rejected the first heavy mass of stone erected to shelter the Paris food supply, which wags of the day dubbed the *"fort de la halle"* (fortress of the market), punning on *"les forts des halles"* (the brawny carriers of sides of beef). It was pulled down to make way for Baltard's umbrellalike functional sheds. The old market would be sheltered under the most "modern" and technologically advanced structures in Paris. Claude Lantier, the young painter-hero of Zola's *Le Ventre de Paris*, passed his life in les Halles and thought the pavilions a manifesto of modern art. "Since the beginning of the century," he says, "only a single original monument has been built, a monument that is not a copy, a monument that has sprung naturally from the soil of the epoque: and that is the central pavilion of Les Halles."[59]

The markets not only reintroduced into the city's core the very congestion and popular culture so ruthlessly obliterated nearby, they created a nightmare for urban circulation to rival the Louvre-Tuileries. Between three and ten in the morning the pulsating market blocked traffic from the central post office (on the rue du Louvre) to the Hôtel de Ville. With its thousands of employees and customers les Halles was a city unto itself. The central markets might have been moved out of the center of the city, as were the meat market and slaughterhouses—to La Villette, in the extreme northeast quadrant of Paris (F-G 2)—or the wine market—originally to a bleak stretch along the eastern Left Bank (F 4), later to an equally bleak spot, at Bercy, on the Right Bank (G 5). The decision to retain les Halles at the site of its creation caused the major bottleneck of Paris. The most passionate arguments for the destruction of les Halles in the twentieth century concerned circulation; but razing the central markets has not wholly alleviated the problem. The delivery trucks no longer clog the center of the city for much of the morning, but because the site of the banished markets remains public space—given over to an underground shopping center and the Pompidou Museum—it is still difficult to get across central Paris. And something infinitely precious has been lost to the city.

We reproach Haussmann for what he destroyed. Contemporaries lamented his timidity. Behind his boulevards the deteriorating old city survived. This contrast provided the sharp edge of moral indignation in the characterizations of Zola and Flaubert. Illusion, trompe l'oeil, so popular as an art form in the Second Empire, was writ large in Paris. It elicited ferocious denunciations. "Haussmann's Paris," wrote Zola, "is an enormous hypocrisy, the falsehood of a colossal Jesuitism."

> The large, unencumbered boulevards lie, they are a connivance: they go from December 2 to Sedan.[60] The squares, the great gardens, with their flowers, have the smile of the hypocrite. They are put there to hide the piles of fermenting filth and to ward off the pestilential fumes of the city.[61]

"Everything was false," Flaubert wrote Maxime Du Camp about the empire, "false army, false politics, false credit, and even [a perfect Flaubertian touch] false courtesans." This brilliantly indignant moral condemnation of the empire and imperial Paris misses Haussmann's achievement: the reinvention of Paris, the successful marriage of the old and the new, the perpetuation of ancient urban patterns despite new foundations. Les Halles anachronistically revivified the medieval markets; the Latin Quarter was left relatively untouched.

To the loud consternation of Left Bank landowners Haussmann preserved the fundamental distinctions between the two sides of the Seine. He cut a good many boulevards, but not enough to transform the Left Bank or any significant part of it into a commercial zone. Property values lagged well behind those across the river. The *grand magasin* Au Bon Marché, the model for Zola's *Au Bonheur des dames*, did not commercially transform more than a block or two of the surrounding neighborhood, any more than the Odéon theater—erected in the eighteenth century—had created a theater district. What the new boulevards of the Left Bank did was facilitate passage to the Right Bank, allowing traffic to move through the Latin Quarter without encouraging it to stop. Commerce remained retarded, rents relatively low, and residential property the main source of income. Across the river fortunes were made from skyrocketing rents on commercial property. Rent increases on the Left Bank were modest, although elevated enough to drive out the traditional artisan population. Local landlords complained bitterly about how little their incomes were enhanced by new, bourgeois residents.[62] Even when the boulevard Raspail became the boulevard par excellence of the early twentieth century—as the boulevard des Italiens had been the quintessential street of the late nineteenth— it did not rival in commercial success several of the Right Bank thoroughfares. Nor did the elegant Hotel Lutétia, with its undulating art nouveau facade and distinguished restaurant, supplant the Right Bank travelers' palaces. Even today the Lutétia seems an isolated phenomenon, a *grand luxe* hotel somehow on the wrong side of the river.

The problem was the boulevard St. Germain, Haussmann's only major east-west street. All the new urban arteries—with the exception of the boulevard St. Michel, which formed the Left Bank component of the *grande croisée*—dead-end at the boulevard St. Germain (D-F 4). Pedestrian and passenger alike must either follow the boulevard around to where it meets the Seine—at the Pont de la Concorde, which joins the famous *place* (on the west), or the pont Sully, which leads to the Place de la Bastille (on the east)—or pick their way to the river through the narrow, labyrinthine streets of the Latin Quarter. Everything to the south of the boulevard St. Germain turns its back on the rest of Paris. This orientation has preserved the charm of the Left Bank. Although incessantly threatened by urban planners who held it as an article of faith that Paris could not function without expanded north-south circulation cut through the Latin Quarter, all plans have been successfully resisted. Despite growing pressure to accommodate the automobile, the Latin Quarter seems, momentarily, safe. The old districts, having successfully resisted haussmannization, both of the master and his disciples, now appear all the more precious.[63]

The enhanced value of the Latin Quarter, of relatively unhaussmannized Paris, came precisely when his Paris was everywhere under attack. The abandonment of the boulevards, turning away from his monumental facades to what lies behind was concomitant with an attack on the city Haussmann bequeathed. Entire neighborhoods have come under the wrecker's hammer and the developer's schemes—large, ugly stretches of the thirteenth and fifteenth arrondissements, for example—leaving new urban patterns of life markedly different from those facilitated, created, or encouraged by the prefect. Wholly new forms of urban dwelling—the high-rise apartment—now dwarf the Second Empire apartment houses built along the boulevards, while the modern sameness has given us an appreciation of the subtle and incessant variations imposed by empire and Third Republic architects. It is the end of the cycle of haussmannization.

Those who lived through the Second Empire spoke with wonder of the changes wrought. The historian Jules Michelet (born in 1798) wrote that he had been born in "the French Paris of 500,000 souls"—was he remembering the city before it became a magnet for tourists?—and would die (in 1874) "in this strange European Paris of 2,500,000 souls." The city of his youth was a place "of workers in wood." The city of his old age was "composed of masons and iron workers."[64] His long life had encompassed an enormous cultural and material change, writ in the city itself. Victor Hugo seriously considered modifying the itineraries, above and below ground, of the characters in *Les Misérables* to conform to Haussmann's changes. He decided against it:

> It has already been many years that the author of this book—forced to speak of it with regret—has been away from Paris [exiled by Louis Napoléon]. Since he has left Paris it has been transformed. . . . I

hope I will be permitted to speak of the past as the present. That said, I pray the reader take note, and I shall continue.[65]

Neither of these elegiac descriptions rejects the new city. For all his philistinism, narrow views, and administrative rigidity, Haussmann expressed a number of the ideals of his age in the most durable and wonderful form: the city of Paris. Grandeur, rational order, purposeful and incesssant movement, progress, cleanliness, an urban life lived in public are the qualities he forcefully imposed on Paris. "A great city," he insisted, "above all a capital, has the responsibility to rise to the level that it enjoys in the country; and when that country is France, when centralization, which is the principle of its strength, has made of its capital both the head and heart of the social body, the capital would fail in its glorious mission if, despite everything, it remained systematically trapped in an antiquated street system."[66] Paris, he declared "is the capital of the Empire, the collective property of the entire country, the city of all the French." It is "the universal foyer of Letters, Science, and the Arts."[67] These are the ideals he fixed into stone. No mean achievement for "a parvenu Parisian . . . out to make a name for himself, even a controversial name, in the beloved city of his birth."

·EPILOGUE·

"One of the Most Important Men of Our Time"

"WHO?"

"Haussmann. Baron Haussmann. The prefect of the Seine during the Second Empire. The man responsible for the *grands travaux*."

"Ah, Haussmann. When did he die?"

"January 1891."

He reached across his desk for a loose-leaf binder, thumbed through some pages, ran his finger down a column of names: "Haussmann. His tomb is in the avenue Principale, fourth section."

I consulted the map of Père Lachaise on the wall before leaving the cemetery office.

There's a stone gatekeeper's house at the entrance on the boulevard de Ménilmontant, where a uniformed city employee will sell you, for a few francs, a small, crude outline map of Père Lachaise cemetery, with several of the famous, or most-visited, graves indicated. Haussmann's is not. Nor could the gatekeeper himself tell me where Haussmann is buried.

Not that he rests in an obscure corner. His grave and the familiar gray stone monument favored in the late nineteenth century—a rectangular, roofed structure maybe ten feet square and fifteen feet high, with an open doorway and unglazed windows—is in one of the prominent *allées* of the cemetery, near the main entrance. Within twenty feet is the tomb of his celebrated contemporary and schoolmate, the poet Alfred de Musset, buried under a willow tree, as he requested. Nearby are other luminaries of the July Monarchy and Second Empire: Generals Lecomte and Clément Thomas, the philosopher Victor Cousin, the composer Auber, the political figures Ledru-Rollin and Achille Fould.

The response of the functionary in the cemetery office whom I asked about the location of Haussmann's grave was typical of virtually all the French citizens, and especially Parisians, I have chatted with over the years. All knew who Haussmann was, knew little about him—was he architect? engineer? city planner?—yet had strong opinions. He had either modernized or ruined Paris, but his abiding goal had been to move cavalry and create clear fields of fire against urban insurrectionaries.

There are no amusing anecdotes, no memorable *mots* to fix the historical personage in the mind or the imagination. Standing at his grave, mounting the few stone steps to enter the funereal monument to read the plaque indicating that the city of Paris has assumed the expense of maintaining Haussmann's final resting place—his wife and daughters are buried here as well—I too could summon no special image or word. He seemed more a type than an individual. I knew what was to be known about Haussmann from the historical record. I had tracked him to every provincial post, gazed at every still-standing subprefecture and prefecture where he had served, been in his house at Cestas, turned over his papers, both public and private, but no moments from his long life came to mind.

He himself had taken pains to present the administrator to posterity, while deliberately obscuring the man. In his *Mémoires* and his works we have the public personage rather than the private person. He wanted to be remembered for his labors; and history has honored his wish, ironically enough, by assuring the obscurity of the individual through the disappearance of his private papers and the partial destruction of the public record, which remains abundant. Yet much that he most valued is forgotten. His reform of the Paris administration, for example, is known only to specialists, while the means he thought amply vindicated by the ends he achieved besmirch his reputation today. The buildings and streets lost to hauss-mannization are only abstractly regretted by the few who today even know what once stood where the boulevard St. Germain or the avenue de l'Opéra is now. But much of the human misery he caused by uprooting entire neighborhoods continues to rankle, and many still deplore the administrative heartlessness of haussman-nization. He made few apologies for his cleansing of Paris, acting with the righteousness of the reformer. In our century the prefect of the Seine is of a species familiar but unloved. He was a bureaucrat.

He had laid violent hands on the city. He drew lines on the first accurate map of Paris, which he had ordered made, obliterating buildings, neighborhoods, streets, and gardens, not to mention his-torical sites like the massacre in the rue Transnonain, the death of Gérard de Nerval, the trial of Louis XVI, with the stroke of a pen. He replaced what he had destroyed with boulevards and monumen-tal, sometimes hideous architecture. To centralize his administra-tion of the city he destroyed *quartiers*, imposed ordered movement on the streets, and created a new center of urban gravity. It was, and remains, the most extensive urban renewal project ever attempted. Yet for all his vigor and violence, his shortcomings of sensibility and taste, his extravagant faith in the capacity of bureaucracy, and his exuberant devotion to capitalism and progress, Haussmann had a deep affection for Paris. He left much of the city intact, not because he loved Old Paris for itself or had a taste for the picturesque, but because he envisioned the city as an organic whole—the body was his favorite metaphor for Paris—having new and old parts, all func-tioning together. His aesthetic preferences, rigid and philistine, were consistent and harmonious, expressed in the serried ranks of similar new buildings he erected, his streets and their complemen-tary architecture spoke the familiar language of French classicism. He continued two centuries of urban and architectural preference. New Paris *looked* familiar.

Historical reputations are often fixed early and prove immune to revision. Haussmann has remained what most of his contemporaries thought him. It is no longer fashionable to call him the Alsatian At-tila, but he will never be a popular let alone an attractive figure. His is not so much a false as an unavoidable reputation. Remaking a city presupposes massive destruction. It is probably best to have someone swing the pick without sentimentality. But if the city be Paris, the destruction can at best be viewed with melancholy. On balance history has not done badly by Haussmann. Anyone who loves Paris will regret his methods and the degree to which he imposed his personality and obsessions on the city. But lovers are generous and indiscriminate: they love Paris, haussmanized warts and all.

What is remembered of Haussmann is his work and the aloofness, indifference, and callousness with which it was accomplished. That he is remembered, albeit imprecisely, as the man who made the boulevards is therefore fitting. Paris and the Parisians have assured the endurance of his name as well as all the ambivalence that attaches to it. Haussmann's work has been metabolized by the city and its inhabitants and softened and humanized in the process. Haussmann's Paris is an abstraction. The living city belongs to the Parisians who then as now have bent the administrator's designs to their own will and needs. He imposed a network of streets and boulevards on the city, created new neighborhoods and redefined old ones, but the great city remains a city of neighborhoods. Parisians still ask which *quartier* one inhabits, and fix it in their mind by some monument or landmark. A parochial sensibility persists.

His place in Père Lachaise perfectly represents Haussmann's reputation. He is prominently placed for eternity, amid the graves of distinguished contemporaries, many now as forgotten as he. Visited, without deep emotion, by very few, he is best remembered by what he did. Take a moment to look down on Paris from the cemetery. It is the best memorial.

·NOTES·

All the references to the *Mémoires du Baron Haussmann* are only to the volume (roman numerals) and page (arabic numerals). All the references to unpublished sources begin with the location (e.g., A.N. [Archives Nationals]). The contents of the several series of cited documents, as well as of individual cartons in some cases, are given in Works Cited, Unpublished Sources. All other references are by author's name. Multiple books or articles by the same author are distinguished by the author's name and a short title. Most collective works and all exhibition catalogs are cited by title only.

Prologue

1. Louise-Octavie died in Paris on December 24, 1890, her husband on January 11, 1891. She was in her eighty-third year, he in his eighty-second. They had been married on October 17, 1838. Unless otherwise noted, all the details given here come from AN, *Inventaire*.
2. M. Daniel Dollfus (the husband of their deceased daughter, Henriette-Marie), Mme Suzanne Salomé Luling, and Mme Louise Ehérise Hecht, the children of this marriage. Valentine received half the estate, the others each received a sixth.
3. Sherard, p. 104. The portrait of the empress does not appear in the Inventory, and there seems some disagreement between the *notaire* and Sherard about which Louis defines the chairs.

4. I have searched every departmental and municipal archive where Haussmann lived or served, as well as the national depositories (the Archives Nationales, the Archives de la Seine, the Bibliothèque Nationale, the Bibliothèque Historique de la Ville de Paris) and have found almost none of his personal correspondence. Nor, it appears, have his personal papers survived in the family. I have contacted as many of his living descendants as I could locate, all of them quite distantly related, for his last direct descendant, his grandson, died in a boating accident in 1909, also to no avail. M. Roland Hecht, who kindly made inquiries of his family in response to my request, assures me there remain no personal papers. Whatever might have existed was destroyed by the Germans, who pillaged the family property, I assume during World War I. One of Haussmann's biographers, André Morizet, says (p. 9): "As for Haussmann's private papers, his descendants destroyed them. One of his descendants confided to me that they contained too many letters from women friends! Another descendant retained some, but they were destroyed in the First World War. The biographer of Haussmann, alas, will discover only ashes in his investigations." Morizet names no names, gives no dates that might support his assertions. Haussmann himself told Sherard (pp. 107–8) he had not saved any of the correspondence he received: "Only think, if I had collected all the papers that came my way, notes from the Emperor, notes from the Empress, from Bismarck, from the King of Prussia, letters from everybody of note and of importance of the century,—I should have had the material for a score of volumes! But I never attached any importance to these documents. I was far too busy to collect them and too careless to preserve them." Haussmann's memory, when he was in his eighties, may not have been the keenest, but the remarkable scarcity of personal documents lends credence to his words.

5. See AN 332 AP 5 for the sums Haussmann paid Baltard for the work he did at Cestas.

6. All the details of Haussmann's indebtedness and the value of Cestas at his death are in the *Résumé* at Cestas and AN 3Q 4964, "Registre de recette. Déclarations des mutations par décès" (1ère partie, no. 6 [1890]).

7. I, xiii.

8. II, 529.

9. I, xv. Sherard, p. 113, repeats this verbatim (although my rendering of the original French differs somewhat from his), attributing it to a meeting with Haussmann: "Another day, *mon ami*? Shall we ever meet again? I may be carried off at any moment by one of those *crises* which you have just witnessed [Haussmann had just recovered from a severe coughing spell]. May it be so. I look forward with confidence to death, and my only hope is that death may find me standing (*debout*) as it found all the strong men of my generation. I shall leave this life," said Baron Haussmann, "if not with an erect head as formerly, at least with a firm heart; and as to the things of the world beyond the grave, full of hope in the merciful justice of the Most High God." Did Hauss-

mann say precisely this? More than likely he said something like it and Sherard supplemented his memory of the conversation with what Haussmann had written in the *Avertissement* to his *Mémoires*. He used this same phrase in a speech to the Corps Législatif (April 13, 1869): "But whenever we leave the Hôtel de Ville, we will leave as we entered, with our head held high and with a strong heart, certain of having conducted ourselves as decent human beings, as men of honor, as dedicated servants, with courage and resolution, but also with loyalty, perseverance, and a devotion beyond reproach."

10. I, viii–ix. According to a note he inserted after the *avant-propos* of 1890 (II, xiv–xv), he wrote the chapters on his career, which volume II comprises, before he thought (or was persuaded) to provide an account of his years before the Hôtel de Ville. The first chapters of volume II "date from July 1886"; some others "were written only a year later." Several chapters are "distinct," having no precise connection with others. He offers these explanations as an apology for "the lack of a chronological method in my accounts." There are a number of overlappings and repetitions.

11. I, v.
12. I, v.
13. I, 1. This is the first sentence of the *Mémoires*.
14. I, ix.
15. I, vi–vii.
16. II, 91–92.
17. I, vii.
18. I, vi.
19. I, xv.
20. I, 34–35.
21. Chapter 20, "Récapitulation," (pp. 507–34 in volume II), is the locus classicus of the prose of haussmannization. Each subheading—"Streets, Promenades, and Plantings," "Water and Sewers," "Religious, Municipal, and Educational Buildings"—contains lists of his achievements: kilometers of streets built, thousands of trees planted, meters of sewer pipe laid, cubic meters of water delivered, dozens of buildings built.
22. I, v–vi.
23. II, ii.
24. *Histoire de la France urbaine*, IV, 77, 93.
25. The best books on what has happened to Paris since Haussmann are Evenson, Chevalier, *Assassination*, Sutcliffe, *Paris*, Olsen, Loyer, and Chaslin.

I. Paris Before Haussmann

1. Rousseau, pp. 146–47.
2. Karamzine, p. 76.

3. Réstif de la Bretonne, p. 185.

4. The far less distinguished critic, François-Joseph Guillotte, took a similar view: "The only rational [*régulières*] cities we have are those that have been burned down." Quoted in Chagniot, p.153.

5. The quotations are, respectively, from "des embellissements de Paris," in Voltaire, XXIII, 297, 298, 302. Published after the peace of 1748 in a volume entitled *Recueil de pièces en vers et en prose par l'auteur de la tragédie de Sémiramis* (1750). Haussmann quotes Voltaire's proposal in his May 20, 1868, *Rapport* to the emperor, which he in turn quotes in his *Mémoires*, II, 531. Voltaire does not otherwise appear in the *Mémoires*.

6. "des embellissements de Paris," in Voltaire, XXIII, 304.

7. Quoted in Chagniot, p. 164, from Montesquieu, II, 1140.

8. Boussard makes the argument for 1110–70 as the time of "the birth of a capital city." I follow him on the transformation of medieval Paris and his account of the reign and urban ideas of Philippe Auguste.

9. Little is known about the bishop's palace. Oddly it had not attracted any attention before it was burned down in the rioting of 1831 and replaced, in 1837, by a square, the first in Paris. Apparently during the centuries when Gothic architecture was scorned, the palace was ignored or despised. A lovely park alongside and behind the cathedral now occupies the space once filled by the palace.

10. The bishop of Paris, it should be noted, did not become an archbishop with his own metropolitan cathedral until the seventeenth century. Before then the archbishopric of Sens was foremost in the hierarchy and Paris remained suffragan to this venerable ecclesiastical city of the Gauls. Maurice de Sully, the bishop who built Notre Dame, traveled to Sens in 1160 for his consecration. But the wealth of Notre Dame of Paris was enormous. She had properties from Champagne to Brittany and south beyond the Loire, forming a great block of land in the center of France, as well as isolated holdings as far away as Provence. The chapter also had a large network of toll bridges and roads and collected a variety of taxes outside Paris. Notre Dame was the single largest real estate owner in the city, receiving a full third of the municipal revenue. The chapter owned an estimated half of the Ile de la Cité and the whole of the Ile St. Louis, as well as hundreds of dwellings and shops, the Grand Pont and part of the Petit Pont, fields and vineyards on the Left Bank, and on the Right a tract of land known as the Bourg-l'Evêque, which extended from the Louvre to what is now the Etoile.

11. The most eloquent statement of this view is Chevalier, *Assassination*.

12. This is the estimate of Pierre Lavedan, in Réau, p. 43, who repeats the estimates made by Verniquet, who made the first geometric map of Old Paris on the eve of the revolution.

13. The suggestion is Evenson's. Everything on one side of the *périphérique* is

Paris, everything on the other is various townships and municipalities. There is more than metaphor here.

14. See the discussion of the relationship among population, urbanism, food, and territory in *Histoire de la France urbaine*, vol. 3, pp. 57ff, and Tilly for a European-wide analysis, Kaplan for Paris itself.

15. Tilly, p. 398.

16. Tilly, p. 447.

17. See the maps in Kaplan, pp. 90–91 for the grain crowns, p. 109 for the location of the markets.

18. For a detailed description of Henri's entry into Paris see Pillorget, pp. 11–15, whom I closely follow for my account of Henri's urbanization of Paris. His description of Henri's determination to make Paris a royal city by locating his government there is on pp. 88–95, an account of Henri's major projects is on pp. 273–337. See Ballon on the same subject, for the perspective of an architectural historian.

19. Sutcliffe, *Paris*, p. 23.

20. A partial list of Henri IV's projects includes the Pont-Neuf, the Place Royale, the Place Dauphine, the Arsenal, the Cours-la-Reine, the Luxembourg palace (and gardens), the Tuileries, significant additions to the Louvre, as well as churches and monasteries, not to mention important private mansions. There is a good account of Henri's transformation of Paris in Pillorget, pp. 273–337.

21. Girouard, p. 174.

22. This is the suggestion of Barbiche, pp. 119–20.

23. Sutcliffe, *Paris*, p. 66

24. The houses rented by Thomas Jefferson as ambassador to France (1784–89) form a useful itinerary of changing Paris preference. He lived always in the most fashionable neighborhoods: on the Right Bank, first in eastern Paris, then northeastern Paris, and his last residence was along the Champs-Elysées, just emerging as a preferred neighborhood.

25. See Pronteau, pp. 312–13 for the decree.

26. For a list of members, see Pronteau, pp. 477–78. My account and the quotations are from this work.

27. A word about all the maps and plans of Paris I shall be speaking of. None of them has survived in its original. Each map in question has its own curious story, and I shall have something to say eventually about the famous map drawn up by Louis Napoléon that was, supposedly, the map used by Haussmann to transform Paris. As to the Plan des Artistes, Verniquet's biographer (Pronteau, pp. 481–82) says the original has disappeared. That indefatigable researcher has been unable to find it in the archives and cannot discover its destiny. Its authors said the map was deposited, in 1797 when the Commission was dissolved, with the bureau of plans maintained by the Ministry of the Interior, whence it was transferred to the Prefecture of the Seine (in the

Hôtel de Ville), where, in theory, it lay along with Verniquet's original map of Paris, which served as the base for the Commission's proposals. The speculation is that it and Verniquet's original burned in the fire at the Hôtel de Ville in 1871 during the Commune. The same hypothesis will be offered for all the missing papers concerning Paris in the nineteenth century. Anyhow, the deliberations of the Commission des Artistes survived—Pronteau does not say where they may be found—and on the centenary of the French Revolution the geometer Bernard reconstructed this famous Plan des Artistes from these discussions and published it in a commemorative atlas.

28. III, 81.

29. This discussion is based on Tulard, pp. 205, 204, 191, 205, respectively.

30. All trace of the elephant has vanished, but it is described by Victor Hugo in *Les Misérables*, IV, vi, chap. 2, p. 1128. He speaks of the elephant as "rude, squat, heavy, unrefined, austere, almost deformed, but nevertheless majestic and having a kind of magnificent and savage gravity." It finally disappeared so that "a gigantic ornamented column" could replace "the somber fortress with its nine towers, in the same way the bourgeoisie replaced feudalism." Quoted in Combes, p. 47.

31. Again Victor Hugo, this time in *Choses vues*, is a trenchant witness. He is quoted by Chevalier, p. 161: "They want to demolish St.Germain-l'Auxerrois in order to align a *place* or a street. Some day they will destroy Notre Dame in order to enlarge the *parvis*. Some day they will level Paris to enlarge the Sablons plain."

II. Haussmann Before Paris

1. The quotation is from Sherard, 109. Touttain, p. 49, n. 2, says Haussmann's dating of his father's birth in 1760 is incorrect (Valynseele, p. 25 follows Haussmann). "I have consulted the death certificate of Nicolas Haussmann in the Archives de la Seine," says Touttain, "[and] he was most certainly born *in 1759*." I have been unable to verify Touttain.

2. The quotations are from I, 6 and 7. The passage on Custine comes from *Rapport fait . . . par Haussmann, l'un de ses commissaires aux armées du Rhin*, p. 3.

3. *Rapport sur la situation de la caisse de l'extraordinaire. . . .*Haussmann's argument is that another 1,600 millions should be printed to add to the existing 1,300 millions. In other words, he advocated further inflation.

4. I, 7 and I, 10.

5. I, 15 and I, 16.

6. See his *Rapport . . . pour l'organisation du district établi à Landau.*

7. See *Rapport . . . pour l'organisation du district établi à Landau*, pp. 1–2, 8, 11–16, 18.

8. See *Dentzel. . .à ses collègues* and *Mémoire . . . au rapport fait par Lacoste et Baudot*. Both were written from prison.

9. Not only did he have to defend himself, but his son became involved in some tricky financial manipulations and his father came to his defense, arguing his son was acting in his father's name and had done nothing illegal. Besides, the charges had not been proved because everything turned on an unsigned, undated letter sent to the son. See *Observations. . .à Messieurs les Membres de la cour*, p. 4.

10. Haussmann's sister married an outspoken Orleanist. His brother-in-law, Nicolas-Louis Artaud, was a professor at the *collège* Louis-le-Grand, one of the most important schools in the country. During the Restoration he wrote for the *Courrier Français*, a newspaper of the liberal opposition. When the reactionary Villèle ministry expelled Guizot, Villemain, and Victor Cousin from their chairs at the Sorbonne, Artaud also lost his position. In the July Monarchy Guizot appointed Artaud *Inspecteur de l'Académie de Paris* and eventually *Inspecteur Général des Etudes*. Louis Napoléon furthered his career, naming him vice-rector of the Academy of Paris, while Haussmann put him on his Municipal Council. He died in 1861. Haussmann's Orleanist connections were of long standing and ran deep. See his appraisal of his brother-in-law, I, 127–28.

11. Of these the most celebrated at the time were a *Lettre à M. Odilon Barrot*, discussed in the text; *Réorganisation ou désorganisation dont est menacée l'Intendance militaire* (1833); *Des subsistances de la France, du blutage et du rendement des farines et de la composition du pain de munition* (1848). He also published an *Annuaire des institutions de crédit financier, commercial et industriel de la France et des principales places de l'Europe* (1853), and collaborated on the *Moniteur de l'armée* and the *Dictionnaire d'administration*.

12. *Lettre à M. Odilon-Barrot*, pp. 23, 8.

13. *Lettre*, pp. 49–50. What was necessary was the right combination of circumstances (pp. 59–60): "a united ministry, a calmer political situation, and a parliamentary majority to give the government the authority and the confidence it needs to control the situation."

14. I, 13. Haussmann's mixture of past and present—Paris as it was when he recounts an anecdote, and Paris as it became when he was prefect of the Seine—is a habit that runs throughout the *Mémoires*. He cannot recollect or describe a place without noting his transformations.

15. Zola, in *La Débacle*, the last of the twenty novels in the *Rougon-Macquart* series, describes the childhood of one of his characters (V, 447), "listening from his cradle, [to] the stories of his grandfather, one of the soldiers in Napoléon's Grande Armée." In *Le Rouge et le Noir* Stendhal has Julien Sorel hearing stories of the disastrous Russian campaign from an old army surgeon.

16. I, 17–18.

17. I, 20.
18. I, 14–15.
19. I, 23, 25, 26–27.
20. The school name followed governments, each of which put its imprint on the institution: Lycée Napoléon under the two empires, Lycée Corneille in 1848 and 1870, and Lycée Henri IV again in 1873; and so it has remained.
21. This institution had been founded by Napoléon and would ultimately, after the Second Empire, be the Lycée Fontanes.
22. I, 26–29.
23. I, 31.
24. I, 32.
25. I, 33.
26. I, 33.
27. I, 34.
28. I, 40–42.
29. Magraw, p. 42.
30. Magraw, p. 42.

III. Climbing the Greasy Pole

1. I, 37.
2. I, 40–42.
3. III, 40. Note again the theme of emerging from the labyrinth of medieval Paris into order, this time the Hôtel de Ville, foreshadowing Haussmann's ordering of all Paris.
4. I, 43–45. Colonel Bro's words are quoted from des Cars, p. 43.
5. AN, F[1b] 162[3], pièces 5 and 6.
6. The document, signed by Haussmann and the prefect, is in AN, F[1b] 162[3], pièce 17.
7. I, 55, 61. He gives few details for so tantalizing an episode, which he describes as arising from an inadvertent faux pas at the theater. Paying court to a lady in her box, he turned his back on the parterre seats, was sharply told to face them, entered into some bantering insults with the unnamed young man who had commanded him to turn around, which resulted in the challenge.
8. I, 67–69.
9. I, 76, 78.
10. The relevant documents are in AN, F[1b] 162[3], pièces 20, 21, 24, 38, 42.
11. I, 87, 91.
12. I, 119.
13. I, 127, 125.
14. George Sand, 5ème partie, chapitre xi. I, 134. She had family connections in

the area and was married to the natural son of a colonel of the empire—from whom she was legally separated—who had been raised by the Baroness Dudevant, where Haussmann often dined. Haussmann presumably read George Sand's memoirs, published in 1854–55, before writing his own. He does not date the episode. Could he and George Sand have discussed Alfred de Musset, Haussmann's old school chum? Her ill-fated trip to Italy with the poet had taken place in 1833–34. The allusions to political differences would have been immediately apparent to George Sand's contemporaries: she had strong socialist leanings.

15. I, 134.

16. See Charles, "Un Exemple de carrière," pp. 229–40, esp. pp. 231–33, where he compares the careers of Haussmann and Baron Neveux, whom he would later succeed at Bordeaux. The latter began higher up on the ladder and came from a more distinguished family. Although he eventually obtained a prefectship a few months before Haussmann, his rise to that post was much slower than that of the protégé of the duc d'Orléans.

17. AN, F[1B] 162[3], pièce 72 (January 14, 1836).

18. He would later reject Libourne as too far from Bordeaux "via a monstrous route across the Entre-deux-Mers." But at the time (I, 207–8) he had no idea he would be stuck in the subprefecture of Blaye for more than six years.

19. AN, F[1B] 162[3], pièce 87 (April 13, 1840), and pièce 88 (April 14, 1840). Both letters were written from Paris.

20. The relevant documents are AN, F[1b] 162[3], pièces 50, 51, 57, 59, 60, 61, 62, 64, 65, 66, 68, 69, 70, 79, 80, 81, 86, 87, 90, 95, 96.

21. AN, F[1B], 162[3], pièce 84 ("A Messieurs les Maires de l'Arrondissement").

22. I, 59.

23. I, 214. The French *avancement*, which I translate literally, is unambiguous.

24. AD (l'Ariège), Série 1 M11[1].

25. AN, F[1B]162[3], pièce 93 (June 11, 1840).

26. AD (l'Ariège), Série 3Z 32*, numbers 459, 462, 496, 503, 518, 555.

27. AD (l'Ariège), Série 3Z 32*, numbers 606, 643, 699, 730, 1631.

28. AD (l'Ariège), Série 3Z 32* number 2461.

29. I, 170.

30. *Il était grand, bien fait, mince, et très élégant;*
    Il avait le teint blanc et rose d'un enfant.
    Les cheveux blonds-cendrés et la barbe soyeuse,
    Le regard doux, voilé, la tourneur amoureuse.
    Et par surcroît, le prestige du rang,
    Que relevait la noblesse du sang!
    Comment, dès lors, ne pas être charmée,
    Comment ne pas désirer d'être aimée
    Par un Monsieur qu'on trouvait si joli!. . .
    Ajoutez qu'il était extrêmement poli,

> *Saluant le premier, parlant à tout le monde,*
> *Mais aux femmes surtout, et toujours à la ronde*
> *Semant, sans les compter, les propos obligeants,*
> *Et, quand c'était le cas, de gentils compliments,*
> *Comme il en débitait aux nobles demoiselles*
> *Aux dames de châteaux, si fières et si belles!*

The *avertissement* speaks of the place of composition and his surroundings: "in a happy mood . . . in the shade of orange trees and surrounded by flowers." And apparently also in the company of his mistress, Francine Cellier.

31. I, 138.

32. According to the *Nouveau guide de l'étranger à Bordeaux* (1856), p. 110, the new church, the work of the architect Courcelles, was opened March 29, 1835. "Its facade, of a noble simplicity, is composed of four doric columns supporting an entablature decorated by a carving of an open Bible. The interior is 34 meters long and 16 meters wide."

33. AD (Gironde), cote 3E 26134. This includes the domain of La Pelette, where Haussmann's château of Cestas was located. Also see the Inventory drawn up at the death of Marie Fanny Texier, June 8, 1862, AD (Gironde), cote 3E 26218.

34. I, 147.

35. I, 382 is representative. When he was posted to Auxerre, in the Var, he left immediately, with "my office manager . . . my secretary . . . and my valet . . . leaving my valiant wife, as usual, the task of setting things in order, selling my horses, and following with our baggage."

36. I, 124, and 225–26.

37. I, 211, 212, 208.

38. I, 527–28. The story requires some slight deconstruction because the Haussmanns were seldom together in Blaye.

39. I, 211–12.

40. I, 212.

41. Jullian, p. 715: "The neighborhoods of Rousselle, le Chapeau Rouge, and Chartrons ruled Bordeaux under the constitutional monarchy [of July] as had the neighborhoods of the rue Neuve and the Pont-St.-Jean under the English."

42. Mme Haussmann's family, especially her father, was attached to an evangelical variety of Protestantism, and Haussmann, some years later (December 30, 1851) wrote to the minister of the interior (AN, F[1b] 162[3], pièce 193) specifically to distance himself from his father-in-law's religious views. He insisted he and his wife "remained attached to the national Protestant church and, consequently, we have been for some time on very delicate terms with her family—as everyone in Bordeaux knows—and since my arrival here, neither my father-in-law nor anyone [of his followers] has set foot in the Prefecture."

43. Born in Bordeaux November 3, 1786, Sers was the son of a businessman who rose to the rank of senator and count in the empire. He had sat with the Girondins during the revolution, survived their purge at the hands of the Jacobins, and eventually returned to Bordeaux. He was Protestant, which helped earn his son Guizot's protection after 1830. He was appointed prefect of the Gironde on October 20, 1838, and served until the end of February 1848, driven from office by the 1848 revolution. He died in Paris in 1862.

44. I, 378.

45. AD (Gironde) 4N, 256. It is likely that Haussmann found much of this in his official residence when he arrived.

46. AD (Gironde), 4N 8 (1823–1938). On May 1839 there is one estimate, and another on August 9, 1856. No work had been done. On September 30, 1823, the minister of the interior had rejected a request for funds. Earlier (April 26, 1823) the departmental architect submitted an estimate to acquire and repair a house in Blaye for the subprefect. After all these schemes failed another was launched (4N 70, 1838–43) to acquire the building and property designated as "le bâtiment de M. Lesparre-Duroc" for the residence and office of the subprefect. This too came to naught.

47. AD (Gironde), 4N 70 (1840–41).

48. AD (Gironde), 2N 175 (1842).

49. AD (Gironde), 2N176 (1843), August 2; 2N 178 (1845), July 30.

50. AN, F1B 162³, pièce 129.

51. AD (Gironde), 2N 176 (1842), 2N 177 (1844).

52. AN, F1B 162³, pièce 114.

53. I, 237. Also see I, 235, and Charles, *La Révolution de 1848*, pp. 54ff. for a commentary.

54. This is what he later told the duke.

55. Tilly and Lees, "The People of June, 1848," in Price, p. 177.

56. Figures from Tilly and Lees, "The People of June, 1848," in Price, pp. 184–85.

57. All figures, and the Renan quotations, from Tilly and Lees, "The People of June, 1848," in Price, pp. 185–86.

58. Gautier, quoted from Dufourg, "La Révolution de 1848. .," pp. 40–41.

59. I, 246–47. See Charles, *La Révolution de 1848*, p. 105. For a comparison of Neveux's career with Haussmann's see Charles, "Un carrière administrative. . .," pp. 229–40.

60. I, 247–48.

61. I, 248.

62. I, 250.

63. See Charles, *La Révolution de 1848*, p. 162, and I, 267–75. Neveux was powerless to remove his rival.

64. Quoted from Dufourg, "La Révolution de 1848. . .," p. 48.

65. I, 263, 266.

66. AN, F1B 162³, pièce 135.

67. See Charles, *La Révolution de 1848*, p. 168.
68. Charles, "Un carrière administrative. . .," p. 234.
69. I, 272. Haussmann's hatred of the Second Republic would last a lifetime.
70. Charles, *La Révolution de 1848*," pp. 178, 219.
71. I, 274.
72. The *Mémorial* newspaper had been founded as a liberal journal during the Restoration. It subsequently supported the government of Louis-Philippe and was the newspaper of the prefecture. It was owned by Sieur Durand, who also ran a service, out of the newspaper office, where rich army recruits could hire replacements to do their service for them. The director of the newspaper, in 1848, was M. Molé and he was the first to come out in favor of Louis Napoléon, exiled in England at the time of the February revolution, who hurried home to take advantage of new opportunities. Molé took the line Haussmann would later follow: the conservative party (as well as the more liberal Orleanists, and even the Legitimists), who loathed and distrusted the republic, would be best served by Louis Napoléon. There was also a Napoleonic Central Democratic Committee in Bordeaux, directed by General Darmagnac and a former officer in Napoléon's Imperial Guard, Durège de Beaulieu, who also used the pages of the *Mémorial*. These were efforts and men too marginal to interest Haussmann.
73. I, 280–81.
74. I, 278–79.

IV. *Paris in Crisis*

1. Tilly and Lees, "The People of June, 1848," in Price, p. 190. Referring to Pierre Caspard, "Aspects de la lutte des classes en 1848: le recrutement de la garde nationale mobile," *Revue historique*, 98 (1974), pp. 81–106, Tilly and Lees (p. 198) add: "Marx and Engels' characterization of the regime's makeshift soldiers as a *lumpenproletariat*, observes Caspard, seems to have erred. Instead, the *garde mobile* came especially from the least privileged (and most unemployed) members of privileged trades. Their opponents, the insurgents of June, drew more heavily on the ordinary workers of intensely organized, large-scale industries."
2. Quoted by Merriman, *Margins of City Life*, p. 76.
3. Amann, p. 17.
4. See Tulard, *Nouvelle histoire*, p. 26 and Pouthas, p. 160.
5. Merruau, p. 350.
6. See Loyer, pp. 52, 53, 54, 56, 57, 58, 59 for contemporary photographs of some remaining buildings, and Cobb, who lovingly records some of these pockets of Restoration and July Monarchy Paris in photographs and commentary.
7. Loyer, p. 61.

8. Merruau, p. 350.

9. Quoted in Olsen, p. 37.

10. Quoted in Tulard, *Nouvelle histoire*, p. 237.

11. Quoted in Morizet, pp. 116–17.

12. Edward l'Anson, "On the Recent Improvements in Paris: Papers Read at the Royal Institute of British Architects," quoted in Olsen, p. 35.

13. Balzac, *Cousin Bette* (Penguin edition), pp. 61–62.

14. Alfred de Musset, *La Confession d'un enfant du siècle*, pp. 58–59, quoted in Kranowski, p. 9.

15. See Girard, *Second Empire*, pp. 136–37. Zola, however, begins his serial novel of *Les Rougon-Macquart*, in the south, in the Provençale town of Plassans (actually Aix-en-Provence).

16. John Merriman, "Introduction: Images of the 19th-century French City," in Merriman, *French Cities*, p. 38.

17. Haussmann changed the numbering of the arrondissements when he incorporated the *banlieue*. I refer throughout to this new system, which still pertains

18. See Girard, *Second Empire*, pp. 139–40, on the segregation of the population, and Réau, pp. 27–28, for the statistics.

19. Morizet, p. 226.

20. Pinkney, p. 7.

21. The same epidemic in London, which was less densely populated and had far better urban services, especially sanitation, killed 5,500 out of 1,778,000. Contemporaries knew, without statistics, that the disease was the most murderous in the poorest, most overcrowded neighborhoods.

22. Olsen, p. 37, for the statistics, and Pinkney, p. 10, for Eugène Sue (his translation).

23. Chevalier, *Choléra*, p. 35. Vigier, p. 84, analyzes the cholera victims by occupation. Comparing deaths in the epidemic to the customary rates of mortality for a given occupation, we see that the "salaried occupations," as the French euphemism has it—day workers, street sweepers, rag collectors—paid the heaviest tribute to the disease.

24. Merruau, p. 191, and Paul-Lévy, p. 99, for *L'Edite de Paris*.

25. Tudesq, p. 566.

26. These articles from the law are quoted in Vigier, p. 138.

27. See Vigier, p. 207, n. 90, with references. Among the several anecdotes about Rambuteau (Réau, p. 9) is that he paid social visits on New Year's Day leaving his calling card, upon which he had written: "*Monsieur de Rambuteau et Vénus*," a frightful and funny gaff. Literally translated it means "M. de Rambuteau and Venus." What he meant to write was "M. de Rambuteau est venu" (M. de Rambuteau paid a visit). Both are pronounced the same.

28. This is the judgment of Loyer, p. 106.

29. Rambuteau, p. 399, "le feu roi était ménager."

30. This is the position of Lamartine. See Vigier, p. 223.
31. Louis Lazare has several chilling descriptions of the wretchedness of the *banlieue* and makes the telling argument that Haussmann's policies have only made the *banlieue* what the center of Paris once was: a disgraceful area unfit for human habitation.
32. See an explanation in Loyer, p. 50.
33. Gaillard, p. 19.
34. Lanquetin, pp. 1, 7, 9–10.
35. Merruau, p. 165.
36. Gaillard, pp. 18–19.
37. Merruau, pp. 346–47.
38. Réau, p. 9, quotes a popular verse of the day:

> *Vive le comte de Rambuteau*
> *Pour les bornes et les fontaines.*
> *Vive le comte de Rambuteau,*
> *Grâce à lui nous aurons de l'eau.*
> (Long live the count of Rambuteau
> For the limits [of the city] and the fountains
> Long live the count of Rambuteau,
> Thanks to him we have water.)

39. Merruau, pp. 77, 344–45.
40. Merruau, pp. 107–8.
41. Merruau, p. 419.
42. Sutcliffe, *Autumn of Central Paris*, pp. 181–82.
43. Merruau, pp. 348–49. Haussmann would inherit the unfinished project and carry it to completion, enveloping the Hôtel de Ville in a massive new urban fabric Rambuteau could not and would not rend.
44. Merruau, p. 349.
45. Literally, the act of piercing, uniformly used for canals, tunnels, streets.
46. Rambuteau, p. 375.
47. Quoted in *Paris-Haussmann*, p. 32.
48. Vigier, p. 190.
49. Merruau, p. 343.
50. Merruau, p. 148, lists projects both begun and envisioned: the creation of a central market, widening the rues Montmartre, St. Denis, de la Harpe, and des Mathurins, and the quai St. Paul, opening new streets to provide access to the railroad stations, enlarging the Sorbonne and the *collèges* Louis-le-Grand and Henri IV, completing the church of Ste. Clotilde and the Lariboisière Hospital, and the construction of a number of *mairies*, or local city halls. Rambuteau had also wanted to join the northern wing of the Louvre to the Tuileries and complete the rue de Rivoli, carrying it at least as far as the Hôtel de Ville.

51. See Vigier, p. 190, n. 46, and the authorities there cited.
52. Loyer, pp. 131, 144.
53. Girard, *Second Empire*, pp. 60–61; Morizet, p. 109.
54. Gaillard, pp. 14, 21; Paul-Levy, p. 104. The neighborhood is described by Balzac in *Les Parents pauvres*.
55. Gaillard, p. 21.
56. The prediction remained true as late as 1968, or at least the authorities thought the connection between pavement and street rebellion permanent. I remember standing in a melancholy crowd, in July 1968, where the boulevard St. Michel meets the entrance to the Luxembourg Gardens, watching crews black-top over the paving stones that had so recently been used to barricade the boul' Mich.
57. Paul-Lévy, pp. 177–78.
58. Quoted in Paul-Lévy, p. 178.
59. Merruau, p. 162.
60. Paul-Lévy, p. 153.
61. Marx, *Eighteenth Brumaire*, p. 75.
62. Merruau, p. 91.
63. See Merruau, pp. 165, 377–78.
64. Merruau, pp. 142–44. The buyout came to more than 13 million francs and this sum was arrived at by calculating how much traffic passed over the bridges in a year. See Féline-Romany, who was the chief engineer of bridges and streets, for details.
65. Gaillard, p. 32.
66. Benevolo, pp. 103–4.
67. Loyer, p. 124.

V. "My *Combative Prefectship*"

1. I, 285. He doesn't specifically repeat the story of Eugène having been his god-father, but the implication is clear enough. The changing governments and their official, historical pedigrees can be tracked in Haussmann's autobiographical emphases: during the July Monarchy he stressed his father's Orleanism and his two grandfathers' opposition to the king's death, hardly mentioning his Napoleonic heritage. During the Second Republic he stressed his grandfathers' revolutionary credentials—both had been elected to France's first republican assembly—and downplayed his Bonapartism. Now it is the Napoleonic connection that he emphasized.
2. Quoted by Machin, "The Prefects and Political Repression," in Price, p. 287.
3. II, 287.
4. AN, F^{1B} 162^3, pièce 143 (January 28, 1849).
5. I, 289–90.

6. Agulhon, *République*, p. 15. The department remained the home of avant-garde republicanism until the twentieth century. The Var elected two Communist deputies (out of five) in 1936, and the choice was seen as typical of the "Midi rouge."

7. Margadant, pp. 8–9.

8. Margadant, p. 11, table 1.1.

9. Margadant, p. 104.

10. Despite his enmity for Haussmann, Ollivier provided one of the most judicious appraisals of his foe. He recognized the prefect's "genius" for administration and expressed some regret that he could not have retained him at the Hôtel de Ville when he became first minister, in 1870: "The Emperor had wanted to retain Haussmann. I myself was reluctant to remove from office a man of such administrative superiority. But to keep him was out of the question." (Ollivier, *L'Empire libéral*, XII, 358–59.)

11. See Agulhon, *Pénitents*, esp. pp. 233–50.

12. Margadant, p. 64.

13. I, 336.

14. I, 339.

15. I, 353–54.

16. I, 360.

17. The suggestion is Agulhon's, "Le Baron Haussmann. . .", pp. 124–62. See p. 144, n. 8 *bis*.

18. Quoted by Agulhon, "Le Baron Haussmann. . .," p. 155.

19. I, 357.

20. Agulhon, "Le Baron Haussmann. . .," p. 158.

21. Agulhon, "Le Baron Haussmann. . .," p. 160.

22. Agulhon, "Le Baron Haussmann. . .," pp. 142–43, quoting Ollivier's *L'Empire libéral*, II, 534.

23. Agulhon, "Le Baron Haussmann. . .," pp. 146–47. And see Agulhon's extended account of the episode in *République*, pp. 316ff.

24. For another example of Haussmann's retrospective myopia, see Agulhon's account of *l'affaire de Vidauban* (*République*, pp. 409–17). Here the issue was Ollivier delivering a series of radical, even inflammatory, speeches in Vidauban as well as in Luc and Draguignan, and the trial that resulted. There are also a number of errors of fact (Agulhon, "Le Baron Haussmann. . .," pp. 145–46). The autobiographer confused two individuals, misidentified one of the local mayors, transformed a lawyer into a worker and a republican into a legitimist.

25. AD (Var), 4 M16.

26. AN, F^{1B} 162^3, pièce 170 (May 16, 1850).

27. I, 380–81.

28. I, 385.

29. The numbers are less impressive than those for the Var. See Margadant, p. 11, table 1.1. There were 2,200 men involved, in twenty-nine communes.

30. Agulhon, *République*, p. 476.

31. Merriman, *Agony*, p. 191. The author considers that the experience of the Yonne "exemplifies this particular sequence, which was most typical of the Midi: radicalization, repression, insurrection, and the final repression."

32. I, 387.

33. AN, F^{1B} 162^3, pièce 174.

34. For details, see Merriman, *Agony*, pp. 191–201.

35. BN, NAF 12295. There are seventy-nine letters addressed to Louis Frémy.

36. I have been unable to find Frémy's replies, presumably lost with the rest of Haussmann's papers.

37. BN, NAF 12295, September 22, 1850, and November 3, 1851.

38. BN, NAF 12295, July 8, 1850, and July 11, 1850.

39. BN, NAF 12295, March 26, 1851, and July 23, 1851.

40. BN, NAF 12295, May 6, 1851, and July 11, 1851.

41. BN, NAF 12295, June 29, 1850, and July 30, 1850.

42. BN, NAF 12295, February 13, 1851; February 20, 1851; February 21, 1851; and March 2, 1851.

43. BN, NAF 12295, March 18, 1851; April 10, 1851; April 20, 1851; and May 6, 1851.

44. I, 434.

45. I, 453–54.

46. See his account in I, 420–23. Here is another instance of his real (or exaggerated) confrontation of a crowd. In Paris, of course, where he did not control the police power, there would be no occasion for such cowboy bravado.

47. AN, F^{1B} 162^3, pièce 181.

48. BN, NAF 1229, November 19, 1850.

49. AN, F^{1B} 162^3, pièce 182. His autobiographical version of the episode is considerably toned down from either of these reactions.

50. BN, NAF 12295, February 14, 1851, and September 19, 1851. This recurring complaint about Legitimist society's avoiding the republic (and later the Second Empire) was a serious problem for Haussmann and all the new prefects. As Theodore Zelden has convincingly argued, the Bonapartists, and particularly the duc de Morny, the architect of a political party to support and sustain Bonapartism, elaborated a strategy to attract all the notables, whatever their political persuasion, to the Bonapartist cause. The ideological lines separating the elites proved quite penetrable. Berger's career, or even Haussmann's, are good examples. Only with the support of the traditional elites could the upstart regime hope to govern. The political behavior of Napoléon III is, in this, identical to that of his uncle, who welcomed all to join his government, however they had behaved during the revolution.

51. BN, NAF 12295 January 29, 1851, and February 7, 1851.

52. BN, NAF 12295, April 1, 1851, and February 14, 1851, and see I, 406.

53. BN, NAF 12295, May 5, 1851.

54. BN, NAF 12295, November 28, 1851.
55. The account is in I, 437–40; the letter to Frémy is BN, NAF 12295, August 4, 1850.
56. BN, NAF 12295, May 26, 1851.
57. The account of this second visit is in I, 447–52. The railroad car episode is I, 449–51.
58. I, 452.

VI. *"This Province I Have So Loved"*

1. Quoted in Charles, "Un exemple de carrière. . .," p. 239.
2. AN, F^{1B} 168^2.
3. Quoted in Dufourg, "Antoine Gautier. . .," p. 80.
4. I, 474.
5. Emile Ollivier confirms this account in his own recollections, including Haussmann's faux pas to Thorigny. See *L'Empire libéral*, II, 449.
6. I, 476.
7. BN, NAF 12295, December 2, 1851.
8. Quoted by Dufourg, "Antoine Gautier. . .," pp. 81, 82.
9. I, 486.
10. *Recueil*, IV, 703 (#311), "Proclamation du Préfet aux habitants du département (Bordeaux, December 4, 1851).
11. *Recueil*, IV, 758 (#317), and *Recueil*, V, 25 (#5).
12. Quoted in Charles, *La Révolution de 1848*, p. 364.
13. I, 496.
14. Quoted in Dufourg, "Antoine Gautier. . .," p. 81.
15. Margadant, p. 302.
16. Wright, "The Coup d'état of December 1851," in Price, pp. 308–9.
17. Riffaud, pp. 36, 42, 43, 47.
18. I, 521–27.
19. Charles, *La Révolution de 1848*, p. 345, citing AN, F^{1C} III (Gironde).
20. Quoted by Charles, *La Révolution de 1848*, p. 349.
21. AN, F^{1C}, III (Gironde) 9.
22. I, 504.
23. I, 528.
24. *Recueil*, V, 58 (#11).
25. Quoted by Charles, *La Révolution de 1848*, p. 354.
26. Charles, *La Révolution de 1848*, p. 355.
27. *Recueil*, V, #31.
28. Charles, *La Révolution de 1848*, p. 356, quoting from AM, FK^6, September 5, 1852.
29. *Recueil*, V, 141 (#21 *bis*), 146 *bis* (#21 *bis*). Haussmann's autobiographical

recollections (I, 564) differ considerably from the official record. "I myself made all the preparations, to the smallest detail," he wrote, "security measures, simple precautions for order, in a word all that could contribute, directly or indirectly, to the punctual execution of the several parts of this complex program. Nothing was neglected on any point to assure success."

30. The decrees are in *Recueil*, deuxième série, IV, 143 *bis* to 146 *bis*.

31. From the Quinconces to the hemicycle, to the cours du XXX Juillet, to the *place* of the Grand Theater, to the Fossés de l'Intendance, to the *place* of the rue Dauphine, to the *cours* d'Albert, the rue Rohan and eventually to the Hôtel de Rohan.

32. Sers, pp. 318–23.

33. I, 569.

34. I, 572.

35. I, 574.

36. I, 528.

37. *Discours . . . au Sénat*, p. 31.

38. Marrying his daughter to Louis François Rouxel, the marquis de Grancey, was an equally brilliant move. The marquis was considerably older than his bride, and his death would add the domains of Grancey to those of Tourny. Louis-Urbain eventually became the comte de Grancey (in 1758), as well as the marquis de Tourny.

39. See Lhéritier, pp. 42–51 for a detailed account of his climb.

40. See Merriman, *Red City*, esp. pp. 12–18, for an evocative description of this unique neighborhood and its place in the city's history.

41. The territory of the *généralité* of Bordeaux or the Basse-Guienne comprised three modern departments: the Gironde, the Lot-et-Garonne, and the Dordogne, and a part of the Gers.

42. Bernadau, pp. 138–39. He adds: "This line [of houses] extends from the hôtel of the Douane to the port de la Grave, in a 1200 meter hemicycle. . . . He built this with his own money and in the space of three years. This great work alone would suffice to insure the glory of this illustrious administrator."

43. Tourny was especially fond of this kind of architectural embellishment. Virtually all the finest buildings in Bordeaux feature elaborate and elegant stone carving, which was done once the stones had been set in place. The most conspicuous example is the three hundred uniform houses along the quays. Each has a different carved head above the door: a vast gallery of portraits, both realistic and fantastic.

44. Its only rival is Bath. Originally an elegant resort, it has burgeoned in recent years to become a substantial provincial center. Although impossible to drive in or park, the city has successfully preserved its eighteenth-century beauty.

45. Lhéritier, p. 445.

46. It was here that the guillotine was erected during the revolution.

47. Bernadau, pp. 139–40, 142.

48. Lhéritier, p. 514. The Paris houses were constructed according to letters patent from the king, dated October 18, 1669, which authorized the chapter of St. Germain l'Auxerrois to enlarge the street, with the provision that only those who agreed to build according to royal plans could purchase land. See Dethan, p. 388, for a picture of the original plan and how it looks today.

49. Bernadau, pp. 106–7.

50. Lhéritier, p. 484.

51. All the intendants were preoccupied with urban improvement, and among the towns significantly altered in the eighteenth century were Reims, Rennes, Dijon, Nantes, and Toulouse. The royal mistress, Mme du Berry (and her relatives who benefited from her elevation), took a keen interest in architecture and buildings, where there was glory to be earned, fortunes to be made. Courting the king through his mistress, by embellishing provincial capitals, became a familiar (and effective) form of advancement.

52. See Lhéritier, pp. 469–71, on Tourny's work in Périgueux.

53. II, 34. There are other examples, but this is characteristic and will suffice.

54. Saalman, p. 16.

55. III, 79.

56. III, 81–82.

57. Quoted by Tulard, *Nouvelle histoire*, p. 431.

58. Olsen, p. 289.

59. Olsen, p. 291. Roche, p. 32, traces this theatricality at least to the eighteenth century, when was "created an immense theater in which the populace rarely performed except through their labor. . . . A unitary organization of space, in which the relationship between public buildings, squares, streets and houses was changed, suggested a theatrical vision of the urban landscape where city-dwellers were experiencing a new social order."

60. "L'Architecture n'étant autre chose que l'Administration." I retain his capitalization of Administration. Quoted by Quéré in *Paris-Haussmann*, p. 222.

61. This building was especially moving to Duc's contemporaries. Viollet-le-Duc wrote admiringly: "The *salle des pas perdus*, on the exterior and the interior, is one of those monuments which will do honor to our times. There everything holds together, everything is connected by a clear thought. The execution . . . responds to the composition, it is beautiful and pure. One senses an artist, rare thing in our times, who respects his art and the public." Quoted in Drexler, p. 429. The indispensable book on the palais and its place in Paris public life is now Taylor.

62. The facade of the Palais de Justice, facing the rue de Harlay, was opened in 1869 and its architect, Louis Duc (1802–79), received a prize of one hundred thousand francs from the emperor for the best work of art produced during the Second Empire. The facade faces the amputated Place Dauphine, which functions, badly, as a kind of parvis. It is not a very successful presentation of an important building. The gare du Nord Haussmann ignored. He was feud-

ing with the Rothschilds, the gare was a privately constructed building, and he did not even provide adequate access streets.

63. St.-Pierre-du-Petit-Montrouge, on the Place Victor-Basch, in the fourteenth arrondissement, is a vast yet harmonious building. Constructed from 1863 to 1872, it is considered one of the masterpieces of Emile Vaudremer. It could hardly be classified as a Romanesque church. Vaudremer successfully blended Romanesque, Byzantine, and Italian Renaissance elements in his church, which was built as part of the urbanization of the commune of Petit-Montrouge, after its incorporation into Paris in 1860.

64. Richard Chafee, "The Teaching of Architecture at the Ecole des Beaux-Arts," in Drexler, p. 88.

65. Pinon, in *Paris-Haussmann*, pp. 97–98. He also points out that when Haussmann wrote the contracts of sale for the Place du Louvre (May 1, 1857), he stipulated that all new buildings had to conform to the facades of the houses already constructed along the rue de Rivoli.

66. Van Zanten, "Architectural Composition at the Ecole des Beaux-Arts from Charles Percier to Charles Garnier," in Drexler, p. 185.

67. I follow Loyer, pp. 240, 251–52, and his marvelous photographs.

68. Loyer, p. 312.

VII. "A State Within the State"

1. Balzac, *Cousin Bette*, translated Marion Ayton Crawford, pp. 60–61.
2. Persigny, p. 248.
3. Persigny, pp. 260–61.
4. Persigny, pp. 250–51.
5. Persigny had selected five of the senior prefects to interview for the position: Le Roy (Rouen), Besson (Lille), de Crèvecoeur (Marseille), Tourangin (formerly of Lyons), and Haussmann, and invited each to dine with him in Paris.
6. Persigny, pp. 252–55.
7. I, 542–43.
8. II, 16.
9. The empress was named after Prince Eugène.
10. II, 50–51. Haussmann regularly repeated this linkage. The emperor, exceptionally jealous of his family—the essence of his authority rested on his descent, which he considered as legitimating as descent from the Bourbons or any other royal family. Haussmann surely knew his connection with Prince Eugène was at best tenuous and probably imaginary. The empress may also have known. Did this particular conversation actually take place? Did Haussmann genuinely believe Prince Eugène was his godfather, and so repeated the anecdote in all innocence? Or in that regime so filled with pretense and illusion, was the connection (as with Haussmann's baronetcy) winked at?

11. See Machin, "The Prefects and Political Repression: February 1848 to December 1851," in Price, p. 287, for the various laws passed to facilitate repression.

12. II, 53–54.

13. Ollivier, III, 83, who had access to the best sources and was a careful and scrupulous writer, is typical: "He himself indicated the major streets," Ollivier wrote, "which have made Paris one of the most beautiful cities of the world, and indicated their order of completion." La Gorce, (I, 130), a contemporary and the historian of the empire, accepts the existence of the plan and avers that "each morning groups of workers spread out through the city. They were the first to execute the imperial plan, grandiose if open to criticism in several of its details." Pinkney, p. 26, merely affirms the plan's existence, without comment beyond its presumed destruction when the Hôtel de Ville burned. Pinon, *Paris-Haussmann*, p. 55, offer some nuance. He says there was a plan that predated 1860—he dates it from the projects indicated—but it was sketchy at best. Sutcliffe, *Autumn of Central Paris*, p. 23, favors a mere sketch, which seems the best compromise position.

14. This explanation for the disappearance of Haussmann's copy is not without problems. Haussmann left the Hôtel de Ville in January 1870, more than a year before the Commune. Although he doubtless left behind some map of Paris for his successor—most likely the map he had made after Paris was triangulated, which he had mounted on a special rolling stand and kept always in his office—for his work was not completed when he fell, and the empire was still the government, there is no good reason to suppose he left behind the emperor's autographed map, which was inaccurate and would have been of no practical use to any future prefect. It is much more likely he would have taken this map, which belonged to him, or at least some kind of copy for himself, if only as a souvenir. But there is no mention of either the original or a copy in the inventories made at his death or in his surviving papers.

15. Persigny, p. 256.

16. Quoted in Lameyre, p. 88.

17. *Histoire de la France urbaine*, IV, 95.

18. II, 202.

19. II, 32.

20. Pinkney, p. 25. The story was originally told by Thomas W. Evans.

21. III, 29. A further problem is here introduced. Which map did Louis Napoléon use for his base? Was it Verniquet's or some other, less accurate map? Louis Napoléon had been exiled from France for some years, and because he is assumed to have indicated the changes he wanted to see while in England, he may have used an outdated map of Paris.

22. III, 74, 79, Pinon, *Paris-Haussmann*, pp. 79–80. Louis Napoléon concentrated his attention on the old core city and had no vision of developing western Paris.

23. Pinon, *Paris-Haussmann*, p. 55.
24. III, 13, 15. There is a smaller reduction of Haussmann's copy of this map in the Bibliothèque Historique de la Ville de Paris: *Atlas Administratif des 20 arrondissements de la Ville de Paris*, publié d'après les ordres de M. le baron G.E. Haussmann, Sénateur, Préfet de la Seine (1868), bound in blue leather, with his coat of arms and a hand-illuminated dedicatory page: "A Monsieur le Baron Haussmann, Sénateur, Préfet de la Seine, hommage respectueux du Service du Plan de Paris. Le Chef du Service du Plan de Paris, [signed] Deschamps."
25. Merruau, p. 365–66.
26. It is difficult to say how close this plan is to the original. Several important projects, well underway or completed by 1867, are missing. The plan given to Frederick William of Prussia does not show the 1860 extension of the city, and western Paris, around the Etoile and Chaillot, is depicted only in sketchy form, the boulevard Haussmann stops at the boulevard Malesherbes, there is no boulevard St. Germain, and the significant esplanades around the Place de la Nation and the Place Voltaire are shown only as projects. At the same time this copy indicates projects that were completed after 1853 and so cannot have been a copy of the emperor's original. Louis Napoléon did give the king a copy of the Deschamps plan along with this version of his original vision, which Morizet found in the Berlin archives and published. I have been unable, despite the efforts of my colleague, Prof. Gregg Roeber, who made inquiries in the former East Berlin, to locate the original reproduced by Morizet; and I have been unable to find a copy of Morizet that contains the plan, tipped into the end of the book. The Bibliothèque Nationale cannot locate its copy, and that in the Bibliothèque Historique de la Ville de Paris has had the map cut out, as have all the copies I have seen in America. Fortunately, the map was earlier reproduced by Werner Hegemann, in 1911 (between pp. 222 and 223), and, from Hegemann, by David Van Zanten, *Building Paris: Architectural Institutions and the Transformation of the French Capital, 1830–1870* (Cambridge: Cambridge University Press, 1994), p. 200. I reproduce this map from Hegemann as well.
27. Merruau, pp. 365–67. The streets are drawn in color: (1) red for those that existed in 1872, and that the emperor wanted built; (2) green for those not yet completed or not undertaken but that he also wanted built; and (3) black for those streets he did not envision but that were built. The plan came to Merruau via Rouher, who accompanied the emperor into exile.
28. Most likely the imperial plan for Paris was at best a visionary sketch. Was it drawn before or after 1848, before or after the June Days injected political and social urgency, even panic, into urban planning? If we knew the answer to this question it would also date the sketch. Was it drawn in Paris or in England?
29. The suggestion is Saalman's, p. 14.

30. The first handsome graphic representation of Paris of the Second Empire was drawn under the Third Republic and appeared in the *Atlas des travaux de Paris*, published on the occasion of the Universal Exposition of 1889.

31. Gaillard, p. 141, n. 2.

32. Earls, pp. 70–71, sums up (rather woodenly) the argument that it was the emperor and not Haussmann who was the creator of Paris: "Haussmann has been called an architect and the first town-planner. He was neither. He has been given credit for designing tree-lined boulevards and for landscaping and creating parks. He did supervise teams of engineers and horticulturists who followed the ideas of Louis Napoléon. He did provide the complicated financial negotiations of the project. He was a shrewd administrator who desired power. There were exceptions when the emperor's plans would not work, problems not foreseen on a drawing board. Few of the original ideas were Haussmann's. However, he was also a St. Simonian; therefore he must have been in basic agreement with the emperor's plans to improve Paris. He realized the St. Simonian concept of industry but it was the emperor who initiated the ideas. Les Halles was constructed of iron and glass because Louis Napoléon demanded the materials. Haussmann has been called a collaborator, supervisor, agent and rebuilder of Paris." A few pages later (p. 74) Earls gives Haussmann a bit more credit, saying, "Together they rebuilt the city."

33. Persigny, 259–60.

34. Vincent Wright, "The Coup d'état of December 1851: Repression and the Limits of Repression," in Price, p. 308.

35. II, 20.

36. Girard, *Politique des travaux publics*, pp. 170–71, 261.

37. II, 155.

38. I, 36–37.

39. Quoted in Lameyre, pp. 54–55. The sneer is especially nasty, for Haussmann never practiced law.

40. I, 117.

41. II, 73, and II, 237, for his explanation of these changes. I have not found any evidence that he was offered and declined the ministry of the interior. As for the other proffered positions, the Paris memoir writers and gossips seem to have elevated rumor into fact.

42. See Blayau, p. 247, for Haussmann's strained relations with several ministers.

43. II, 226.

44. Persigny, 260.

45. II, 155, 156. Haussmann does not explain what "fact" it was he reported to the emperor that caused this show of temper. And the testimonial, for which Haussmann gives no source, may be edited. The emperor remained loyal to Haussmann almost to the end of the empire. It is difficult to imagine what not recognizing his political worth might mean, unless Haussmann took it as

testimony that Louis Napoléon came to understand that he should have earlier followed the political advice of his prefect.

46. II, 53.
47. II, 58–59.

VIII. *"The Implacable Axes of a Straight Line. . ."*

1. Writing in the *Revue générale de l'architecture*.
2. III, 41. Haussmann also cut down the last remaining tree of liberty, planted in 1793, near the Feuillants pavillion of the Tuileries. No historical epoch stayed Haussmann's hand.
3. Quoted in Pinon, *Paris-Haussmann*, p. 65.
4. III, 47–48.
5. III, 49.
6. Sutcliffe, *Autumn of Central Paris*, p. 33, quoting Conseil Général, *Procès verbaux*, November 24, 1856, pp. 13–14.
7. III, 54. "This was the gutting of Old Paris, of the neighborhood of riots, of barricades, accomplished by a large central street, piercing, from one end to the other, this almost impassible labyrinth, and connected with transverse arteries whose continuation ought to complete the work thus begun."
8. II, 318.
9. Quoted in Gaillard, p. 38.
10. III, 54.
11. Vandam, p. 159.
12. Gaillard, pp. 39, 35.
13. Harvey, *Urban Experience*, p. 165, and see especially Jacquemet, pp. 161–70.
14. III, 54–55.
15. An Architect, "An Epistolary Chat from Paris," *Builder*, June 1852, p. 380.
16. Sherard, 106–7. These sketches, too, have disappeared.
17. *La Curée, Oeuvres*, I, 332.
18. II, 488.
19. II, 524.
20. Sherard, p. 115. Yet another part of Old Paris sacrificed to haussmannization, the memory of the poet's death is preserved only in Nanteuil's lithograph.
21. II, 487.
22. Gaillard, p. 14.
23. III, 28.
24. See II, 485–86 for Haussmann's extended explanation of the several jurisdictions involved in gathering the courts in one building, and how he managed the complicated financial arrangements.
25. III, 535–36.

26. Gaillard, p. 66.
27. Saalman, p. 114.
28. Sutcliffe, *Paris*, p. 41.
29. See his description in III, 75–76.
30. III, 76.
31. The obvious irony was intentional. December 10, 1848, was the date of Louis Napoleon's election to the presidency of the Second Republic, by an overwhelming majority. September 4, 1870, was the proclamation of the Third Republic: the beginning and end of the second Napoleon.
32. Louis Lazare, *Publications administratives*, vol. 4 (Paris, 1864), pp. 312–14, quoted by Pinon, in *Paris-Haussmann*, p. 197.
33. II, 226.
34. See Mead, pp. 55–58.
35. Chaix d'Est Ange, "Avis de la Commission d'Enquête," p. 20, quoted in Mead, p. 57: "the project placing the Opera in the center of Paris, in the richest and most lively quarter, and near the boulevard [des Capucines] presents . . . the best conditions."
36. Claudin, pp. 16–19.
37. Girard, *Le deuxième République*, p. 173, quoting the *Bulletin de statistique municipal* (1865), p. 252.
38. Daumard, p. 154, and the graphs, pp. 151–53.
39. Sutcliffe, *Autumn of Central Paris*, p. 155.
40. Gaillard, p. 529.
41. Quoted by Mead, p. 61.
42. Quoted by Mead, p. 3. Louise Garnier's account is in *L'Architecture*, 38 (1925), p. 382.
43. Quoted by Mead, p. 4.
44. Mead, p. 129.
45. Mead, p. 74.
46. Mead, pp. 133–34.
47. See the lament in Chevalier, *Assassination*, p. 53.
48. Quoted from *Les petits Bourgeois*, by Morizet, p. 201. The unfinished novel, mostly written in 1847–48, was published posthumously in 1856.

IX. "The Vice-Emperor Is the Prefect of the Seine"

1. Because Paris has had a mayor, a development of the last twenty years or so, there has not been a prefect of Seine. In a sense the same problem of the extraordinary importance of Paris in France continues and the mayor, presently Jacques Chirac, is a figure of national significance, the leader of one wing of the old Gaullist Party, which splintered into groups whose leaders contested the heritage.

2. Quoted in Tulard, *Paris et son administration,* p. 185.

3. Tulard, *Paris et son administration,* p. 188: "No text fixes the holding of sessions [but] there should be one regular annual session of fifteen days consecrated to the examination of the budget as well as exceptional sessions, convoked by the prefect of the Seine. At the opening of each session the Council was to elect a president and secretary. The majority of its work would be done by special commission or *en bureau* [by the members separately]. The prefects had the right to be present at these meetings."

4. I, 471–72.

5. AM, Paris (BHVP), cote 4746, série 110.

6. II, 38.

7. Gaillard, p. 259.

8. II, 219–20.

9. II, 236.

10. Ollivier, *L'Empire libéral,* V, 83 (November 1860).

11. I, 117.

12. II, 212–13.

13. "De l'Organisation municipale de Paris," AN, 45AP 19 (Papiers Rouher). The folder is marked "Ville de Paris, Organisation Municipale, REP 165B, II, 22."

14. II, 200, 204.

15. II, 85.

16. Haussmann, *Discours* (April 13, 1869), p. 4.

17. II, 311.

18. See Caro, who dislikes his hero but presents the best picture of his work.

19. Haussmann (II, 24–26) has a long digression on the merits of Merruau, not least of which was his fine literary style, which the prefect had often to translate into the turgidities of administrative prose. " 'Very well,' I told him, 'that is perfect. I will with pleasure keep on, as permanent witness of my acts, a functionary . . . whose sentiments could not be suspected of disloyalty toward me!'"

20. II, 85–87.

21. II, 257.

22. AN, F^{1}C III (Seine) 31, letters of December 28, 1858, and January 26, 1859. On another occasion (May 7, 1869), he informed the minister he had to reject the request to construct a "military panorama" near the boulevard Mazas because "the city . . . only owns in this neighborhood a single plot of land and it is destined for the construction of a school."

23. AN, F^{1}C III (Seine) 31, October 29, 1858.

24. II, 218–19.

25. AN, F^{1}C III (Seine) 31, July 31, 1862.

26. AN, F^{21}825, July 20, 1853.

27. AN, F^{21}825, April 30, 1868.

28. AN, F^{21}825, June 12, 1858. This entire series contains letters of the same kind.

29. AD (Seine), 5AZ 25 (November 27, 1865).
30. AD (Seine), GAZ 104/3 (November 6, 1869).
31. Silverman, p. 44. See de Coetlogon and Tisserand, I, 98–99, 155–64, 189–92, for Haussmann's part.
32. III, 9. Zola has a description of this very chicanery in *La Curée*, where Saccard wanders familiarly into the various offices at the Hôtel de Ville, peeking at the plans. Zola does have a character based on Haussmann, Baron Hartmann. There are resemblances and differences between the historical and fictional creations. Hartmann—who does not appear in *La Curée* but in *Au Bonheur des dames*—is "an old man, about sixty" (Haussmann would have been that age in 1869) but physically he is "a small and energetic man," endowed with "a large Alsatian head and whose broad face was lit by the flame of intelligence." He is a devious creature, always on the alert.
33. II, 543. A few pages later in the *Mémoires* (II, 546), he recorded a conversation with Louis Napoléon in which he told the emperor how he had refused a bribe of 600,000 francs. Once again he named no names. Lavedan, in Réau, p. 51, says: "He left the Hôtel de Ville less rich than when he entered."

X. Money

1. Quoted in La Gorce, II, 61. Robert Moses would later use the same technique, with equal effectiveness: start work and the funds will be found.
2. II, 31.
3. II, 36.
4. *Mémoire. . .à la commission municipale* (session ordinaire, 1859), p. 1. "In effect," he wrote in his first *Mémoire. . .à la commission municipale* (session ordinaire, 1854), p. 2, "order is the principle and the law of economy."
5. II, 36. "*Eureka!* I found it!" he announced a few pages later (II, 42), "the support that would allow me to lift, not the world, but the enormous burden I had assumed." He returned to the Archimedean image (II, 273): "Archimedes, who said he could make a lever to raise the earth, asked only a place to support his terrible engine. My point of support, I have said, will be a surplus of receipts, still very modest, that I have been able to separate from the confusion of the city's accounts. My lever will be the gradual growth of revenues, on which I believe I can count."
6. The sums Haussmann was able to raise without taxes during the seventeen years of his prefecture are impressive. Morizet, p. 284, gives some figures: 820 million francs beyond what was needed for the daily running of Paris. Including extraordinary income, along with state subventions and the resale of confiscated land, the sum rose to 1,380 million.
7. Girard, *Travaux*, p. 85.
8. See Persigny, pp. 439–57, where he reprints his report of May 21, 1868, to

Louis Napoléon on his economic ideas. Note the relatively late date for the report, considering that deficit spending on urban transformation had been going on for more than a dozen years, originally modeled on the Crédit Mobilier of the Péreire brothers, which had at first been used to finance the railroad boom. Persigny wanted to apply the same methods to perpetuate the Paris building boom. He sought a prefect to replace Berger who would be sympathetic with his ideas. He surely deserves credit for the initiative. What seems to have happened, and it is not uncommon for Haussmann, is that he so thoroughly incorporated the ideas about deficit spending that they soon seemed his own. He would later do precisely the same thing with the water supply and the sewers of Paris, making Belgrand's ideas his own and taking almost complete credit. Pinkney, pp. 180–81, gives Persigny the priority. Contemporary opinion is well expressed by Ollivier, *L'Empire libéral*, XI, 423–24: "If Haussmann did not have the initiative of the idea, he had the merit of applying it with a mixture of brutality, finesse, indomitable vigor fruitful in expedients, and he endowed it with his veritable administrative genius." This seems the best explanation. Without Haussmann's complete conversion and bureaucratization of the idea, it would never have been realized. In doing so, however, he always gave himself more credit than he deserved. Of modern writers Giradet, p. 278, gives Haussmann the priority over Persigny, but he is a bit hesitant.

9. Merruau, pp. 65–66. He estimated total receipts at 47,429,921 francs, of which 34,576,630 came from the *octroi*.

10. Figures from Morizet, p. 284.

11. AN, 45 AP 21 (Papiers Rouher), September 15, 1867.

12. AN, 45 AP 20 (Papiers Rouher), "Note pour M. le Préfet." See also AN, 45 AP 19, "Relevé du produit des droits d'entrée et d'octroi sur les vins pendant les années 1866, 1867 et le 1er trimestre de 1868." Municipal income from the tax went from 19,085,082 francs in 1859 (before annexation), to 22,747,118 in 1860, to 38,339,126 in 1866.

13. See the table in Girard, *Deuxième République*, p. 198.

14. See the figures in Girard, *Politique*, p. 331, n. 257.

15. Saalman, p. 23, argues that in a final accounting, "it must be acknowledged that Haussmann's idea of deficit financing proved correct. The tax base of Paris grew along with the economic expansion made possible by the city's transformation, and surplus income eventually covered the outlay may times over. By the time of Haussmann's death in 1891, when the political clamor of the 1860s had died down, it was generally admitted that Paris could not only afford to do what was done, it could not have afforded not to do it."

16. Harvey, *Consciousness*, p. 97.

17. Harvey, *Urban Experience*, pp. 88–89.

18. Harvey, *Consciousness*, p. 89.

19. II, 327: "It varied from 4.87% for the loan of 1855, and 4% for the several loans of 1860, to about 5% for the loan of 1865."

20. Ollivier, *L'Empire libéral*, V, 41–42.
21. Girard, *Politique*, p. 166.
22. Gaillard, p. 394.
23. Gaillard, pp. 393–94.
24. Sutcliffe, *Autumn of Central Paris*, p. 42.
25. Girard, *Politique*, p. 392.
26. See Morizet, p. 329. The loan of 1855, for the first *réseau*, was paid off September 1, 1897; the loan of 1869, reimbursement for the advances made by the Crédit Foncier to the Caisse des Travaux, was paid off July 31, 1909. The repayment on annuities for repurchasing concessions was paid off between 1899 and 1922; and the loan of 1865, for annexations, was the last to be paid off, July 31, 1929.
27. *Histoire de la France urbaine*, IV, 93.
28. Quoted in Merruau, p. 78.
29. Pinon, *Paris-Haussmann*, p. 97.
30. II, 51–52.
31. II, 311.
32. III, 9.
33. AD (Seine), 7AZ 296 (June 26, 1854).
34. du Camp, VI, 337.
35. Sutcliffe, *Autumn of Central Paris*, p. 25.
36. II, 308.
37. *La Curée, Les Rougon-Macquart*, I, 88.
38. Harvey, *Urban Experience*, p. 89.
39. AM, Paris (BHVP), Cote 3392, November 18, 1861.
40. II, 500–501.
41. Gaillard, p. 46. For the purposes of comparison, Haussmann paid an average of 443 francs per square meter to get the land needed for a continuation of the rue de Rivoli in 1854. See AN, F¹ᶜIII (Seine) 31, "Mémoire à la Commission Municipale" (19 mai 1854).
42. II, 303–4.
43. III, 64.

XI. *"Lackey of a Good House"*

1. Merruau's contemporary and detailed description of the Hôtel de Ville, which I follow, is on pp. 5–12. The pages here referred to are pp. 19–20; the quotation comes from p. 31.
2. Rambuteau, p. 395.
3. The two leading, and antagonistic, schools of painting were thus represented: Delacroix, the leading exponent of romanticism; and Ingres, the old master

of neoclassicism. See Mainardi, especially pp. 49–61, for an account of the Universal Exposition of 1855 and the artistic rivalries.

4. There should have been a mural of Henri IV in the series. More than François I, he put his stamp on Paris, while Clovis, although central to the myth of the origins of the French monarchy, had little to do with Paris.

5. Lameyre, p. 272.

6. II, 99–100.

7. II, 64, 100–101.

8. Rambuteau, p. 398.

9. II, 101.

10. II, 102.

11. Des Cars, p. 233, for the brooch. Lameyre, pp. 259–60, for the public balls.

12. The menu, reprinted by Lameyre, p. 271, is worth quotation. See p. 266 for another menu, this one for the son of Leopold I of Belgium. Although the capacity and eating habits of the nineteenth century seem sometimes staggering, this sumptuous menu offered choices in each category. It is not a list of what the guests were expected to consume:

SOUPS:

Bisque d'Ecrevisses
Printanier

FIRST COURSE:

Turbot, sauce Hollandaise
Quartiers de Chevreuil

WARM HORS-D'OEUVRE:

Croustades à la Portugaise
Bouchées aux Crevettes

MAIN COURSE:

Filet de Boeuf à la Provençale
Suprêmes de Poulardes aux Truffes
Caisses de Mauviettes à la Financière
Caille de Vigne à la Jardinière
Homards à l'Américaine
Mayonnaises de filets de Soles

ROASTS:

Dindonneaux aux Truffes, sauce à la Périgueux
Faisans de Bohême et Bécasses

Buissons d'Ecrevisses du Rhin
Timbales de foies gras au Malaga

SWEETS:

Petits pois à la Française
Patates d'Espagne au Malaga
Truffes au vin de Champagne
Suprêmes de pêches
Gelées d'Ananas à l'Orientale
Gâteaux ambroisie glacés

DESERTS:

Fruits, raisins, ananas, compotes, pâtisserie, etc.

WINES:

Madère frappé
Château d'Yquem frappé
Château d'Issan
Romanée
Château Montroze
Chambertin
Rudesheimer
Xérès
Champagne frappé
Léoville Poyféré
Château Laffitte
Malaga
Porto

13. Quoted in Lameyre, p. 272–3.
14. AD (Seine), 2AZ 180, number 11 (March 14, 1867).
15. AD (Seine), 2AZ 180, number 10 (February 22, 1867).
16. II, 104.
17. Ollivier, *Journal*, I, 332–33, tells the story as he heard it from Jules Favre, who was present. Leclerc d'Osmonville's words were, "Il est fâcheux que M. le Préfet de la Seine fasse entrer l'Opéra partout où il ne devrait pas être." There are other sources for the episode, which all Haussmann's biographers repeat, but without attribution.
18. Lameyre, p. 274.
19. Viel-Castel, II, 61. Fronsac Baroche was the son of the minister Baroche.
20. Quoted in Lameyre, p. 275.

21. BN, NAF, 24624 (#237), October 28, 1857.

22. As a child, in 1848, she lived at 4 rue de Chabrol, a shabby neighborhood behind the gare de l'Est. She then moved to 37 rue St. George, a decided improvement. Then to 30 rue Bleu, and next to a new apartment, part of Haussmann's transformation, at 79 boulevard de Sébastopol. When she was engaged by the Vaudeville Theater she moved to 38 rue Notre-Dame-des-Champs, where she remained from 1863 to 1868. Next, she moved to 83 boulevard Malesherbes.

23. Lameyre, p. 276.

24. Des Cars, p. 294. The nasty bon mot that described her as "a puppet who had swallowed a music box" denigrates a respectable talent.

25. AN, *Inventaire*, cote 106 (11 items).

26. Quoted in Touttain, p.72.

27. II, 181–82. Henriette-Marie's dowry consisted of a trousseau of dresses, and linen valued at 20,000 francs, and a sum of 300,000 francs in cash, payable as 100,000 francs in cash the day of the marriage, and the rest (with 5 percent interest), "after the celebration of the marriage" in three payments. This was fully paid. Valentine's dowry was identical, but she was divorced before the entire amount was paid.

28. Quoted by Des Cars, p. 295.

29. Des Cars, p. 296.

30. Quoted in Valynseele, p. 59, n. 62:

> *Haussmann à Pernety vient d'accorder sa fille,*
> *Quoique l'hymen soit beau, je plains le marié.*
> *Je craindrais, en entrant dans pareille famille,*
> *D'être, comme mari, trop vite exproprié!*

31. Quoted by Haag, p. 38.

32. I, 35.

33. Des Cilleuls, II, 539.

34. Quoted in Lameyre, pp. 295–96. Claudin's observation is confirmed by Alfred des Cilleuls, the historian of the Paris administration. Claudin also provides the interesting detail that for all the crosses and medals that decorated the coats Haussmann habitually wore, attached to his vest was "a small gold chain which was worth maybe 18 francs. He never wore another."

35. III, 40.

36. Fournier, p. ii.

37. *La Curée, Les Rougons-Macquart*, I, 387–88.

38. II, 455.

39. Morizet, p. 185.

40. Olsen, p. 50.

41. I, 151.

42. See *Alexandre-Théodore Brongiart*, for a catalogue of his works and their fate.

43. Quoted in Lameyre, p. 248.

44. *M. Bergeret à Paris*, quoted by Morizet, p. 277.

45. III, 85.

46. Dusolier is representative. Haussmann's insistence on the rectilinear is the culprit. Why couldn't the rue de Fleurus—familiar to many Americans from Hemingway's description of Gertrude Stein's apartment there in *A Moveable Feast*—not make a slight "detour of less than 100 meters" instead of running directly into the rue de l'Abbé-de l'Epée?

47. Hugo, *Actes et Paroles*, quoted by Morizet, p. 278.

48. Chambre des Députés, session of Wednesday, July 29, 1879, *Discours prononcé par M. le Baron Haussmann, député de la Corse. . .*, pp. 7–8.

49. Unidentified clipping, January 12, 1891, in one of the files, AD (Seine), GAZ 1014.

50. II, 33.

51. Pinon, *Paris-Haussmann*, p. 90.

XII. *"Organs of the Large City"*

1. Quoted in Reid, p. 20.

2. The *Rapport* is undated so cannot be attributed to Berger's or Rambuteau's administration.

3. AN, F^{1}C III (Seine), 31.

4. *Cousin Bette*, p. 344.

5. Girardet, p. 296.

6. II, 514–15.

7. II, 517.

8. II, 514–15.

9. II, 517.

10. II, 517.

11. III, 111–12.

12. III, 117.

13. Pinkney, pp. 110–11. Belgrand wanted the water brought to Paris at ten meters above what was necessary. He estimated this would cost another three million francs. Haussmann told the Municipal Council it would be "a little more than two million."

14. Edwin Chadwick, the British advocate of public health, is said by his biographer to have told Louis Napoléon: "Sire, they say that Augustus found Rome a city of brick, and left it a city of marble. If your Majesty, finding Paris fair above, will leave it sweet below, you will more than rival the first Emperor of Rome." Quoted in Reid, p. 29, from Benjamin Ward Richardson, *The Health*

of Nations: A Review of the Works of Edwin Chadwick, 2 vols. (London, 1887), I, lxiii.

15. III, 382.
16. III, 403.
17. III, 350.
18. Reid, p. 29.
19. *Mémoire sur les eaux de Paris* (1854), pp. 52–53.
20. III, 356–57.
21. III, 359–62.
22. See the description of these boats, fitted with special outworks, in I, 219.
23. III, 110. Haussmann points out that these boats were introduced during the reign of Louis XIII by workers imported from Holland. Reid, pp. 30–33 has a description, with photographs, of the technique.
24. Quoted in Reid, p. 41.
25. Reid, p. 41.
26. Pinkney, p. 104. He adds that "these forty-seven acres together with other parks in the city ordinarily open to the public provided an acre of recreation for every 5,000 inhabitants; in 1870 there was an acre for every 390 inhabitants. The Regional Survey of New York in 1928 recommended one acre of park for 300 to 500 inhabitants as a reasonable standard, and in 1925 Manhattan had only one for every 1,130 of its residents."
27. Not only did Haussmann specify 95,577 trees where there had previously been 50,466 (II, 513), he added: "Moreover, one cannot make any comparison between the care they received from specialists, where previously they were cared for by some city employee or other."
28. *Histoire de la France urbaine,* IV, 170–71.
29. III, 177.
30. III, 179–80.
31. III, 183.
32. III, 231.
33. The most notable are the square St. Jacques (1854), square du Temple (1857), square des Arts et Métiers (1857), square des Innocents (1859), square Ste. Clotilde (1859), square Louvois (1859), square Ventimille (1859), square Montholon (1862), square Louis XVI (1862), square des Invalides (1865), square de la Trinité (1866), square Laborde (1866), square de l'Observatoire (1866), square Monge (1868), square des Ménages (1869); and in the new arrondissements, square des Batignolles (the largest), square de Belleville, square de Montrouge, square de la Chapelle, square de la Réunion, square Victor, and square de Grenelle.
34. III, 17. He celebrates the engineering involved, which necessitated putting the tower up on wooden blocks while a new foundation was excavated and constructed. He also placed a statue of Pascal there, "to recall the experi-

ments having to do with the weight of air and falling bodies, which he had
conducted in this tower."

35. III, 182. Note the pedantic enumeration of the plants involved.

36. III, 182.

37. Morizet, pp. 190–91.

38. Originally published in two oversize volumes (Paris, 1867–73) containing 487
    woodcuts, eighty steel engravings (of remarkable quality, most evident in the
    elegant shadings obtained), and twenty-three color lithographs, the work not
    only contains careful descriptions and wonderful plates and plans but also de-
    picts the machinery used, some of it especially designed to accomplish the
    work: tree planters, various watering systems and apparati, stone sifters, and
    tree braces. There is also an extensive historical introduction, learned and
    well illustrated, developing the principles of Alphand's work.

39. Alphand's funeral took place on December 11, in Notre Dame. The cortege,
    assembled at the Champ-de-Mars, crossed the Paris he had been so instru-
    mental in embellishing. His eulogy of Haussmann was, incidentally, not read
    and printed until December 26, 1891, nearly a year after the great prefect's
    death. There are two streets named for Alphand in Paris, one a simple *rue*,
    the other an avenue, and he early had a memorial statue. Haussmann's statue
    was not erected until 1989.

40. Merruau, p. 367.

41. Quoted in Lameyre, p. 52.

42. III, 122–23.

43. III, 201–2. As with all his technical innovations he was quite proud of his in-
    genuity, his use of technology to solve aesthetic problems.

44. III, 124.

45. III, 197.

46. Olsen, p. 170, quoting the *Builder* for 1869: "land, the value of which did not
    exceed from 1 franc 50 centimes to 6 francs the *mètre*, is now worth from 20
    francs to 100 francs the *mètre*. . . . On the surrounding land 487 châteaux or
    expensive villas . . . have been built."

47. Evans, p. 35: "I have been with him there myself, with M. Alphand, the chief
    engineer, when, having proposed some changes, the Emperor has taken a
    hammer from a workman, and planted a number of pickets with his own
    hands, to mark the line that in his opinion should be followed. He seemed to
    take great pleasure in indulging his taste for this kind of work."

48. III, 198. He goes on to specify that there were 612,511 meters covered in bro-
    ken stone, 189,400 meters of sanded pathway, 275,500 meters of paths that
    were not paved in any way, which together made 1,074,411 meters, or a total
    length of about 95 kilometers.

49. III, 185.

50. Quoted in Morizet, p. 192.

51. II, 514.

52. *Les Rougon-Macquart*, II, 1379.

53. Girard, *Travaux publics*, p. 168.

54. See Jacquemet, pp. 153–54.

55. Jacquemet, pp. 98–101. The population had a growth of 82 percent between 1836 and 1841, 67 percent between 1851 and 1856.

56. Quoted in Jacquemet, pp. 141–42.

57. Girard, *Deuxième République*, p. 123.

58. AN, C1063 (Préfecture de la Seine), "Documents relatifs à l'extension des limites de Paris" (1859), dossier 177, #19, "Rapport à l'Empereur," pp. 6, 8–9.

59. The prefects of Hautes-et Basses-Alpes, Lozère, and Pyrénées-Orientales administered, respectively, 130,000, 150,000, and 180,000 citizens. The Paris suburbs contained nearly as many residents as these three departments combined.

60. *Mémoire . . . sur l'extension*, pp. 24–25.

61. *Mémoire . . . sur l'extension*, p. 29.

62. *Mémoire . . . sur l'extension*, p. 29.

63. *Mémoire . . . sur l'extension*, p. 79.

64. Girard, *Deuxième République*, p. 126.

65. The report incorporated in his *Mémoire . . . sur l'extension* is an inquiry on annexation, in AN, F²II, 36–37.

66. Girard, *Travaux publics*, p. 168.

67. AN, 45AP 20, Haussmann to Rouher (September 15, 1867).

68. Evenson, p. 221. It was not until the years following World War I that the rapid growth of the suburbs took place. The War had enormously augmented the industrial development of Paris, with an accompanying increase in population and a consequent worsening of the housing problem. The eight-hour day (legislated in 1919) made long-distance commuting feasible, and improvements in low-cost commuter trains stimulated the movement out of Paris.

69. Lazare, pp. 95–112 records a long interview with a married couple who experience these dislocations.

70. Dalotel, Faure, Freiermuth, pp. 74–75.

71. Gaillard, p. 104.

72. Olsen, p. 146.

73. Gaillard, p. 67. The enhanced value of old houses due to the construction of new streets makes up 1,500,000 francs of this total.

74. Quoted in Olsen, p. 114.

75. Olsen, p. 114.

76. Quoted in Olsen, p. 181.

77. Fournel, pp. 71–72.

78. Misery in the countryside drove the rural population to Paris. "Paris thus gained 300,000 persons in fifteen years, from 1851 to 1866," according to Gaillard, p. 195. They sought "in the capital a stability that the town or the village had not given them."

79. Harvey, *Urban Experience*, p. 145.
80. *Conseil général* minutes (1857), p. 13, quoted by Sutcliffe, *Autumn of Central Paris*, p. 117.
81. Fournier, *Splendeurs*, II, 59.
82. Foucher de Careil, p. 134.
83. Gaillard, p. 213.
84. Gaillard, p. 211.
85. BN, NAF, *Papiers Picard*, 24370, #55 (March 22, 1861).
86. II, 457.
87. II, 459.
88. II, 461.
89. The characterization of urbanism by regulation is Françoise Choay's in *Histoire de la France urbaine*, IV, 168.
90. He treated hospitals with the same indifference. Girard, *Deuxième République*, p. 155, points out that the number of hospital beds remained unchanged under the empire, and no new structure was built after the Hôpital Lariboisière (1846–54). At the same time the number of sick seeking treatment increased steadily throughout the Second Empire.
91. *Mémoire . . . sur l'extension*, p. 10.
92. II, 453.

XIII. "The Vandalism of Triumph"

1. Dalotel, Faure, Friermuth, p. 105.
2. Dalotel, Faure, Friermuth, p. 98.
3. II, 233. Haussmann was describing the minister, Pierre-Jules Baroche, but the characterization was generic for him.
4. Ollivier, *L'Empire libéral*, XI, 426. He goes on to explain the tangle of financial arrangements Haussmann made to keep his work going.
5. Ernst Theodor Amadeus Hoffmann (1776–1822), famous for his bizarre tales. His *Phantasiestücke* of 1814 had been translated into French as *Contes fantastiques*, in 1830. In 1851 it was a successful play in Paris. Jacques Offenbach's last and most enduring opera, *The Tales of Hoffmann*, was first presented in 1880, three months after his death.
6. Ferry, p. 5.
7. Ferry, p. 62. A Marxist scholar, Harvey, *Urban Experience*, p. 10, makes much the same argument but using Marxist categories: "Such a system had its limits. It is hard to maintain surveillance and control in an economy when the circulation of capital is given free rein, where competition and technical progress race along side by side, sparking all manner of cultural movements and adaptations."
8. Haussmann's estimate (II, 335) is 1,088,979,394 francs. Cadoux, *Les Finances de*

la ville de Paris (quoted by Morizet, p. 328), gives a slightly higher figure (1,475,799,082 francs), and Cilleuls, again quoted by Morizet, p. 328, an even higher figure (2,904,313,409 francs). Haussmann's figure is probably too low, Cilleuls's too high. Cadoux, if one adds (as he suggests) another 43,000,000 francs—"to take account of the loan of 1869"—is closest with a sum of 1,518,799,082 francs. Morizet, p. 329, calculates the debt at 1,524,322,324 francs. He takes a memoir of the prefect Léon Say, himself an economist concerned with Haussmann's financial buccaneering, adds to it 57 million francs for the annuities that resulted from buying out various concessions (such as the toll bridges), and another 80 million francs for the annual charges included in Haussmann's budget. The enormous debt, incidentally, did not fall to his contemporaries to pay. The cost of rebuilding Paris was borne by the Third Republic.

9. See Ferry, p. 35, for the *bons de délégation*; p. 54 for his calculations of the city's debt; pp. 65–66 for his summary of municipal finances.

10. Claveau, I, 344: "The famous libel of Jules Ferry, *Les Comptes fantastiques d'Haussmann*, did not for an instant disturb his serenity."

11. Ferry, p. 17.

12. Ferry, p. 43.

13. Ferry, p. 67.

14. The phrase *douce tenacité* is Ollivier's, *L'Empire libéral*, XI, 423.

15. Mme Baroche, p. 492.

16. I quote all the speeches from Lan (p. 251), a convenient collection of the important speeches (pp. 250–327).

17. Lan, p. 255.

18. Lan, p. 253.

19. Claveau, I, 67, tells the anecdote, as do a few other contemporaries.

20. Lan, p. 256.

21. Lan, p. 257.

22. Lan, p. 269.

23. Lan, p. 271.

24. Lan, pp. 272–73. The criticism of the rue de Rennes is disingenuous. The reason it stopped short of the Seine is that to continue it from the boulevard St. Germain to the river would have meant tearing down Louis Le Vau's marvelous Institut, one of the finest seventeenth-century buildings in Paris. Even Haussmann balked at the prospect.

25. Lan, p. 272. Haussmann liked the remark well enough to repeat it in his *Mémoires* (II, 394) and insisted it was intended ironically. He prints a slightly different version than the one Thiers actually delivered: "They call M. Rouher vice-emperor; they flatter him. The vice-emperor is the prefect of the Seine." Haussmann's version is quoted by those who have not troubled to look at the debates.

26. Lan, p. 286.

27. Lan, p. 289.

28. Ollivier, *L' Empire libéral*, XI, 434.
29. Claveau, I, 346.
30. Ferragus, the director of the weekly *La Cloche*, wrote (April 24, 1869) unfairly but brilliantly, "In truth, M. Haussmann abuses the right of making fun of the Parisians. . . . His speech to the senate, as long as the rue Lafayette, as boring as the rue de Rivoli, as ornate as the new Opéra, as sentimental as certain locations, such as the Park Monceau, was, in the last analysis, as useless as the Park Buttes-Chaumont!" Quoted in Lameyre, p. 78.
31. Lan, p. 296.
32. Lan, p. 297.
33. Lan, pp. 303–5.
34. Lan, p. 316.
35. Lan, p. 318.
36. Lan, p. 319.
37. From a letter to Louis Napoléon, August 7, 1857, on the elections of that year. Quoted by Zeldin, *Political System*, p. 76.
38. II, 166–67.
39. II, 462.
40. See Ollivier, *L'Empire libéral*, XII, 357–58: "The Emperor had wanted to retain Haussmann. For my part I was against removing from government service a man of such administrative superiority." Claveau, I, 346–47, attributed this devotion to Haussmann's loyalty and wrote "it was born, they say, from a favorable impression that his presence of mind made upon Louis Napoléon, when he was president of the Republic, in a situation when Haussmann's height played the major role. They toured Bordeaux in an open carriage, and the prince was so diminutive next to his immense prefect that the population, the curious crowd wanting to catch a glimpse of [the prince-president] could hardly see him. He remarked on the contrast—for which his interlocutor was doubtless prepared for he responded immediately: 'It is perhaps the drum major they see when it is the general they are looking for!'"
41. Girard, *Deuxième République*, p. 397.
42. Girard, *Deuxième République* , p. 398.
43. From an undated note on Paris finances, BN, *Nouvelles acquisitions françaises*, 24.372, quoted in Gaillard, p. 68.
44. Claveau, I, 68.
45. Claveau, I, 242.
46. II, 64.

XIV. *Haussmann After Paris*

1. Quoted in Schnerb, p. 266.
2. Claveau, I, 343–44.

3. Halévy, II, 40. Chevreau was a senator, the prefect of the Rhone, and the *mayor central* of Lyons.

4. Baroche, pp. 571–76, is a source for all these details. She had access to a number of important officials of the empire, her husband having been one of Louis Napoléon's ministers.

5. Ollivier, *Journal*, II, 416.

6. Ollivier, *L' Empire libéral*, XII, 358–59.

7. II, 174.

8. Ferry, p. 5.

9. II, 185–87 is the entire address to the council. "Ah, Messieurs," he continued, "one must have courage and devotion to undertake public functions in France, to consecrate [to the public] efforts and abilities which, in the liberal professions, earns one independence and money at the same time, but which often only lead here to bitterness and scorn." Baroche, p. 575, quotes this speech from the *Constitutionnel*.

10. In II, 557, he quotes the speech made before the Senate on April 13, 1869, in the midst of the debates on the budget: "At whatever moment we leave the Hôtel de Ville, we will leave as we entered, head held high and with a firm heart, certain of having conducted ourselves as decent men, men of honor, faithful servants, with courage and resolution, and also with a tenacious loyalty and a devotion beyond reproach." He repeated the formula to Sherard in the last months of life.

11. Which of his numerous decorations did he wear on this occasion? A mere catalogue of those he had received is impressive. Grand-Croix of the Imperial Order of the Legion of Honor; Grand-Croix of the Order of St. Stanislas (Russia); Grand-Croix of the Order of Charles III (Spain); Grand-Croix of the Order of Notre-Dame of the Conception of Villa-Vicoza (Portugal); Grand-Croix of the Order of Guada Lupa (Mexico); Grand-Croix of the Order of Saints Maurice and Lazare (Italy); Grand-Croix of the Order of the Lion of Zaehringen (Baden); Grand-Croix of the Order of the Lion of the Sun (Persia); Grand-Croix of the Order of Danebrog (Denmark); member of the Order of the Red Eagle (Prussia); Grand commander of the Order of the Crown (Bavaria); commander of the Royal Order of Wasa (Sweden); commander of the Order of St. Louis (Parma); commander of the Order of Francis 1 (Naples), to name only the more notable.

12. II, 559–60. Baroche (pp. 573–75) tells this story as well, and with as many details. Did she lift it from Haussmann's *Mémoires* or have it on some other authority? The first explanation seems more likely.

13. Quoted in Lameyre, pp. 306–7.

14. Baroche, p. 603.

15. II, 564–66.

16. II, 568–69.

17. Ollivier, *L'Empire libéral*, XIII, 524–25. Through her secretary, Franceschini

Pietri, he inquired about the veracity of Haussmann's account. "The extract from [Haussmann's] *Mémoires* that M. Ollivier sent . . . is as inexact as that part [of the *Mémoires*] where it is said I was held at the baptismal font by Prince Eugène. It is absurd! The Emperor has always been loyal and a man of his word. As for myself, I do not remember having seen M. Haussmann and I have neither considered nor helped in the overthrow of the ministers." Pietri added to the empress's note: "For my own part, at no time did I know about the interview in question in this note." Haussmann had something of an obsession about being held at the baptismal font by Napoleon's son-in-law. Having invented an imperial lineage for himself, he then embellished it by insisting the same hands had held the empress: a kind of laying on of hands. Filon, p. 110, relates an anecdote from later in the year. "During the night of 8–9 [August 1870], around 2 a.m., being unable to sleep, she [the empress] summoned me and discussed, with perfect lucidity, the different available choices. How many names were put forward in the last forty-eight hours! How many combinations were proposed, imagined, rejected, taken up again and again rejected! Haussmann had been spoken of: the Right did not want him." Filon was another of Eugénie's secretaries and a man of probity. The anecdote raises the possibility of Haussmann's return to power. The Right, in this instance, are the dyed-in-the-wool Bonapartists, with whom Haussmann was never intimate. I don't think this bit of evidence alters my hypothesis that Haussmann heavily embroidered the interview with the emperor; but it does indicate that there was at least the possibility of reestablishing the authoritarian empire, and Haussmann was considered for some role. That his name came up only on the eve of the debacle of the Franco-Prussian War indicates it was a desperate, and perhaps impossible, proposal.

18. Halévy, II, 4.
19. II, 183.
20. In AN, *Inventaire* (cote 54) is a certificate stating that M. le Baron Haussmann is entitled to an annual civil pension of six thousand francs, payable the first of March, June, September, and December.
21. Zeldin, *Ollivier*, p. 106, quotes Napoleon III on Ollivier—from H. Oncken, *Die Rheinpolitik Kaisers Napoleon III von 1863 bis 1870* (Stuttgart, 1926), iii, 337): "Ollivier is certainly a man of talent: he is young still: he has a future before him and could achieve great things if he is properly guided. . . .[He] has two precious qualities which make me forget his defects. He has faith in me and he interprets my ideas eloquently, above all when I let him think they are his own." This could easily be a description of Haussmann.
22. Quoted in Lameyre, p. 310.
23. Quoted in Lameyre, pp. 312–13.
24. AN, $F^{1B}162^3$, pièces 259 and 262.
25. AD (Seine), GAZ 1014/11 (January 22, 1871).
26. AD (Seine), GAZ 1014/11 (February 22, 1871). The Prince Napoléon here is

Louis Napoléon's cousin, a mercurial and unreliable character whom Hauss-mann disliked and against whom he would later stand as a candidate for the Chamber of Deputies. Hence the exclamation point, for ironic emphasis.

27. II, 553.

28. My colleague, Prof. Marion Miller, kindly searched the Rome archives for the map and any Haussmann correspondence and found nothing of interest.

29. II, 554.

30. Evenson, p. 265.

31. The avenue de l'Opéra and the boulevard Henri IV were soon completed. The boulevard Raspail, begun in 1866, was not completed until 1913. The boulevard Haussmann was completed only in 1927.

32. BN, NAF, 12295 (February 17, 1871).

33. BN, NAF, 12295 (May 24, 1871).

34. Lameyre, p. 325. Des Cars is skeptical about this. I have been unable to verify the fact, one way or the other, but I incline toward Lameyre's account. I have found him not only a very well-informed biographer but a reliable one as well.

35. Marie Fanny Texier, Mme Haussmann's mother, died June 8, 1862. The *inven-taire* of the contents of the Château de Cestas, which were sold at her death, is in the AD (Gironde), 3E 26218, where the building itself is described as "in the chartreuse style with sub-basement and vaulted cellar, with a formal salon, a dining room, and diverse [other] rooms." Mme G. Dupin, a "member of the archeological society of Bordeaux," deposited in the Archives munici-paux de Bordeaux a nineteen-page typescript (the pages are unnumbered)— its *cote* is $S^{ix-c}/12$—on Cestas and adds some details. The structure was surrounded by woods and grassland, and had some grape vines. Dumas's son later sold the place, which eventually, passing through two intervening own-ers, was bought by Alphonse Daniel de LaHarpe, Mme Haussmann's father. Françoise Bellemer, the daughter of the current owner of the château, consid-ers this typescript inaccurate, but the details I mention here conform to other sources and appear to be based upon them.

36. This was the château de Rouillac and the domaine de Camparian, which had originally been owned by Paul Loret, the *président* of the Parlement of Bor-deaux (AD [Gironde], 3E 26228). The woods, which rounded out his hold-ings, were located at Argileyres and Croisière. These details are from a manuscript *résumé* of nearly seven hundred pages (pp. 8, 9, 16), drawn up at Haussmann's death and the settlement of his affairs. It is in the possession of the present owner of Cestas, Mme Bellemer, who kindly gave me access.

37. II, 539.

38. When I visited in 1991, the only original furniture remaining was Hauss-mann's enormous desk and map case, and the dining room table (that opened to seat forty-eight guests). The original chandeliers were gone, as were wall sconces and some pieces of external decorative ornament. The bookcases were empty, the only remaining volume from his library—which judging from

the shelves had been considerable—was a set of printed scenes of Paris, of no great interest. Mme Bellemer recalled the library filled with books bound in blue leather stamped with Haussmann's coat of arms when she was a child growing up here. The *résumé* of 1891 (p. 641-B/2) does not specify how many books there were, referring only to "the books contained in the libraries," which were excluded in the sale of the estate. The Bellemers did not recall any personal papers when their family acquired the château in the 1920s. The *résumé* (p. 644) additionally specifies the following items that were not included in the sale of Cestas: "a Louis XVI pendulum clock in M. le Baron Haussmann's study, two Louis XIV arm-chairs, with cushions covered in old silk, a set of Louis XV [furniture] from the square salon, including two *canapés*, four cushions and four arm-chairs, a porcelain service consisting of 189 plates, four soup tureens, three salad bowls, four sugar bowls, and thirty-eight plates, decorated with garlands and green ornamentation, and, from the office at the entry, a wall chronometer." Also excluded from the sale were the wines stored in Haussmann's cellar. Espagnet, otherwise uninformative, has very good photographs of the château when she visited on February 26, 1970, before the robbery, and some useful physical details. What I describe in the text of the furnishings and decorations is drawn from this source, from photographs made, alas, after the robbery, and from the *résumé*. Haussmann himself provided no physical description of Cestas in his *Mémoires*.

39. The use of these arms, granted originally to his maternal grandfather by Napoléon I, was, as with his title of baron, strictly speaking inappropriate. He was claiming to be recuperating the title, but in French law titles could not be passed through the maternal parent, and Napoléon III had never confirmed either title or arms. See a description of the arms in Valynseele, p. 35, and the photograph of the arms over the door of Cestas reproduced therein.

40. Françoise Bellemer, still shocked at the robbery that stripped the house, would not allow these to be photographed and reproduced, lest they attract other thieves. She told me of a racket practiced by thieves. They would examine the photographs of grand houses in the region offered for sale by real estate agents. If the pictures revealed furnishings or decorations worth stealing, they would burgle the unoccupied house.

41. AN, *Inventaire*, March 27, 1891. For Baltard's work see the papers relating to Cestas in AN, 332 AP5 (*Papiers Baltard*). There are fifteen separate items, including drawings, letters, and accounts. There are no personal letters from Haussmann to Baltard. Although Haussmann had known Baltard since their school days together, he did not directly correspond with him. Théodore Duphot, a Bordeaux architect, was in charge of the actual work at Cestas and apparently conveyed Haussmann's wishes. Yet another broken or nonexistent paper trail. I have found no substantial collection of letters from Haussmann to any of the architects he worked with.

42. AN, 332 AP5 (*Papiers Baltard*) (Cestas), "Relevé des comptes réglés par M.

Duphot, architecte, pour travaux executés sous sa direction aux châteaux de Cestas et de Rouillac, à Monsieur le Baron Haussmann." The orangery (letter of November 21, 1867) cost 29,407 francs, a tower on the main building 33,959 francs (and he thought it would cost even more when finished).

43. AN, *Inventaire*, cote 84, 85, 86, 90, 93, 96, 103. Unfortunately, those making the inventory only describe these letters—which have since vanished—in the most general terms (subject and number of letters).

44. Cited in Larousse, *Grand Dictionnaire universel au XIXème siècle*, XVI (deuxième partie), 941.

45. Claveau, I, 68.

46. Haussmann, *Les ruines des Tuileries*, pp. 2, 7–8.

47. Sherard, p. 103.

48. Larousse, *Grand Dictionnaire universel au XIXème siècle*, XVII (troisième partie), p. 1369.

49. AN, 400 AP 192, (August 15, 1888), from his speech to the Comités Impérialistes Napoléonniens de Paris et de la Seine.

50. There are fourteen letters from Haussmann to Victor Napoléon, four letters from Victor Napoléon to Haussmann. All are in AN, 400 AP 192.

51. AN, 400 AP 192 (Cestas, September 19, 1887).

52. AN, 400 AP 192 (Paris, December 6, 1887), to Ernest-Edmond Blanc.

53. AN, 400 AP 192 (Paris, March 30, 1888).

54. AN, 400 AP 192 (Cestas, October 29, 1889).

55. AN, 400 AP 192, speech to Comités Impérialistes Napoléonniens, August 15, 1888.

56. AN, 400 AP 192 (Paris, April 18, 1888).

57. Quoted in Lameyre, p. 331.

58. The two letters, undated, are in the AD (Seine), GAZ 1014/9 and 1014/10.

59. Sherard, p. 113.

60. Quoted in Lameyre, p. 334.

61. This account is taken from *Le Temps*, January 16, 1891, which is the most detailed description of Haussmann's funeral. M. Delaborde, the perpetual secretary of the Académie des Beaux-Arts, spoke at the graveside, as did M. Blanche, Georges Berry, and Marius Martin (the former a deputy for Paris, the latter a municipal counsellor).

62. Haussmann had been elected to the academy on December 7, 1866. Mme Baroche remarked in her diary: "How was he so easily selected for admission? Nothing is easier to understand: the prefect has each year an infinite number of paintings and sculpture to commission. It is in everyone's interest to flatter him." Quoted in Lameyre, p. 75.

63. *Discours de M. Alphand sur M. le Baron Haussmann* (lu à l'Académie des Beaux-Arts, le 26 décembre 1891), reprinted in *Mémoires*. The passages quoted are, respectively, III, v, viii, and iii.

64. I, ix.

65. I, v–vi.

XV. Paris After Haussmann

1. These figures, reached by comparing the various estimates, are from Rials, p. 135. The author points out that Strasbourg was far more severely bombarded, suffering twelve thousand shells in five days. Howard, p. 361, adds: "For this attack on the civilian population, as for that at Strasbourg, there was no military reason. Its only excuse, and it was to be one increasingly used by belligerents of all lands with equally little justification, was that by directly attacking their morale it would incline the stubborn Parisians the earlier to peace." The shelling, he confirms, "did astonishingly little damage" and "Parisians at first flocked curiously to the Left Bank, which bore the brunt of the bombardment, and were disappointed to find how little could be seen."

2. Rials, pp. 137–8. Along with the rue Monge, the rues du Tombe-Issoire, de la Chaussée-du-Maine, and du faubourg St. Jacques were the others seriously damaged. Otherwise the damage to houses was scattered and relatively minor. Of the public buildings, nine barracks, five convents, and eight schools were hit, among the latter the Collège de France, the *grands écoles* Normale and Polytechnique, and the Sorbonne. The seventeenth-century dome of the Sorbonne was seriously damaged. Seven churches were hit, including the Panthéon, whose marvelous dome was damaged, and St. Germain-des-Prés (the oldest church tower in Paris). Sixteen hospitals were hit, including the great seventeenth-century dome of the Val-de-Grâce, as were six museums. The damage suffered by the collections of the Luxembourg Palace, as well as the loss of its outbuildings, was irreparable. Four Paris prisons also suffered damage. For a fuller account see Sarrepont, which Rials cites. The Prussian gunners targeted the monuments of Paris, clearly visible from their emplacements, none of which had any military significance.

3. Lefebvre, p. 258.

4. Lefebvre, p. 261.

5. All these details are from Lefebvre, pp. 272–74.

6. Dalotel, Faure, Freiermuth, p. 122.

7. Dalotel, Faure, Freiermuth, p. 98.

8. Quoted from an article in *Le Sémaphore de Marseille*, for which Zola was the Paris correspondent, in February-May 1871, by Furet, p. 489. There are no accurate figures of Communards killed during Bloody Week. Estimates range from 15,000 to 40,000, with 25,000 being a frequent choice of historians. Most died in the actual street fighting, which by the end had become suicidal for the Communards. Many who survived were summarily shot.

9. The column had a full history. On its site had originally stood a statue of Louis XIV, the builder of the *place*. This was destroyed in 1792. Napoléon's

monument, officially named the "Column of Austerlitz," in commemoration of his greatest victory, was built between 1806 and 1810, and modeled after the column of Trajan, in Rome. Its 266 bronze bas-relief plaques, depicting scenes from the battle, spiraled up the column. They were cast in metal melted from captured canon. In 1814 the statue of Napoléon was taken down and replaced by a gigantic fleur-de-lis, surmounted by a white flag, the symbols of the just restored Bourbon kings. In 1830 these symbols were in turn removed and another statue of Napoléon, this time in greatcoat and cocked hat, was erected. The July Monarchy, favorable to a rehabilitation of Napoléon, reintegrated him into the nation's history. Around the same time his remains were returned to France from St. Helena and buried in the church of St. Louis, at the Invalides. The Second Empire replaced the simple statue of Napoléon in the Place Vendôme with another depiction of the first emperor as Roman hero. It is this last representation of Napoléon that was thrown down. The column was rebuilt by the Third Republic and eventually a version of the original Roman Napoléon was placed atop the monument, where it remains.

10. See Blanc for a description of these lost treasures. Haussmann wrote Frémy (BN, NAF, 12295, May 24, 1871) of his fear "that the energy of M. Thiers, overexcited at the moment by the ruin of his house, was not equal to the task" of recapturing Paris, for which he would need not only all his energy but "all the energies of the great party of order, without distinction of opinions or precedents."

11. Descriptions, contemporary photographs, and bibliographical references are in Rials, pp. 471–80.

12. Marx, *Civil War*, p. 94.

13. Louis Enault, *Paris brûlé par la Commune* (Paris, 1871), quoted by Rials, p. 471.

14. To this incomplete list should be added the following, taken from Rials, pp. 482–83: the Palais Royal (only slightly burned); the Assistance publique (avenue Victoria); the Théâtre-Lyrique; the Direction de l'Artillerie, Poudres et Salpêtres (Place de l'Arsenal); the grain storehouses d'Abondance in the boulevard Bourdon, the rue de Crimée, and the Quai de la Loire; the Protestant Temple (rue St. Antoine); part of the Luxembourg Palace; part of the barracks in the Quai d'Orsay (formerly the hôtel d'Egmont); the archives of the Cour des Comptes; the Hôtel de Praslins (rue de Lille); the Théâtre de la Porte St. Martin; the Théâtre des Délassements comiques (boulevard Voltaire); part of the Magasins Réunis; the Eglise de Bercy; the Entrepôt des Denrées Coloniales; the Usines Lapostolet; the Magasins Trottot; and some minor damage to the gares Montparnasse and d'Orléans. For the historian the greatest losses were the city and departmental archives, stored in the Hôtel de Ville, a building of considerable historical and artistic value. A good deal of the evidence for Haussmann's prefecture was destroyed at this time, as

well as all that the Hôtel de Ville contained, including a library of 100,000 volumes, and a unique collection of plans and maps—plausibly including the famous sketch by the emperor. For an account of what was burned in the Archives de la Seine, see Lamouroux for the details.

15. There was also considerable destruction in the rues du faubourg St. Honoré, Royale, St. Martin, de la Tacherie, de la Coutellerie, du Bac, Vavin, de Bondy, du faubourg St. Martin, de Crimée, the avenue Victoria, and the boulevards Mazas, Sébastopol, Beaumarchais, des Amandiers, the quais de Gèvres and de Valmy, the places du Château d'Eau and Hôtel de Ville, and the Porte de Bercy. Without counting those houses in western Paris destroyed by bombardment, two hundred individual houses were also burned during the street fighting.

16. Rials, p. 509 (author's italics). See pp. 495–509 for a discussion of the evidence and the historiography. Karl Marx, p. 93, passionately pleads the Communard case: "The Commune used fire strictly as a means of defense. They used it to stop up to the Versailles troops those long, straight avenues, which Haussmann had expressly opened to artillery fire; they used it to cover their retreat, in the same way as the Versaillais, in their advance, used their shells which destroyed at least as many buildings as the fire of the Commune."

17. *La Curée, Les Rougons-Macquart*, I, 387–88. The most famous panoramas of Paris in Zola are those in *Une Page d'amour, Les Rougons-Macquart*, II, 845–55, 902–12, 964–74, 1024–34, and 1083–92. The novel is cast in five parts, each containing five chapters, each of which concludes with a panorama from the Trocadéro (except the last of these, which is a view of Paris from the Père Lachaise cemetery). About 20 percent of the novel is given over to descriptions of Paris. Zola considered these bird's-eye reveries, especially the first, among the best pages he had written. Flaubert, otherwise favorably disposed toward Zola, thought them exaggerated. See Kranowski, p. 49. None of these descriptions, incidentally, speaks specifically of Haussmann's Paris as an act of destruction, although monuments erected by him or during the grands travaux—the Opéra, Ste.-Clothilde, St. Augustin—are singled out.

18. Quoted by Lameyre, p. 279.

19. Sherard, p. 102.

20. Quoted by des Cars, p. 282.

21. From his *Paris in Old and Present Times* (London, 1892), quoted by Olsen, p. 231.

22. Olsen, p. 219.

23. Chevalier, *Assassination*, pp. 44–66, has the best discussion of the impact of the car and what the disappearance of trees has meant for Paris. Not only has the city been deforested in favor of stone, but pedestrian space has been consistently sacrificed to the car. Cornu, pp. 94–95, describes another recent phenomenon, the dislocation of population by commerce. Between 1876 and 1936 banks and commercial enterprises drove 17 pecent of the population of

the ninth arrondissement to new *quartiers*, a good part of whom were the bourgeoisie who had thronged the boulevards. The forced emigration was enough to change the nature and composition of boulevard life in this neighborhood, the home of the Grands Boulevards.

24. *Confession d'un enfant du siècle*, Musset, *Oeuvres complètes*, XI.

25. Quoted by Russell, pp. 106–7.

26. Quoted in Olsen, p. 223, from *La Duchesse de Langeais*.

27. Russell, p. 213.

28. *Illusions perdues*, Balzac, *La Comédie humaine*, IV, 257.

29. Russell, p. 111.

30. Nord, p. 70.

31. Nord, p. 97.

32. See Nord, p. 83, for a list of the shops near Au Bon Marché that thrived. The "politics of resentment" is his designation for characterization of the ideology of those who joined the right-wing *Ligue Syndicale*.

33. Gaillard, p. 560. Haussmann mistakenly feared insurrection would come from the city gates and the factories located in the outer arrondissements. But in the Commune the fighters were not drawn from this source. They came, rather, from the old working-class neighborhoods of St. Antoine and St. Marcel, which had furnished street fighters since the days of the French Revolution.

34. Sutcliffe, *Autumn of Cental Paris*, p. 27.

35. Olsen, p. 230.

36. Gaillard, p. 224.

37. Gaillard, p. 622, n. 16.

38. His much cited line, "The old Paris is no more (the form of a city/Alas, changes more quickly than a human heart);" from the poem "The Swan," in *Les Fleurs du mal*, can be read not so much as a lament over the destruction of Old Paris, which he seems not to have regretted, as a more general lament about our difficulties in coming to terms with the present, the inevitable clash between ourselves and our physical universe.

39. Baudelaire, II, 110–13.

40. Quoted in Tulard, *Nouvelle histoire*, p. 432.

41. Quoted in Gaillard, p. 12.

42. *Mémoire presenté. . .sur l'extension des limites de Paris*, p. 29.

43. AN, AP 452, (Papiers Rouher), December 15, 1857.

44. Merriman, *Red City*, p. xiii: By the end of the century "Paris had become more frequently a scene of nationalist demonstrations than left-wing insurgency."

45. The most outspoken are Jeanne Gaillard and Pierre Lavedan, often quoted in these pages, and Richard Sennett.

46. Loyer, p. 219.

47. Loyer, p. 325.

48. Girard, *Deuxième République*, p. 241.
49. Saalman, p. 116.
50. Cornu, p. 34.
51. *Lettres à Viollet-le-Duc*, June 6, 1867, p. 211. The French word is *meublera*.
52. Quoted by Pinon, *Paris-Haussmann*, p. 181.
53. *La Curée, Les Rougons-Macquart*, I, 332.
54. Lortsh, p. 33. Quoted by Evenson, p. 153 (her translation).
55. Loyer is the most persuasive proponent of urban complexity and subtlety and sums up a long reconsideration of Haussmann's work. The architect Paul Maigmont, a professor at the Ecole des Beaux-Arts, told an interviewer for *Connaissance des arts* (1979): "I wanted simply to say that there are certain qualities [in Haussmann's architecture] that we ought to rediscover. It had the capacity to express the difference of the epoch. Maybe this was not what was sought, but it is there in Haussmann's architecture. There is a perfectly sympathetic mixture of genres. There is always harmony, and this is what we have forgotten."
56. *Paris*, in *Oeuvres complètes* (*Politique*), p. 11. Hugo wrote this essay in 1867 for inclusion in a collection of essays by the great French writers issued on the occasion of the universal exposition held in Paris that year.
57. Bacon, p. 193.
58. There is no more eloquent, passionate, or erudite lover of Paris than Louis Chevalier, who believed the destruction of the markets in the 1970s—he has movingly written the funeral oration for les Halles—meant the death of Paris itself. See *Assassination*, pp. 237–45.
59. *Le Ventre de Paris, Les Rougon-Macquart*, I, 799. The 1937 *Guide Bleu* recommended reading *Le Ventre de Paris, Au Bonheur des dames*, and *L'Assommoir* for the markets, the *grands magasins*, and the neighborhood of Goutte d'Or, respectively.
60. From Louis Napoléon's coup d'état to his defeat in the Franco-Prussian War.
61. Zola, *La Cloche*, "Le nettoyage de Paris sous Haussmann," June 8, 1872, in "Lettres parisiennes," II, 78.
62. Gaillard, pp. 86–87, 91.
63. Evenson, p. 71: "the historic and aesthetic value of the Latin Quarter at last seemed sufficient to counterbalance the need for expanded traffic circulation."
64. From his *Notes de vieillesse*, quoted by Gaillard, p. 562.
65. Quoted in Combes, p. 77.
66. II, 32.
67. II, 196.

· WORKS CITED ·

UNPUBLISHED SOURCES

Archives Nationales (AN)

AB XIX (fonds divers)	Papers found in the study of Napoléon III in the Tuileries, September 1870.
AB XIX 2837	Dossier 3, undated letter from Haussmann.
AB XIX 3301	Dossier 9, undated letter from Haussmann.
AB XIX 3323	Dossier 3, undated letter from Haussmann, letter from Mocquart.
AB XIX 3326	Dossier 1, letter from Mocquart.
AB XIX 3357	Dossier 1, undated letter from Haussmann.
AB XIX 3375	Dossier 7, letter from Mocquart.
BB³⁰ 366	Miscellaneous documents, including reports to the minister of the interior from the prefect of police on conditions in Paris (1851–59).
BB³⁰ 366	Report from prefect of police (autumn 1856) on high price of food, on unemployment, and papers relative to the demolitions in the zone.
BB¹¹ 4056 7095	Valentine's will (cannot be consulted).
C 1058 (dossier 169)	Haussmann's *Mémoire* on new streets, some *procès ver-*

	baux of the Municipal Council. Letter from Haussmann to president of the Conseil d'Etat on the boulevard Malesherbes and the rue de Rome.
C 1063	Documents on the extension of Paris, including notes for Haussmann's *Mémoire* on the extension.
C 1067	Some documents on the Crédit Foncier.
C 1146	Collection of *Mémoires* by Haussmann to the Municipal Council and Devinck's reports on the Caisse des Travaux.
C 1077	Documents on the Opéra.
C 1102	Authorization to borrow 250 million *livres* (1865).
C 1147	Documents relating to the *grands travaux*, immediately after Haussmann's sacking.
ET/XVII/1456	The inventory made after Haussmann's death.
ET/XXXI/1302–1307	Documents relating to Haussmann's will.
F^{1B} 162^3	Haussmann's official file and dossier.
F^{1C} I 3^7	Contains a few reports from Haussmann as prefect of the Gironde.
F^{1C} III (Gironde) 6	Several official reports in Haussmann's hand on the political, moral, material, economic, and administrative situation in Bordeaux (December 1851–June 1853).
F^{1C} III (Gironde) 9	Letters to minister of the interior on reorganizing the police in Bordeaux, political conditions in Bordeaux, defending his actions on the Commission Mixte, on touring his department, building a railroad from Bordeaux to Bayonne, opposing the emperor's clemency.
F^{1C} III (Seine) 30	A few letters to Haussmann at the beginning of his tenure as prefect of the Seine.
F^{1C} III (Seine) 31	Documents on the rue de Rivoli, jurisdictional conflicts between the prefect of police and the prefect of the Seine, "Rapport sur la salubrité de l'eau de la Seine, entre le pont d'Ivry et St. Ouen, considérée comme eau potable." A number of these documents are accompanied by Haussmann's written responses.
F^{12} CIII 31	Documents on the relations of Haussmann with other public authorities, and the construction of the rue de Rivoli.
F^{12} 2370–74	Documents on salaries, some correspondence of Devinck with members of the *chambres syndicales ouvrières* in 1867

and petitions, a number of them concerning salaries, from those employed on the *grands travaux*.

F¹⁴ 10912/143 — Register of deliberations of the General Council of Bridges and Roadways (1862).

F²¹ 825 — Documents concerning jurisdiction over the equestrian statue of Henri IV on the Pont-Neuf, the equestrian statue of Louis XIV in the Place des Victoires, and other public monuments.

3Q 4964 — Registre de Recette. Déclarations des mutations par décès. The settlement of Haussmann's estate at his death.

45 AP — Rouher papers. (45 AP 2) contains correspondence with the emperor; (45 AP 3) contains two letters from Haussmann; (45 AP 6) contains documents on reunions and strikes; (45 AP 18) is an unsigned analysis of city finances; (45 AP 19) is an unsigned analysis of the principles of Bonapartism as applied to the government of Paris; (45 AP 20) contains correspondence with Haussmann; (45 AP 24) contains documents on the new Opéra and plans for the Universal Exposition of 1867.

87 AP 7 — Letter from Baron Travot.

112 AP 2 — Letters of Mocquard (1853–60).

115 AP 7 — Letter from Marcotte de Quivières.

116 AP — Morny papers (only a list of prefects).

160 AP — Papers of Cardinal Donnet.

223 AP 6 — Letter from Mocquard (February 25, 1855).

246 AP 5 — Nine letters from Mocquard (1853–56).

332 AP 4 — Baltard papers (decorations at the Hôtel de Ville, abbatoirs at la Villette, reconstruction of the Hôtel de Ville).

332 AP 5 — Baltard papers (work at Cestas).

400 AP 192 — Correspondence with the prince imperial.

Archives Departemental (AD)

l'Ariège

1M 111 — Sous-préfets of St. Girons.

5M 62 — Political attitudes of various functionaries.

5M 132 — Carlist refugees (1816–1908).

3Z 32*   Sous-préfecture of St. Girons: transcription of the correspondence with the prefect (July 1838–March 28, 1840).

3Z 62*   Sous-préfecture of St. Girons: transcription of the correspondence with the mayors and functionaries (December 10, 1839–May 4, 1841).

Gironde

3E 26134   Haussmann's act of marriage.

3E 26228   Purchase of the house and property of Rouillac (October 6, 1864).

3E 26240   Land transaction involving Cestas.

5K 80–83   Registers of the Conseil de Préfecture, recording routine business (Haussmann never attended).

2N 174–79   Procès-verbaux of the deliberations of the council of Blaye.

2N 198–99   Reports of the heads of bureaux, with some correspondence (Blaye).

4 N 8   Documents on buildings in Blaye.

4N 70   Documents concerning the acquisition of property for the sous-préfet's residence (Blaye).

4N 103   Documents concerning construction of the Civil Tribunal (Blaye).

4N 256   Inventories, upkeep, acquisitions to public buildings (Blaye).

4N 277   Documents relating to the Palais de Justice (Blaye).

4N 278   Documents relating to the Tribunal de Commerce (Blaye).

Lot-et-Garonne

M 2 B   Documents relating to the sous-préfets of Nérac. Unclassified and not available for consultation.

Seine

D^7 P^2 91 (dépôt IV)   Registers (18) concerning demolitions, new construction, and the change in tax liability (1846–54).

DQ 12236–38   Haussmann's "succession."

DZ[17]	Lazare Collection of contemporary newspaper clippings and brochures on the transformation of Paris.
GAZ 1014	Letters (18) from 1862–84.
VD⁶ 486	"Déplacement de la population vers la rive droite," description of changes in neighborhood that became the new seventh arrondissement.
2 AZ 180 (10)	Letter.
2 AZ 180 (11)	Letter.
2 AZ 272 (1)	Report to minister of interior on Caisse de Travaux.
2 AZ 272 (3)	Letter.
2 AZ 272 (8)	Letter.
3 AZ 161 (11)	Letter.
3 AZ 161 (12)	Letter.
4 AZ 1380 (1)	Letter.
4 AZ 1380 (8)	Letter.
5 AZ 25	Letter.
7 AZ 250 C 159	Letter.
8 AZ 1101 C 196	Letter.

Var

4 M 1–60	Documents on *"police politique."*
4 M 16	Correspondence on *"l'esprit public,"* on the Revolution of 1848, and on political activity.

Archives Municipales (AM)

Bordeaux

Antoine Gautier	Eighty-four manuscript volumes (1832–81) of his *Memorandum*.
Fonds Delpit, série B	Engravings of nineteenth-century Bordeaux.
S^{ix-c}/12	Typescript on Haussmann château, Cestas.

Paris (BHVP)

1070, Fol. 280	Haussmann's order to strike commemorative medals.
1134, Fol. 265	Haussmann's order to print atlas of Paris.

3392   Letter.

3456   Note on neighborhood near the Louvre.

3636   Documents relating to the construction of the church of
                         St. Vincent de Paul. Letters (39) to Haussmann from
                         Hittorff.

4746 (série 110)   Letters to Haussmann requesting invitations to social
                         events at the Hôtel de Ville. Manuscript report (33
                         pages) arguing for suppression of dual prefectship of
                         Paris, and a letter from Haussmann.

Bibliotheque Nationale (BN)

NAF (Nouvelles acquisitions françaises)

NAF 449 13–14   Letter.

NAF 12295   "Lettres de G.-E. Haussmann, préfet de l'Yonne
                        (1850–51) au secrétaire du ministère de l'Intérieur
                        Frémy." 133 *feuillets*.

NAF 13581 #47   Letter.

NAF 22554   Letter.

NAF 22553 #268   Letter to Haussmann.

NAF 24208   Three notes.

NAF 24370–72   Picard Papers, containing some information on Hauss-
                        mann as prefect.

NAF 24638 #190   Letter.

NAF 24642 #237   Letter on behalf of Mlle Cellier.

Printed Official Documents

Archives départementale de la Gironde, Répertoire numérique détaillé de la série M.
          2 vols. Bordeaux, 1979. Contains Haussmann's letter to
          the minister of the interior distancing himself from his
          father-in-law's evangelical views.

Recueil des actes administratifs du département de la Gironde, nos. 257 to 319
          (1851).

———, deuxième série, tome IV (n.d.).

———, deuxième série, tome V (1852). Contains Haussmann's orders for Louis
          Bonaparte's Bordeaux visit.

———, deuxième série, tome VI (1853).

Sessions de la Commission Départementale de la Seine. Bibliothèque Administrative de l'Hôtel de Ville. One volume for each year.

Miscellaneous

The current owners of Cestas, the Bellemer family, have a bound manuscript volume of more than seven hundred pages containing notarial records of the settlement of the estate at Haussmann's death. This appears to be, at least in part, the family's copy of many documents in Haussmann's "succession" filed in Paris at his death.

Henriette Espagnet, *Le Baron Haussmann par lui-même . . . dans le cadre du château de Cestas, au cours de la visite des domaines d'Haussmann* (Bordeaux, 1971), contains a dozen photographs of the house as it was in 1970, before the robbery.

PUBLISHED SOURCES

Alexandre-Théodore Brongniart, 1739–1813. Architecture et décor. Musée Carnavalet, 22 avril–13 juillet 1986. Paris, 1986.

Atlas des anciens plans de Paris: reproduction en fac-simile des originaux les plus rares et les plus intéressants pour l'histoire de la topographie parisienne. Paris, 1880.

Atlas des travaux de Paris. Paris, 1889.

Charles Marville, photographie de Paris de 1851–1879: Bibliothèque historique de la Ville de Paris, 21 novembre 1980–31 janvier 1981. Paris: Bibliothèque historique de la Ville de Paris, 1980.

Eloge de M. de Tourny, ancien intendant de la Guyenne, discours par F. J. . . . T. Perigueux, 1809.

Histoire de la France urbaine, tome 3, *La Ville classique, de la Renaissance aux révolutions.* ed. Emmanuel Le Roy Ladurie. Paris: Editions du Seuil, 1981.

Histoire de la France urbaine, tome 4, *La Ville de l'âge industriel, le cycle haussmannien.* ed. Maurice Agulhon. Paris: Editions du Seuil, 1983.

L'Ancien Hôtel de Ville et la place de Grève. Exposition. Musée Carnavalet, juin–août 1975. Paris, 1975.

L'Illustration. Journal universel. Paris, 1843ff.

Les Grands Boulevards. Musée Carnavalet, 25 juin–20 octobre 1985. Paris, 1985.

Nouveau guide de l'étranger à Bordeaux. Bordeaux, 1856.

Nouveaux conducteur de l'etranger à Bordeaux. Bordeaux, 1843.

Paris dans sa splendeur, 2 vols., Paris, 1861.

Paris-Haussmann, "Le pari d'Haussmann." ed. Jean Des Cars and Pierre Pinon. Paris: Editions du Pavillon de l'Arsenal, Picard, 1991.

Agulhon, Maurice. *La République au village: Les Populations du Var de la Révolution à la deuxième République.* Paris: Editions du Seuil, 1979.

———. "Le Baron Haussmann, préfet du Var (1848–50) d'après ses *Mémoires.*" *Provence histoire,* VI, no. 24 (1956).

———. *Pénitents et francs-maçons de l'ancienne Provence: Essai sur la sociabilité méridonale.* Paris: Fayard, 1984.

Alphand, Alphonse. *Les Promenades de Paris,* 2 vols. Paris: Rothschild, 1867–73.

Amann, Peter H. *Revolution and Mass Democracy: The Paris Club Movement in 1848.* Princeton: Princeton University Press, 1975.

An Architect. "An Epistolary Chat from Paris." *Builder* (June 1852).

Bacon, Edmund N. *Design of Cities.* New York: Penguin, 1974.

Ballon, Hilary. *The Paris of Henri IV: Architecture and Urbanism.* Cambridge, Mass: MIT Press, 1991.

Baltard, Victor and Callet, Félix-Emmanuel. *Monographie des Halles centrales de Paris construites sous le règne de Napoléon III et sous l'administration de M. le Baron Haussmann, sénateur, préfet du département de la Seine.* Paris: Morel, 1863.

Balzac, Honoré de. *La Comédie humaine.* Texte établi et préface par Marcel Bouteron, 11 vols. Paris: Gallimard (Pléiade), 1949–59.

Balzac, Honoré de, trans. Marion Ayton Crawford. *Cousin Bette.* London: Penguin, 1965.

Barbiche, Bernard. *Sully.* Paris: A. Michel, 1978.

Baroche, Mme Jules. *Second Empire, notes et souvenirs.* Paris: Editions G. Crès, 1921.

Baudelaire, Charles. *Les Fleurs du mal.* Paris: Poulet-Malassis, 1857.

Belgrand, Eugène. *Les Travaux souterrains de Paris.* 5 vols. Paris: Dunod, 1873.

Benevolo, Leonardo, trans. Judith Landry. *The Origins of Modern Town Planning.* Cambridge, Mass.: MIT Press, 1963.

Bernadau, Pierre. *Histoire de Bordeaux.* Bordeaux, 1837.

Bernard, Leon. *The Emerging City. Paris in the Age of Louis XIV.* Durham: Duke University Press, 1970.

Bertier de Sauvigny, Guillaume. *Nouvelle Histoire de Paris: La Restauration, 1815–1830.* Paris: Hachette, 1977.

Billy, André, trans. Margaret Shaw. *The Goncourt Brothers.* New York, 1960.

Blanc, Charles. *Le Cabinet de M. Thiers.* Paris: Renouard, 1871.

Blayau, Noël. *Billault, ministre de Napoléon III, d'après ses papiers personnels, 1805–1863*. Paris: Klincksieck, 1969.

Boussard, Jacques. *Nouvelle Histoire de Paris: De la fin du siège de 885–886 à la mort de Philippe Auguste*. Paris: Hachette, 1976.

Cadène, J. *L'Eglise réformée de Bordeaux, aperçu historique*. Bordeaux, 1892.

Caro, Robert A. *The Power Broker: Robert Moses and the Fall of New York*. New York: Knopf, 1975.

Caspard, Pierre. "Aspects de la lutte des classes en 1848: Le recrutement de la garde nationale mobile." *Revue historique* (1974).

Cavignac, Jean. *Les vingt-cinq Familles: Les négociants bordelais sous Louis-Philippe*. Bordeaux: Les Cahiers de l'I.A.E.S., 1985.

Cerdá, Ildefonoso. *La Théorie générale de l'urbanisation*. Présentée et adaptée par Antonio Lopez et Aberasturi. Paris: Editions du Seuil, 1979.

Chagniot, Jean. *Nouvelle Histoire de Paris: Paris au XVIIIème siècle*. Paris: Hachette, 1988.

Chapman, J. M. and Brian. *The Life and Times of Baron Haussmann: Paris in the Second Empire*. London: Weidenfeld & Nicholson, 1957.

Charles, Albert. "L'Isolement de Bordeaux et l'insuffisance des voies de communication en Gironde au début du Second Empire." *Annales du Midi* 72, no. 49 (janvier 1960).

———. "La modernisation du port de Bordeaux." *Revue historique de Bordeaux et la Gironde* (1962).

———. *La Révolution de 1848 et le Second République à Bordeaux et dans le département de la Gironde*. Bordeaux: Delmas, 1945.

———. "Portrait intellectual d'un grand bourgeois bordelais du milieu du siècle dernier, d'après ses impressions de lecture et de théâtre." *Revue historique de Bordeaux et du département de la Gironde* (1961).

———. "Un Exemple de carrière administrative dans la première moitié du siècle dernier: Le Baron Neveux, préfet de la Gironde de 1848 à 1851." *Revue historique de Bordeaux et du département de la Gironde* (1954).

Chaslin, François. *Les Paris de François Mitterrand*. Paris: Gallimard, 1985.

Chevalier, Louis, trans. David P. Jordan. *The Assassination of Paris*. Chicago: University of Chicago Press, 1993.

———. Collection présentée par. *La Choléra: La première Épidémie du XIXème siècle*. La Roche-sur-Yon, France: Bibliothèque de la Révolution de 1848, 1958.

Clark, T. J. *The Painting of Modern Life: Paris in the Art of Manet and His Followers*. Princeton: Princeton University Press, 1984.

Claveau, Anatole. *Souvenirs politiques et parlementaires d'un témoin*, 2 vols. Paris: Plon, 1913.

Cobb, Richard. *The Streets of Paris*. London: Duckworth, 1980.

Coetlogon, A. de and Tisserand, L. M. *Histoire générale de Paris, collection de documents publiée sous les auspices de l'édilité parisienne. Les armoiries de la ville de Paris, sceaux, emblèmes, couleurs, devises, livrées et cérémonies publiques*. Paris: Imprimerie Nationale, 1874.

Combes, Claudette. *Paris dans* Les Misérables. Nantes: Editions CID, 1981.

Cornu, Marcel. *La Conquête de Paris*. Paris: Mercure de France, 1972.

Dabot, Henri. *Souvenirs et impressions d'un bourgeois du quartier Latin, de mai 1854 à mai 1869*. Paris: Péronne, 1899.

Dalotel, Alain; Faure, Alain; and Freiermuth, Jean-Claude. *Aux Origines de la Commune: Le Mouvement des réunions publiques à Paris, 1868–1870*. Paris: François Maspero, 1980.

Daumard, Adeline. *Maisons de Paris et propriétaires parisiens au XIXème siècle (1809–1880)*. Paris: Cujas, 1965.

Dentzel, Georges-Frédéric. *Dentzel, Représentant du peuple à ses collègues*. n.p., n.d.

———. *Mémoire du citoyen Dentzel, Représentant du peuple à la Convention nationale, en réponse au rapport, fait par Lacoste et Baudot, représentants du peuple près de l'armée de la Mozelle et du Rhin sur la conspiration de Landau*. n.p., n.d.

———. *Observations présentées à Messieurs les membres de la Cour de Pairs, par le Général Baron Dentzel; pour son fils, le Lieutenant-Colonel Dentzel*. n.p., n.d.

———. *Rapport fait à la Convention nationale par Dentzel, député du Bas-Rhin, et envoyé par elle le 3 juillet 1793, l'an deux de la République française, en qualité du représentant du peuple, pour l'organisation du district établie à Landau et adjoint par le même décret aux commissaires de l'armée du Rhin avec les même pouvoirs*. Paris, n.d.

des Cars, Jean. *Haussmann, la gloire du Second Empire*. Paris: Perrin, 1988.

des Cilleuls, Alfred. *Histoire de l'administration parisienne au XIXème siècle . . .*, 3 vols. Paris: Honoré Champion, 1900.

Dethan, Georges. *Nouvelle Histoire de Paris: Paris au temps de Louis XIV, 1660–1715*. Paris: Hachette, 1990.

Drexler, Arthur, ed. *The Architecture of the Ecole des Beaux-Arts*. New York: MIT Press, 1977.

Du Camp, Maxime. *Paris, ses organes, ses fonctions et sa vie dans la seconde moitié du XIXème siècle*, 6 vols. Paris: Hachette, 1875.

Dufourg, Robert. "Dans les Souvenirs d'Antoine Gautier." *Revue historique de Bordeaux* (1954).

————. "La Révolution de 1848 à Bordeaux dans les Mémoires d'Antoine Gautier." *Revue historique de Bordeaux* (1953).

Dupin, Marcelle. *Le Château Haussmann à Cestas.* Cestas, 1977.

Dusolier, Alcide. *Les Spéculations et la mutilation du Luxembourg.* Paris: Libraire du Luxembourg, 1866.

Earls, Irene Anne. *"Napoleon III as a Patron of Architecture."* Ph.D. diss., University of Georgia, 1975.

Espagnet, Henriette. *Le Baron Haussmann par lui-même . . . dans le cadre de Cestas, au cours de la visite des domaines Haussmann.* Bordeaux: Documents Girondins, 1971.

Evans, Thomas W., ed. Edward A. Crane. *Memoirs of Thomas W. Evans*, 2 vols. New York: Unwin, 1905.

Evenson, Norma. *Paris: A Century of Change, 1878–1978.* New Haven: Yale University Press, 1979.

Féline-Romany. *Notice historique sur les ponts de Paris.* Paris, 1864.

Ferry, Jules. *Les Comptes fantastiques d'Haussmann* and *Les Finances de l'Hôtel de Ville par J.-E. Horn.* Paris: Guy Durier, 1979.

Filon, Augustin. *Souvenirs sur l'impératrice Eugénie.* Paris: Calmann-Lévy, 1920.

Flaubert, Gustave. *L'Education sentimentale.* Paris: Garniers Frères, 1964.

Fletcher, Banister. *A History of Architecture on the Comparative Method.* London: Althone Press, 1896.

Foucher de Careil, comte Louis Alexandre. *Les Habitations ouvrières.* Paris: E. Lacroix, 1873.

Fournel, Victor. *Paris nouveau et Paris futur.* Paris: A. Delahays, 1865.

Fournier, Edouard. *Paris démoli*, revue et augmentée, avec une préface par M. Théophile Gautier, 2d ed. Paris: Auguste Aubry, 1855.

————. *Splendeurs de Paris.* Paris, 1864.

France, Anatole. *Monsieur Bergeret à Paris.* Paris: Calmann-Lévy, 1901.

Furet, François. *La Révolution: De Turgot à Jules Ferry, 1770–1880.* Paris: Hachette, 1988.

Gaillard, Jeanne. *Paris, la Ville, 1852–1870: L'Urbanisme parisien à l'heure d'Haussmann.* Paris: Honoré Champion, 1977.

Garnier, Charles. *Le Nouvel Opéra de Paris*, 2 vols. Paris: Ducher, 1878–81.

Girard, Louis. *La Politique des travaux publics du Second Empire.* Paris: Armand Colin, 1952.

————. *Napoléon III.* Paris: Fayard, 1986.

———. *Nouvelle Histoire de Paris: La deuxième République et le Second Empire.* Paris: Hachette, 1981.

Girardet, Philippe. *Les Réalisateurs.* Paris: O. Lesourd, 1943.

Girouard, Mark. *Cities and People: A Social and Architectural History.* New Haven: Yale University Press, 1985.

Haag, Paul. "Haussmann, préfet de la Seine." *Revue politique et parlementaire* (1955).

Halévy, Ludovic. *Carnets.* Publiés avec une introduction et des notes par Daniel Halévy, 2 vols. Paris: Calmann-Lévy, 1935.

Hamerton, Philip Gilbert. *Paris in Old and Present Times, with Especial Reference to Changes in its Architecture and Topography.* Boston: Roberts, 1885.

Hamon, Philippe, trans. Katia Saison-Frank and Lisa Maguire. *Expositions: Literature and Architecture in Nineteenth-Century France.* Berkeley: University of California Press, 1992.

Harvey, David. *Consciousness and the Urban Experience: Studies in the History and Theory of Capitalist Urbanization.* Baltimore: Johns Hopkins University Press, 1985.

———. *The Urban Experience.* Baltimore: Johns Hopkins University Press, 1989.

Haussmann, Georges-Eugène. *Chambre des députés, séance du mardi 29 juillet 1879. Discours prononcé par M. le Baron Haussmann, député de la Corse, sur la proposition de loi tendant à faire disparaître les ruines des Tuileries.* Paris, 1879.

———. *Dans les Bois, pensées d'un forestier.* Cestas, 1882.

———. *Discours prononcé au sénat par M. le Baron Haussmann, sénateur, préfet de la Seine, au sujet des pétitions ayant pour but l'annulation du décret du 9 janvier 1861, extrait du* Moniteur *du 7 juin.* Paris, 1861.

———. *Discours prononcé au sénat par M. le Baron Haussmann . . . au sujet de la pétition contre le projet de percement d'une rue d'isolement du jardin du Luxembourg.* Paris, 1861.

———. *Discours prononcé au sénat par M. le Baron Haussmann, sénateur, préfet de la Seine, au sujet de la pétition de M. Baudin fils, contre le décret du 11 août 1867 déclarant d'utilité publique l'ouverture d'une rue nouvelle à travers une partie du cimetière du Nord. Séance des 10 et 11 janvier 1868.* Paris, 1868.

———. *Discours prononcé au Sénat par M. le Baron Haussmann . . . sur le projet de loi ayant pour objet d'approuver les traités passés entre la ville de Paris et le Crédit Foncier de France. Séance du 13 avril 1869.* Paris, 1869.

———. *Discours prononcé par M. le Baron Haussmann sur le projet de loi ayant pour objet la déclaration d'utilité publique et la construction du canal du Havre à Tancarville.* Paris, 1880.

———. *L'infini.* n.p., 1887.

———. *Le joli sentier.* Clagny, 1885.

———. *Les Fleurettes*. Paris, 1882.

———. *Mémoire présénté par le préfet de la Seine à la Commission municipale* (session ordinaire de 1854). Paris, 1854.

———. *Mémoire présenté par le préfet de la Seine à la Commission municipale* (session ordinaire de 1859). Paris, 1859.

———. *Mémoire présenté par M. le sénateur, préfet de la Seine au Conseil Municipal de Paris au sujet d'une convention entre l'état et la ville, relative à l'ouverture de nouvelles voies publiques*. Paris, 1858.

———. *Mémoire présenté par M. le sénateur, préfet de la Seine, au Conseil Municipal de Paris au sujet de l'extension des limites de Paris*. Paris, 1859.

———. *Mémoire presenté par M. le sénateur, préfet de la Seine à la commission départementale sur l'extension des limites de Paris* (session extraordinaire de 1859). Paris, 1859.

———. *Mémoire sur les eaux de Paris, présentés au Conseil Municipal, le 20 avril 1860*. Paris, 1860.

———. *Mémoires du baron Haussmann*, 3 vols. Paris: Havard, 1890.

———. *Mémoires sur les eaux de Paris, présenté au Conseil Municipal, le 4 août 1854 et le 16 juillet 1858*. Paris, 1858.

———. *Recherches statistiques sur la ville de Paris et le département de la Seine. Recueil de tableaux dressés et réunis d'après les ordres de M. le baron G.-E. H.* Paris, 1860.

———. *Regrets fidelès, stances adressés à une mère inconsolable de la perte de sa fille*. Cestas, 1876.

———. *Saint-Girons, une campagne administrative dans les Pyrénées*. Nice, 1876.

Haussmann, Nicolas. *Rapport fait à la Convention nationale par Haussmann, l'un de ses commissaires aux armées du Rhin, des Vosges et de la Moselle*. Paris, 1793.

———. *Rapport sur la situation de la caisse de l'extraordinaire, et sur une nouvelle émission de petits assignats, fait à l'Assemblée nationale le premier novembre au nom des comités réunis de la dette publique, de la caisse de l'extraordinaire, et des assignats et monnoies*. Paris, 1791.

Haussmann, Nicolas-Valentin. *Annuaire des institutions de crédit financier, commercial et industriel de la France et des principales places de l'Europe*. Paris, 1853.

———. *Des subsistances de la France, du blutage et du rendement des farines et de la composition du pain de munition*. Paris, 1848.

———. *Lettre à M. Odilon-Barrot, membre de la chambre des députés, sur l'affranchissement des communes et sur la décentralisation*. Paris, 1832.

———. *Réorganisation ou désorganisation dont est menácée l'intendance militaire*. Paris, 1833.

Hautecoeur, Louis. *Histoire de l'architecture classique en France*, nouvelle éd., 7 vols. Paris: A. et J. Picard, 1963.

Hegemann, Werner. *Der Städtebau nach den Ergebnissen der allgemeinen Städtebau-Ausstellung in Berlin nebst einem Anhang: Die internationale Städtebau-Ausstellung in Düsseldorf.* Verlag Ernst Wasmuth. 2 vols. Berlin, 1911.

Howard, Michael. *The Franco-Prussian War.* New York: Macmillan, 1962.

Hugo, Victor. *Oeuvres complètes*, 16 vols. Paris: Robert Laffont (Bouquins), 1985.

Huppert, Ellen Taylor. "The Image of the City: The Paris of the Novelists from Stendhal to Zola." Ph.D. diss., University of California, Berkeley, 1970.

Jacquemet, Gérard. *Belleville au XIXème siècle, du faubourg à la ville.* Paris: Jean Touzot, 1984.

Jullian, Camille. *Histoire de Bordeaux, depuis les origines jusqu'en 1895.* Bordeaux: Feret et Fils, 1895.

Kaplan, Steven Laurence. *Provisioning Paris, Merchants and Millers in the Grain and Flour Trade during the Eighteenth Century.* Ithaca: Cornell University Press, 1984.

Karamzine, Nikolai, ed. A. Legrelle. *Voyages en France, 1789–1790.* Paris, 1885.

Kranowski, Nathan. *Paris dans les romans d'Emile Zola.* Paris: Presses Universitaires de France, 1968.

La Gorce, Pierre de. *Histoire du Second Empire*, 7 vols. Paris: Plon (reprinted AMS Press), 1899.

Lameyre, Gérard-Noël. *Haussmann, "Préfet de Paris."* Paris: Flammarion, 1958.

Lamouroux, Alfred. *Rapport . . . au nom de la 4ème commission sur la situation des archives.* Paris: Imprimerie municipale, 1893.

Lan, Jules. *Parallèle entre le marquis de Pombal (1738–1777) et le Baron Haussmann (1853–1869).* Paris: Amyot, 1869.

Lanquetin, Jacques-Séraphin. *Question du déplacement du Paris. Opinion d'un membre de la commission ministérielle chargée d'examiner cette question.* Paris: Vinchon, 1840.

Lapouyade, Meandre de. "Essai d'iconographie du Marquis de Tourny." *Revue historique de Bordeaux et du département de la Gironde* XII (1919).

Laronze, Georges. *Le Baron Haussmann.* Paris: F. Alcan, 1932.

Lavedan, Pierre. *Les Villes françaises.* Paris: Vincent, Freal, 1960.

———. *Nouvelle Histoire de Paris: Histoire de l'urbanisme à Paris.* Paris: Hachette, 1975.

———. *Paris.* Paris: Presses Universitaires de France, 1964.

Lazare, Louis. *Les Quartiers pauvres de Paris: Le 20ème arrondissement.* Paris: Bureau de la Bibliothèque municipale, 1870.

Le Clère, Bernard and Wright, Vincent. *Les Préfets du Second Empire*. Paris: Armand Colin, 1973.

Lefebvre, Henri. *La Proclamation de la Commune: 26 mars 1871*. Paris: Gallimard, 1969.

Leroy-Beaulieu, Paul. *L'Administration locale en France et en Angleterre*. Paris, 1871.

Lhéritier, Michel. *L'Intendant Tourny*. Paris: Félix Alcan, 1920.

Lortsh, Charles. *La Beauté de Paris: Conservation des aspects esthétiques de la ville de Paris*. Paris: Bernard Tignol, 1911.

Loyer, François. *Paris XIXe siècle, l'immeuble et la rue*. Paris: Hazan, 1987.

Lucan, Jacques. *Haussmann . . . un viaduc*. Paris: Institut de l'environment, 1973.

Magraw, Roger. *France 1815–1914: The Bourgeois Century*. Oxford: Oxford University Press, 1983.

Mainardi, Patricia. *Art and Politics of the Second Empire: The Universal Expositions of 1855 and 1867*. New Haven: Yale University Press, 1987.

Margadant, Ted W. *French Peasants in Revolt: The Insurrection of 1851*. Princeton: Princeton University Press, 1979.

Marx, Karl. *The Eighteenth Brumaire of Louis Bonaparte*. New York: International, 1963.

Marx, Karl and Engels, Frederick. *On the Paris Commune*. Moscow: Progress, 1971.

Mead, Christopher Curtis. *Charles Garnier's Paris Opéra: Architectural Empathy and the Renaissance of French Classicism*. Cambridge, Mass.: MIT Press, 1991.

Merimée, Prosper, ed. Pierre Trahard. *Lettres à Viollet-le-Duc*. Paris: Champion, 1927.

Merriman, John M. *The Agony of the Republic: The Repression of the Left in Revolutionary France, 1848–1851*. New Haven: Yale University Press, 1978.

———, ed. *French Cities in the Nineteenth Century*. London: Holmes & Meier, 1981.

———. *The Margins of City Life: Explorations on the French Urban Frontier, 1815–1851*. New York: Oxford University Press, 1991.

———. *The Red City: Limoges and the French Nineteenth Century*. New York: Oxford University Press, 1985.

Merruau, Charles. *Souvenirs de l'Hôtel de Ville de Paris (1848–1852)*. Paris: Plon, 1875.

Middleton, Robin, ed. *The Beaux-Arts and Nineteenth-Century French Architecture*. Cambridge, Mass.: MIT Press, 1982.

Montesquieu, Baron de (Charles de Secondat). *Oeuvres complètes*, 3 vols. Paris: Gallimard (Pléiade), 1950.

Morère, P. *Haussmann, sous-préfet de St. Girons*. Paris, 1925.

Morizet, André. *Du vieux Paris au Paris moderne.* Paris: Hachette, 1932.

Moses, Robert. "What Happened to Haussmann." *Architectural Forum* (July 1942).

Musset, Alfred de. *Oeuvres complètes d'Alfred de Musset.* édition ornée de 28 gravures. 11 vols. Paris: Charpentier, 1876.

Nord, Philip G. *Shopkeepers and the Politics of Resentment.* Princeton: Princeton University Press, 1986.

Ollivier, Emile. Texte choisi et annoté par Theodore Zeldin et Anne Troisier de Diaz. *Journal,* 2 vols. Paris: Julliard, 1961.

———. *L'Empire libéral. Etudes, récits, souvenirs,* 16 vols. Paris: Garnier Frères, 1895.

Olsen, Donald J. *The City as a Work of Art: London, Paris, Vienna.* New Haven: Yale University Press, 1986.

Patte, Pierre. *Mémoires sur les objets les plus importants de l'architecture.* Paris: Rozet, 1769.

Paul-Lévy, Françoise. *La Ville en croix: De la révolution de 1848 à la rénovation haussmannienne.* Paris: Librarie des Méridiens, 1984.

Persigny, duc de. *Mémoires du duc de Persigny.* Publié avec des documents inédits, un avant-propos et un épilogue par M. H. de Laire, comte d'Espagny. Paris: Plon, 1896.

Pillement, Georges. *Destruction de Paris.* Paris: B. Grasset, 1944.

Pillorget, René. *Nouvelle Histoire de Paris: Paris sous les premiers Bourbons, 1594–1661.* Paris: Hachette, 1988.

Pinkney, David H. *Napoleon III and the Rebuilding of Paris.* Princeton: Princeton University Press, 1958.

Pouthas, Charles-Henri. *La Population française pendant la première moitié du XIXe siècle.* Paris: Presses Universitaires de France, 1956.

Price, Roger, ed. *Revolution and Reaction: 1848 and the Second French Republic.* London: Croom Helm, 1975.

Pronteau, Jeanne. *Edme Verniquet, 1727–1804.* Paris: Imprimerie municipale, 1986.

———. *Notes biographiques sur les membres des assemblées municipales parisiennes et des conseils généraux de la Seine de 1800 à nos jours.* Paris: Imprimerie municipale, 1958.

Rambuteau, Claude-Philibert de. *Mémoires du comte de Rambuteau.* Publiés par son petit-fils. Paris: Calmann-Lévy, 1905.

Réau, Louis et al. *L'Oeuvre du baron Haussmann, préfet de la Seine (1853–1870).* Paris: Presses Universitaires de France, 1954.

Reid, Donald. *Paris Sewers and Sewermen: Realities and Representations.* Cambridge, Mass.: Harvard University Press, 1991.

Restif de la Bretonne, Nicolas. *Monsieur Nicolas, ou le coeur humaine dévoilé*, 6 vols. Paris, 1959.

Rials, Stéphane. *Nouvelle Histoire de Paris: De Trochu à Thiers, 1870–1873*. Paris: Hachette, 1985.

Riffaud, Emile. *Aide-mémoire du Baron Haussmann, souvenir d'une polémique . . .* Bordeaux, 1890.

Roche, Daniel, trans. Marie Evans and Gwynne Lewis. *The People of Paris*. Berkeley: University of California Press, 1987.

Rousseau, Jean-Jacques, ed. Michel Launay. *Les Confessions*. Paris: Garnier, 1968.

Russell, John. *Paris*. New York: Abrams, 1983.

Saalmam, Howard. *Haussmann: Paris Transformed*. New York: Braziller, 1971.

Saint-Georges, Marie de. *Essai historique sur l'administration de Monsieur le Marquis de Tourni, conseiller d'état, intendant de Bordeaux*. Brussels, 1782.

Sand, George. *Oeuvres autobiographiques*. Texte etabli, présenté et annoté par Georges Lubin. Paris: Gallimard (Pléiade), 1970.

Sarrepont, Major H. de. *Le Bombardement de Paris par les Prussiens . . .* Paris: Didot, 1872.

Schivelbusch, Wolfgang. *The Railway Journey: The Industrialization of Time and Space in the Nineteenth Century*. Berkeley: University of California Press, 1986.

Schnerb, Robert. *Rouher et le Second Empire*. Paris: A. Colin, 1949.

Sennett, Richard. *The Fall of Public Man*. Cambridge: Cambridge University Press, 1977.

Sherard, Robert H. *Twenty Years in Paris*. Philadelphia: George W. Jacobs, n.d.

Silverman, Debora L. *Art Nouveau in Fin-de-Siècle France: Politics, Psychology, and Style*. Berkeley: University of California Press, 1989.

Simon, Jules. *Premières Années*. Paris: Flammarion, 1901.

Stevenson, Norah W. *Paris dans la Comédie humaine de Balzac*. Paris: Georges Courville, 1938.

Sutcliffe, Anthony. *The Autumn of Central Paris. The Defeat of Town Planning, 1850–1970*. Montreal: McGill-Queen's University Press, 1971.

———. *Paris: An Architectural History*. New Haven: Yale University Press, 1993.

Taylor, Katherine Fischer. *In the Theater of Criminal Justice: The Palais de Justice in Second Empire Paris*. Princeton: Princeton University Press, 1993.

Temko, Allan. *Notre-Dame of Paris*. New York: Viking, 1955.

Texier, Edmond. *Tableau de Paris*, 2 vols. Paris: Paulin et le Chevalier, 1852.

Thezy, Marie de, ed. *Paris, la rue, le mobilier urbain du Second Empire à nos jours à travers les collections photographiques de la Bibliothèque Historique de la Ville de Paris.* Paris: Société des amis de la Bibliothèque historique, 1976.

Tilly, Charles, ed. *The Formation of National States in Western Europe.* Princeton: Princeton University Press, 1975.

Touttain, Pierre-André. *Haussmann, artisan du Second Empire, créateur du Paris moderne.* Paris: Gründ, 1971.

Trollope, Frances. *Paris and the Parisians in 1835.* Paris: A. and W. Galignani, 1836.

Tudesq, André. *Les Grands Notables en France (1840–1849): Etude historique d'une psychologie sociale,* 2 vols. Paris: Presses Universitaires de France, 1964.

Tulard, Jean. *Nouvelle Histoire de Paris: Le consulat et l'empire.* Paris: Hachette, 1983.

———. *Paris et son administration: 1800–1830.* Paris: Imprimerie municipale, 1976.

Valynseele, Joseph. *Haussmann, sa famille et sa descendance.* Paris: Editions Christian, 1982.

Vandam, Albert D. *An Englishman in Paris,* 2 vols. New York: D. Appleton, 1893.

Vapereau, G. *Dictionnaire universel des contemporaines,* 4 vols. Paris, 1893.

Viel-Castel, Comte Horace de. *Mémoires du Comte Horace de Viel-Castel sur le règne de Napoléon III, 1851–1864,* avec un avant-propos et des notes par Pierre Josserand, 2 vols. Paris: Guy le Prat, n.d.

Vigier, Philippe. *Nouvelle Histoire de Paris: Paris pendant la Monarchie de Juillet.* Paris: Hachette, 1991.

Voltaire. *Oeuvres complètes,* nouvelle éd., 52 vols. Paris: Garnier, 1877.

Zeldin, Theodore. *Emile Ollivier and the Liberal Empire of Napoleon III.* Oxford: Oxford University Press, 1963.

———. *The Political System of Napoleon III.* London: Oxford University Press, 1958.

Zola, Emile, ed. Henri Mitterand. *Les Rougon-Macquart,* "Lettres Parisiennes," *Oeuvres complètes,* vol. 14. Paris: Cercle du livres précieux, 1970.

———, ed. Henri Mitterand. "Lettres parisiennes." *Oeuvres complètes,* vol. 14. Paris, 1970.

· INDEX ·

Abbey St. Victoire, 37
Agen, 148
Ajaccio, 331, 332
Alexander II, 276
Alphand, Adolphe, 151, 164, 238,
    242, 279, 280, 281, 282, 283,
    318, 329, 337, 339
Alsace, 41
Angoulême, 59, 76, 149
Arago, Etienne, 56
Arc de Triomphe (Etoile), 39, 175,
    178, 199, 205, 206, 244, 283,
    344
Arras, 9, 156
Asnières, 269, 274
Association internationale des
    travailleurs, 298
Au Bon Marché, 352, 363
Au Louvre, 352
Au Printemps, 210, 352, 353
Auber, Daniel-François-Esprit, 257,
    258, 370
Augustus Caesar, 184, 273
Austerlitz, Battle of, 139
Auvergne, 59
Avallon, 127, 270, 271
Ave-Marie, l', 37
Avenues
    de l'Impératrice (Avenue Foch),
    206, 283

de l'Opéra, 207, 208, 210, 213,
    332, 371
des Gobelins, 175
Foch (*see* Avenue de
    l'Impératrice)
Portalis, 198

Baltard, Victor, 46, 196
Balzac, Honoré de, 29, 51, 95, 96,
    189, 213, 223, 262, 269, 248,
    249, 350, 351
Banlieue, 102, 110, 231, 245,
    285–290, 294, 307, 343, 350,
    354, 355, 360
Banque de Paris, 233
Barcelona, 9, 281
Barot, Odilon, 45
Bastia, 332
Batignolles, 358
Baudelaire, Charles, 280, 352, 354
Beauharnais, Eugène de, 47, 119,
    171, 191, 334
Beaumont, Elie de, 51
Belgrand, Eugène, 164, 243,
    270–272, 276, 280
Belleville, 195, 272, 286, 289
Bercy, 221, 362
Berger, Jacques, 112, 113, 169, 174,
    227, 228, 229, 230, 281, 313,
    360

Berlioz, Hector, 51–52
Bernini, 25
Beudant, François, 51
Beychevelle, 71, 74
Bibliothèque Nationale, 29, 163, 195
Blanqui, Auguste, 298
Blaye, 71, 74, 76, 143
Bois de Vincennes, 10, 278, 281, 283
Bonapartism, 46, 139
Bons de délégation, 235, 304
Bordeaux, 1–3, 8, 9, 16, 59, 69–74, 76, 79, 80, 82–89, 118, 120–122, 134, 138–159, 161, 166, 171, 172, 181, 207, 212, 215, 230, 247, 254, 255, 258, 281, 299, 323, 326, 328, 333–335, 342, 356
    Louis Napoléon's coup d'état in, 140–142
Boulanger, Georges, general, 336
Boulevards
    de Strasbourg, 90, 115, 120, 169, 189, 190, 193, 195, 199, 200, 223, 341, 343, 351, 357, 361
    des Capucines, 78
    du Palais, 200
    Diderot, 192
    Friedland, 46
    Haussmann, 46
    Malesherbes, 175, 198, 208, 233, 243, 244, 257, 262, 357
    Morland, 29
    Richard Lenoir, 191, 194, 195, 291
    St. Germain, 161, 175, 197, 262, 363, 371
    St. Michel, 189, 190, 200, 363
    Voltaire, 182, 191, 197, 244, 345
Boulevardier, 347, 349
Bourbonnais, 24

Bourse, 29, 87, 105, 149, 153, 170, 180, 263, 281, 351
Bouscat, 71
Briez, Philippe-Constant-Joseph, 42
Bro, Colonel, 57
Brongniart, Alexandre-Théodore, 263
Brun, Jean Adrien, 62, 63
Bruneseau, Pierre-Emmanuel, 267
Bullant, Jean, 222
Burger, Marie-Madeleine, 41
Burgundy, 24, 101, 108, 347
Buttes Chaumont, 278

Café de la Paix, 351, 352, 355
Caisse des Travaux de Paris, 234
Calley de Saint-Paul, 306
Calliat, P.-V., 201
Calvin, Jean, 65
Camden Place, 328, 334
Campoformio, Treaty of, 45
Cardinal Lemoine, collège de, 37
Caserne de la Cité, 201
Casimir-Périer, 57, 65, 66
Cauchy, Augustin, 51
Cavaignac, Louis-Eugène, general, 81, 88, 89, 173
Cellier, Francine, 256, 257
Cestas, 1, 3, 223, 280, 315, 318, 322, 323, 325–328, 330, 331, 370
Chabanais, 59
Chaillot, 39, 269
Chalgran, J. F. T., 205
Champ-de-Mars, 32, 178
Champagne, 272
Champs-Elysées, 15, 38, 39, 153, 178, 189, 206, 326, 351
Changarnier, Nicolas-Anne-Théodule, general, 181
Charenton, 286
Charles V, 22, 190

Charles X, 77–79
Charron, Pierre, 43
Château d'Yquem, 74
Chaussée d'Antin, 31, 203, 262, 291
Chaville, 41, 59
Cherubini, Luigi, 51
Chevalier Negra, 324
Chevallier, M., 79
Chevandier de Valdrôme, Jean-Pierre-Napoléon-Eugène, 315, 316, 323
Chevreau, Henri, 315
Chinese baths, 349
Chopin, Frédéric, 61
Claudin, Gustave, 209, 213, 261
Claveau, Anatole, 307, 315
Clemenceau, Georges, 264, 333
Clermont-Ferrand, 59
Cluny, 37, 204
Cobden-Chevalier Treaty, 298
Colbert, Jean-Baptiste, 15
Cologne, 41
Commission des Artistes, 36, 37, 39, 176
Compiègne, 179, 254, 259
Conciergerie, 201
Conservative Alliance of the Gironde, 333
Conservatoire des Arts et Métiers, 192
Considérant, Victor, 188
Cornu, Marcel, 358
Cousin, Victor, 370
Convention Assembly, 41
Cour de Cassation, 240, 242
Cours-la-Reine, 17, 29
Crédit Foncier, 233–235, 304
Crédit Industriel et Commercial, 233
Crédit Lyonnais, 233
Crédit Mobilier, 232, 233, 327

Crugy, Emile, 143
Crystal Palace, 231
Custine, Adam Philippe, comte de (general), 42

D'Arbouville, General, 140
Danton, Georges, 43
Daumier, Honoré, 99, 192
Davioud, Gabriel, 200, 212, 278, 332
Debret, François, 207
Delacroix, Eugène, 76, 77
Delangle, C.-A., 286
Delmas, Jean-François-Bertrand, 44
Dentzel, Caroline (*see* Haussmann, Caroline)
Dentzel, Georges-Frédéric, 43
Departments
  Ariège, 64, 66
  Bas-Rhin, 44
  Charente, 76, 151
  Creuse, 59, 93
  Gironde, 63, 71, 144
  Haute- Loire, 59
  Lot-et-Garonne, 59
  Seine-et-Oise, 41
  Var, 144
  Vienne, 58
  Yonne, 144
Deschamps, Eugène, 176, 243, 280, 281
Dhuys, 270–273
Diet, A.-S., 201
Donnet, Ferdinand-François-Auguste, archbishop, 73, 146, 148
Drouyn de Lhuys, Edouard, 148
Du Camp, Maxime, 111, 241, 362
Dupin, Aurore (George Sand), 60, 61, 260, 263, 348
Durkheim, 43

Ecole des Beaux-Arts, 164, 196
Ecole Militaire, 31, 32, 178
Edinburgh, 9, 271
Eiffel Tower, 166, 178
Elizabeth I, 185
Elysée Palace, 139
Engels, Friedrich, 294
Espinasse, Esprit-Charles-Marie, general, 214
Eugénie, empress, 2, 48, 143, 171, 179, 209, 211, 254, 255, 258, 319, 321, 329, 338
Expiatory Chapel, 344
Faubourg du Roule, 43
Faubourg St. Antoine, 14
Faubourg St. Marceau, 13
Faubourg St. Germain, 29, 32, 161
Faucher, Léon, 90, 117, 119, 120, 131, 132, 133
Favre, Jules, 294, 304
Ferry, Jules, 301–304, 313, 316, 332, 342
Fifth arrondissement, 50
Flaubert, Gustave, 80, 241, 362
Fould, Achille, 210, 313, 370
Foix, 66
Fontaine, Pierre-François-Léonard, 38
Fontainebleau, 24, 254
Fourier, Charles, 298
Fournier, Edouard, 293
Fracasti, 349
Franco-Prussian War, 238, 319, 321, 324, 327
François I, 22, 24, 189, 249, 251
Frémy, Louis, 127, 128, 129, 130, 132, 133, 135, 140, 233, 235, 313, 318, 324, 325, 327
French Revolution, 41
Frochot, Nicolas, comte, 355
Froissart, Jean, 58

Galos, Henri, 143
Gare de l'Est, 195, 199, 200
Gare du Nord, 162, 163, 359
Gare St. Lazare, 208, 210
Garnier, Charles, 162, 163, 178, 207, 210, 211, 212, 304, 359
Garnier-Pagès, Louis-Antoine, 304
Gautier, Antoine, 138, 140, 142, 144
Gautier, Jean-Elie, 73
Gay-Lussac, Joseph, 51
Gilbert, Emile, 201
Glasgow, 9, 271
Gobelins, Les, 175, 345, 346
Goncourt brothers, 348
Grand Hôtel (de la Paix), 351, 352
Grands-Augustins, convent of the, 37
Grands Boulevards, 94, 207, 208, 210, 213, 338, 347, 349–351, 354
Grands magasins, 210, 352, 353
Grange, Marquis de la, 73, 76
Gros Caillou, 188
Grouchy, Emmanuel, marquis de (general), 145
Guienne, 152, 153
Guizot, François, 65, 78

Halle aux Bleds (Blé), 32
Halévy, Ludovic, 315
Hamerton, Philip Gilbert, 349
Hamilton, Duke of, 175
Haussmann, Balthazar, 41
Haussmann, Caroline Dentzel (Haussmann's mother), 43, 46, 336
Haussmann, Christian, 41
Haussmann, Fanny-Valentine (Haussmann's daughter), 70

Haussmann, Georges-Eugène
  after his fall, 324–328, 331, 332,
    334–336
  and Commune of, 1871, 326, 327
  and George Sand, 61
  and the marquis de Tourny, 149,
    155–157, 314
  annexation of banlieue, 231,
    286–290
  appointed prefect of the Seine,
    171
  as administrator, 212, 215,
    217–224, 261
  at the Hôtel de Ville, 252–255
  attack on his budget, 300–303,
    304–309
  Bonapartism, 47, 48, 88, 118,
    126, 127, 129, 132, 136, 138,
    143, 145, 147, 334, 335
  Bonapartist from the cradle, 47
  Bordeaux, 299
  boulevards, 178, 348–352, 354
  Cestas, 328–331
  confiscation of Orléans property,
    143
  death, 337, 338
  delicate health of, 48
  demolitions, 262
  desire for a ministry, 182
  difficulties with superiors, 62, 63
  dislike of romanticism, 49
  education, 49, 50, 51
  expropriations, 240, 241
  finances, 228–233, 234,
    235–239, 243, 299, 300
  Franco-Prussian War, 322, 323
  friends, 73
  friendship with duc de Chartres,
    50
  harshness, 144
  fall of, 313–318
  fastidiousness, 48, 280, 288
  first appointment, 58
  flawed memory of, 48
  funeral, 338
  housing, 291, 293–295
  influence of Bordeaux, 158
  interest in mental illness, 68
  interpreting Louis Napoléon's
    ideas, 175
  last meeting with emperor,
    318–322
  lineage, 41
  Louis Napoléon's coup d'état,
    139–142, 146
  love of nature, 49
  love of music, 51
  Luxembourg Gardens, 263–265
  map of Paris, 176
  marriage, 69, 70
  meeting Napoléon, 47, 48
  Mémoire sur les Eaux de Paris, 271
  Mixed Commission, 142, 143, 146
  obsessive cleanliness, 48, 49, 220,
    274
  on Alfred de Musset, 50
  on Berlioz, 52
  on his birth, 46
  on his maternal grandfather, 43,
    48, 49
  on his mother, 46
  on his paternal grandfather, 42,
    45
  on Old Paris, 50, 159
  pageantry for Louis Napoléon,
    147–149, 151
  parks, 277, 278, 282, 283
  personality, 224, 259, 260
  prefect of the Gironde, 138, 144,
    145
  prefect of the Seine, 152, 247, 248
  préfet à poigne, 144
  private life, 256, 257
  qualities of mind, 49

Haussmann, Georges-Eugène
(*continued*)
reading, 60
relationship with Louis
Napoléon, 179, 181, 184–186
restoring Tuileries, 332, 333
Revolution of 1830, 56, 57, 77
Revolution of 1848, 172
sewers, 274–275
subprefect of Blaye, 71, 74, 75, 76
subprefect of Nérac, 59, 60
subprefect of St. Girons, 64, 65,
67
subprefect of Yssingeaux, 59
taste, 279, 359
three réseaux, 244, 245
wine expertise, 74
Une campagne administrative dans
St. Girons, 68
urban ideas, 172, 177, 232, 248,
276, 278, 295, 296, 312, 354,
357, 358
urban regulation, 292
water supply, 271–273
Haussmann, Henriette-Marie
(Haussmann's daughter), 78,
258
Haussmann, Mme (Laharpe,
Louise-Octavie de,
Haussmann's wife), 69, 70,
139, 145, 253–255, 258, 337
Haussmann, Nicholas
(Haussmann's grandfather),
41–42
Haussmann, Nicolas-Valentin
(Haussmann's father), 41, 56
Lettre à M. Odilon Barrot, 45–46
Haussmannization, 6, 10, 161, 162,
165, 201, 203, 238, 245, 247,
261, 267, 276, 277, 289, 299,
302, 311, 312, 324, 327, 346,
352, 364, 371

Hazlitt, William, 350
Henri IV, 25–27, 30, 38, 49, 50, 59,
61, 66, 102, 156, 184, 185,
197, 222, 249, 288, 332, 350
Henri IV, collège de, 50, 66
Hittorff, Jacques-Ignace, 162, 163,
195, 359
Hospice des Enfants-Trouvés, 201
Hôtel Carnavalet, 222
Hôtel d'Harcourt, 203
Hôtel de Choiseul, 207
Hôtel de Rohan, 148, 149
Hôtel de Sens, 22
Hôtel de Ville, 20, 33, 56, 77, 79,
97, 103, 105, 106, 109–114,
117, 159, 169, 173, 193, 200,
202, 212, 217, 219, 222, 223,
227, 229, 236, 239, 244, 248,
249, 251, 253–256, 260, 273,
288, 299, 304, 316, 323, 332,
333, 339, 342, 345, 346, 360,
361
Hôtel-Dieu, 201–203, 354
Hôtel Laffitte, 242
Hugo, Victor, 51, 181, 202, 264,
268, 276, 297, 360, 364
Hyde Park, 175, 278, 282

Ile St. Louis, 29, 35, 113, 156, 188,
197
Ismail Pasha, 281

Jena, 43
Johnston, Nathaniel, 73
Julius Caesar, 184
July Column, 38
Jumilhac, Dumont de, 64

Karamzine, Nicolai, 14

La Chapelle, 110, 286, 356
La Courtille, 286

La Défense, 206
La Rochefoucauld, 59
La Villette, 33, 291, 345, 346, 361
Laubadère, General, 44
Labrouste, Henri, 163
Lafayette, Marquis de, 77
Laharpe, Henri de, 69
Laharpe, Louise-Octavie de (*see*
    Mme Haussmann)
Lamartine, Alphonse de, 80, 89
Lamorcière, Christophe-Louis-
    Léon Juchault de, general,
    181
Landau, 43
Laubadère, General, 44
Lazare, Louis, 208, 289, 292
Le Nôtre, André, 29
Le Réole, 148
Le Temps, 56
Le Vau, Louis, 29
Lecomte, Claude-Martin, general,
    342, 370
Ledoux, Charles-Nicolas, 33, 263,
    288
Ledru-Rollin, Alexandre-Auguste,
    79, 85, 89, 120, 122, 370
Left Bank, 16, 19, 27, 29, 32, 34,
    35, 37, 38, 103, 109, 161, 175,
    188–190, 193, 197, 199, 200,
    203, 244, 248, 297, 305, 312,
    341, 349, 354, 358, 362, 363
Legislative Assembly, 41
Lescot, Pierre, 25, 222, 360
Lesseps, Ferdinand de, 328
Leszczynski, Stanislas, 156
Les Halles, 20, 22, 23, 32, 34, 35,
    96, 106, 163, 195, 196, 203,
    210, 211, 330, 360–362
Les Invalides, 32
Libourne, 63
Limoges, 59, 79, 153, 356
Liverpool, 271

Loire River, 272, 313
London, 9, 15, 172, 175, 177, 271,
    278
Lortsch, Charles, 359
Louis, Victor, 32, 149, 207
Louis Napoléon, 12, 78, 85, 88–90,
    92, 95, 108, 112–115,
    118–121, 123, 126, 127, 129,
    132–136, 138–141, 143, 144,
    146, 147, 149–152, 158, 168,
    169, 171–173, 175–177, 179,
    180, 182–186, 188–190,
    195–197, 208, 209, 211, 213,
    214, 221, 224, 228, 250, 251,
    260, 274, 277, 281, 283,
    298–300, 303, 308, 311, 313,
    314, 316, 318–322, 337, 356,
    360, 361
  Bois de Boulogne, 278, 281–283
  confiscates Orléans property, 143
  coup d'état, 138, 139, 143, 144
  death, 328
  foreign policy blunders, 312, 313,
    320
  Liberal Empire, 298
  map of projects, 173, 175, 177
  on Haussmann, 183, 184
  social ideas, 228, 229
  "The Empire is peace!", 151
  urban ideas, 172, 174, 356
  visits Bordeaux, 147–151
Louis VII, 195
Louis XIII, 25, 27, 29
Louis XIV, 15–17, 25, 26, 29, 31,
    37, 93, 108, 110, 152, 155,
    175, 190, 205, 221, 222, 227,
    250, 251, 284, 285, 288
Louis XV, 2, 8, 9, 31, 32, 211
Louis XVI, 2, 36, 42, 44, 109, 189,
    211, 249, 333, 344, 371
Louis-Philippe, 45, 50, 78, 79, 102,
    172, 216, 249

Louvel, Louis-Pierre, 207
Louvre, 15, 16, 21, 22, 24–26,
    28–31, 33, 38, 39, 43, 95, 96,
    109, 110, 113–115, 117, 163,
    165, 168, 169, 178, 189, 193,
    196, 207, 208, 211, 229, 244,
    249, 261, 276, 332, 333, 345,
    352, 353, 360, 361
Lusignan, marquis de, 63
Lusson, A.-L., 291
Luxembourg Palace, 27, 263

Magne, Auguste-Joseph, 148
Madeleine, Eglise de la, 41, 178,
    198, 207, 208, 262, 277
Magasins Généraux, 327
Maison Haussmann frères, 41
Maleville, Léon de, 64, 71
Manchester, 271
Manège, 189
Marat, Jean-Paul, 267
Marché des Champeaux, 19
Marché St. Martin, 221
Marseilles, 79
Marx, Karl, 112, 238, 345
Maximilian, Archduke, 298, 313
Médoc, 74
Ménilmontant, 271–273, 286,
    369
Mercier, Louis-Sébastien, 15
Mérimée, Prosper, 259, 359
Merruau, Charles, 97, 103,
    105–107, 112, 174, 175, 177,
    190, 219, 231, 281
Michelet, Jules, 364
Miller-Richer, Hippolyte, 294
Mocquard, Jean-François-
    Constant, 119, 148
Moltke the elder, 177
Montesquieu, Charles Secondat,
    baron, 16
Morizet, André, 189

Morny, Charles-Auguste, duc de,
    139, 140, 142
Moses, Robert, 11, 219, 230
Municipal Council (Conseil
    Municipal de la Ville de Paris),
    97, 100, 101, 103–107, 114,
    130, 173, 179, 181, 212, 215,
    216, 240, 250, 251, 259, 271,
    303, 309, 310, 316, 333
Musset, Alfred de, 50, 61

Nadar (Félix Tournachon), 277
Naples, 325
Napoléon I, 2, 8, 9, 12, 22, 25,
    36–39, 45–48, 55, 72, 76, 78,
    85, 88–90, 92, 95, 97, 101,
    104, 106, 108, 112–115,
    118–121, 123, 126, 127, 129,
    132–136, 138–141, 143, 144,
    146, 147, 149–152, 158, 162,
    164, 168, 169, 171–177, 179,
    180, 182–186, 188–190,
    195–197, 205, 207–209, 211,
    212, 211, 213, 214, 221, 224,
    228, 250, 251, 254, 255, 260,
    269, 274, 277, 281, 283, 284,
    288, 298–300, 303, 308, 311,
    313, 314, 316, 318–322, 324,
    331, 334–338, 356, 359–361
Napoléon, Jérôme (Plonplon), 254,
    255, 324
Napoléon, Victor, 334, 335, 336,
    338
Nash, John, 177
National Workshops, 92
Nérac, 60, 62, 69, 72, 73
Nerval, Gérard de, 51
Neuilly, 79
Neveux, Alexandre-Eugène,
    84–87, 138, 140
9 Thermidor, 44
Nohant, 61

Notre Dame, 18, 22, 77, 94, 159, 163, 201–203

Odéon, théâtre de la, 17, 161, 363
Ollivier, Emile, 79, 122, 125, 126, 144, 214, 215, 294, 304, 309, 310, 313, 315, 321, 322, 327, 335
Opéra, l', 8, 151, 159, 162, 163, 178, 191, 206–214, 245, 248, 256–258, 349–353, 359
Orléans, Ferdinand-Henry-Joseph, duc de Chartres, then duc d', 50, 57, 58, 61, 65, 66, 143
  aids Haussmann's career, 58, 66
Orsini, Felice, 208, 214

Palais de la Légion d'Honneur, 345
Palais-Bourbon, 79
Palais-Royal, 17, 27, 32, 34, 149, 244, 262
Panthéon, 32, 50, 81, 103, 179, 197, 203, 204
Parc Louvois, 269
Parc Monceau, 33, 196, 243, 278
Parc Montsouris, 278
Parent-Duchâtelet, André-Jean-Baptiste, 267, 268, 275
Paris (*see also* Avenues; Boulevards; *Places*; Rues)
  bombardment, 326, 341
  boulevard life, 348–352, 354
  cholera epidemics, 268
  classical city, 159
  compared to Bordeaux, 158
  destruction during Commune, 344–346
  Haussmann's urban ideas, 159
  hostility to Second Empire, 311
  housing, 291–294
  Old and New contrasted, 93
  organization in hubs, 159

population, 358
sewers, 268, 270, 271, 274–277, 280, 287
water supply, 268–271
Pauillac, 71
Pavillon du Louvre, 345
Pelletan, Eugène, 313
Père Lachaise (cemetery), 3, 338, 369, 372
Péreire brothers, 161, 230, 231
Périphérique, 22, 159
Perrault, Claude, 15
Persigny, Victor-Fialin, duc de, 169, 170, 171
Petit de Bantel, 64
Peyre, Marie-Joseph, 17
Philippe-Auguste, 195, 251, 287, 288, 360
Places
  Dauphine, 28, 153, 156, 201
  d'Italie, 159
  de France, 28
  de Grève, 20, 106, 249
  de la Bastille, 35, 38, 39, 81, 109, 114, 159, 178, 190, 191, 193, 197, 363
  de la Concorde (Place Louis XV), 2, 31, 95, 104, 139, 159, 178, 190, 269, 276, 338, 344
  de la Madeleine, 198, 277
  de la Nation (Place du Trône), 31, 178, 182, 262, 159, 192, 197
  de la République (Place du Château d'Eau), 159, 178, 194, 197, 208, 277
  des Victoires, 16, 156, 205, 206, 221
  des Vosges (Place Royale), 27–29
  du Château d'Eau (*see* Place de la République)
  du Châtelet, 200, 203, 212, 244

Places (continued)
　du Théâtre-Français, 210, 277
　du Trône (*see* Place de la Nation)
　Louis-le-Grand, 35
　Malesherbes, 277
　Pigalle, 342
　Royale (*see* Place des Vosges)
　St. Michel, 200
　Vendôme, 344
Plaine de Monceau, 243, 262
Plan des Artistes, 35, 36, 190
Poitiers, 58
Pont-Neuf, 16, 20, 26, 27, 222, 269
Ponts
　au Change, 200, 203
　d'Ivry, 269
　Royal, 29
　St. Michel, 37, 200, 203
　Sully, 197, 363
Port de Bercy, 221
Port St. Antoine, 31
Port-Royal, 29
Porte St. Eustache, 203
Prefecture of police, 201, 212, 213, 345, 346
Prefecture of the Seine, 211–213
Pressensé, Edmond de, 298
Printemps, Au, 210, 352, 353
Propylées, 33
Protestation des Journalists, 45
Proust, Marcel, 29, 283
Prudhomme, Pierre-Joseph, 298

Quai de la Rapée, 192
Quinze-Vingts (hospital), 189
Quatre-Nations, collège de, 16

Rambuteau, Claude-Phibert Barthelot, comte de, 100–102, 104–109, 113, 115, 117, 195, 239, 251, 253, 269, 284, 360
Raspail, François-Vincent, 181

Raymond, J. A., 205
Regent Street, 177
Réstif de la Bretonne, 14
Richelieu, rue de, 27, 56, 204, 305, 349, 351
Richelieu, Cardinal de, 27
Richelieu, quartier, 29
Riffaud, Emile, 142
Right Bank, 16, 17, 19, 20, 22, 35, 37, 97, 103, 161, 189, 207, 262, 347, 350, 362, 363
Robespierre, Maximilien, 42
Rochfort, Henri, 289
Roederer, P.-L., 356
Rohault de Fleury, Charles, 209
Rome, 8–10, 15, 16, 19, 39, 47, 212, 273, 313, 323, 324, 328
Rothschild, James, baron de, 79
Rouher, Eugène, 192, 214, 219, 231, 259, 300, 305, 306, 308, 313, 315, 328, 356
Rousseau, Jean-Jacques, 13
Rues
　Auber, 208, 209
　Chauchat, 338
　Danton, 200
　de Cluny, 204
　de Grenelle, 221
　de l'Hirondelle, 203
　de l'Odéon, 17
　de la Grande-Truanderie, 20
　de la Hachette, 203
　de la Harpe, 50, 203
　de la Michodière, 349
　de la Roquette, 345
　de Lille, 345, 346
　de Mazas, 192
　de Rennes, 161, 193, 305
　de Rivoli, 34, 39, 93, 106, 111, 113–115, 169, 192, 193, 200, 207, 208, 229, 244, 250, 332, 338, 345, 360

de Tourtille, 286
de Turenne, 356
des Ecoles, 169, 193
des Grés, 204
des Lavandières, 203
des Maçons-Sorbonne, 203
Doyenné, 95, 189
du 4 Septembre, 208
du Pont-Neuf, 20
Grenelle, 139
Halévy, 208, 209
Lafayette, 208, 242
Lepelletier, 207
Montmartre, 105, 203
Mouffetard, 175, 193
Soufflot, 179
St. Antoine, 39, 189
St. Denis, 35, 203, 241
St. Honoré, 203
St. Jacques, 189
St. Martin, 35, 241
Transnonain, 98, 192, 371

Sacré-Coeur, 178
Saint-Junien, 59
Saint-Just, Louis de, 43
Saint-Léonard, 59
Saint-Marc Girardin (Marc
    Girardin), 93
Saint-Simon, Claude-Henri, comte
    de, 228
Salle Lepelletier, 207–209
Salle Wagram, 334
Sand, George, 60, 61, 260, 263,
    348
Scot, Mr. (Haussmann's friend), 73
Sedan, Battle of, 321, 323, 336,
    362
Sers, Jean-André, baron de, 73
Sévigné, Mme, 222
Sherard, Robert H., 196, 200, 333,
    334, 337, 348

Société Générale, 233
Sorbonne, 29, 50, 51, 199, 203
Soufflot, Germain, 32, 50, 179
St. Augustin (eglise), 50, 159, 198,
    203, 243, 337
St. Cloud, 171, 318–321, 344
St. Eustache, 203, 360
St. Germain l'Auxerrois, 39
St. Germain-en-Laye, 24
St. Gervais, 16
St. Girons, 64, 66, 69, 71
St. Jacques la Boucherie, 280
St. Julien, 74
St. Pierre, 74
St. Sulpice, 16, 104, 269
St. Vincent de Paul, 195
Ste. Chapelle, 201–203
Ste. Geneviève (eglise), 117, 179,
    193, 197, 203, 360
Ste. Geneviève (montagne), 179,
    193, 197, 203, 360
Stendhal (Pierre Beyle), 47, 55
Sue, Eugène, 51, 97
Surcnscs, 79

Temple, 37, 82, 94, 262, 269, 336
Tennstedt, 41
Théâtre de la Comédie Française,
    207
Théâtre des Arts, 207
Théâtre français, 56, 57
Thénard, Jacques, 51
Thiénot, Catherine-Thérèse, 41
Thiéron, Colonel, 145
Thiers, Adolphe, 98, 102, 181, 244,
    304, 305, 307, 310, 323, 343,
    344
Thirteenth arrondissement, 354
Thomas, Clément, general, 84, 85,
    86, 342, 370
Thorigny, Pierre-François-Elisabeth
    Leullion de, 139

Tourny, Louis-Urbain Aubert,
    marquis de, 8, 9, 147, 149,
    152–160, 166, 313, 314
  Allées de Tourny, 153
  building in Bordeaux, 153, 154
  his methods, 155, 156
  urban ideas, 158–160
Travot, Jean-Pierre, baron, 73
Tribunal de Commerce, 159, 163,
    200, 201
Trocadéro, 178, 304, 332
Tuileries, 2, 15, 24, 25, 29–31, 33,
    38, 39, 47, 79, 109, 110,
    113–115, 169, 178, 189, 207,
    208, 211, 227, 229, 244, 261,
    264, 332, 333, 345, 346, 361
Turin, 45

University of Paris, 19, 20
Urban hygiene, 48

Val-de-Grâce, 29
Vannes, 143

Vendôme Column, 332
Verdon, 71

Verniquet, Edme, 33
Versailles, 16, 26, 29–31, 41, 45, 47,
    93, 249, 343, 344
Victoria, Queen, 254
Vie boulevardière, La, 347
Villejuif, 14
Villemain, François, 51
Villers Cotterets, 24
Viollet-le-Duc, Eugène-Emmanuel,
    106, 211, 359
Voltaire, 15, 16, 24, 37, 93, 117,
    156, 182, 191, 192, 197, 244,
    296, 309, 345, 350

Wailly, Charles de, 17
Wall of the Tax Farmers, 22, 32,
    37
Wilhelm I of Prussia, 177
Wren, Christopher, 15

Yssingeaux, 59
Yvon, Adolphe, 250, 288

Zola, Emile, 47, 196, 241, 242, 261,
    283, 304, 344, 347, 353, 359,
    360, 361, 362, 363

· PICTURE CREDITS ·

Moving the Colonne du Châtelet: (c) 1995 Artists Rights Society (ARS), New York/SPADEM, Paris.

Place du Châtelet: (c) 1995 Artists Rights Society (ARS), New York/SPADEM, Paris.

Boulevard Henri IV: (c) 1995 Artists Rights Society (ARS), New York/SPADEM, Paris.

Théâtre du Luxembourg: (c) 1995 Artists Rights Society (ARS), New York/SPADEM, Paris.

Rue de Rivoli: BHVP.

Night Work: Phot. Bibl. Nat. Paris.

Rue de Rivoli: (c) 1995 Artists Rights Society (ARS), New York/SPADEM, Paris.

Avenue de l'Opéra: (c) 1995 Artists Rights Society (ARS), New York/SPADEM, Paris.

Avenue de l'Opéra: (c) 1995 Artists Rights Society (ARS), New York/SPADEM, Paris.

The Arcueil Aqueduct: (c) 1995 Artists Rights Society (ARS), New York/SPADEM, Paris.

Capturing the Dhuis Waters: (c) 1995 Artists Rights Society (ARS), New York/SPADEM, Paris.

INSERT 3

Massacre at the Rue Transnonain: Phot. Bibl. Nat. Paris.

Rambuteau: (c) 1995 Artists Rights Society (ARS), New York/SPADEM, Paris.

Berger: (c) 1995 Artists Rights Society (ARS), New York/SPADEM, Paris.

Haussmann "Voleur": (c) 1995 Artists Rights Society (ARS), New York/SPADEM, Paris.

Haussmann "Prefect": (c) 1995 Artists Rights Society (ARS), New York/SPADEM, Paris.

Louis Napoléon: Phot. Bibl. Nat. Paris.

Emile Ollivier: Phot. Bibl. Nat. Paris.

Old and New Paris: (c) 1995 Artists Rights Society (ARS), New York/SPADEM, Paris.

Les Halles [street scene]: (c) 1995 Artists Rights Society (ARS), New York/SPADEM, Paris.

The Sewers: Phot. Bibl. Nat. Paris.

The Grand Théâtre: Archives Municipales de Bordeaux.

Cestas [exterior]: Ministère de la Culture, Commission régionale d'inventaire, "Aquitaine."

Cestas [interior]: Ministère de la Culture, Commission régionale d'inventaire, "Aquitaine."

INSERT 4

Hôtel de Ville in Ruins: Phot. Bibl. Nat. Paris.

Boulevard des Italiens: (c) 1995 Artists Rights Society (ARS), New York/SPADEM, Paris.

The Grand Hotel: (c) 1995 Artists Rights Society (ARS), New York/SPADEM, Paris.

Avenue de l'Opéra: (c) 1995 Artists Rights Society (ARS), New York/SPADEM, Paris.

The Opéra Under Construction: Phot. Bibl. Nat. Paris.

Boulevard Promenade: (c) 1995 Artists Rights Society (ARS), New York/SPADEM, Paris.

Haussmann's Dreariness: Photograph (c) 1994, The Art Institute of Chicago. All Rights Reserved.

Dismal Paris: (c) 1995 Artists Rights Society (ARS), New York/SPADEM, Paris.

St. Augustin: BHVP.

Eglise de la Trinité: (c) 1995 Artists Rights Society (ARS), New York/SPADEM, Paris.

Paris Landlords: (c) 1995 Artists Rights Society (ARS), New York/SPADEM, Paris.

Haussmann Lampooned: Phot. Bibl. Nat. Paris.

Haussmann in his Glory: Phot. Bibl. Nat. Paris.

Haussmann at the End: (c) 1995 Artists Rights Society (ARS), New York/SPADEM, Paris.